# Collecting and Restoring Antique Bicycles

## by G. Donald Adams

# Collecting
## and
# Restoring
# Antique
# Bicycles

## by G. Donald Adams

Pedaling History—the Burgwardt Bicycle Museum
Orchard Park, New York, USA

*Book Design by Michael Höhne*
*Frontispiece Illustration by George Retseck*
*Cover Photo by Carl Burgwardt*


Collecting and Restoring Antique Bicycles

Second Edition     First Printing     March, 1996

Printed in the United States of America

Library of Congress Catalogue Card Number: 96-67123

**Publisher's Cataloging in Publication**
*(Prepared by Quality Books, Inc.)*

Adams, G. Donald.
     Collecting & restoring antique bicycles / by G. Donald Adams. — Rev. 2nd ed.
     p. cm.
     Includes bibliographical references and index.
     ISBN 0-9649537-0-6  (hc.)
     ISBN 0-9649537-1-4 (pbk.)

     1. Bicycles—Conservation and restoration. I. Title.
II. Title: Collecting and restoring antique bicycles.

TL430.A43 1996                              629.2'272
                                            QBI96–84

ISBN 0-9649537-0-6 hardcover (previously published by TAB, ISBN 0-8306-9676-8)
ISBN 0-9649537-1-4 softcover (previously published by TAB, ISBN 0-8306-1256-4)

To

# Robert McNair

and his fellow bicycle history enthusiasts,
who in 1967 founded The Wheelmen.

# Contents

# Acknowledgements

Foremost, I am grateful to the entire membership of The Wheelmen whose support of the first edition paved the way for this one. I am especially grateful to Carl Wiedman for his photographic assistance with this edition, Michael Höhne for his excellent editing and publishing perseverance, and Carl and Clarice Burgwardt and Pedaling History–the Burgwardt Bicycle Museum, who made this edition possible. I also want to thank Fred Fisk, who introduced me to the fascinating topic of bicycle history and Lowell Kennedy, who nurtured my appreciation of the high level of design and manufacturing perfection that was achieved by bicycle designers and builders before the turn-of-the-century—a benchmark that probably will not be significantly surpassed before the century turns again.

# Introduction

Transportation vehicles always have intrigued collectors, but until 1967, when The Wheelmen was formed, American enthusiasts functioned independently of each other and did not have many opportunities to convey to potential collectors the excitement, fascination, and historical worth of their hobby.

Antique bicycle collecting in America is the story of the early collectors and the formation of The Wheelmen. It is the story of riders who are totally enchanted by ordinaries, which are the high wheel bicycles of 1871 to 1892. It is the story of people and technologies from many nations that contributed to the refinement of one of the most successful machines ever developed.

Having been in a position for many years to answer questions from prospective collectors and to provide reference material to restorers, I felt the strong need for a book written from their point of view.

Although the emphasis is on antique bicycle collecting in America, the story is heavily involved with and applies equally to collecting anywhere in the world. To help assure accuracy, primary research sources such as manufacturers' catalogs are used. To make the story current, I discuss the collecting of special interest bicycles manufactured from 1900 to the present day.

If this book creates an interest that leads you to become a collector, if it causes you for the first time to appreciate the importance of the bicycle in American history, and if it becomes a principal reference in support of your enjoyment of the marvelous hobby of preserving and riding antique bicycles, its goal will have been achieved.

G. Donald Adams

## Chapter 1:
# The Collector

oseph Collings probably was the first American to realize the historic worth of antique bicycles. In 1889 he entrusted his velocipede to the Smithsonian Institution.

A moderate interest in early bicycles also was shown by some of the cycling magazines of the 1890s. Occasionally they cast a disparaging glance backward at the hobby horse and boneshaker.

Sometimes a sturdy boneshaker or an elegant high wheeled ordinary would be exhibited at one of the gala bicycle shows of the 1890s "to show how far we have come."

Some manufacturers took a scornful look backward in their advertisements. The Pope Manufacturing Company in 1893 pictured a hobby horse with the notation "One of the FIRST and WORST bicycles." That same year Pope exhibited Expert Columbia serial number 8524 which Thomas Stevens of Colorado rode around the world, departing from San Francisco April 22, 1884, and arriving back in San Francisco in January, 1887. Fanciful art showing a modern bicycle rising out of a smoldering pile of boneshakers and ordinaries with the notation: "From the ashes of the past comes the TRIUMPH of the PRESENT" was featured in the 1897 advertising of the Stover Bicycle Manufacturing Company of Freeport, Illinois (Fig. 1-1).

The venerable veteran machines did not fare any better at the pens of the 1890s cartoonists. "Father Time" was shown with his ordinary in one cartoon; "prehistoric" man was shown riding another.

In the 1890s used boneshakers and ordinaries seldom were advertised for sale, probably because they brought very little money. Many early machines were unceremoniously retired to the scrap pile. A few were relegated to such places as hay lofts and crawl spaces under houses from which they would surface in varying stages of deterioration many years later.

*Fig. 1–1.* 1897 Stover bicycle advertisement.

By 1917 Englishman Horace Wilton Bartleet, who bought his first ordinary new in 1886, had collected 20 antique bicycles and had resolved to make them the nucleus of a collection he would present to the city of Coventry. No one knows if he was the first antique bicycle collector, but it is known that interest in antique bicycles was seldom publicly expressed.

In 1925 Roger Johnson of South Hadley, Massachusetts, asked his uncle, who owned an antique shop, to hold for him a high wheel bicycle he had come across. Wanting only to relive the pleasure of riding an ordinary—he had ridden one to school when he was a boy at the turn of the century—he later formed one of the most comprehensive American collections of antique bicycles and cycling memorabilia. His machines were a popular attraction at New England parades beginning in the late 1920s.

During the 1920s there were isolated examples of private collecting of antique bicycles in Europe and in America and the hobby horse had made it to the silver screen with Buster Keaton riding a replica in the 1924 picture *Our Hospitality.* The duplicated 1818 Denis Johnson hobby horse that he rode is now owned by the Smithsonian Institution.

In the late 1920s auto magnate Henry Ford, a cyclist since 1893, purchased examples of most major types of antique bicycles for his village and museum in Dearborn, Michigan. Barney Oldfield gave his famous 1899 Tribune Blue Streak racing bicycle (Fig. 7-1) to Ford. Bartleet sold him an 1886 Kangaroo. When the village was dedicated October 21, 1929, President Herbert Hoover and Thomas Edison were entertained by a costumed museum employee riding an ordinary.

Robert B. Morrison, a Jersey City, N.Y., former captain of the Harlem Wheelmen, redirected attention to the long-forgotten ordinary bicycle when he rode his across New York's George Washington Bridge in December, 1932.

In 1933 Ernest Knight (Fig. 1-4) of Raymond, Maine, bought a Columbia Expert high wheel bicycle from Roger Johnson. Thirty-four years later he would become the first vice commander of the American antique bicycle club, The Wheelmen.

Charles Murphy, first to go a mile a minute—a feat he accomplished June 30, 1899 while riding a Tribune Blue Streak bicycle behind a railroad car on a platform between the rails—regaled audiences with his memories at the 1939 New York World's Fair. A replica of Scotsman Kirkpatrick Macmillan's 1839 velocipede, (Fig. 1-3) the first two-wheeler with which the rider could keep his feet entirely off the ground while in motion, was exhibited at the Fair.

Over the next 30 years, growing collections of antique bicycles found their way into museums and into the basements and garages of a few private collectors in America and Europe. Interest in them was so limited they could be purchased for a song, or perhaps simply could be picked off the junk heap.

## VETERAN CYCLE CLUB FOUNDED

It was 1955, with the establishment of the Southern Veteran Cycle Club (SVCC) of England, that enthusiasts for old bicycles began to gain stature as collectors of worthwhile antiques. In August of that year, 13 enthusiasts, eight on antique bicycles, made the first SVCC club run. That same month Derek Roberts (Fig. 1-2) began publication of The Boneshaker, the SVCC magazine, and the first in the world to be devoted to antique bicycle collectors. Other small antique bicycle clubs had existed in Europe previously, but none was as serious of purpose as the SVCC.

When the SVCC began publication of its newsletter, News and Views, in October 1959, antique bicycle collectors had a publication in which they could advertise what they wanted to buy or sell.

In 1958 American Roland Geist attended the 75th anniversary parade of the Swiss Velo Union at Lucerne, Switzerland, where he became fascinated seeing the antique bicycles ridden. Upon his return, he, Roger Johnson, and Washington, DC, collector Henry Mathis founded the Antique Bicycle Club of America. Although the club did not involve many collectors, it did establish the American Bicycle Hall of Fame in 1959 at Staten Island, N.Y., where it exhibited antique bicycles and cycling memorabilia in the Richmondtown Historical Museum.

## HISTORIC WORTH ESTABLISHED

Authors took to their typewriters as interest grew, turning the funny old bicycles into fascinating subjects of technical and social interest. It was the

printed page that revealed to collectors the historic worth of their machines, and it was H. W. Bartleet who led the way, through his *Bartleet's Bicycle Book* published in 1931. In 186 pages of prose and photos, Bartleet produced a valuable reference for antique bicycle collectors.

In 1955 C. F. Caunter described the expansive London Science Museum bicycle collection, comprising machines built from 1819 to 1950, in his book *Cycles, A Handbook of the Collection.*

Arthur Judson Palmer, an American, was next to put it all together for collectors in his well-illustrated 1956 volume, *Riding High.* Certainly many collectors can trace their interest in antique bicycles back to their first trip through Palmer's pages of primitive hobby horses, elegant tricycles, and sophisticated safeties.

By 1965 antique bicycles had become significant enough to be offered in London by the prestigious auction house of Messrs. Sotheby

*Fig. 1–2.* Derek Roberts riding a c. 1898 Crypto Alpha Bantam.

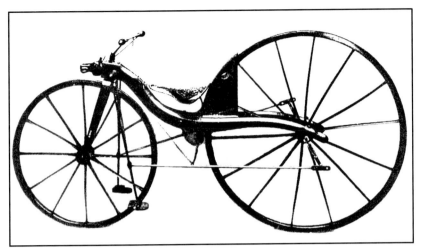

*Fig. 1–3.* Replica of Macmillan's 1839 velocipede.

and Company. Some of the most important machines extant, including two hobby horses, a Michaux boneshaker and a James Starley rotary tricycle, virtually the first commercially successful vehicle for women, were sold at the November 5 auction and at a second Sotheby auction in July of 1966.

Also in 1965, Derek Roberts was instrumental in founding The Fellowship of Cycling Old Timers. Based upon the Fellowship of Old Time Cyclists, founded in England in 1916 for those who had ridden before 1890, the new club was for any cyclist age 50 or over. The Fellowship's magazine, edited for many years by Roberts, publishes letters in which members give first-hand accounts of their cycling experiences, past and present, and reproduces pen and ink drawings by cycling's important early illustrators.

The antique bicycle activity of the 1950s and 60s in England and America set the stage for recreating America's cycling heritage.

### WHEELMEN FOUNDED

When he became a member of the Southern Veteran Cycle Club in 1956, Roger Johnson of Springfield, Massachusetts, probably was the first American to join an antique bicycle club.

But there were many Americans who shared his love for antique bicycles, twelve of whom, spearheaded by Philadelphian Robert McNair, (Fig. 1-5) met at Hoopes Park, Delaware, October 15, 1967, to form a national organization dedicated to the enjoyment and preservation of America's bicycling heritage. Emphasizing riding, collecting, restoring, research, and history, the organization was named The Wheelmen.

Not only would The Wheelmen bring American antique bicycle collectors together for the first time and help serve their needs, it would also recreate the color and pageantry of The League of American Wheelmen (LAW) which had been founded May 31, 1880, continued in operation until 1942, and was re-established to serve modern cyclists in 1965.

Reviving the form and function of the LAW as it had existed from 1880 to 1900 required an understanding of the conditions leading to its creation, its purpose, and the organization and procedures by which those purposes were fulfilled.

The story began in the spring of 1876 when English racing cyclist John Keen appeared in New York stirring interest in a new bicycle with a high front wheel. It would become known as the ordinary. That summer one was exhibited at the Philadelphia Centennial Exposition and intrigued many, including retired Civil War Colonel Albert A. Pope. The following summer Pope learned to ride a high wheel bicycle made by his English friend John Harrington. Convinced of the machine's worth, Pope ordered eight English Duplex Excelsiors for study and sale. Soon he placed an order with the Weed Sewing Machine Company of Hartford, Connecticut, for 50 similar bicycles to sell at the September Framingham, Massachusetts, fair. Their success led Pope to buy the necessary patents and turn his Connecticut plant over to producing his new Columbia bicycle beginning in the spring of 1878.

*Fig. 1–4.* Ernest Knight with the ordinary he bought in 1933.

As Columbias and their imported counterparts began to appear on the streets in increasing numbers, a public clamor arose against them. Teamsters claimed they scared horses. Pedestrians felt they were endangered by them. Many localities passed ordinances banning them from streets and public parks and imposed heavy fines on riders.

Immediately Pope fought these restrictive ordinances in the courts. He also helped establish the Boston Bicycle Club, the first of many city bicycle clubs that riders organized for their own protection from those who would force them off the roads.

Irving Leonard explained in *The Wheelmen* magazine, summer 1970, that by 1880 there were 40 bicycle clubs in Massachusetts, Connecticut, Rhode Island, New York, New Jersey, and Pennsylvania. Kirk Munroe, captain of the New York Club and a popular writer of children's books, convinced Truman Burdick, mayor of Newport, Rhode Island, to allow a grand parade of 100 cyclists to be part of the city's May 31, 1880, Decoration Day festivities. At 10 o'clock that morning at Newport's municipal skating rink, Munroe called to order delegates of 32 clubs and read the proposed constitution of a national League of American Wheelmen.

Following the unanimous adoption of the LAW constitution, 133 uniformed cyclists advanced down Newport's main street on their bicycles. They rode into an American scene that the LAW would change through its pioneering efforts as the first organization in America to be serious about lobbying for good roads, marking road dangers and routes, publishing maps, issuing road condition reports, approving hotels and taverns, and influencing legislation to ban illegal tolls and ordinances that prevented riding.

The colorful LAW parades, tours, races, and riding demonstrations participated in by Wilbur and Orville Wright, Commodore Vanderbilt, Diamond Jim Brady, and 102,633 other members left the American scene after 1900 when the automobile began capturing the attention of the same adventure seekers who had taken to the bicycle. The adventure and pageantry of early LAW club riding in America would not be enjoyed again until 1967 when The Wheelmen was formed.

The growth of The Wheelmen was swift and sensational. As in the tradition of the LAW of nearly 100 years before, a national commander and a vice commander were elected. Robert McNair, whose accomplishments also included authoring a book of interest to young people, the Boy Scouts of America whitewater canoeing manual, was elected the first national commander. In 1971 he was credited in a citation naming him Wheelmen Commander Emeritus, as being most influential in establishing the organization. Ernest Knight of Raymond, Maine, was elected the first vice commander.

By summer of 1970, when the first issue of *The Wheelmen* magazine was published, there were 110 members who reported ownership of 531 ordinaries.

From the outset, McNair urged Wheelmen members to conform as much as possible to the traditions of the LAW. Thus American bicycling history repeated itself in 1971 when Edward Berry, Jr. pedaled his 1886 Columbia ordinary 3,400 miles in 48 days from San Francisco to Boston. He made the trip, he said, to show Americans that one can cross the country by bicycle, seeing the scenery and not polluting the air. Also he commemorated Stevens' 1884 ride which required 105 days to cross the United States following a similar route.

## COLLECTING INTEREST GROWS

By 1970 the antique bicycle collecting climate had changed in America. In the same way that new books on the subject had established the historical significance of antique bicycles in the 1950s, publicity generated interest in riding and collecting in the 1960s.

*Fig. 1–5.* Robert McNair being interviewed at a Wheelmen meet.

A series of important stories about The Wheelmen started with the July 5, 1970, issue of Parade, the popular magazine included with Sunday newspapers across the nation. In color on the cover of that issue was Philadelphia Wheelman George Garrettson and his daughter Carla. Garrettson was resplendent in the Wheelmen uniform that had been adopted by the Pennsylvania Chapter.

The June, 1971 *Yankee* magazine published a detailed article about a Wheelmen gathering at Roger Johnson's farm in Massachusetts. With relish, *Yankee* regaled its readers with an account of the colorful parade in which riders responded in crisp military precision to signals blown on a brass bugle by Commander McNair. The bugle signals are those used in the 1880s by the LAW for such instructions as attend wheels, prepare to mount, mount, quicken pace, and dismount.

Writers of stories published in *Americana* magazine, the *New York Times* and countless newspapers across America were astonished to learn about the 100 mile "century rides" members of The Wheelmen were making on high wheel bicycles. Most articles explained that to be a voting member of The Wheelmen, one must ride an official high wheel tour of ten miles minimum at a club meet. They also emphasized that anyone with an interest in antique bicycles could be an associate member simply by paying dues and that ownership or riding of an antique bicycle was not a requirement to be a part of the organization.

Perhaps most interesting to chroniclers of this new enthusiast group were the riding demonstrations at which Wheelmen showed how to mount and dismount each type of antique bicycle. They even showed how to ride an ordinary while seated sidesaddle and while standing on the top of the seat, tricks that also had delighted spectators in the 1880s.

Photographers were quick to capture the exciting patterns cast by long straight rows of high wheel bicycles lined up for Wheelmen judging. Then there was the visual spectacle and excitement of such unorthodox Wheelmen field events as no-hands races, the likes of which hadn't been attempted since the 1880s.

The beauty of early bicycles also found expression in television specials, most notable of which was The Ballad of The Bicycle, written by Val Clery of Toronto and seen on the CBC television network in 1975.

In 1970 a morning *Today Show* on the NBC television network had the charm of a late 1890s bicycle shop when Eugene Sloan had a selection of antique bicycles on camera to promote his *Complete Book of Cycling*.

To say the least, being in the public limelight markedly changed antique bicycle collecting in America.

Suddenly The Wheelmen were getting many requests to appear in major parades. They planned and practiced impressive parade formations reminiscent of those used in the 1880s by the LAW and they were seen by millions who watched in person or on television. The Wheelmen rode in the Philadelphia Mummers Parade, the Cherry Blossom Festival Parade in Washington, DC, Macy's and Hudson's Christmas Parades in New York City and Detroit, Michigan, the Indianapolis 500 Memorial Day Parade in Indianapolis, Indiana, the Kentucky Derby Parade in Louisville, Kentucky, the Disneyworld Easter Parade in Florida, and the Schlitz Circus Parade, Milwaukee, Wisconsin. Revenue from parades was used to help pay for *The Wheelmen* magazine.

Robert Trepanier of California in the early 1970s staged a show of antique bicycles that was seen in shopping malls across the country to the accompaniment of much publicity.

In 1972 Finn Wodschow of the Dansk Veteran Cycle Club invited The Wheelmen to join him and Cyril Mundy of England in establishing an International Society of Bicycle Collectors involving England, Holland, France, Denmark, Sweden, and the United States. Although The Wheelmen pledged support of the new organization, nothing further was heard about it.

In 1986 the International Veteran Cycle Association was formed. It produces events and a magazine titled *The International Veteran Cyclist.*

A few American museums brought their antique bicycles out of storage for permanent exhibit in the 1960s and 70s. Others refurbished their collections for the first time in many years. In September of 1977, Cincinnati, Ohio's Taft Museum opened a one-month special exhibit showing antique bicycles as art forms. The Smithsonian Institution staged a traveling antique bicycle exhibit entitled *Ride On!* that was seen in many major cities. Henry Ford Museum, Dearborn, Michigan, refurbished and re-exhibited its antique bicycle collection and Burlington County, New Jersey, residents spruced up the mansion and manufacturing buildings of the Star Bicycle Company, acquiring historic status for the Smithville facility and opening it to the public.

As ordinaries and their antecedents neared the 100 years-of-age mark and the artistry of their fine design and workmanship passed under the appreciative eyes of museum goers, collectors of fine antiques became interested in old bicycles.

The antique bicycle's return to public view coincided with a fascination for Victorian antiques which swept the nation in the 1970s. Collectors soon realized that perhaps there was no more dramatic expression of Victorian exuberance than the antique bicycle.

Occasionally members of The Wheelmen were invited to exhibit their antique bicycles at gatherings sponsored by the numerous antique car collectors' clubs. Indeed it was The Wheelmen's inclusion in the annual antique car meet in September 1969 at the Indianapolis Speedway in Indiana that introduced the organization to the midwest section of the country. In 1970 antique bicycle demonstrations were incorporated into the Greenfield Village Old Car Festival in Dearborn, Michigan, and have been a part of that annual affair since.

Through involvement with the antique car fraternity, it was not long before car collectors became aware of and interested in old bicycles. This was a reversal of what had happened at the turn of the century when Americans abandoned pedals for horseless carriages.

Bicycling in general captured the imagination of American adults in the 1960s and 70s to a degree not equalled since the 1890s. A new emphasis on ecology and a clean environment coupled with the beginnings of a stale period in America's love affair with the automobile, gave bicycles and cycling a new lease on life. Daniel Behram in his 1973 book, *The Man Who Loved Bicycles,* expressed what an increasing number of Americans were thinking—it is time to make use of the bicycle.

The Smithsonian *Ride On!* exhibit poster pointed out that the first contemporary bicycle route in America was developed in Homestead, Florida, in 1961. It was called a "bicycle safety route." In 1971 Oregon required its State Highway Commission cities and counties to begin spending at least one percent of total highway revenue on footpaths and bicycle trails. In 1972, for the first time in 60 years, bicycles outsold automobiles in America. The Federal Highway Act of 1973 earmarked $120 million for bicycle facilities over three years.

Meanwhile two American bicycle magazines, *Bicycle Spokesman* and *Bicycling!,* sought and found an audience of cyclephiles who were ten-speed pedaling in every corner of the nation. In their pages the magazines chronicled the development of The Wheelmen and created among riders of modern bicycles an interest in their cycling heritage.

By the 1970s the LAW, re-established in 1965 in Chicago, again had become a national force in encouraging fitness through cycling and in supporting cyclists' rights for safe roads. Affiliated with the LAW, The Wheelmen rode in support of such LAW activities as the opening of new bikeways and the promotion of bikeathons for charity.

It was a diversified group of people which included the collector of fine antiques, the student of Victoriana, the collector of antique automobiles, the modern cyclist, and the physical fitness and ecology advocate that came together in the 1970s to form The Wheelmen into an organization with wide appeal and a growing membership that would establish old bicycles as antiques worth preserving and collecting.

Its success as the only American antique bicycle organization enabled The Wheelmen to organize its first major club tour in 1976. Leaving from the replica Independence Hall tower at Henry Ford Museum, July 4, (Fig. 1-6) Wheelmen completed over 700 miles on high wheels arriving at Pennsylvania's original Independence Hall in Philadelphia 14 days later. The one woman and 16 men rode in tribute to the nation's 200th anniversary and in commemoration of the 100th anniversary of that first showing of an ordinary in America at the Philadelphia Centennial Exposition in 1876.

*Fig. 1–6.* The Wheelmen depart on their bicentennial tour from Henry Ford Museum to Independence Hall in Philadelphia. *(courtesy of Henry Ford Museum, Dearborn, MI)*

## Chapter 2:
# The Hobby Horse: 1817-1821

Although there was a variety of claims that two-wheeled muscle-powered machines existed in Paris as early as 1791, Baron von Drais of Sauerbrun, Germany, generally is credited with developing in 1817 the first one that was at all practical. It was described (Fig. 2-1) in an 1819 issue of *Ackermann's Magazine* as a seat upon two wheels propelled by the two feet acting upon the ground in a motion similar to skating. The saddle was fixed upon a perch on two short wheels running after each other. To preserve the balance, support the arms, and rest the shoulders, a small stuffed and covered board was placed before the rider on which the arms were rested. A guiding pole was held in hand to direct the route, the article explained.

A landscape gardener of distinction, von Drais was master of the forests of the Grand Duke of Baden. He used this new device as an aid in getting around the grounds. Soon a German newspaper took notice of his machine and in February, 1818 von Drais was granted a five-year French patent, according to Andrew Ritchie in his *King of the Road*.

Englishman Denis Johnson improved the von Drais machine by making it lighter and by allowing for adjusting the height of the saddle and arm rest. He introduced it in England, first as the "pedestrian curricule." Although it also was referred to as the "swift walker" and derisively as the "dandy horse," because it often was ridden by fashionable youngbloods called dandies, most people referred to it as the hobby horse.

In 1819 a hobby horse, of the type produced by Johnson, was introduced in New York City. It was made by the firm of Davis and Rogers of Troy, New York. In April 1819 the *Boston Weekly Messenger* noted that Ambrose Salisbury of Boston, Massachusetts, had made a hobby horse. The May 17, 1819, issue of the *New England Palladium and Commercial Advertiser* mentioned Salisbury again, noting that he had two hobby horses available for inspection. In June 1819

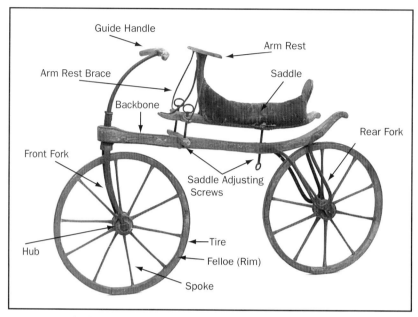

*Fig. 2–1.* c. 1818 hobby horse, also referred to as a velocipede, draisine, swift walker, dandy horse, and pedestrian curricle. *(photo courtesy of the Smithsonian Institution)*

William K. Clarkson was granted a United States patent for an improvement to the hobby horse, but records of what the patent covered were destroyed in the Washington, DC, Patent Office fire of 1836.

In America use of the hobby horse was most prevalent in Troy and Saratoga, New York, New York City, Philadelphia, and Boston according to Charles Pratt in his 1880 edition of *The American Bicycler*. He also noted that wear and tear on shoe leather was so great when riding a hobby horse that one enterprising manufacturer advertised "a special shoe with iron-clad sole to withstand the pit-pat on the roads." The trials and tribulations of the hobby horse rider are well illustrated by European cartoon prints of 1817 to 1819 that ridicule the heavy machine (Fig. 2-2).

Interest in the hobby horse declined abruptly after 1820 in the United States and the machine would not be seen again in America until after 1869 when a few would be resurrected with cranks and pedals added so they could be used as boneshakers. In Europe, however, tinkerers continued to work at improving the muscle powered two-wheeler.

### MAJOR MAKERS

**Baron Karl von Drais, Sauerbrun, Germany** (Fig. 2-3). Authorized by French patent to manufacture machines from 1818 to 1823, he promoted sales by demonstrating the machines at the Luxembourg Gardens and on public highways.

**Denis Johnson, 75 Long Acre, London, England.** (Fig. 2-4). More refined, lighter, and simpler in design than the draisienne, the Johnson hobby horse provided for adjusting the height of the saddle and arm rest. Deluxe models were hand painted to order, according to Ritchie in *King of the Road*. It is not known for how long the Johnson machines were made or how many were produced. Judging from the number of period cartoons that illustrate Johnson machines and from records of raw material costs that were revealed by Ritchie, we can determine that Johnson was the major manufacturer of hobby horses.

**Davis and Rogers, Troy, New York.** Nothing is known about this American producer of hobby horses except that Charles Pratt in *The American Bicycler* notes that Davis and Rogers manufactured a number of machines in 1819 and rented them to young men of Troy, N.Y., for 25 cents an hour. He claims to have known many men who rode them in Boston. None of the hobby horses known to exist today is marked as having been produced by Davis and Rogers.

The lack of makers' marks and the variety of construction and design details of the few surviving hobby horses indicate that the greatest number probably were crafted by makers of varying skill. Most were one-off models for personal use or were built in very small numbers for limited sale.

### SELECTED EXAMPLES

**1818 hobby horse,** unmarked, (Fig. 2-5) is owned and exhibited by the London Science Museum, England. As described by Caunter in *Cycles*,

*Fig. 2–2.* German hobby horse cartoon. *(courtesy of Henry Ford Museum)*

Fig. 2–3. Baron von Drais with his hobby horse.

*Handbook of the Collection,* it belonged originally to one of the Dukes of Marlborough and consists of a wooden backbone, strengthened by iron, and supported by light iron work upon two wheels. The rider sat astride the saddle, pressed his elbows into the well-padded arm rest, and thrust backward upon the road surface with both feet while maintaining his balance by steering with the guide handle. He raised his legs to coast when possible. A stay rod, forerunner of the kick stand, was linked to the backbone and held the machine upright when not in use. A speed of ten miles per hour was claimed on level surfaces. Front wheel was 25.5" diameter, rear wheel, 27" diameter, wheelbase 39.5", weight 38 pounds.

    c. 1818 hobby horse, unmarked, owned and exhibited by the Museum of History and Technology, the Smithsonian Institution, Washington, DC (Fig. 2-1). As described by Berkebile in *Wheels and Wheeling,* it is believed to be of French origin. It consists of a spliced wood backbone, originally probably of one piece, to which a saddle is mounted on a separate bar elevated above the backbone by three adjusting screws. The two forward screws are fixed between two short crossbars situated near the front of the saddle. A firmly padded saddle is covered with maroon mohair. The saddle assembly can be elevated from 30 to 33 inches above the ground. The front wheel is held by an iron fork. A coil spring around the guide handle stem bears upward against a pin through the stem taking up vertical play in the head. Tires are iron. Traces of the original light green

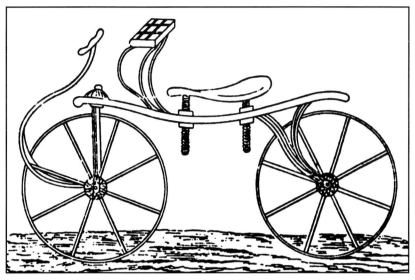

*Fig. 2–4.* Patent drawing, Denis Johnson pedestrian curricle.

finish with yellow and black striping are visible. Front and rear wheels are 24" diameter, wheelbase is 38".

**c. 1819 T. Sisson hobby horse** (Fig. 2-6) is in a private American collection and was auctioned by Sotheby and Company, London, November 4, 1966. It has a shaped wooden backbone, padded saddle and arm rest, and a steering bar mounted on a scrolled iron bracket. The backbone is stamped "T. Sisson, 1852." The 1852 is not believed to be the year of manufacture. It has an adjustable saddle, and iron tires. The dark green finish may not be original.

*Fig. 2–5.* Unmarked hobby horse exhibited by the London Science Museum.

*Fig. 2–6.* Hobby horse marked T. Sisson, 1852.

**c. 1819 hobby horse,** unmarked, (Fig. 2-7) was sold by Sotheby and Company, London, November 5, 1965. Horse legs form forks to wheels. The backbone is embellished with horsehair mane and tail. It is steered by a guide handle passing through the horse's neck. Note unusual spokes, no adjustment for height, and no arm rest. Wood frame parts are natural finish, wheels are

*Fig. 2–7.* Unmarked hobby horse.

*Fig. 2–8.* Unmarked hobby horse, private Canadian collection.

faded yellow paint with thin blue stripe. Some paint at horse's hoofs suggests that originally there was more detailing.

**c. 1819 hobby horse,** unmarked (Fig. 2-8). Handsome lines based upon the Denis Johnson pedestrian curricle, and marvelous craftsmanship distinguish this example. Pear shaped guide handle grip is unusual. The wood frame is

*Fig. 2–9.* Unmarked hobby horse.

*Fig. 2–10.* Henry Ford Museum hobby horse. *(courtesy of Henry Ford Museum and Greenfield Village)*
*Fig. 2–11.* Detail shows the origin of the term "head tube" on modern bicycles.

reinforced with iron strips. Wheels are 29" diameter rear, 27¼" front with 1½" wide iron tire. Wheelbase is 41". The machine measures 26" from the ground to the top of the backbone and 30" to the saddle when it is adjusted in a low position. The frame and forks are finished in black with a red stripe. The leather saddle appears to be original.

c. 1819 hobby horse, unmarked, (Fig. 2-9). Sold at the November 4, 1966, Sotheby and Company auction, it is probably of English origin. Adjustment for height is by means of relocating axles through a series of parallel holes in the forks. It has a natural wood finish with a rear fork support of ornamental spiralled iron and a leather covered padded saddle and arm rest. Wood spokes attach directly to the iron tires with no wheel felloes, a feature indicating it was made by someone not skilled as a wheelwright.

c. 1819 hobby horse, marked only with the initials RVR, (Fig. 2-10) owned and exhibited by Henry Ford Museum, Dearborn, Michigan. The backbone is shaped from one piece of wood and fronted by a carved bird's head (Fig. 2-11). The heart-shaped wood saddle is padded and covered with leather. Wheels are wood discs studded with decorative nail heads and pierced by heart-shaped openings. Iron tires are fitted. The initials RVR are painted on the front wheel

(Fig. 2-12). Traces of original red paint and black stripe remain on the wheels. Construction details indicate maker was not a wheelwright, but had an artistic eye and was a carver. There is no height adjustment or arm rest. Wheelbase is 46½". Front and rear wheels are 23" diameter.

## ESTABLISHING AUTHENTICITY AND CONDITION

Hobby horses probably are the most difficult antique bicycles to authenticate because so little is known about them. Few are marked with a maker's name and most period illustrations are cartoons with varying degrees of artistic license.

Some hobby horses are found incomplete. Others have been modified with such additions as cranks and pedals incorporated into the hub of the front wheel.

Replicas are known to circulate among collectors in recent years. The replacement of components such as the original hand-wrought bolts should arouse age suspicions even with some hobby horses exhibited by museums.

Considering the great rarity of original hobby horses, collectors should be especially cautious about examining one to be certain it is an original. Here are some guidelines to assist you.

☞ Look closely at nuts and bolts. If they are 1817–1821 period they should be hand-wrought. Especially examine the threads to determine if they are cut perfectly as if by machine, or if they have the variances of a hand-wrought

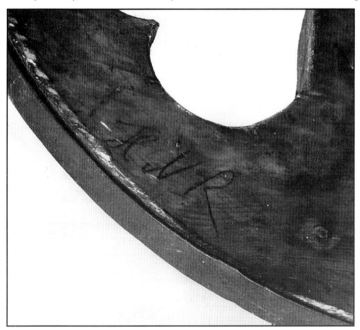

*Fig. 2–12.* Initials "RVR" on wheel of Henry Ford Museum hobby horse. *(courtesy of Henry Ford Museum and Greenfield Village)*

piece. If you cannot determine if bolts are original, try to have a person who does blacksmithing look at them for you.

☞ Examine the wood for separations along the grain that can indicate age. Machine cut marks should not be evident anywhere. Examine the interior walls of holes that have been drilled in the wood. Are they smooth like a machine cut hole or do they have the bore marks of a hand drill? Perhaps a collector of 18th century furniture who is accustomed to analyzing wood and is familiar with joining methods could be helpful.

☞ Look very carefully, outdoors in good light, for any evidence of old paint. Does the paint that remains match that of other components?

☞ Is the machine so large that you cannot comfortably be seated and extend your legs to the ground? Oversize machines, especially if their frames are largely iron, may be boneshakers with cranks and pedals removed to make them look like the much rarer hobby horses.

In summary, hobby horses with the maker's name or a symbol identifying a particular maker are best. Identification may be stamped into the wood or metal.

Original finish, even if only faint traces remain, is preferable to new paint. Those equipped with an arm rest are better than those without. Machines with an adjustable seat are preferable to those without. Fine carving also adds to the desirability.

## FURTHER RESEARCH

Henry Ford Museum, the Museum of American History at the Smithsonian Institution, and several museums in Europe, including the London Science Museum, have hobby horses that may be examined.

Cartoon caricature prints from 1819 by Leech, Alken, Cruikshank, and Rowlandson as well as a number of drawings from the period, define the basic design concepts employed by hobby horse makers. Although often the cartoon machines are exaggerated and fanciful, they can assist in documenting a hobby horse.

Many of these prints plus general information on hobby horses are reproduced in the Summer 1972 and Summer 1973 issues of *The Wheelmen* magazine and in the following books described in the bibliography: *King of the Road; Bicycle People; Riding High, A Social History of the Bicycle;* and *Wheels and Wheeling.*

## Chapter 3:
# The Boneshaker: 1865-1871

Although Kirkpatrick Macmillan's famous lever-driven machine had been developed in Scotland about 1839 and Englishman Willard Sawyer had developed a successful line of treadle-driven quadricycles by 1858, the evolution of the adult bicycle really began with the attachment of cranks and pedals to the front axle in about 1865.

Some collectors hold that this machine, once called the velocipede, but popularly known as the boneshaker, was the first true bicycle (Fig. 3-1).

The invention of a rotary crank propulsion system which is essentially the same as that used on today's bicycles, is credited to the Paris shop of Pierre Michaux. Debate continues, however, as to whether it was Michaux himself (Fig. 3-3), his son Ernest, or his associate, Pierre Lallement, who actually originated the idea.

In *The American Bicycler* Pratt notes that Lallement worked passage to Connecticut in 1866 where he made and rode the first American boneshaker (Fig. 3-2). His machine was seen by James Carroll of New Haven, Connecticut, who induced Lallement to join with him in obtaining a patent. Dated November 20, 1866, it is the first complete patent obtained anywhere in the world for a boneshaker.

Lallement soon returned to France, having done nothing with the patent. He sold it to Calvin Witty of New York City who had commissioned a patent investigation in late 1868, shortly after initiating his own velocipede production. The transaction was completed in early 1869 after confirmation from France that it was a valid patent. In February, 1869, Witty notified the more than 20 American boneshaker makers, most of whom had been producing boneshakers only about six months, that they must cease further production and settle with him for all past infringements. Many were carriage makers who obtained regional rights to manufacture and sell boneshakers.

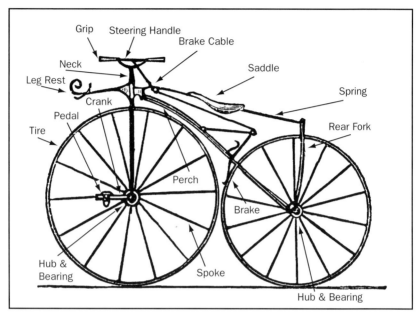

*Fig. 3–1.* c. 1869 Wood Bros. boneshaker, also called a velocipede.

Meanwhile Lallement and Michaux were among several makers who were popularizing the boneshaker in Europe. According to Ritchie in *King of the Road*, Michaux's workforce reached a high of 300 probably in late 1868 or 1869.

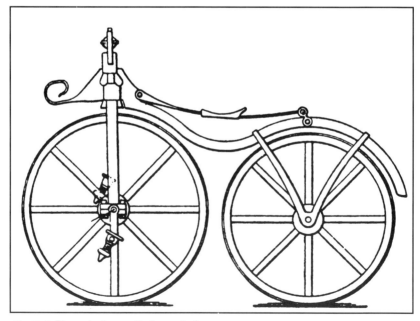

*Fig. 3–2.* Pierre Lallement's boneshaker.

*Fig. 3–3.* Pierre Michaux with his boneshaker.

A race to register patents for boneshaker improvements began in March, 1868 when Louis Riviere of France described a machine with front wheel larger than rear, thus establishing a direction that eventually would lead to the development of the high wheel bicycle.

Four months later the Hanlon brothers of New York City patented such boneshaker improvements as slotted cranks to make pedals adjustable to leg length, and seats that would slide forward and back for the same purpose. Also, according to Berkebile in *Wheels and Wheeling*, they suggested rubber rings to fit over the iron tires to make the machine noiseless and to help prevent side slipping. The following year they patented a mudguard for the front wheel and a brake controlled by a twist of the steering handle and operating against the rear tire.

As the year drew to a close, American C. K. Bradford made the suggestion of a hard rubber tire to replace the iron tire and Englishman Edward Cowper introduced wire spoke wheels and anti-friction bearings, according to Pratt's *The American Bicycler.*

American enthusiasm for the boneshaker peaked in 1869, but the heavy and hard to ride machines soon lost favor. By 1871 there was hardly a boneshaker seen in the United States except for the occasional one being ridden by a boy.

One boneshaker problem, as described by Berkebile in *Wheels and Wheeling* was "...the rider's position far behind the pedals created an awkward angle of thrust for the legs which tended to push him back and away from the pedals when the going became heavy." Along with the bad roads, pedestrians who felt threatened by the machine and passed ordinances preventing its use contributed to its rapid demise.

Boneshakers had a minor revival in the early 1880s when they were useful in learning how to ride a bicycle before attempting the more dangerous high wheel.

## MAJOR AMERICAN MAKERS

*(Descriptions of boneshakers are based on "Velocipedes, The American Outlook in 1868" by Carl Wiedman, Summer 1974 The Wheelmen.)*

**William P. Sargent & Co., Boston,** was a well known manufacturer of high-grade carriages. The Sargent (Fig. 3-4) was patterned after Michaux's French design, but was claimed to embody all available American improvements in form, materials, and thoroughness of construction. The rear wheel turned on the axle bar preventing friction problems that arose with machines on which the axle turned with the wheel. The neck at the upper part of the front fork was wrought in one piece, and the neck swivel was wrought iron instead of the cast

*Fig. 3–4.* Sargent boneshaker.

brass that was normally used. They alleged these features provided great durability in the most vulnerable parts of the machine.

Messrs. Sargent and Company made every effort to construct a light, noiseless, and smooth-running velocipede. They also manufactured a cheaper $55 machine without the spring that extended across the upper part of the frame and to the rear wheels. It was used by learners in halls and on rinks.

**Kimball Bros., Sudbury St., Boston,** secured the first license granted in America under the Lallement patent. They obtained the exclusive right to manufacture boneshakers in Maine plus the right to sell them throughout the United States. They employed the same high standards of production in making velocipedes as they had in the sleighs and carriages for which they had become well known. Patterned after Michaux's French design, the Kimball boneshakers had wrought iron frames, composition and gunmetal bearings, and superior saddles. They ranged from $75 to $175 depending upon style and finish. The most expensive had mud guards, a lamp, and a silver plated brake.

**William H. Brownell & Co., New Bedford, Mass.** produced inexpensive $70 to $90 boneshakers without springs or metal bearings. During one three month period in 1868, their sales exceeded $40,000 with a demand greater than their supply.

**The Wood Brothers, 596 Broadway, New York,** (Fig. 3-1) based their machine on the Michaux design, but improved upon it with steel tires and axles and gun metal bearings upon the rear wheel. Pedals were attached to slotted cranks so they could be adjusted. The Wood had a brake operating on the rear

*Fig. 3–5.* David Metz riding his Pickering and Davis boneshaker.

wheel, rests for the legs when coasting, and a well-finished saddle supported by steel springs. Typical price was $135.

**Calvin Witty, 638 Broadway, New York,** had the advantage of controlling the Lallement patent and, of course, did not have to pay the license fee of $10 per machine as did other manufacturers. He could sell at prices in the range of $90 to $130.

**Messrs. Pickering & Davis, 1441 Green Street, New York,** built a machine differing materially from Michaux's French model (Figs. 3-5, 3-10). Like the Hanlon, the frame was a single member that ran to the rear axle and provided the support for the saddle. On some of the Pickerings, the rear of the saddle itself was used as a brake so that pressing forward on the steering handle and rocking backward on the saddle forced the brake against the rear tire. The Pickering's perch was made of hollow hydraulic tubing and had gunmetal bearings attached in such a manner that they could be replaced when worn. The axle was so constructed as to constitute in itself an oil box. Cotton lamp wick was placed in the tubular axle and the oil was fed by this means through small holes in the center of the axle to the bearing surfaces. The steering handle was constructed with a spring steel portion so the hands were relieved from the jolts of riding over rough roads.

Pickerings were popular throughout the United States and in England where they were known as the American velocipede. They varied in price from $110 to $155.

*Fig. 3–6.* J. Shire boneshaker c. 1879. *(courtesy of Henry Ford Museum)*

**J. Shire and Company, Detroit,** (Fig. 3-6) at a late date for this type of machine, (late 1870s) produced a boneshaker designed to combine a large driving wheel for speed with a low saddle for safety and ease of mounting. Perhaps Shire sensed that the newly introduced high wheel bicycle would intimidate some riders and that they would turn to his machine. Judging by the large number of Shires in collections today, he must have produced a great quantity of this rakish boneshaker. Brightly painted and elegantly striped, Shires were equipped with a brake operating on the front wheel and a front fork similar to those in use on high wheel bicycles.

**The Hanlon Brothers of New York City,** distinguished acrobats and the first Americans to patent significant boneshaker improvements, continually refined their machine. It is not known how many they produced. Period sources did not consider the Hanlon to be among the best American boneshakers, but the simple upright frame design was distinctive enough to cause collectors today to categorize similar boneshakers as Hanlon types (Fig. 3-7).

*Fig. 3–7.* Hanlon boneshaker. *(courtesy of Henry Ford Museum)*

*Fig. 3–8.* Irving T. Thornton's boneshaker. *(courtesy of Henry Ford Museum)*

## THE ONE-OFF BONESHAKERS

Several amateur mechanics built one-off boneshakers for their personal use or a few copies for limited sale. So many Americans applied for boneshaker improvement patents that they deluged the Patent Office in Washington. The John Wilkinson Company of Chicago did a thriving business selling wood wheels in 14 sizes for those who wanted to make their own boneshaker. Period literature gave building instructions.

Some amateurs built machines based upon illustrations in Scientific American magazine. Others like Irving T. Thornton of Orchard Park, New York, were among those who developed boneshakers based on unique European models. Built in 1871 and once exhibited at Henry Ford Museum (Fig. 3-8), Thornton's was based on the British Phantom manufactured by Reynolds and May. Its unique pivoting frame, with both front and rear wheels steering, was designed to solve the problem of a front wheel and steering handle that would spin around unexpectedly when the rider encountered deep ruts and other road obstacles. The linked front and rear steering prevented the front wheel from being thrown abruptly to the left or right and in theory made the machine safer and easier to ride. In practice, double steering boneshakers were very difficult to steer and balance.

### ESTABLISHING AUTHENTICITY AND CONDITION

A considerable number of original boneshakers have survived. It is unlikely you will find a reproduction. Nevertheless each machine should be exam-

*Fig. 3–9.* Reynolds and May Phantom boneshaker.

ined for indications of natural aging, using the same criteria as for the hobby horse.

Wheels should be built close to the perch and spokes, felloes, and hubs should match front and rear. On most boneshakers the tire should clear the front fork by not much more than one inch. If the wheel is considerably smaller, chances are it is not original. Front wheels should not exceed 40" in diameter. Iron parts throughout the machine may be highly burnished or tinned, but most likely were not plated originally. Normally the machine should weigh 40 to 60 pounds. American boneshaker steering handles usually are straight and about 25" wide.

Boneshakers marked with the maker's name are the most desirable. The mark usually will be on a plate attached to the spring or will be stamped into the spring or fork. Often heavy paint conceals the maker's mark. Some makers stenciled their name in paint on the machine.

American boneshakers usually are preferred by American collectors, but French machines by Michaux and Lallement are especially desirable because of the pioneer role played by their makers. English Phantoms (Fig. 3-9) are desirable for their unique double steering and because their maker scored the first radical departure in boneshaker design with his wire spoke suspension wheels and rubber tires. (In "suspension" wheels, the weight of frame and rider is suspended from the uppermost portion of the rim by the spokes above the hub.

Wooden spoke wheels carry the load on the spokes which are immediately beneath the hub.)

In his 1869 book, *The Velocipede,* Goddard ranked as best those boneshakers made by Pickering and Davis; Wood Brothers; Mercer and Monad; Calvin Witty; Sargent; and Kimball. Other American makers not previously mentioned whose marks you may encounter include: Merrill and Sons; J. N. Hazelip; Pearsall Brothers; Laubach; Van Anden Dexter; Sheridan; Buell American Spring Velocipede; G. C. Elliott; J. M. Quimby; Datzell and Sons , G. F. Perkins; Tomlinson, Demarest and Company; Topliff and Ely; Stephen W. Smith; Chicago Velocipede; and D. W. Gosling.

The highest quality boneshakers should be fitted with a leg rest fronted by an ornamental scroll forward of the handlebar and a friction brake operated by a steering handle that twists pulling a cord that runs to the rear brake, pressing it against the tire. The brake arm should be fitted with a spring return and the cord should move on rollers wherever it changes direction. Springs should return the steering handle to its normal position when the brake is released.

Handle grips should be of a pleasing shape formed from some durable material such as bone, bakelite, or ivory. Pedals should be a bronze ornamental casting or wood and should be either three-sided or should have an acorn shaped weight so they always will be in riding position. They should be adjustable up and down on the crank arm either by sliding them in a slot or by relocating the pedal shaft into alternative crank holes. The saddle should be shaped much like today's, padded and covered either with leather or carpet cloth. It should loosen with wing nuts so it can be slid fore and aft on the spring to adjust the reach to the pedals.

Many of these features, however, may have not been included on lower grade boneshakers. Look carefully for mounting brackets and other evidence that accessory components originally were fitted, but now are missing.

Original finish, which usually was red, blue, cream, or green and boldly decorated with wide stripes such as those used on horse-drawn commercial vehicles, is preferable to a repainted finish.

#### FURTHER RESEARCH

Museums and books cited in the preceding chapter for hobby horse research also contain boneshaker material. In addition, the book *Velocipede,* published in 1869 by "Velox" and reprinted in 1971, is useful.

You can often see excellent examples of original boneshakers at meetings of The Wheelmen and in numerous small museums and private collections.

*Fig. 3–10.* Pickering and Davis boneshaker pedals and bearings *(courtesy of Henry Ford Museum)*

# Chapter 4:
# The Ordinary: 1871-1892

In 1870 when Englishmen James Starley and William Hillman patented their unique Ariel bicycle, they could not have anticipated that it would be the prototype for most of the world's bicycle production over the next 20 years.

The Ariel (Fig. 4-3) was the first all-metal bicycle and the first to have tension wheels. A tangential pull could be transmitted to the rims, moving them around until they tightened the spokes and made the wheel rigid (Fig. 4-4). Tension wheel spokes were threaded through eyes riveted into the rim. The ends of the spokes were bent at right angles and passed through holes in the hub which gripped the turned-over ends against the hub flanges.

Equally important, the Ariel was one of the first to abandon the nearly equal sized front and rear wheels that were common on the hobby horse and bone-shaker. The Ariel had a 50" front wheel rotating inside a front fork to which was attached a backbone. The 50" drive wheel was available with a speed gear which made it revolve at twice the speed of the pedals. The backbone followed the curve of the large wheel until it straightened to accommodate a rear fork holding a 14" wheel.

It was widely known that the larger the wheel, the farther and faster it would go with each turn of the pedals. It was this fact that led to the adoption of the large front wheel. The backbone, with mounting step and small rear wheel, was an ingenious solution to the problem of how to provide for a rider to reach the lofty saddle which was positioned directly over the large wheel. Also, reducing the size of the rear wheel saved weight.

The machine that resulted was surprisingly pleasant and comfortable to ride and could be coaxed up to 20 miles per hour. Its major problem was that it pitched forward without warning when the front wheel was stopped by a road obstruction. The rider, his legs pinned beneath the handlebar, pivoted over the

*Fig. 4–1.* The Header. *(courtesy of Henry Ford Museum)*

wheel landing on his extended arms and hands, or worse, on his head in a spectacular fall from which the expression "header" derived (Fig. 4-1).

Frequent serious injuries from "headers" caused manufacturers to become preoccupied with how to make the ordinary safer. A series of bicycles was developed in the United States and in Europe that in varying degrees solved this problem. Described in the next chapter, they were called safeties.

American bicycle riders always preferred the Ariel type design, though not with the geared wheel; thus the large front, small rear wheel bicycle driven by rotary cranks was the ordinary bicycle of the day, so referred to at the time to distinguish it from the growing number of unique safety bicycles.

Although high wheel safeties frequently and sometimes successfully challenged ordinaries at races and hill climbs, the ordinary usually was faster. Its simpler and lighter mechanical components made it less prone to friction and easier to pedal. Moreover, many club members thought the ordinary to be more "manly" to ride than the often smaller high wheel safeties.

Riding the ordinary was and continues to be one of life's pleasures. The smoothness and responsiveness that results from pedaling a wheel that is driven directly with no mechanical loss from a chain or other mechanism is exhil-

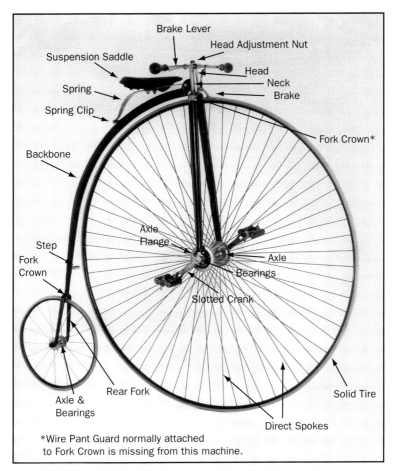

Brake Lever
Head Adjustment Nut
Suspension Saddle
Head
Neck
Spring
Brake
Spring Clip
Fork Crown*
Backbone
Axle
Flange
Step
Fork
Crown
Axle
Bearings
Slotted Crank
Rear Fork
Solid Tire
Axle &
Bearings
Direct Spokes
*Wire Pant Guard normally attached
to Fork Crown is missing from this machine.

*Fig. 4–2.* 1884 Expert Columbia. *(courtesy of Henry Ford Museum)*

arating. With no chain the ordinary is silent, the whoosh of the wind in the spokes and the rubber on the pavement being the only sound.

Riding is easy and comfortable on today's smooth paved roads once you master the art of mounting and dismounting. The long spokes in the large front wheel, coupled with the solid rubber tires that are fitted to nearly all metal wheeled ordinaries, cushion bumps remarkably well. There is something to be said for the erect riding position which provides good leverage on the pedals. The elevation from which you view your surroundings is stimulating. Indeed, why one wanted to be mounted lower than a man on a horse was a question raised by riders when in the 1890s small wheeled safety bicycles began to become popular.

The Ariel's success led numerous manufacturers in Europe and America to engage in the production and refinement of ordinaries. But by 1890 the faster and safer chain driven safeties had captured the market. The most colorful period

Fig. 4–3. The Ariel.
Fig. 4–4. (Inset) Ariel wheel showing spokes pulling wheel into tension.

in cycling history came to a close in 1892 when most of the principal American manufacturers discontinued production of their ordinary bicycles.

## THE EVOLUTION OF THE ORDINARY

The evolution of the ordinary was described as follows in a series of articles in the 1897 *LAW Bulletin and Good Roads.*

"It became constantly a lighter, stronger, easier running, more graceful, and in every way a better machine. Experience in its use and manufacture showed the weak points in the early patterns. In the late eighties it reached a high degree of perfection. Narrow handle bars were lengthened to 26" and had T or spade grips; cranks had an inch added to them, and became, in rare cases, 6" long. Spokes changed from nippled and nutted to direct and then to tangent; in number they rose from 36, 'spokes for inches' (same number of spokes as diameter of wheel) to as high as 90 and finally settled at from 60 to 70 according to size of wheel. Tires were reduced from 1¼" and 1⅛" solid rubber to as low as ¾" and then settled at ⅞" and 1". Sometimes with a hollow core, they were usually cemented on, but could be vulcanized, and occasionally were held by wires running throughout their length."

For purposes of examination, I will divide the ordinary era into three time periods: Early – 1871 to 1882, Mid – 1883 to 1890, and Late – 1890 to 1893.

### The Early Period, 1871–1882

Still smarting from their losses when riders abruptly lost interest in bone-shakers, American manufacturers did not produce ordinaries until 1878 even though they had been available in Europe at least since September, 1871 when the British Ariel went into production in Coventry.

In 1872 Englishman W. H. S. Grout put into production an ordinary that was an improvement upon the Ariel. It had a hollow front fork and solid rubber tires vulcanized to the rim.

*Fig. 4–5.*
Radial spoking on a Standard Columbia.

That same year, James Starley developed radial spoking (Fig. 4-5) in which the flattened heads of each spoke were secured in holes in the rim and held at the hub by nipples which screwed into flanges on the wheel hub. This "spider wheel," as it was called, was very popular with many manufacturers throughout the early period because it easily could be trued by tightening and loosening the nipples.

As riders became less fearful of the ordinary, the front wheel was offered in diameters up to 63" and was limited only by the rider's leg length.

*Fig. 4–6.* Coventry Spider.

Although everyone wanted to ride as large a wheel as possible, the 52" and 54" sizes were most popular. As a service to customers, each manufacturer published tables specifying suggested wheel sizes. It was always noted that it was safer and more comfortable to ride a bicycle slightly too small than one too large. Gormully and Jeffery's size table was as follows:

| *Diameter of front wheel* | *Length of leg: inside measure to sole of foot* |
|---|---|
| 48" | 31½" |
| 50" | 32½" |
| 52" | 33½" |
| 54" | 34½" |
| 56" | 35½" |
| 58" | 36½" |
| 60" | 37½" |

Plain, parallel, or cone bearings, and later ball bearings, made wheels rotate more freely. Gradually, hollow backbones and front forks were developed to make ordinaries lighter.

In 1874, Tinsley Brothers of London published *Bicycling, A Text for Riders* which was republished in 1970. It noted that among the 20 British ordinaries being manufactured, the best known were Sparrow of London, Keen of Maidenhead, Humber of Nottingham, and Coventry Machinists' Company of

Coventry. The book illustrated a Coventry Spider (Fig. 4-6) which in the following ways was typical of early period ordinaries:

☞ Straight, narrow handlebar.

☞ Relatively small front wheel, perhaps 50" diameter maximum, solid rubber tires glued on, solid rims usually of a V-shaped cross section.

☞ Solid front fork of narrow cross section.

☞ Solid backbone of small diameter.

☞ "Spider" wheel with spokes, adjustable by tightening nuts at hub.

☞ Seat spring extended forward of the handlebar.

☞ Brake activated by twisting the handlebar as with the boneshaker. This tightened a cord that would press a friction brake onto the rear tire, not locking the wheel, but rather retarding its movement.

☞ Burnished rather than plated bright work enhanced by glossy black finish ornately striped.

In 1874, James Starley developed an important innovation, the tangent spoke wheel (Fig. 4-7). As you recall, the spokes of the spider wheel radiated straight from the hub to the rim. The tangent wheel had spokes set at a slant so each pair crossed each other at an angle. Tangent spoking proved to be more rigid than direct spoking.

*Fig. 4–7.* Tangential spoking of a New Rapid wheel. Note portions of spokes nearest hub are nickeled.

*Fig. 4–8.* 1878 Columbia.

By 1876, production of ordinaries in Europe had increased immensely with nearly 200 manufacturers in England alone. The ordinary also was popular in France where it retained a greater resemblance to the boneshaker with not so large a front wheel and not so small a rear wheel as the English ordinary. The French ordinary also had the saddle farther back on the backbone. According to Pratt, the best French makers were Michaux, Meyer, and Truffault.

There were a few ordinaries in the United States that had been brought back by Americans traveling abroad, but it was not until 1876, when several European manufacturers exhibited ordinaries at the Philadelphia Centennial Exposition, that the machines attracted much attention outside of Europe.

In November 1877 the Boston firm of Cunningham, Heath and Co. became the first American importer of ordinaries. Cunningham specialized in British machines and operated a popular riding school on Pearl Street. Cunningham imported the following English ordinaries beginning in 1877:

| | |
|---|---|
| Eclipse | John Keen, Clapham Junction |
| Grout Tension | WHS Grout, London |
| Hallamshire | R. A. Hill and Co., London |
| Stanley | Hydes and Wigfull, London |
| Excelsior & Duplex Excelsior | Bayliss Thomas & Co., Coventry |
| Premier | Hillman, & Herbert, Coventry |

A month later Frank Weston began publishing *The American Bicycling Journal*. In February 1878 the Boston Bicycle Club was founded. It was the first of a series of city clubs that would lead to the formation of the League of American Wheelmen and to the popularization of cycling in America.

In January 1878 the Pope Manufacturing Company opened warehouses for the sale of Challenge and Special Challenge ordinaries imported from Singer and Co. of Coventry. Pope also operated a riding school in conjunction with his business.

His success led him by mid-1878 to contract with the Weed Sewing Machine Co. to produce his new Columbia bicycles based on the Duplex Excelsior of the Coventry, England, firm Bayliss Thomas and Co.

The Weed Co., located in Hartford, Connecticut, had mastered the principle of parts interchangeability which it applied to the Columbia ordinary giving it a distinct advantage over many of its European competitors whose components were not standardized.

The 1878 Columbia was well constructed and reasonably priced at $90 for the 50" size. The ways it differed from the previously described 1874 Coventry Spider also described the state of the ordinary's development by 1878 (Fig. 4-8).

☞ Wider handlebar

☞ Front wheel sizes available up to 58" diameter

☞ Larger diameter hollow seamless steel tubing for backbone

☞ Shorter saddle spring adjustable by sliding on backbone

☞ Optional nickel plating

☞ More spokes in the wheels

☞ Pant guard added

☞ Better bearings, lighter construction

In 1879 Englishman James Sturmey described 325 different English ordinaries in his *Indispensable Bicyclist's Handbook*. One named the Portable and made by Grout in London folded and fitted into a carrying bag.

During the remainder of the ordinary's early period, the exporting of English ordinaries to America continued successfully. Cunningham and Co. was the first American importer to commission an English company to produce a special ordinary for them to sell exclusively in the United States. Calling it the Harvard, Cunningham claimed it combined the best qualities of several English makes.

A. M. Gooch of Newton, Massachusetts, began the custom making of bicycles in 1880 and in 1881 R. P. Gormully of Chicago engaged in manufacturing his bicycle called the Ideal. It was produced under license from Pope who had purchased all applicable patents.

Pope continued to promote and refine his product. In 1882 he claimed that of the 12,000 bicycles in use in America there were twice as many Columbias as all the imported brands combined. His 1882 offering differed from the 1878 Columbia in the following ways (Fig. 4-9):

*Fig. 4–9.* 1882 Standard Columbia.

☞ Three models were offered—Standard, Special, and Expert.

☞ Major differences in the 1882 Standard, which is most comparable to the 1878 Columbia, were a friction brake operated by lever on the front wheel, detachable cranks, refinements in the head, larger front wheel hub flanges for greater strength, and the availability of ball bearings.

☞ The Special, introduced in 1880, had the new U-shaped rims that were lighter, a lighter, neater, and better protected closed head, narrower front fork, standard adjustable ball bearings for the front wheel, and spokes threaded directly into the hubs.

☞ The Expert, introduced in 1882, represented the state of the art in American ordinary design and featured hollow elliptical shaped front forks, double butted spokes that were thicker at the ends where the greatest strength was needed, and a wider handlebar better shaped for rider comfort.

**The Mid Period, 1883–1890**

During the mid-period the ordinary reached its peak of refinement and popularity in America. The many city bicycle clubs and the LAW generated enthusiasm for ordinaries among all types of people, but particularly city dwellers who could not afford to keep a horse and carriage. For them, the bicycle was the first personal transportation vehicle they could own and they took to it in astonishing numbers.

Pope continued to expand his line in 1885 and introduced a Light Roadster that had tangential spokes and hollow rims. Also he offered a 22½ pound racing ordinary with the hope that its accomplishments on the track would help promote the entire Columbia line.

In 1885 Albert H. Overman of the Overman Wheel Co., Chicopee, Massachusetts, manufacturers of adult tricycles since 1882, became one of Pope's strongest competitors when he introduced the Victor Light Roadster. It featured interchangeable parts, adjustable ball bearings, hollow rims, and tangential spokes. Two innovations distinguished it from the Columbia: tires compressed into the rim rather than glued on and a "swing saddle" that allowed the rider to sit very close to the backbone thus making it possible to ride a wheel larger than his leg length normally would allow (Figs. 4-10, 4-11). The rider could easily remove the leather saddle from the spring and take it with him to discourage a

*Fig. 4–10.* Victor swing saddle with leather in place.

*Fig. 4–11.* Victor swing saddle with leather removed.

*Fig. 4–12.* Otto boy's bicycle.

thief from hopping on the bicycle and taking off. The 1885 52" Victor Light Roadster was priced at $127.50 compared to its Columbia Light Roadster counterpart which was $135. The controversy rages to this day as to whether the Victor or the Columbia was the better ordinary bicycle.

The third major American manufacturer, the Gormully and Jeffery Co. of Chicago, Illinois, in 1885 offered two ordinaries, the American Challenge and the American Ideal. They also produced a high wheel safety which will be discussed in the next chapter.

The American Challenge was heavier than its Columbia counterpart by more than 17 pounds, but it was $61 less expensive. Part of the Challenge's low cost was achieved by having as options, features that were standard equipment on most Columbias and Victors. For example, the very desirable ball bearings for front and rear wheels and ball bearing pedals were $20 extra.

The American Ideal was even less expensive. It was available only in wheel sizes from 38" to 50". At a time when most bicycles were painted black or nickel plated, standard finish for the Ideal until 1887 was maroon with gold leaf striping.

In 1886 Gormully and Jeffery introduced the American Champion, a higher grade, lighter weight ordinary available in all sizes. This was followed the next year by a still lighter and more competitive American Light Champion.

Like the American Ideal, a few ordinaries were available only in small wheel sizes and were intended primarily for boys and small men. Dress styles of the time restricted most women to adult tricycles. The most popular small ordinaries were the Otto, (Fig. 4-12) which along with the St. Nicholas, was available with wood or metal wheels, and the Horsman, Arlington, Hecla, Fairfield, Spalding, Wilkinson, Apollo, and Acme. Few families could afford to buy these small ordinaries for their children so they are very rare today.

In 1887 William Read & Son, Boston, introduced the New Mail light roadster (Fig. 4-13) built by the Ames Manufacturing Co., Chicopee, Massachusetts. It incorporated all the latest advances and illustrated the ordinary at its highest level of refinement. The New Mail differs from the previous example of an 1882 Columbia in the following ways:

☞ Handlebar wider; spade grip for better grasp.

☞ Head containing ball bearings for maximum smoothness in steering (Fig. 4-14).

*Fig. 4–13.* 1887 New Mail light roadster.

☞ Backbone oval (elliptical) shaped and thicker near the neck gradually tapered to a thinner wall where it attached to the rear fork, thus providing maximum strength where necessary with minimal weight. A similar construction was used for the front fork with the thickest portion nearest the head (Fig. 4-15).

☞ Rims hollow and seamless with thickened section at the bottom for rigidity.

☞ The saddle was longer so the rider could slide forward when needing maximum leverage over the pedals when climbing hills or riding against wind and back to shift weight toward the rear when riding on bumpy roads or descending hills.

☞ Tangent spokes were used and were tied where they crossed to prevent rattles. Spokes easily adjustable by means of nipples at the rim that could be tightened or loosened with a spoke wrench.

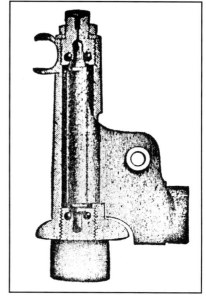

Fig. 4–14. 1887 New Mail "Trigwell" ball bearing head.

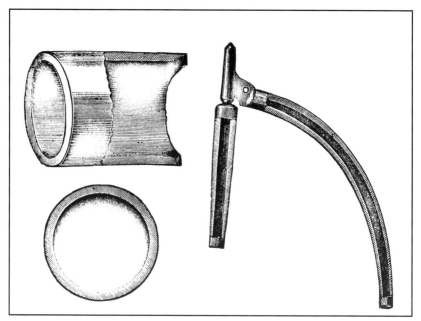

Fig. 4–15. 1887 New Mail "Perfection" double butted backbone and fork.

☞ Pedal rubber shaped with a large flat surface for better purchase.

☞ The 1887 New Mail was priced at $130 compared to $127.50 for the 1882 Expert Columbia. The 1887 Columbia Light Roadster, Pope's counterpart to the New Mail, was sold at the same price as the New Mail.

### The Late Period, 1890–1892

By 1890 most bicycle manufacturers were producing chain driven safeties, retaining ordinaries only as secondary offerings in their lines. Yet the preference for ordinaries persisted among many riders. For them and perhaps to reduce the inventory of slow selling ordinaries, Pope introduced a "rational" option on his Expert and Volunteer Columbias beginning in 1890. A 22" rear wheel four inches larger than standard and an increased rake to the front fork were incorporated in the rational to shift the rider's weight toward the rear to discourage headers.

As described by G. Lacy Hillier in his 1887 Badminton Library *Cycling*, the rider of the ordinary bicycle, before the days of the high wheel safety, considered it necessary to have his saddle very close to the head in order to put him well over his work and to bring the handlebar close to him. In riding the new high wheel safeties he soon found his handlebar and pedals could be further in front without reducing his power.

Ordinary riders then positioned their saddles further back on the backbone giving greater safety from headers while retaining all the advantages of the ordinary. But they discovered that the vibration from a small insufficiently tired rear wheel was an immense drawback. It was to remedy this situation that the larger rational rear wheel was introduced.

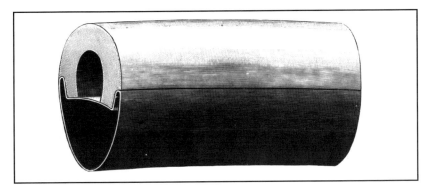

*Fig. 4–16.* Victor cushion tire on a hollow rim.

Overman introduced a Victor Rational Light Roadster in 1891 which was modified from the regular ordinary by a front fork of increased rake and rear wheel of 22" or 24" diameter. Instead of having the usual solid rubber tires, it was fitted with the Victor cushion tire, a simple arch of rubber extending from edge-to-edge of the rim, its side walls were held against spreading by flanges at the edges of the hollow rim. The tire's elasticity cushioned the ride (Fig. 4-16).

Overman and Pope discontinued their ordinaries with the conclusion of the 1892 model year.

### Principal American Ordinaries

American Challenge, 1885–1890, Gormully & Jeffery, Chicago, IL
American Champion, 1886–1890, Gormully & Jeffery, Chicago, IL
American Light Champion, 1887–1890, Gormully & Jeffery, Chicago, IL
American Ideal, 1886–1890, Gormully & Jeffery, Chicago, IL
Centaur, est. 1887, St. Nicholas Mfg. Co., Chicago, IL
Columbia, 1878–1880, Pope Mfg. Co., Boston, MA
Special Columbia, 1880–1882, Pope Mfg. Co., Boston, MA
Standard Columbia, 1880–1889, Pope Mfg. Co., Boston, MA
Expert Columbia, 1882–1892, Pope Mfg. Co., Boston, MA
Columbia Light Roadster, 1885–1892, Pope Mfg. Co., Boston, MA
Columbia Semi Roadster, 1886–1892, Pope Mfg. Co., Boston, MA
Columbia Racer, 1886–1891, Pope Mfg. Co., Boston, MA
Volunteer Columbia, 1888–1892, Pope Mfg. Co., Boston, MA
Gooch, 1880–1889, A. M. Gooch, Newton, MA
Mustang, 1881–1883, Pope Mfg. Co., Boston, MA
National, est. 1889, St. Nicholas Mfg. Co., Chicago, IL
Otto, est. 1881, Western Toy Co., Chicago, IL
Rival, est. 1887, Western Toy Co., Chicago, IL
Victor, 1885–1887, Overman Wheel Co., Boston, MA
Victor Light Roadster, 1887–1891, Overman Wheel Co., Boston, MA
Victor Junior, 1888–1891, Overman Wheel Co., Boston, MA
Warwick, est. 1889, Warwick Cycle Mfg. Co., Springfield, MA

### English Ordinaries Most Popular in America

Club, Coventry Machinists' Co., Ltd., Coventry
Harvard, Bayliss Thomas Co., Coventry for Cunningham & Co., Boston
Humber, Humber & Co., Beeston, Nottingham
New Rapid, St. George's Foundry Co. for S. T. Clarke Co., Baltimore, MD
Premier, Hillman, Herbert, Cooper, Coventry
Royal Mail, Royal Mail Mfg. Co., Ltd., Birmingham
Rudge, D. Rudge & Co., Coventry
Sanspareil, W. Andrews Ltd., Birmingham
Shadow, Thomas Smith & Co., London, for A. G. Spalding Bros., Chicago
Singer, Singer & Co., Coventry
Spalding, Hillman, Herbert, Cooper Coventry, for A. G. Spalding Bros.
Yale, Surrey Machinery Co., London for A. G. Spalding Bros.

## ESTABLISHING AUTHENTICITY AND CONDITION

After your initial excitement in finding an ordinary has subsided, the first thing you should do is identify it. Pope's Columbias and Gormully and Jeffery's Americans had their names and patent information on the dust shield on the head. Because now these shields often are painted or rusted, it is important to know how to identify them by shape (Fig. 4-17). Columbias will be as pictured with a clasp at the base. If the handlebar is attached as shown in Fig. 4-18 and the dust shield is as illustrated, it is one of the American series by Gormully and Jeffery. Victors do not carry maker information on the dust shield, but have

*Fig. 4–17.* c. 1891 Columbia Light Roadster dust shield and head.

a name plate shaped as pictured in Fig. 4-19 attached to the backbone below the saddle bracket. The New Mail nameplate (Fig. 4-20) is mounted on an oval backbone. Its dust shield is shaped as illustrated in Fig. 4-21. The Rudge will have the maker's name stamped into the neck (Fig. 4-22). Bearings and pedals may contain script on many bicycles, but it is not always indicative of the maker because large suppliers of such components sold to several manufacturers.

*Fig. 4–18.* American Ideal dust shield, head, and handlebar clamping device. This 1888 model is equipped with a two-speed hub gear shifted by the right handlebar.

*Fig. 4–19*. Victor name plate.

You can determine from patent dates only that the machine was made after the most recent date. It may be several years newer than the latest date.

*Fig. 4–20*. New Mail name plate.

If it is not possible to find a maker's name or some other identifying criteria, move on to a close examination of the ordinary's condition. If you buy it, you will succeed eventually in identifying it and you'll enjoy the research.

Begin your close look by stepping back and looking at the bicycle's profile from the side. The backbone should fit closely, about 1½" to the edge of the front tire, and the curved portion should match the curve of the rim. If there is too much space between tire and backbone, the ordinary probably has the wrong front wheel (Fig. 4-23). Most ordinaries have the wheel size stamped at the top of the front fork near the rim or at the top of the head. If you can locate the stamping, measure the wheel diameter to double check. The correct measure is from outside edge of tire to outside edge of tire.

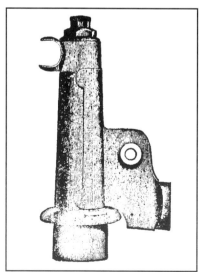

*Fig. 4–21*. New Mail dust shield.

*Fig. 4–22*. Rudge stamped neck.

*Fig. 4–23.* This hybrid ordinary has too much space between the wheel and the backbone, indicating it has the wrong front wheel.

*Fig. 4–24.* This ordinary has had the backbone bent rearward.

Be certain that the spoking pattern corresponds to what was offered originally on the bicycle, i.e., if an Expert Columbia has semi-tangential spokes, its wheels have been switched with another bicycle.

If the backbone does not follow the radius of the front wheel and if it allows the distance between the front and rear tires to exceed about 2", the backbone either has been bent toward the back (Fig. 4-24) or it is the wrong one and is too large for the wheel. If the front fork does not have a slight rake toward the front, the bicycle has been fitted with a backbone that is too large. Many ordinaries have a serial number stamped on the neck of the backbone or on the head that is repeated on the front fork at the back of the head below the dust shield or under the fork where it curves over the wheel or just above the bearings at the end of the fork. If you can find the serial numbers, check whether they match.

*Fig. 4–25.* The too-small rear wheel is noticeable on this ordinary which is being ridden by Robert Menker in a Wheelmen meet obstacle course run.

If the angles of each side of the front fork or rear fork do not match, then the forks have been bent.

The rear wheel was the first component to wear out and thus frequently has been replaced. If it is correct, the tire will fit close within 1½" to the top of the rear fork (Fig. 4-25).

Looking at the ordinary from the front, the shape of the handlebar should be symmetrical and the brake lever should approximate the curve of the bar. Look for cracks, bends, and bad welds on the often-damaged handlebar. If you have determined by its appearance that the bicycle was made in the mid-period, it is unlikely that it would have had a straight bar. Often straight replacement bars were fitted because they were the easiest to make. The front fork should be perfectly true and straight, its distance from the wheel being exactly the same on both sides. It is not unusual for forks to be bent from falls. Have someone lift the bicycle and spin the front wheel while you observe whether the axle is bent. Some wobble at the rim is to be expected in an ordinary that has not had the wheel trued in many years.

Looking at the ordinary from the back, the backbone should align with the front wheel. If it angles to one side, it is bent. If the rear wheel angles slightly to the right or left and does not align exactly with the front wheel, the rear fork is bent. Again, sight down the bicycle and be sure the wheels align.

Having made this initial inspection, now look closely for cracks in the metal, especially in the area of the neck and the head. If there is deep pitting on places such as the handlebar, satisfactory plating will be impossible or very costly. If saddle hardware is missing or incorrect or if the pedals are missing they probably will have to be machined by hand. There are practically no spare parts available.

Check all rims for cracks and bad seams that indicate improper repair. Hollow rims are prone to severe rust damage. Peel back the tire and see if the inner portion of the rim is badly rusted. If it has rusted thin or broken through, a costly new hollow rim will have to be made.

The spokes are most apt to rust near the rim and the hub. Usually ordinary spokes are double butted, which means they are thicker at the hub and at the rim than through the rest of their length (Fig. 4-26). If they have rusted badly, it will be noticeable and each spoke will break when tightened.

Two things are especially important in an ordinary: the absence of cracks and deeply pitted rust, and the completeness and correctness of all the major components. If you find an ordinary with correct and serviceable saddle hardware, handlebar, brake, pedals, wheels, forks, and backbone and if it has only

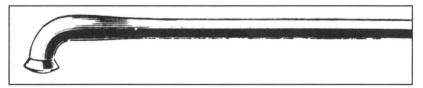

*Fig. 4–26.* A butted end spoke.

surface rust, you have a very restorable bicycle. You can largely disregard missing tires, handlebar grips, saddle leather, and a few broken spokes. These components are the easiest to replace with the exception of spokes that are broken off flush with the hub flange; they have to be drilled out.

*Fig. 4–27.* The Fox reproduction ordinary.

## THE REPRODUCTION ORDINARY

A few individuals skilled at machine work have made ordinaries in numbers less than a dozen for their own use and for limited sale. Certain machines, such as those made by the Greenfield Village Early Engine Club are very convincing in appearance. One important difference that exists on all known reproduction machines is that modern bearings, rather than the original adjustable type, are fitted. This book shows the principal bearings used originally on ordinaries for your reference in examining a machine that may be a reproduction.

Be cautioned that many children's ordinaries are reproductions. The most authentic appearing are made by the Kennedy Machine Shop, Defiance, Ohio, and will bear the name Kennedy stamped into the forward edge of the head.

Following are reproduction ordinaries made in numbers less than a dozen.

**The Fox,** (Fig. 4-27) made by Melvin Fox, Napoleon, Michigan in the early 1970s. Flat stainless rims, modern saddle and pedals, large hub with center same diameter as outside flanges, high cylindrical head, straight handlebar, no taper to backbone.

The **Greenfield Village Early Engine Club** members made about 12 duplicates of the 1884 Expert Columbia owned by Henry Ford Museum. These come close to copying an original, but are unlikely to be found as so few were made and they have stayed within the club membership. Look for a brass dust shield marked Greenfield Village Early Engine Club, an absence of stamped serial number on the top edge of the neck, and modern bearings.

**Allen Polhill,** Milledgeville, Illinois, in the early 1970s made seven reproduction Columbia ordinaries. They closely approximate the original but have modern bearings.

Following is a list of reproductions that have been made in larger numbers:

**The Boneshaker,** manufactured first by Boneshaker Inc., Cleveland, then by Wayne McCutty, Columbus, and later offered by Smith-Edwards, Temple, NH. Modern saddle, cranks, pedals, handlebar, and stem, no taper to backbone, high cylindrical head, a nameplate on some of their models reading "The Boneshaker," generally small wheel sizes 48" or less. Some available with large wheel in rear.

**High Step,** by High Step Bicycle Co., Milwaukee, WI (Fig. 4-28). 48" front, 24" rear wheels, flat rims, modern handlebar and saddle, no taper to backbone, spring loaded plunger brake operating on front wheel, step mounted on right instead of customary left, rear fender.

*Fig. 4–28.* The High Step reproduction ordinary.

*Fig. 4–29.* Two Kennedy reproduction ordinaries and owners Charles Sheets (left) and Ted Sheets (right) of Toledo, OH.

**The Kennedy,** (Fig. 4-29) Kennedy Machine Shop, Defiance, Ohio, resembles the open head Standard Columbia. Brake, front and rear forks, tapered backbone, crescent shaped rims, straight or cow horn handlebar, brake lever and spoon, hubs, and step all are close approximations of original ordinary components although it is not intended to copy a single machine. The word "Kennedy" is stamped into the forward edge of the head. Kennedys are available in any wheel size and can be equipped with direct or tangential spokes that are stainless steel or painted. Handlebars and other components may have nickel or chrome plating.

**Ucceline Manufacturing Company,** Greencastle, Pennsylvania, offers a reproduction that resembles an early Expert Columbia with closed head, straight handlebar, suspension saddle, and front fork that in pictures looks authentic. It is fitted with flat rims, non-tapered backbone, and modern pedals.

The Falcon, produced by Wheel Goods Corp. in Britain in the 1960s, has a modern saddle and handlebar, flat rims, a distinctive cross brace at the head, and an L-shaped seat post welded to the non-tapered backbone.

Please note: the Kennedy Machine Shop also has built Eagle-style reproductions and the Spillanes of Madison, Connecticut, sell reproductions of the Eagle. They also sell the Whitney, a reproduction of the 1884 Victor. Reproduction Eagles also have been built by Gary Woodward of Ann Arbor, Michigan.

## FURTHER RESEARCH

Among recent books, those of most value in researching ordinaries are: *Bicycles and Tricycles* (technical); *Wheels Across America; Wheels and Wheeling; King of the Road; Bicycles and Tricycles of the Year 1886;* and *The Story of the Bicycle.* Don't overlook public libraries. Excellent source books may be found in even the smallest library.

Original catalog descriptions are the best source for correct specifications. The Wheelmen Library contains nearly complete runs of Pope, Victor, and Gormully and Jeffery catalogs and numerous dealer catalogs describing most popular American and European ordinaries. A catalog copying service is offered

*Fig. 4–30.* 1879 Standard Columbia.

*Fig. 4–31.* 1880 Standard Columbia.

to Wheelmen members. Catalog reprints occasionally are advertised in The Wheelmen Newsletter.

Museums listed in the appendix that exhibit antique bicycles offer excellent opportunities to view ordinaries and Wheelmen meets attract ordinaries in great numbers.

### COLUMBIA ORDINARY DATING GUIDE

*(based on catalogs and data compiled by Charles Hetzel for Summer 1972 and 1973 and Winter and Summer 1974 issues,* The Wheelmen *magazine)*

### Standard Columbia 1879–1889

1879     (Fig. 4-30) Columbia seal stamped on saddle spring— Friction brake operating on

*Fig. 4–32.* The longer saddle spring in the 1880, 1881 Standard Columbia.

*Fig. 4-33.* 1880 Special Columbia.

front tire—One round mounting step at crown of rear fork—Serial numbers up to 1091 found at base of left crank for 1878 and 1879. 1879 models had Duplex Excelsior type head, adjustment nut center of pin (Fig. 4-62)

1880–81   (Fig. 4-31) Head adjusted by threaded bolt through the top—Brass oval nameplate fixed to side of backbone— Longer saddle spring (Fig. 4-32)—Detachable cranks—Round mounting step on backbone (Fig. 4-82)—Ball front wheel bearings available late 1881

1882   Parallel front wheel bearings, ball bearings optional
Larger 4½" front wheel hub flange

**Later Standards**

1883   52" and over and 1884 to 1888, 50" and over, had U shaped rims, direct spokes threaded and screwed into the hub flange, 22" to 25" handlebar, parallel bearings front wheel and pedals, cone bearings rear wheel, brass shield with maker's name and patent dates on head facing rider.

1883   50" and under, 1884 to 1888, 48" and under, same as preceding except early shaped rims, spokes thread into lock nuts at hubs

*Fig. 4–34.* 1885 Expert Columbia.

**Special Columbia**

1880–82    Closed head—adjustable Aeolus ball bearings front hub, cone
bearing pedals—locknuts at hub—1⅜" diameter backbone
—U shaped rims (Fig. 4-33)

**Expert Columbia**

1882–92    (Figs. 4-2, 4-34, and 4-37)

**Handlebars**

1882–85    Straight

1883–85    Bent bar optional (Fig. 4-55)

1885       23" to 30" widths, cowhorn bar optional (Fig. 4-57)

1886–92    Cowhorn bar with 2½" drop standard, 1¼" drop optional

1888       28" to 30" widths

**Pedals**

1882–83    Bown's Aeolus ball pedals optional

1882–85    Parallel bearing pedals standard (Fig. 4-69)

1883–85    Columbia ball pedals optional

1886–92    Columbia ball pedals standard

**Saddles**

1882–85    Suspension saddle

*Fig. 4–35.* 1885 Columbia Light Roadster. *(courtesy of Henry Ford Museum)*

1886–92   Hammock saddle
1886       First pattern Kirkpatrick (Fig. 4-48)
1887       Second pattern Kirkpatrick (Fig. 4-49)
1888–89   Third pattern Kirkpatrick (Fig. 4-50)
1890–92   Fourth pattern Kirkpatrick (Fig. 4-51)
**Handlebar Grips**
1882–86   Pear shaped
1886–88   Spade optional (Fig. 4-58)
1887–88   Double grip standard (Fig. 4-59)
1889–92   Spade standard, any earlier type grip optional
**Steps**
1882–87   Oblong, fixed (Fig. 4-80)
1888–92   Oblong, adjustable (Fig. 4-83)
**Rear Forks**
1882–84   Tubular (Fig. 4-86)
1885–86   Rounded crown, open and semi-tubular (Fig. 4-87)
1887–92   Square crown, open and semi-tubular (Fig. 4-89)
**Head Adjustments**
1882–86   Single screw spindle adjustment

*Fig. 4–36.* 1888 Columbia Light Roadster.

| | |
|---|---|
| 1882–85 | Dome-shaped locknut (See Fig. 4-55) |
| 1886 | Hex locknut (See Fig. 4-57) |
| 1887–92 | Double screw adjustment |

**Columbia Light Roadster** (Figs. 4-35 and 4-36)

**Saddles**

| | |
|---|---|
| 1885 | Suspension |
| 1886–88 | Suspension optional |
| 1886–92 | Hammock standard |

**Pedals**

| | |
|---|---|
| 1885 | Parallel bearings, ball optional (Fig. 4-90 and 4-96) |
| 1886–92 | Ball standard, parallel optional |

**Grips**

| | |
|---|---|
| 1885–86 | Pear |
| 1886–88 | Spade optional |
| 1887–88 | Double grip |
| 1889–92 | Spade standard, pear or double grip optional |

**Steps**

| | |
|---|---|
| 1885–87 | Fixed, oblong |
| 1888–92 | Adjustable, oblong |

*Fig. 4–37.* 1890 Expert Columbia.

**Head**
1885–86   Single screw adjustment
1887–92   Duplex screw adjustment
**Rear Fork**
1885–86   Rounded crown, open, semi-tubular
1887–92   Square crown, open, semi-tubular

**VICTOR ORDINARY DATING GUIDE**
(based on catalogs and data compiled by Charles Wilson)

**1885 Victor Bicycle** (Fig. 4-38)
Two bolts hold handlebar to head (Fig. 4-63)
Pear shaped hollow grips
Fixed mounting step (Fig. 4-88)
Skirted saddle instead of pant guard
Clip at front of saddle rather than pommel spring
Oval plates on ends of pedals (Fig. 4-92)
Tangential spokes with three crossings (Fig. 4-70)
All backbones and forks painted black

*Fig. 4–38.* 1885 Victor bicycle.

    Domed nut for head adjustment
    Early bearing style (Fig. 4-71)
    Available 48" to 58"
**1886 Victor Bicycle** (Fig. 4-39) (same bicycle in **1887** called **Victor Roadster**)
    Less curve to handlebar
    Collar holds handlebar to head (Fig. 4-64)
    Grey rubber tires
    Solid black rubber pear grips
    Dust cover attached by screw
    Adjustable step
    Saddle pommel spring optional
    Backbones and fork sides available nickel plated
    60" available
**1887 Victor Light Roadster** (Fig. 4-40)
    Handlebar curvature less pronounced, enters stem at angle
    Handlebar collar adjustable at rear (Fig. 4-65)
    Later type bearing and hub (Figs. 4-73 and 4-72)
    Spade handles on all models
    Conventional screw and hex nut head adjustment
    Cross shaped end plate on pedals (Fig. 4-93)

*Fig. 4–39.* 1886 Victor.

Saddle pommel spring standard
Pant guard replaces skirted saddle

**1888** and **1889 Victor Light Roadster**
No change except long crank with 6¾" slot optional

**1890 Victor Light Roadster**
Unchanged except for greater rim depth

**1891 Victor Light Roadster Rational**
Rear wheel enlarged to 22" or 24" rims
1½" front, 1¼" rear cushion tires

**1892 Rational**
Square shouldered forks front and rear, full tubular rear fork,
plunger actuated brake with a coil return spring

#### AMERICAN ORDINARY DATING GUIDE
*(based on catalog descriptions)*

**American Ideal 1881–1890**
Although information on early Ideals is sketchy, please note from
Fig. 4-41 that pre-1885 models were virtually the same as the
Standard Columbia. They were built under license from the Pope
Mfg. Co.

*Fig. 4–40.* 1887 Victor Light Roadster.

1885 (Fig. 4-42)
> Dropped one-piece handlebar
> Solid iron forks
> Parallel bearings front wheel and pedals, ball bearings optional
> (Fig. 4-74) 38" to 50" wheel diameter, closed head except on small-
> er sizes which continued with Standard Columbia pattern open
> head, rubber handlebar grips, adjustable step on all larger than 42"
> (Fig. 4-81), cone rear wheel bearings
> 16" diameter rear wheel on 44" to 50"
> 14" diameter rear wheel on 38" to 42" and 12" on 30" to 34"

1886     Wheel sizes 30" to 50" available

1887     (Fig. 4-43) Gormully and Jeffery patent handlebar clamp
> (Fig. 4-60) Cowhorn handlebar standard, dropped or straight
> optional (Fig. 4-56). Maroon finish discontinued, black with gold
> leaf stripe substituted

1888–89   Cobblestone saddle standard, ram's horn handlebar optional
> (Figs. 4-52 and 4-61)

1890     Spade handlegrips

*Fig. 4–41.* A pre-1885 American Ideal.

**American Challenge, 1885–1890**

1885 (Fig. 4-46)
        Suspension saddle
        1½" diameter backbone
        Adjustable step
        Cone bearing rear wheel
        Maker's name on dust shield, closed head
        One piece handlebar available dropped, straight, or cowhorn
        Solid forks
        Parallel bearing pedals, balls optional, white pedal rubber (Fig. 4-91)

1886     Sizes 48" and 50" incorporated into regular line, smaller and intermediate sizes continued to be available. Gormully and Jeffery handlebar clamping device, new step (Fig. 4-85)

1887     Lillibridge hammock saddle optional (Fig. 4-53)

1888–89  Lillibridge hammock saddle standard, Wonder (Fig. 4-54) or Cobblestone saddles optional, ram's horn handlebar optional

1890     Split sleeve over socket screw (Fig. 4-66)

*Fig. 4–42.* 1885 American Ideal.

**American Champion, 1886–1890**
**1886 American Champion** (Fig. 4-45)
      48" to 60" wheels, also available in smaller and intermediate sizes
      Hollow forks
      Molded red tires
      Ball bearings front and rear wheels, deeply recessed hub (Fig. 4-75)
      Cowhorn handle bar with ebonite spherical grips
      High backbone neck to increase bearing surface (Fig. 4-67)
      Solid comfort hammock saddle
      Ball bearing pedals (Fig. 4-94)
      Adjustable step
      17" diameter rear wheel 52" and above, 16¾" below 52"

| | |
|---|---|
| 1887 | Lillibridge saddle standard, spade grips optional |
| 1888 | Ram's horn handlebar, rat trap pedals optional, new design adjustable step |
| 1889 | Perfect fit grips optional, Light Champion fork ends (Fig. 4-77) Cobblestone saddle standard |
| 1890 | Rational pattern with shorter backbone and 20" rear wheel optional, ball pedals with pointed rather than rounded ends, split sleeve over head socket screw |

## American Light Champion, 1887–1890

**1887 American Light Champion** (Fig. 4-47)

Ram's horn handlebar, ebonite grips, ball bearing head (Fig. 4-68) 60" available, hollow forks, red molded tires, tangent spokes tied seven times, ball bearings front and rear wheels, corrugated front hubs (Figs. 4-76 and 4-79), Lillibridge saddle, ball bearing pedals, rat trap optional (Fig. 4-95 and 4-97), light adjustable step as in Fig. 4-84, 17" diameter rear wheel 52" and above, 16" for rest, all nickel finish including rims optional.

1888    Light fork end, light head, hollow rims

1889    Perfect fit grips optional

          Wonder saddle standard, and G & J saddle optional

1890    Split sleeve over head socket screw

*Fig. 4–43.*
Jane Adams
riding an
unusual 1887
American Ideal
with two-speed
freewheeling
hub made by
the Simonds
Gear Co.

*Fig. 4–44.* Spade handle grips were featured on the 1890 American Ideal.

*Fig. 4–45.* 1886 American Champion.

*Fig. 4–46.* 1885 American Challenge.

*Fig. 4–47.* 1887 American Light Champion.

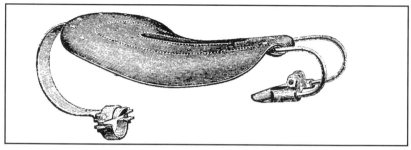

*Fig. 4–48.* First pattern Kirkpatrick saddle, Columbia.

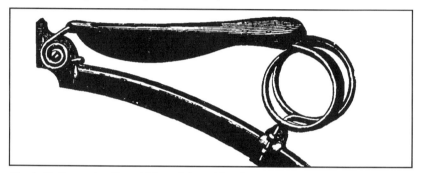

*Fig. 4–49.* Second pattern Kirkpatrick saddle, Columbia.

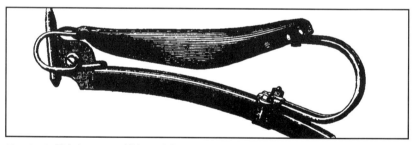

*Fig. 4–50.* Third pattern Kirkpatrick saddle, Columbia.

*Fig. 4–51.* Fourth pattern Kirkpatrick saddle, Columbia.

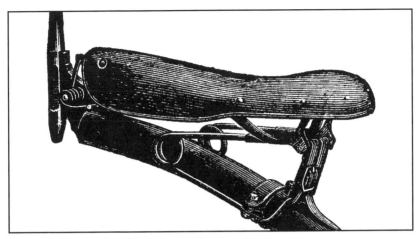

*Fig. 4–52.* Standard Cobblestone saddle, American Ideal.

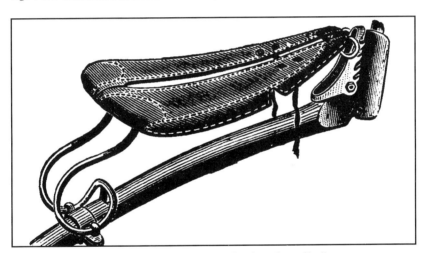

*Fig. 4–53* Optional Lillibridge hammock saddle, American Challenge.

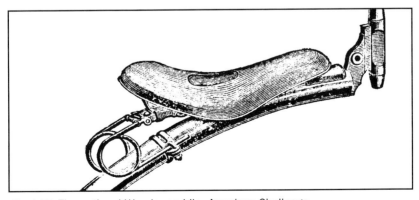

*Fig. 4–54.* The optional Wonder saddle, American Challenge.

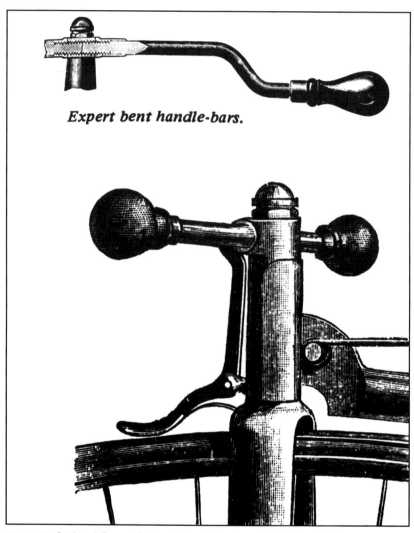

*Fig. 4–55.* Optional Expert Columbia bent bar top, straight bar bottom.

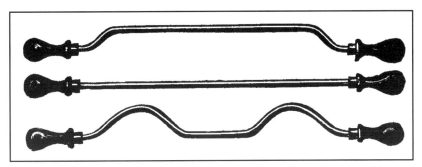

*Fig. 4–56.* Dropped, straight, and cowhorn handlebars for the American Ideal.

*Fig. 4–57* Optional cowhorn handlebar, Expert Columbia.

*Fig. 4–58.* Optional Spade grip, on a Columbia.

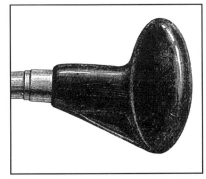

*Fig. 4–59.* Standard double grip, Columbia.

*Fig. 4–60.* Patented handlebar clamp by Gormully and Jeffery, American Ideal.

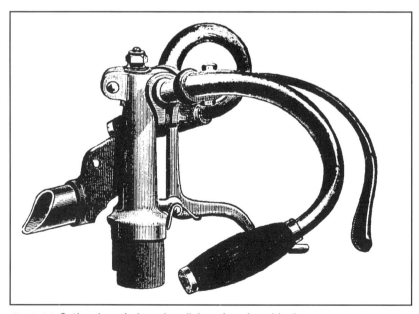

*Fig. 4–61.* Optional ram's horn handlebar, American Ideal.

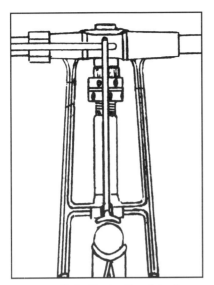

*Fig. 4–62.* Note Duplex Excelsior type head, adjustment nut off center of pin on 1879 Standard Columbia.

*Fig. 4–63.* Two bolts hold handlebar to head; Victor.

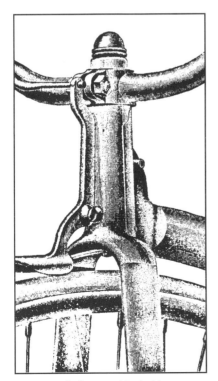

*Fig. 4–64.* Collar used to hold handlebar to head; Victor.

*Fig. 4–65.* Adjustable handlebar collar.

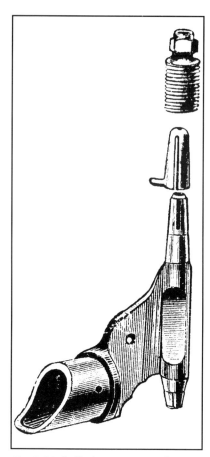

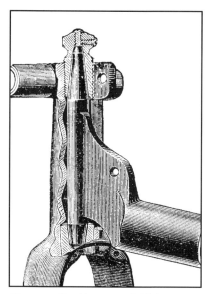

*Fig. 4–67.* Backbone neck high; American Champion.

*Fig. 4–66.* Split sleeve over socket screw; American Challenge.

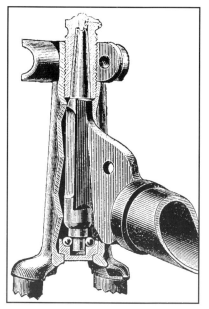

*Fig. 4–68.* Head has ball bearings; American Light Champion.

*Fig. 4–69.* Closeup of standard parallel bearing pedals of a Columbia Expert. *(courtesy of Henry Ford Museum)*

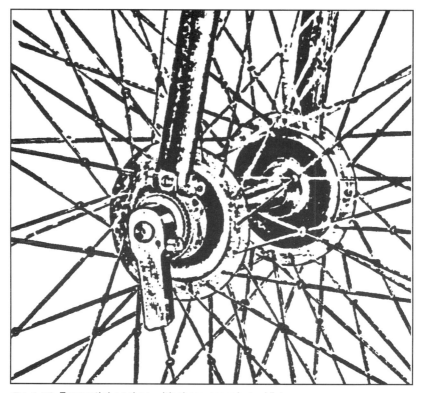

*Fig. 4–70.* Tangential spokes with three crossings; Victor.

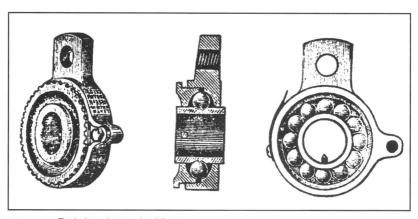

*Fig. 4–71.* Early bearing style; Victor

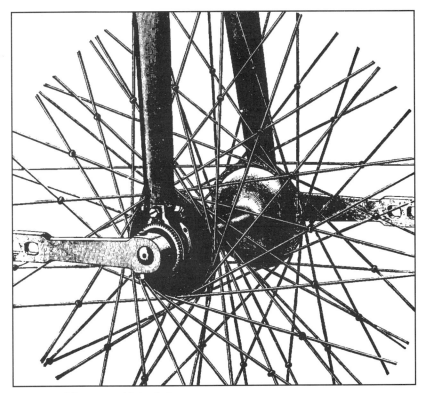

*Fig. 4–72.* A later type Victor hub.

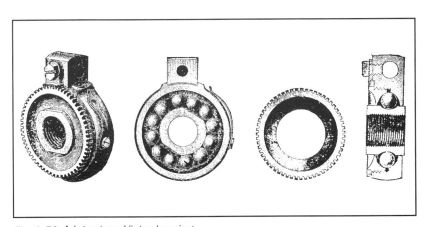

*Fig. 4–73.* A later type Victor bearing.

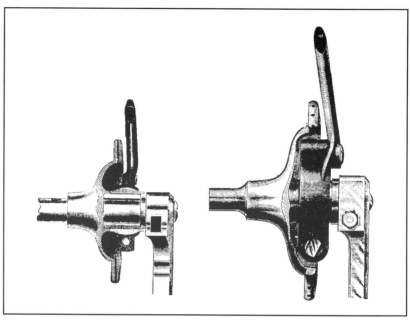

*Fig. 4–74.* Parallel bearings for front wheels and pedals, left. Optional ball bearings, right; American Ideal.

*Fig. 4–75.* Deeply recessed front hub; American Champion.

*Fig. 4–76.* Ball bearings front and rear, corrugated front hub; American Light Champion.

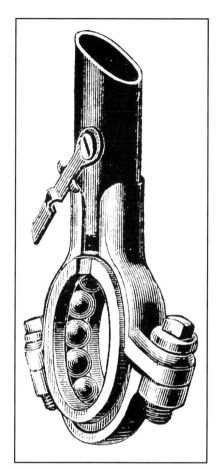

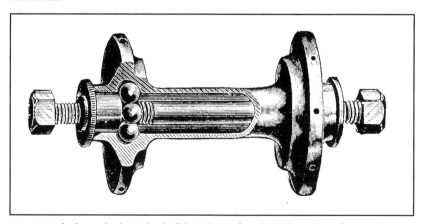

*Fig. 4–78.* Columbia rear hub with ball bearings.

*Fig. 4–77.* American Light Champion fork ends.

*Fig. 4–79.* A closer look at the ball bearings of an American Light Champion rear hub.

*Fig. 4–80.* Oblong, fixed step; Columbia.

*Fig. 4–81.* Adjustable mounting step on American Ideal models larger than 42".

*Fig. 4–82.* Closeup of the round mounting step on backbone; Standard Columbia.

*Fig. 4–83.* Oblong, adjustable step; Columbia.

*Fig. 4–84.* New light adjustable mounting step on an American Light Champion.

*Fig. 4–85.* American Challenge 1886 pattern mounting step.

*Fig. 4–86.* Tubular rear forks of a Columbia.

*Fig. 4–87.* Rounded crown, open and semi-tubular; Columbia.

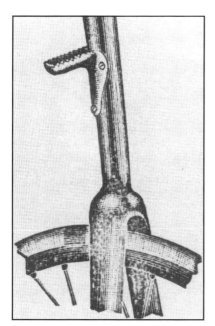

*Fig. 4–88.* Fixed mounting step on a Victor.

*Fig. 4–89.* Square crown, open, and semi-tubular; Columbia.

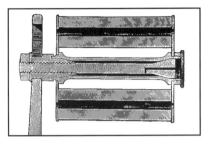

*Fig. 4–90.* Columbia pedal with parallel bearings.

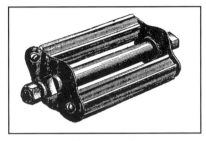

*Fig. 4–91.* Rubber was white on American Challenge pedals.

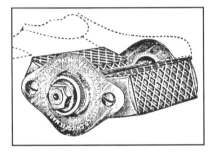

*Fig. 4–92.* Oval plates on ends of Victor pedals.

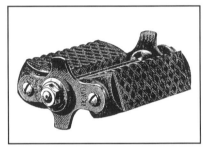

*Fig. 4–93.* Cross-shaped end plate on Victor pedal.

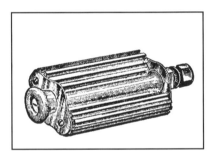

*Fig. 4–94.* American Champion ball bearing pedal.

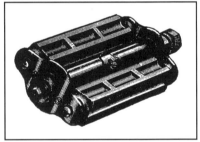

*Fig. 4–95.* American Light Champion Ball bearing pedals.

*Fig. 4–96.* 1886–92 Columbia standard ball pedal.

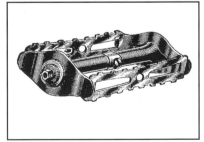

*Fig. 4–97.* American Light Champion's optional rat trap pedal.

# Chapter 5:
# The High Wheel Safety: 1876-1891

While most bicycle makers concentrated on refining the ordinary for greater speed and ease of pedaling, some, led by J. Beale of England, spent their efforts in a quest for safety. The high wheel safeties they produced were the most interesting bicycles of the period. Using various approaches to prevent headers, these machines were distinguished from the common ordinaries by such features as smaller drive wheels and larger trailing wheels, raked back front forks, and unusual drive mechanisms.

Although it is not certain who made the first high wheel safety, Englishman H. J. Lawson in about 1876 built the Sussex Giant with a huge 84" rear wheel driven by levers from a small 24" front wheel over which the rider sat. The rear wheel was reduced to 60" to keep it from swaying before it was unsuccessfully marketed by Singer and Company. Bicycle historian Derek Roberts asserts that Singer's 1878 Xtraordinary Challenge was the first high wheel safety to be patented.

By 1880 there was a proliferation of high wheel safeties in England and the first American patent for one had started a wave of activity in the United States. Several ordinary manufacturers soon added safeties to their lines and suddenly cycling had a new dimension with riders arguing the merits of safeties versus ordinaries and challenging one another for speed and distance.

Typically the several different approaches to safety bicycles all had more moving parts than the ordinary, thus increasing friction, weight, and pedal effort. Most riders simply were not willing to give up the ordinary's relative ease of running for the harder pedaling safety.

Also, American club riders of the period enjoyed the spirit of adventure that came with mastering the ordinary. The ever-present danger of a header added to the challenge and excitement of the ride. Safeties, which often had smaller wheels, were seen by many as being just for the old or timid. Undoubtedly, it must have seemed to the rider of the day that the new high wheel safeties just didn't look like bicycles.

By focusing continuously on the challenge of making a safe bicycle and by developing innovative gear and chain mechanisms, the safety manufacturers and riders helped pave the way for the modern bicycle.

Today, high wheel safeties are one of the most sought after categories of antique bicycles. Their relative rarity, coupled with their interesting drive mechanisms, have only now given them the attention and respect their manufacturers sought nearly 100 years ago.

## THE PRINCIPAL HIGH WHEEL SAFETIES
### The Facile

The Facile, (Fig. 5-1) manufactured 1880 to about 1892 by Ellis & Co., Ltd., Coventry, was patented Jan. 25, 1878 by John Beale. There is general agreement that this was the first commercially successful high wheel safety. The front wheel ranged from 36" to 52" in diameter with an average size of 42". The rear wheel always was 22". The front fork raked back 2" and the saddle was placed well down on the backbone. As described in the March 4, 1898 *LAW Bulletin,* the front fork extended down and forward 12" below the hub. 18" levers were joined to the fork ends and secondary pedal levers were joined to these. The pedal motion was not rotary, but formed an arc of a circle.

*Fig. 5–1.* c. 1887 Facile.

According to the March, 1885 Facile catalog, three factors were responsible for its safety. These applied in varying ways to all front driving high wheel safeties. The reduced front wheel lowered the center of gravity allowing the machine to tip much further before overbalancing either forward or sideways. It was noted that the Facile need tip only a few inches sideways before the rider's feet reached the ground. The enlarged back wheel increased the weight at the rear, and most importantly, the foot was always between the wheels and below and behind the axle.

On ordinaries, pressure was applied forward of the axle or at the center. This tended to lift the back wheel and cause the machine to tip forward. On the Facile, it was claimed, the pressure was always and wholly applied below and behind the center of the axle, thus holding down the back wheel.

The 1885 Facile catalog went on to explain that frequently a bicycle cleared a stone with the front wheel but struck it with the back. With the ordinary this could push the back wheel to one side which was equivalent to turning the front wheel. If done suddenly and unexpectedly, this was liable to upset the rider. On the contrary, the large back wheel of the Facile rolled over an obstacle and was another reason for its greater safety.

Likewise a step 3" lower than a typical ordinary made the Facile easier to mount and dismount. Its overall smaller size further contributed to the ease of learning to ride and also shortened any fall from the saddle. Its reluctance to tip forward permitted harder use of the brake to slow the front wheel. The Facile was so safe, the catalog touted, that not even winter weather would deter it.

*Fig. 5–2.* Geared Facile drive mechanism.

This high wheel safety was offered in Extra Special, Special, and Standard models. Beginning in 1885 a speed gear was an available option (Fig. 5-2).

The Extra Special, produced first in 1884, had hollow back forks and hollow rims and could be as light as 33 lbs. in racing trim.

The Special had solid crescent-shaped rims, direct spokes, and ball bearings throughout. A 40" Special weighed 42 lbs. and cost $132 in 1885.

The Standard had parallel bearings front, cone bearings rear, and a different saddle.

The gear drive mechanism is essentially a sun and planet configuration, with the larger driven wheel attached directly to the wheel axis at one end. This larger "sun" gear is turned by a smaller planetary gear affixed so that it cannot rotate. As the small gear goes around, its projecting teeth carry the large wheel with it, and as its orbit progresses propelling the large gear, the teeth of the planet gear mesh continuously so that new tooth positions are in contact as it moves around. The effect is that as the planetary gear goes around the sun gear, the sun is driven faster by the progressing teeth.

By 1884 geared Faciles were in production sporting a severely raked front fork and large rear wheel positioned well behind the small front wheel.

In actual riding, a good-condition Facile is smooth in operation. The position of the lever is adjustable for varying leg lengths, but the rider must use the tips of his feet on the pedals. This is awkward and tires the ankles. The Facile is well made and unique and sporting in appearance. It is much sought after by collectors.

### Xtraordinary Challenge, 1878 to about 1888

Patented by G. Singer, October 24, 1878, this unique machine (Fig. 5-3) was immediately put into production by his Singer & Co. of Coventry.

Offered in sizes 48" to 54", the Xtra had a front fork that raked back about 9". Precise steering was secured by bending the fork forward at the head (Fig. 5-4) so the line of the steering head pointed to the spot where the front wheel touched the road. It was driven by long bent levers, connected with the cranks and attached at the upper end to short arms which worked on universal joints on the sides of the forks (Fig. 5-5). Safety was assured by the rider's position which placed the application of power so far back of the axle.

The 1887 Singer catalog claimed the Xtraordinary Challenge was the only front-driving safety in which it was possible to use a large driving wheel, thus enabling the rider to sit at nearly the same height as when riding an ordinary.

In actual use, the Xtra's numerous bearings wore quickly and were difficult to keep in adjustment. The complex drive mechanism created friction at several bearing points and the machine tended to be slow and heavy.

By 1884 the Xtra sold for $172.50 in America, making it the most expensive high wheel safety. Nickel plated finish, tool bag, and rubber handlebar grips were extra. It is prized today for its rakish appearance and the intriguing motion

*Fig. 5–3.* c. 1886 46" Xtraordinary Challenge.

*Fig. 5–4.* Xtra fork is bent forward of the head. *(courtesy of Henry Ford Museum)*

*Fig. 5–5.* Xtra drive mechanism. *(courtesy Henry Ford Museum)*

were extra. It is prized today for its rakish appearance and the intriguing motion of its drive levers.

### The Star, 1881–1892

Patented by George W. Pressey of Hammonton, New Jersey, October 26, and November 23, 1880, the Star was put into production by the H. B. Smith Machine Co. of Smithville, New Jersey in the spring of 1881. Its name derived from the double star shaped spoke pattern on the earliest models (Fig. 5-6).

The front wheel of the Star was about 18" and was the steerer. Rear wheels of 42" to 60" diameter were driven by levers and a ratchet gear. The levers carried the pedals on their forward ends, and were hinged at the rear to projections on the lower rod of the frame behind the hub. At the bend of the levers, below the hub, leather straps were attached to pins. These straps passed around

*Fig. 5–6.* 1883 American Star.

drums on the driving wheel axle (Fig. 5-7). Pressure on the levers drew down the straps and rotated the drums which drove the wheel through a ratchet arrangement. A spring within the drum wound up the strap and raised the lever to make it ready for the next stroke. The levers could be depressed alternately or, when a burst of speed was desired, simultaneously.

The Star was the first American safety and the only major American innovation in the general design configuration of the bicycle. It eventually became quite popular despite a slow start in 1881 when customers complained about non-adjustable spokes which were riveted into the rims, a frame that was exceedingly heavy, and the lack of a brake.

The 1882 model eliminated these problems and started the Star on a course of continued refinement that would incorporate the hollow frames and rims, tangential spokes, and improved saddles of the best ordinaries.

Because the Star rider sat over the back wheel, the Star could not be made to take a header, a point dramatically promoted by such activities as riding one down the steps of the Capitol Building in Washington, D.C., and by playing polo while mounted on Stars (Fig. 5-8).

The lack of weight on the front wheel caused the Star's steering to be very uncertain on loose gravel, tending to pitch the machine backward if the front wheel unexpectedly hit or was stopped by an object in the road. Lateral slipping of the front wheel also caused frequent falls to the side. The spring in the axle drum could not be made strong enough to lift the foot at the end of the power stroke and thus the foot had to be lifted after each stroke. This made the

*Fig. 5–7.* Star drive mechanism. Note two attachment pins for drive strap.
*(courtesy of Henry Ford Museum)*

Star tiresome on long tours. Although by 1889 the weight of the 48" Racing Star had been reduced to 30 lbs., most models were heavier than their ordinary counterparts.

*Fig. 5–8.*
Star polo.

Nevertheless, the Star was not without advantages. That it was the only bicycle other than the Eagle that allowed the rider to stand on the levers for a surge of power on hills was the major factor in its astonishing success at holding all records for competitive hill climbs. Also it was not unusual for the Star to perform admirably in competition with ordinaries on timed distance runs and in races. It nearly always won in speed competition with other high wheel safeties. Another advantage was the adjustability of the Star drive mechanism to the leg length of the rider, thus making it possible for one machine to be ridden by anyone in the family.

Stars were available in six models. All but the 39" x 24" and the Rover could be had in standard or Pony sizes. The Pony had a driving wheel of 40", 42", or 45" diameter. The hinged ends of the levers dropped lower on the Pony than on standard size models. Ponys were recommended by riders and the manufacturer as the most comfortable Star to ride.

The American Star was the only model with a coil spring directly over the front wheel and a plated rod covering the steering shaft. It had gravity pawls.

The Semi Racing Star had an exposed steering rod, silent pawls, and longer spring over the rear wheel.

*Fig. 5–9.* c. 1889 39" x 24" Star.

The Special Star had an oscillating coil attached to the front of a long flexible seat spring.

The Star Racer had hollow framing, levers, and rims and tangential spokes.

The 39" x 24" Star was introduced in 1889 with 24" front and 39" rear wheels and a lighter construction. It was safer and less apt to pitch backward. Late versions could be fitted with pneumatic tires (Fig. 5-9).

The Rover Star was introduced in 1892 with 39" rear, 30" front wheels. It was claimed to combine all the advantages of the low wheel safeties with the speed and comfort of a high wheel.

### Kangaroo, 1884 to about 1888

In 1884 Hillman, Herbert and Cooper of England introduced the "dwarf safety" bicycle called a Kangaroo (Fig. 5-10) which they claimed had been designed by Mr. Hillman. In fact, such a machine was described in an Otto and Wallis patent of July 11, 1878, and the same year Kousseau built one in France. In 1881 Joseph Hall of Sheffield, England marketed for one year a bicycle that was very similar.

The Kangaroo was made in "dwarf" sizes with front wheel usually 36", rear 22". The front fork, instead of running directly to the front wheel bearings passed 2½" behind them, was supported by brackets, and was continued about

*Fig. 5–10.* 1885 Kangaroo. *(courtesy of Henry Ford Museum)*

eight inches lower than the axle. At the fork ends were bearings, sprockets, and cranks. The lower sprockets were connected by chains with smaller sprockets on the hub (Fig. 5-11). The Kangaroo thus was driven with two short chains and steered like the ordinary.

Its safety derived from the low position of the rider and its small size and balanced weight. Its speed was demonstrated by Englishman George Smith September 27, 1884. He covered 100 miles in 7 hours, 11 minutes, and 10 seconds beating the existing record by 4 minutes, 8 seconds. Its speed capability resulted from its use of sprockets by which the rotation of the drive wheel could be increased or decreased relative to the rotation of the driving pedals by having different numbers of teeth on the sprockets. Kangaroos with 35" wheel usually were geared to be the equivalent of a 53" ordinary; 36" to 48" or 54"; 38" to 50" or 57".

It was well made with hollow forks, a strong head, good adjustable ball bearings, and a saddle spring that could be adjusted 3" in height to accommodate different size riders.

Lacy Hillier, in his 1889 edition of The Badminton Library, *Cycling,* criticized the Kangaroo for excessive vibration caused by the rider sitting on so small a wheel and by the wheels being so close together. He also noted a great tendency for the machine to wobble caused by the alternate pressure of the feet on the long cranks and the gearing of the driving wheel.

*Fig. 5–11.* Drive mechanism 1885 Kangaroo. *(courtesy of Henry Ford Museum)*

*Fig. 5–12.* 1886 Columbia Safety.

Perhaps the greatest tribute accorded the Kangaroo was that its design was copied by nearly every bicycle manufacturer in England, by Walsh in Germany, and by the Pope Mfg. Co. in America.

Called the Columbia Safety, the Pope machine (Fig. 5-12) was introduced in 1886 at $140 with ball bearings throughout and 42" front, 20" rear wheels. It was available through 1888.

Kangaroos were imported by several American dealers. In 1885, H. B. Hart of Philadelphia offered any size Kangaroo at $130 with ball bearing pedals $7 extra.

Collectors value the Kangaroo as a transitional bicycle using chain drive in an ordinary bicycle design configuration. Despite their popularity in the 1880s and the number of makers who produced them, they are difficult to find today and are much sought after.

**American Safety, 1885–1889**

Produced by the Gormully and Jeffery Company of Chicago and totally different from, but often confused with the Xtraordinary Challenge which depended on fork rake and large rear wheel for safety, the American (Fig. 5-13) had a standard sized rear wheel and normal fork rake. It was based on the earlier English Devon.

The front wheel was available in sizes from 42" to 46". The rear was 20" in diameter.

Ordinary bicycle pedals were attached to levers that were hung below and extended to the end of the cranks. The connection from the front end of the levers to a swinging tubular rod caused the pedals to move in an oval pattern.

The American's safety qualities were due to the comparatively small wheel size and the low, rearward position from which the power was applied.

Offered in its first year of production for $76 in the 42" size, the American required its buyers to pay $15 extra for ball bearings on front and rear wheels.

*Fig. 5–13.* 1885 American Safety.

By its last year of manufacture, a lower handlebar, longer suspension saddle, and rear fender had been added and the price had been reduced to $71.

In 1887 Gormully and Jeffery marketed the American Light Safety (Fig. 5-14) retaining the design of the earlier model which was still offered, but incorporating ball bearings throughout, ram's horn handlebar, and imported weldless steel tubing. In 1888 the Light Safety wheels were changed to tangential spoking, but without hollow rims.

*Fig. 5–14.* 1888 American Light Safety.

Although Gormully and Jeffery machines generally were of a less expensive grade, the American Safety was a smooth-operating and comfortable bicycle.

### Springfield Roadster, 1887–1889

The Springfield Bicycle Manufacturing Co. of Boston claimed headers were impossible with their Springfield Roadster (Fig. 5-15).

Instead of cranks, the Springfield was fitted with levers (Fig. 5-16) and a clutch which oscillated on a fixed axle. Large gears rotated constantly on the axle after the power had been applied. The motion of the gears was transmitted to the driving wheel from a fixed shaft. The clutch was noiseless and gripped instantly when power was applied. It formed a ¾" roll bearing for the gears. The bearing case was lapped over the forks with 1⅜" parallel bearings on each side. The motion of the levers downward and forward was 13".

By 1889 the Springfield Roadster catalog offered models designated simply Number 1, Number 2, and Number 5.

Number 1, at $75, had parallel bearings on the large wheel, cone bearings on the rear, and pear shaped grips on a cowhorn handlebar.

Number 2, at $100, had adjustable ball bearings all around and spade handlebar grips.

Number 5, at $110, featured hollow rims with tangential spokes.

*Fig. 5–15.* 1888 Springfield Roadster.

*Fig. 5–16.* 1888 Springfield Roadster drive mechanism. *(courtesy of Henry Ford Museum)*

The Springfield's up and down lever action required the rider to lift the weight of his leg after the pedal stroke. This, combined with the fact that many of the Springfields in use today are not equipped with ball bearings, has given the machine a reputation for being hard to pedal. However, if a person is properly conditioned for the vehicle's leg movement and is riding a good condition ball bearing equipped bicycle, the Springfield Roadster should be a suitable mount for tours.

Springfields are sought after as a bicycle with one of the very few American high wheel safety drive mechanism innovations.

### The King, 1886–c. 1890

Introduced in 1886 by the King Wheel Co., New York, N. Y., the ratchet drive King safety bicycle (Fig. 5-17) was driven by levers and chains. The drive levers were pedaled up and down in a motion similar to the Star. Each lever was attached to the axle shaft by chains and to a second shaft that pulled the opposite lever back into position by a second chain. Well built with hollow rims, tangential spokes, and even a supply of extra spokes provided with each machine at the factory, this rare high wheel safety was invented by the Rev. Homer A. King of Springfield, Massachusetts, and was made by the Ames Manufacturing Co. The maker offered a one-tenth discount to clergymen.

*Fig. 5–17.* c. 1886 King.

## Eagle, 1889–1891

Patented by L. B. Gaylor of Stamford, Connecticut in 1886, the Eagle was the only high wheel safety that retained the light weight and simple rotary crank drive and large wheel of the ordinary while incorporating the header-free design of the Star (Fig. 5-18).

Because there was no provision for a step, it was mounted with difficulty by riding a pedal high enough to swing onto the saddle. The Eagle was very well made and, as with the Star, riders could gain speed by standing on the pedals.

*Fig. 5–18.* 1889 46" Eagle.

Like the Star, a lack of weight on the front steering wheel caused it to be unsteady on loose surfaces and to be prone to "backward headers." The Eagle's greatest problem may have been that it was introduced too late. By 1889 the small wheel chain safety was becoming well established.

By 1891 three Eagle models were offered; the Roadster, 44 lbs. with direct spokes, solid rims, and ball bearings throughout, and all except spokes and rims nickeled for $130; the Light Roadster, 37 lbs., with frame enameled, balance nickeled, tangential spokes, and hollow rims for $132; and the Racer, 23 lbs. for $140.

A boy's model was listed in the 1891 catalog at $40. The option of cushion tires for any Eagle was offered at $5 per machine, but was not recommended because it made the Eagle slow and heavy.

Eagles are well thought of by collectors today who appreciate their fine work-manship and simple design and by riders, especially young and adventurous ones, who use it to advantage on long distance Wheelmen tours and in club speed events.

### ESTABLISHING AUTHENTICITY AND CONDITION

The manufacturers of most high wheel safeties can be easily identified because of the unique design features. You must exercise caution, however-er, in identifying Kangaroo type chain driven dwarfs, because of the similarity of those offered by various manufacturers. As with ordinaries, when identify-ing dwarfs, look for information on head dust shields and stampings on forks and backbone necks.

When examining the high wheel safety for authenticity and condition, much of the same advice that was given for examining ordinaries applies with a few exceptions. Year of manufacture is more difficult to determine. Certain charac-teristics of early period ordinaries, such as narrow straight handlebars, mark high wheel safeties as being early. But they changed less frequently than ordi-naries and early models tended to be continued in the line for many years. It is best to study other similar machines and the limited available literature to deter-mine the year a high wheel safety was manufactured.

Faciles and Kangaroos were not always built with the wheel as close to the backbone as on the ordinary. Many high wheel safeties are apt to have the rear wheel extended farther behind the front wheel with a resulting larger space between front and rear wheels than on the ordinary. Also some Facile, Kangaroo, and Springfield Roadster backbones may appear to be bent back, not following the radius of the front wheel as closely as on the ordinary. Carefully study original illustrations of high wheel safeties as a guide to how they should look.

Advice on the trueness and symmetry of forks and frames, the importance of looking for cracks and deep pits that weaken the metal in frames, rims, and spokes applies equally to all antique bicycles.

It is not unusual for the uniquely shaped Star solid rims (Fig. 5-19) to break apart. Look carefully for rim cracks. Stars may have the front wheel turned backward so the front fork angles away from instead of toward the back wheel. This easily can be corrected simply by turning it around. Eagle hubs are prone to warping, probably because the cranks could easily bend them in a

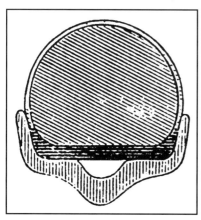

*Fig. 5–19.* Star rim, cross-section.

fall. Also the head, where it attaches to the handlebar, frequently is bent on this particular make. Kangaroo chains sometimes are worn and do not seat well on the sprocket teeth. Xtraordinary Challenge levers often are bent and bearings frequently are worn beyond use.

Most high wheel safeties had more components than ordinaries; thus they are more likely to be missing important pieces that will be costly to reproduce. On the other hand, since in most cases each maker's machine was unique, there was much less switching of parts. The greater value of the safeties often makes it worthwhile to machine the missing components.

### Reproductions

Convincing reproductions of high wheel safeties have not been made with the exception of Eagles made by Gary Woodward (Fig. 5-20) and the Spillane family.

Because of the complex castings and numerous parts in most high wheel safeties, it is unlikely they will be reproduced in the future.

### FURTHER RESEARCH

All recent book sources listed for further research on ordinaries also contain references to and illustrations of high wheel safeties. Likewise museums listed in the ordinary section also exhibit high wheel safeties.

Also, there are high wheel safety catalogs in The Wheelmen library. A series of articles on the Star and frequent references to all high wheel safeties have been published in The Wheelmen magazine.

*Fig. 5–20.* Gary Woodward with reproduction Eagles he made.

# Chapter 6:
# The Solid Tire Safety: 1885-1894

The development of the truly safe and efficient bicycle was long in coming, but when Englishman John Kemp Starley, nephew of James Starley of Ariel fame, and his partner William Sutton introduced their Rover in 1885, a pattern was cast that would apply to nearly every bicycle henceforth.

There were earlier attempts at safeties driven from the rear wheel by belts or chains connecting sprockets located midway between the front and rear wheels and at the rear hub, but none was commercially successful.

In 1876 , at a time when the ordinary and high wheel safeties were gaining in popularity in America, Thomas Shergold of Gloucester, England fashioned a heavy chain drive safety and Henry Bate of Croyden, England built his Flying Dutchman. On Bate's machine, the rear wheel was driven by an endless cord from a sprocket positioned midway between the front and rear wheels. According to the March 25, 1898 *LAW Bulletin* a person who saw it remarked: "It is the most curious machine in appearance ever produced and forms a perfect safety bicycle" (Fig. 6-2).

In 1879, H. G. Lawson refined Bate's idea by substituting a chain for the endless cord creating a machine he called the Bicyclette (Fig. 6-3) which went into production in 1880. The chain and sprockets geared the 24" rear driving wheel to 48". A backbone connected the head with the rear axle, and a long spring above it, supported at the rear by upright arms, carried the saddle. The front forks were very slightly raked and it was necessary to use connecting rods between the front fork and handlebar to bring the handlebar near enough to the rider.

Despite all the publicity the new bicycle received through exhibits and advertising, the public looked upon it with derision calling it the "Crocodile" because of its clumsy and awkward appearance when contrasted to the graceful ordinary.

In 1884 a Mr. Rudling of England made another step forward with his experimental safety built by the New Howe Co. Its front fork was sufficiently raked

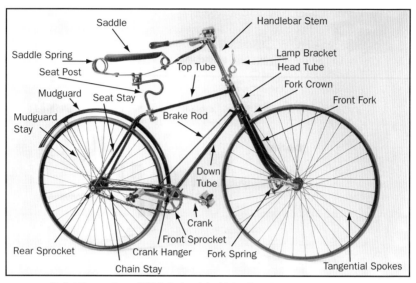

Fig. 6–1. Solid tire safety. 1892 Columbia Light Roadster.

back to bring the handlebar in reach of the rider, thus eliminating the rods that connected the steering fork to the handlebar on the earlier secondary steering machines. Rudling's lighter and more precise front fork steering continues on bicycles to this day. Had this Englishman given his machine a longer wheelbase and equal sized wheels, he would have achieved the design of today's bicycle. As it was, the vehicle was so short there was no space for the front sprocket between the wheels. Thus the distance between the pedals had to be very wide so the front wheel would clear them when turning and the chain had to run outside the frame.

A. J. Wilson, one of Britain's most experienced riders, reported when he tried the Marvel bicycle (Fig. 6-4) made by Rucker and Company in 1884 based on Rudling's design, that it was almost impossible to steer.

John Kemp Starley in 1883 introduced a tricycle called the Rover which positioned the rider behind the main axle and almost directly over the pedals. Finding that power could be applied to great advantage, especially in climbing hills, he set to work on a safety bicycle of similar principles.

The 1897 *LAW Bulletin, Evolution of the Bicycle,* speculated that Starley most probably was familiar with Rudling's Marvel, Lawson's Bicyclette, and Bate's Flying Dutchman when he constructed his Rover bicycle in 1884 (Fig. 6-5). It had a 36" front steering wheel, a 30" rear driving wheel geared to 55", ⅝" and ¾" solid tires, a vertical front fork, and secondary steering connected with the top of the fork by two rods. According to the *Bulletin,* the machine ran easily, but the steering was not firm or steady and the frame was far from rigid.

As with its predecessors, the 1884 Rover's ungainly appearance was not well received. The 1885 model (Fig. 6-6) was much improved with forward sloping

*Fig. 6–2.* Bates' Flying Dutchman.

forks that were curved forward in the manner of today's bicycles and provided for direct steering. The frame, although it was curved, also approximated today's bicycle design. In the post-ordinary history of the bicycle, this machine was most important in establishing the direction of future bicycle development.

Immediately, the 1886 Rover ridden by Englishman George Smith set new speed and distance records. The successful sale of Rovers was launched.

According to the April 1, 1898, *LAW Bulletin,* the success of the Kangaroo the previous year had opened the way to public favor for safety bicycles and a great rush was being made for the ultimate "dwarf" safety of 1884. Nearly every maker was turning out machines of the Kangaroo type and their popularity was at its zenith. In this context, the Rover proved a still greater success and focused attention on the driving and steering defects of the Kangaroo.

*Fig. 6–3.* Lawson's Bicylette.

*Fig. 6–4.* Rucker's 1884 Marvel.

The article went on to note that within a year the Kangaroo generally was displaced by the Rover and every maker was engaged in manufacturing the "Rover type" machine. Indeed, these new machines being produced by several manufacturers were not at first designated safeties, but rather were called "Rovers."

The "Rover type" safety was based on two wheels of about 30" diameter, the rear geared up by means of an endless chain. The rider was positioned over the cranks between the wheels. The connecting of the wheels, the shape of the forks and handlebars, and the attachment of the crank hangers was by whatever design that occurred to the manufacturer.

## FRAME VARIATIONS

By 1887 most manufacturers were making rear driven safeties with simple cross frames. The earliest ones had no rear fork or stay rods (Fig. 6-7). The rear axle, largely unsupported, was mounted at the back end of the down tube, and the front fork was perfectly straight.

### The Cross Frame

Breakage of early cross frames was very frequent, so in 1888 light bolted-on stay rods were attached to the down tube some few inches back of the neck and

*Fig. 6–5.* 1884 Rover.

*Fig. 6–6.* One of the two or three different model 1885 Rovers.

connected to the crank hanger and rear axle. This greatly reduced down tube breakage and contributed to the rigidity and ride quality of the machine. A hinged head, in which the neck of the down tube pivoted, was in common use

*Fig. 6–7.* 1888 cross frame with one stay rod.

(Fig. 6-8). A plunger type brake, operating a spoon on the front wheel, began to replace the pull type that was popular on the ordinary.

Although 1888 improvements were significant, the lightweight ¼ " stay rods which were in common use were too weak and often loosened and rattled. Thus the wholly unsupported saddle post was vulnerable to breakage.

**The Semi-Diamond Frame**

In a quest for adequate frame bracing, two solid rods attached to the head tube were tried in 1889 resulting in the diamond shaped frame which remains the standard bicycle frame design to this day.

As described by the April 8, 1898, *LAW Bulletin,* the first of these safeties had such a short head that the two front frame tubes came together almost in a

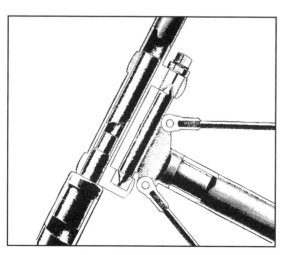

*Fig. 6–8.*
A Union bicycle hinged head. Note threaded stay rods and head cone bearings.

point at the neck. As the head became more open, the shape of the diamond also became more open and the pattern less discernible.

The *LAW Bulletin* explained that at first the diamond frame was very low and the seat tube connecting the top tube and chain stay was curved to follow the lines of the rear wheel (Fig. 6-9). The steering head often was still of the hinged type. By the year 1890, ball and socket steering had become very popular (Fig. 6-10).

### The Ladies' Drop Frame

As early as the hobby horse period, drop frame machines had been designed and constructed to accommodate long dresses. Riding them was cumbersome and was not done in public partly because exercising by women was frowned upon.

*Fig. 6–9.* Low diamond frame with curved seat tube.

The first rear-driving bicycle designed for women was created by Frenchman E. V. de Forville and patented in 1870 (Fig. 6-11). In 1870, Englishman S. W. Thomas built a lady's ordinary with a backbone that half way down curved abruptly to the left so the small rear wheel did not track with the front one, but ran a foot over on its left side. The saddle was placed over the rear wheel and the front wheel axle was extended to the left of the wheel making it double cranked.

In 1874 James Starley introduced his ladies' Ariel (Fig. 6-12) which closely followed Thomas' design, but the frame was jointed so the back portion could be used on one side or in the center. If used at the center, seats could be placed on both sides of the rear wheel making it a side-by-side companion bicycle.

Fig. 6–10.
Victor ball and socket
steering.

An American innovation was a next step in the development of a safety for women. George W. Pressey, October 26, 1880, patented his original Star design. As with later production Stars, it had the large driving wheel behind a small steering wheel. It was claimed that there was enough space between the front wheel and the steering rod for a woman's dress, which was protected from the large driving wheel by a woven skirt guard. A long rod, pivoted to the frame, held the machine upright when the woman mounted it (Fig. 6-13).

A Mr. E. E. Sewall, in the October 7, 1898, *LAW Bulletin*, reported a story about a Mr. Stevens in America who in 1882 built a drop frame safety similar to de Forville's. It was driven by a ratchet and lever device and had a wood frame. Mrs. Stevens learned to ride it on secluded streets after dark under strict pledge that no one should know about it. Feeling that the frame should be stronger, Mr. Stevens planned to construct another of metal and apply for a patent, but his wife assured him that no lady would ever ride a bicycle in public.

American E. G. Latta patented a drop frame "Rover type" safety on February 12, 1886 (Fig. 6-14). Although it was a true drop frame and was perfectly suitable for use by women, the inventor explained: "I thought of modifying the

*Fig. 6–11.* E. V. de Forville's bicycle for women patented 1870.

frame to make it more roomy and of specially adopting it for women's use, but, thinking it would be impossible to induce any considerable number of women to ride a bicycle, did not describe it as being adapted to their use."

Dan Albone of England also in 1886 built the ladies' Ivel which turned out to be the prototype for most ladies' safeties of the future, but he did not put it into production.

British inventors continued to develop the drop frame solid tire safety, but for the purpose of making it safer in a fall rather than for use by women.

By January 1888, American William E. Smith had completed and exhibited three ladies' bicycles (Fig. 6-15) and Mrs. Smith had ridden down Pennsylvania Avenue in Washington, DC. According to the October 14, 1898, *LAW Bulletin*, this probably was the first public ride on a solid tire safety by an adult female. It set a precedent and led to the organization of a women's bicycle club in that city.

Mrs. Smith, claiming to be the first woman in America to ride a bicycle, exhibited her pioneer machine at the 1901 Chicago World's Fair.

In a September 1902 *Ladies' World* magazine article, Mary Sargent Hopkins explained that at the time William Smith built his wife's bicycle "… women's trade was neither sought for nor catered to in this country, and I know of one manufacturer who declared he would go out of business if he had to make a woman's bicycle."

In 1887 and 1888 major American patents for drop frame safeties were issued to G. T. Warwick, to H. S. Owen who collaborated with J. M. Starley to secure a patent for the "Psycho" frame, and to Sterling Elliott, whose Elliott Hickory today is one of the most collectible American solid tire safeties.

*Fig. 6–12.* James Starley's 1874 ladies' Ariel.

### The Tandem Frame

The first representation of a two-wheeled tandem appeared in prolific British caricaturist George Cruikshank's 1819 aquatint print of a man and woman seated on and propelling a hobby horse. It is very doubtful though that such a machine existed except in his mind.

Two-seated boneshakers were built and are known to exist today, but none was commercially successful.

In 1887 a description of a duplex tandem (Fig. 6-16) signed by a G. G. C. was illustrated in *Ixion* magazine. The new vehicle consisted of the wheels of two ordinaries of the same make joined by a "duplex connecting iron." The advantages compared to two ordinaries were the saving of 35 pounds, ample driving power and a lessening of friction by 40 percent. It did not, however, interest any manufacturers.

Others tried a similar approach to a tandem including Rucker who in 1883 developed a connecting bar to join two ordinaries. A straight bar was hinged and allowed both wheels to turn. The front rider found the steering easy, the December 16, 1898 *LAW Bulletin* reported, but the rear rider had a desperate time trying to follow the leader.

*Fig. 6–13.* George W. Pressey's originalStar.

*Fig. 6–14.* E. G. Latta's 1886 safety.

By placing a second saddle in front of the head, the Kangaroo lent itself to tandem use through the utilization of Whatton handlebars which bent around the back of the front rider, and the splitting of the lower ends of the front fork

*Fig. 6–15.* W. E. Smith's 1888 Dart.

so as to carry the extra chains (Fig. 6-17). Although such an adaptation was patented by Rucker, it never was put into general use.

These early tandem attempts were experimental. Derek Roberts asserts that the 1886 Wilson/Albone was the first practical tandem.

That same year William E. Smith of Washington, D. C. developed a tandem on which a lady could ride. In 1887 the Starley brothers brought out their Psycho with a deep U shape front frame for ladies, a straight frame in the rear, and a connecting bar on the right side to join the ends of the handlebars to permit either rider to steer.

*Fig. 6–16.* 1875 Duplex tandem.

*Fig. 6–17.* 1884 Rucker Kangaroo tandem.

Also in 1887 Englishman J. W. Hall designed a double diamond "Lightening" tandem built by J. H. Dearlove. Both these machines closely approximated the basic configuration of today's tandems.

In 1889 Colonel Pope introduced the first American solid tire tandem safety (Fig. 6-18), but the machine's inability to cope with the stresses imposed by two riders made it and others of the period weak and hard to pedal. In 1890 a reaction developed against tandems and Columbia discontinued theirs with the end of the 1890 model year.

Their unpopularity and consequently short production run have made solid tire tandem safeties one of the rarest categories of antique bicycles today.

*Fig. 6–18.* 1889 Columbia tandem.

## THE SOLID TIRE SAFETY IN AMERICA

"The experience with safeties over the past three years has proved that a bicycle which is safe in fact as well as name and can be used for night riding and rough roads by elderly and heavy weight riders is a most valuable acquisition to cycling." Thus began the catalog description of the 1887 Victor Safety, the first Rover type solid tire safety to be offered by a major American manufacturer (Fig. 6-19).

### The Overman Wheel Company — Victor

Noting that this safety's construction rendered a backward or forward fall impossible, the catalog went on to explain that the Victor's new spring front fork revolutionized the safety bicycle.

Despite their solid rubber tires, ordinaries and high wheel safeties rode smoothly because the long spokes of the large wheel cushioned the bumps and vibrations.

The short spokes in the new solid tire safeties with low wheels averaging about 30" in diameter did not provide a cushion effect and manufacturers rushed to develop spring suspension systems for the forks and frames.

The Victor's spring fork, in its earliest form, consisted of four curved springs that joined the head and front axle. They were held in place by a stay jointed with bearings at the top. It was claimed in the 1887 catalog that the Victor spring fork was the only device ever applied to a bicycle that gave an abundance of vertical spring to absorb vibration while preserving perfect rigidity in every direction.

The catalog also stressed that with the adjustability of the new Victor safety's saddle, cranks, and handlebar, one size bicycle would fit all.

Offered at $140 and geared to 54", the first Victor safety had two 30" diameter wheels with a ⅞" solid tire on the rear, ¾" solid tire on the front. This was different from many bicycles of the period that had a wider tire and a larger wheel at the front to help steady the steering over loose and irregular surfaces.

The cross frame was strengthened by a stay rod connecting the head to the crank hanger. The block chain was adjustable at the crank hanger. Spade grips, a front wheel brake actuated from the handlebar by a pull lever, and an adequately sprung saddle were standard equipment.

In 1888 Victor changed the angle of the steering bar thus decreasing the vagueness of the 1887's steering, and the cross frame was abandoned in favor of its version of the Rover type curved frame with double tube support to the head and frame support to crank hanger and rear axle (Fig. 6-20). The brake was changed to operate on the rear wheel making the bicycle much safer. A partial mud guard was provided behind the frame over the rear wheel. Small footrests for coasting were added to each side of the spring front fork. The wheel bearings were mounted at the ends of the axles which at the rear allowed the chain

*Fig. 6–19.* 1887 Victor.

to run between the bearings. The manufacturer claimed this gave a stronger and smoother operation.

The 1889 Victor safety featured hollow rims and the number of balls in its numerous bearings totaled 176.

*Fig. 6–20.* 1888 Victor.

Although use of the bicycle by women was not mentioned, if the rider did not weigh over 150 pounds it was possible to order a light spring in the front spring fork and a low saddle could be provided for shorter riders.

Fig. 6–21.
Victor spring fork.

In 1890 Victor placed the safety for the first time in the front of its catalog, relegating the ordinaries to the back. The catalog noted that the 9 feet of steel rod in the spring fork was of the same quality as was used in sword blades (Fig. 6-21). This was to squelch stories being spread by competitors that Victor spring forks broke. (To the best of the author's knowledge, no Victor has been found with broken fork springs.) Gearing was available from 51" to 60". It was announced that a lightweight Victoria would be available by summer for ladies and light men and boys.

Led by the new ladies' Victoria, an immense proliferation of the Victor line occurred in 1891. Overman's trump card though, was his new cushion tire; it was far superior to a similar one offered by Pope and he expected it to revolutionize cycling.

The purpose of the cushion tire was to provide more elasticity than the traditional solid rubber tire. Victor's was a simple arch of rubber extending from edge to edge of the rim. Its side walls were held against spreading by side flanges on the rim which had rounded edges. Other makers' cushion tires consisted only of larger diameter solid rubber tiring with a larger open core. Most often these tires were molded to the rim.

The cushion tire did improve the ride, but it enjoyed a very short vogue before it was made obsolete by the pneumatic tire. Because cushion tire safeties were offered such a short time and because the tires wore faster and often were not replaced, those with original serviceable tires are very rare today.

Selling at $135 the Victoria (Fig. 6-22) had 28" wheels geared to 50", solid tire front and the new cushion tire rear, hollow rims, spring fork, ball bearings throughout, and a perforated metal skirt guard for the rear wheel and chain. The cushion tire also could be had on the front at no extra cost.

In addition to the new ladies' Victoria, Victor in 1891 continued to offer the earlier Rover type calling it the Model A and introduced a new diamond frame model available with a solid front fork as the Model B and with the spring fork as the Model C. Making certain to cover all the bases with offerings to meet

*Fig. 6–22.* 1891 Victor Victoria.

everyone's preference, Victor also introduced a modified cross frame called the Model D when fitted with a rigid front fork and the Model E when equipped with a spring fork. All the aforementioned models were priced at $135 and all except the Model A had the adjustment for taking up chain slack moved from the crank hanger to the rear hub as on today's bicycles.

Also in 1891, Victor introduced a new line of less expensive safeties: the Credenda (Fig. 6-23) in ladies' and gents' models at $90 and the Nonpareil (Fig. 6-24) with 26" wheels for boys. The gents' Credenda had a Rover type frame but with straight tubes. Both had rigid front forks and plunger brakes operating on the front wheels, solid rims, and cushion tires. The ladies' model had a woven string skirt guard.

The boys' Nonpareil had a cross frame, hinged fork, and solid rubber tires.

*Fig. 6–23.* 1891 Credenda.

Having long waged personal and sales battles with Colonel Pope, Overman was frustrated that he had let Pope beat him by one year in bringing out a ladies' bicycle. But Overman's runaway sales success with his cushion tire was in his words "enough to strike terror to the heart of a competitor."

*Fig. 6–24.* 1891 Nonpareil.

In 1892 the Victor Model A was dropped; Models B and C were lightened and the front fork angle was increased. Model D was unchanged and new Models G with spring fork and F with rigid fork were introduced with a distinctive racquet frame. Made in an elliptical form and laced with fine steel wire, the racquet frame Victor was claimed to embody the same suspension principle as the suspension bicycle wheel and to give great strength and stiffness with decreased weight (Fig. 6-25). Derek Roberts suggests that Victor made the racquet frame

*Fig. 6–25.* 1892 Victor racquet frame Model G.

under license from the Euclidia Company of England. Diamond framed Models D and E and the ladies' Victoria remained essentially unchanged.

### The Pope–Overman Wars

As related in the October, 1969 issue of *American Bicyclist and Motorcyclist* magazine, these wars had begun in 1884 over patents. In 1886 Pope secured an attachment against Overman's property and a court injunction prevented him from selling bicycles. Stopped in his tracks, Overman, appealed to cyclists through an advertisement in *Bicycling World* magazine, where he charged that Pope was afraid to come into competition with the new Victor bicycle. Overman also appealed to the courts and won.

The 1891 battle broke out over an Overman advertisement which listed questions such as "What maker in America made the first high grade bicycle with tangent spokes, hollow rims, dropped handlebars...?" It concluded with the statement "We have the documents in hand to prove that there is one answer which fits each of the above questions and that answer is The Overman Wheel Co."

After this ad had appeared three times, Pope had had enough. In his next Columbia ad, he announced a deposit of $1,000 with *Bicycling World* magazine in a challenge to Overman who was also directed to deposit $1,000. Each was to choose a referee, who in turn would choose a third. They were to reach a decision in 30 days, the money going to the LAW road improvement committee.

"Apparently Overman wasn't that sure of his facts. Instead of accepting the challenge," according to *American Bicyclist and Motorcyclist* magazine, "they (the Overman Wheel Co.) opened their next ad with an apology for the bad taste of personal mention of a competitor's name, pleading they 'were simply compelled to adopt such methods by the continued and unwarranted use of our name by the Pope Mfg. Co...' (who had never mentioned them before.)"

The battle ended when Overman raised the ante to $5,000 and asked that all material ever printed by both companies totaling more than 100,000 pieces be examined by a committee.

Pope's only answer was to point out in his next advertisement that no one had accepted the earlier challenge. Pope had the last word and Overman could not tolerate it.

In the words of *American Bicyclist and Motorcyclist*, "A month later Pope made a minor slip that Overman blew into a mountain of revenge." *Bicycling World* had reproduced a scroll of Chinese characters sent in by a Pope advertising man and said to be a testimonial to Columbia bicycles sent all the way from China.

"The following week Overman's front page ad reproduced it exactly with the caption 'We will pay $100 to the first person sending us a correct translation of the above letter. '"

The Overman challenge continued for three weeks, finally offering to pay $1,000 for the correct translation of the letter.

In the fourth week Overman had his revenge when he published the contents of two letters received from Chinese speaking men who said "I cannot make anything out of the paper. It is meaningless. They must be written by some American who imitates not to perfection." The second letter said no Chinese could make out its meaning.

The sweetest part of Overman's revenge, the magazine concludes "...must have been imagining the torture of Pope's hapless promotion man during the four excruciating weeks of the build up."

### The Pope Manufacturing Company — Columbia

By introducing in 1888 its first solid tire safety, the Veloce (Fig. 6-26), The Pope Mfg. Co., which had led the trade in ordinaries, followed Victor by one year in competing for the growing safety market.

Uncertain how customers would react to the solid tire safety, Pope devoted only one sentence to the new Veloce in the catalog introduction of his 1888 line.

Priced at $135, weighing 51 lbs., and geared to 52", this safety had a cross frame with light stays, hinged neck, and an unusual rear mud guard that actually was part of the frame. Rims were solid with direct spokes and solid rubber tires. The Ewart detachable link chain was adjustable at the crank hanger.

In his catalog of the next year, Pope noted that he had devoted his most careful attention and study to safeties during the previous year knowing that the success of this type was unquestionable and its effect upon the interest in cycling was apparent.

*Fig. 6–26.* 1888 Veloce Columbia.

Replacing the Veloce in 1889 was the new Columbia Light Roadster safety (Fig. 6-27). Also added to the line was the unique Columbia tandem safety (Fig. 6-18).

The new Light Roadster safety, weighing 51 lbs., geared to 54", and priced at $130, had 32" diameter front and 30" rear wheels with hollow rims and a low curved diamond frame that incorporated a rear fender as part of the frame structure.

Pointing a finger at Victor's spring fork, Pope described the Columbia's spring jointed front fork (Fig. 6-28) as relieving the frame and handlebar from vibration without affecting the positivity of the steering or the neat appearance of the fork.

As with the first year's model, chain slack was taken up at the crank hanger (Fig. 6-29).

The following year, Pope claimed that more 1889 Columbia Light Roadster safeties had been sold than any other bicycle in one season.

*Fig. 6–27.* 1889 Columbia Light Roadster. The original equipment front fender is missing. *(courtesy of Henry Ford Museum)*

*Fig. 6–28.* 1889 Columbia spring fork. *(courtesy of Henry Ford Museum)*

Unique in the 1889 line was the tandem safety, the only solid tire chain driven safety to be offered by an American manufacturer and among few that were made in the world. None is known to survive today.

At $190, 82 lbs., and with tangent spokes on 30" solid rims, the tandem offered a greater degree of "sociability", especially with a lady on the front seat, than any other bicycle, the catalog suggested. An adjustable plunger brake worked on the front tire while a lever spoon brake working on the rear tire was under the control of the back rider.

*Fig. 6–29.* 1889 Columbia chain adjustment at crank hanger.

Unfortunately design, construction, materials, and technology left much to be desired in the tandem's handling, rigidity, and durability thus rendering it unsuccessful until its reintroduction as a pneumatic tire bicycle in 1895.

In 1890 Pope moved the safety to the front of his catalog; addressed the first section to "each individual of the large and ever increasing army of wheelmen and wheelwomen" and introduced his first Columbia ladies safety (Fig. 6-30).

The ladies' safety, priced at $130 with 28" wheels, solid tires, and hollow rims with tangential spokes had dress guards fashioned from wire over the chain and rear wheel and a friction brake operating on the rear wheel. The frame was the usual loop style, but with two tubes rather than the customary one connecting the head to the crank hanger.

Turning for the first time to the potentially huge new market of women riders, Col. Pope explained in his 1890 catalog that appreciating as he did the benefit conferred by those ladies who had added themselves to the rank of cyclists he could do no less than turn his best efforts and resources to the preparation of a safety bicycle particularly suited to their needs. He added that while the new machine was in the first instance intended for ladies, it would be largely used by youths.

*Fig. 6–30.* 1890 Columbia Ladies' Safety as found by a collector. It is missing the brake hardware.

In 1891 the Columbia low diamond frame was replaced by one Pope described as a double diamond. It used all steel forgings with no castings. Cushion tires of 1¼" diameter were offered, but the rider was warned that any cushion tire could be expected to wear at a faster rate than a solid tire. Geared to either 53" or 57", the 1891 Columbia models used the new Elliott self-oiling block chain with felt in each block to hold enough oil to run 500 miles without renewal (Fig. 6-31). When oil was needed, the mechanic tipped the bicycle on its side and squirted ten to twelve drops through the openings in the sides of the chain.

In 1891 Columbia also offered its first racing safety. It weighed 23 lbs. and had a curved diamond frame.

*Fig. 6–31.* Eliott self-oiling block chain.

In 1892, the Light Roadster (Fig. 6-1), ladies and racing safeties were continued but the star of the Columbia line was the new Century, featuring pneumatic tires which were available optionally on all models.

### Gormully & Jeffery Manufacturing Company, Chicago, Illinois

Referring to it as a novelty, Gormully and Jeffery introduced its American Rambler solid tire safety in 1888 (Fig. 6-32). "So simple is it in construction, that we have succeeded in making it from six to ten pounds lighter (at 44 lbs.) than any of its rivals with no loss in strength" the catalog exclaimed.

Priced at $120, geared to 48" or 60" with a 30" rear wheel and 26" front, it was based on the J. Depard Paroy C frame made in France. However, beginning in 1889, the American Rambler had the addition of a large coil spring connecting the end of the frame under the saddle with the rear fork. It was jointed at the crank to allow it to pivot when the spring was compressed.

Although most makers had included springs on the front fork, G & J claimed that nearly all vibration caused by trolley tracks, cobblestones, and curbs was prevented from being communicated to the rider by its unique springing of the rear wheel.

Admitting in the 1889 catalog that it was not satisfied with the 1888 safety, G & J introduced in that year an improved American Rambler and an American Ideal Rambler that "… while combining all the elements which were so popular in last year's wheel, admits of its being ridden by a lady."

*Fig. 6–32.* **1888** American Rambler safety.

*Fig. 6–33.* 1890 American Rambler that is identical to 1889 except that it has a stay rod joining the head with the seat tube.

The 1889 American Rambler (Fig. 6-33), geared to 54" and priced at $130, replaced the C frame with a single loop drop frame with skirt guards at the chain and rear wheel when specified. The chain stay continued to be hinged to

*Fig. 6–34.* 1890 American Light Rambler.

the bottom bracket. A spring connected the seat tube with a unique seat stay that did not join the seat tube.

The American Ideal Rambler simply was a smaller and less expensive version of the Rambler. It was marketed for ladies of less than 125 lbs. as well as for girls and boys. It had a 26" rear wheel and cost $65.

In 1890 G & J moved its safeties to the prominent front position of its catalog, but it was noted that: "Many wheelmen, particularly those living in the large cities, err in their estimates of the comparative number of safety and ordinary bicycles in use. It is true that the safety has met with extraordinary favor among metropolitan riders, but the ordinary has by no means been crowded to the wall and will always retain a preferred position among younger cyclists."

The 1890 emphasis at G & J was on the new American Light Rambler with tangential spokes, hollow rims, and a weight of 35 lbs. (Fig. 6-34). A special lady's saddle of reduced length with lighter springing was offered for the first time and a child's seat which mounted to the head tube was available for $6. The American Rambler and American Ideal safeties were continued with little change.

The 1891 American line remained largely unchanged in preparation for the new pneumatic tire bicycle to be introduced in 1892.

## UNUSUAL AMERICAN SOLID TIRE SAFETIES
### The Bronco

The Bronco was manufactured by the White Cycle Company of Westboro, Massachusetts, for $135. Basically a cross frame safety, it pedaled from cranks directly on the rear axle which were geared two to one giving the 30" rear wheel a gear of 60". The wheels were located very close together because there was no crank bracket separating them (Fig. 6-35).

The 1890 Bronco catalog claimed it was the easiest handling, easiest steering, and greatest trick riding safety ever built. It was emphasized that there was no greasy chain to catch dirt, bind, or twist and that it had fewer pieces than any other safety. It had all the advantages of an ordinary without any of the disadvantages.

"Life will take on a new brightness, and existence will have a charm hitherto unknown," the catalog extolled, but my experience with the Bronco is that it is uncomfortable to ride because the pedals are located slightly in back of the rider and because of the high gearing.

An improved Bronco was introduced in 1892 incorporating a system of levers to connect to the cranks after the pedals were removed. The levers enabled the rider to pedal considerably forward of the rear axle in a more natural position. A Bronco tandem was produced, at least one of which is in a private American collection.

*Fig. 6–35.* Don Adams riding an 1890 Bronco.

## The White Flyer

About 1890, the same White Cycle Co. adapted the Bronco front fork and handlebar along with some other components and produced a unique safety called the White Flyer (Fig. 6-36).

Noting in their catalog that: "… they had a class of gentlemen-sportsmen to deal with who … are constantly educated as to what is what," the manufacturer presented a machine that was ridden by operating pedals connected by chain pulleys to a geared rear axle. As one pedal was pushed down it correspondingly raised the opposite one. As described by the catalog, "the swing or guide frame hanging from the backbone on which the pedals move up and down can be thrust while the rider is in motion to almost any angle. Thus if he wishes a vertical tread, the frame can be swung so the pedals come well under the saddle. If he wishes to use the thigh muscle, he can swing the frame toward the front wheel." When the driving pedal was on top of the guide frame and in the beginning of a stroke, the construction was such that the rider had more leverage than at any other point. The leverage lessened as the pedal moved down.

*Fig. 6–36.* 1890 White Flyer.

We do not know how many White Flyers were produced, but at least one is known to survive.

### Springfield Roadster Volant

Introduced in 1889 at $115, geared to 67", the Volant was made by the Springfield Bicycle Manufacturing Company, of Boston (Fig. 6-37). It incorporated the Springfield Roadster high wheel safety drive mechanism and transmitted power to the rear wheel by chain. The catalog of that year explained that the company had been induced to build this bicycle especially for beginners and for those who had a fear of mounting a high wheel.

### The Star Safety

Introduced by the H. B. Smith Machine Company of Smithville, New Jersey for $135 in 1889, the Star Safety (Fig. 6-38) incorporated the ratchet drive mechanism from the Star high wheel safety. This safety was built on a cross frame with a support rod from the hinged head to the base of the seat tube. Solid tires were mounted on solid 32" rear, 30" front rims with direct spokes.

A later solid tire Star Safety used the curved diamond frame. A still later version used pneumatic tires and was offered with a ladies' drop frame.

*Fig. 6–37.* 1889 Springfield Roadster Volant.

### The Elliott Hickory

Manufactured by the Elliott Hickory Cycle Company, Newton, Massachusetts, the Elliott Hickory (Fig. 6-39) was made in its initial form from 1888 until about 1893. It was a unique design using hickory wood for the chain stay and seat tube which arched over the rear wheel and served as a mud guard. Also made of wood were the front mud guard, the spokes and felloes of the 31"

*Fig. 6–38.* 1889 Star safety.

rear drive wheel and the 25" steering wheel. It was geared to 54" and was supplied with ¾" solid rubber tires. The brake was applied to the rear wheel via a steel chain passing entirely inside the tubular frame. Weighing 45 lbs. and costing $100, the Elliott Hickory was advertised for either men or women. It was claimed that the wood parts of the frame were elastic and provided adequate spring effect. Later when drop frames became strongly identified with women's bicycles, Elliott brought out a gents' diamond frame of steel tubing with wood wheels and pneumatic tires.

### SELECTED ADDITIONAL MAJOR AMERICAN MAKERS OF SOLID TIRE SAFETIES

Union, Union Cycle Mfg. Co., Highlandville, MA
Lovell Diamond, John P. Lovell Arms Co., Boston, MA
Sterling, Charles F. Stokes Mfg. Co., Chicago, IL
New Mail, William Read & Sons, Boston, MA
Paragon, Stover Bicycle Mfg. Co., Freeport, IL. Featured sprung seat tube.
Imperial, Ames and Frost Co., Chicago, IL
Juno, Western Wheel Works, Chicago, IL
Gendron, Gendron Iron Wheel Co., Toledo, OH
Meacham, E. C. Meacham Arms Co., St. Louis, MO
Clipper, Grand Rapids Cycle Co., Grand Rapids, MI
Warwick, Warwick Cycle Mfg. Co., Springfield, MA
Hartford, Hartford Cycle Co., Hartford, CT

*Fig. 6–39.* 1891 Elliott Hickory. *(courtesy of Henry Ford Museum)*

*Fig. 6–40.* Three gents, Michael Höhne, Dave Metz, and Willis Koehler, with solid tire safeties as extras on the set of Martin Scorsese's *Age of Innocence* showing yet another fun aspect of the old bikes.

# Chapter 7:
# The Pneumatic Tire Safety: 1892-1900

Recognizing as a result of his work perhaps, how important it was that man and horse be properly shod, Irish veterinarian John Boyd Dunlop in 1888 created a hollow tire which he filled with air under pressure. A thin endless rubber tube held the air and a tough outer casing made of canvas and rubber covered and enclosed the air tube. This was cemented to the rim, thus providing an air cushion.

Although it is unclear how much Dunlop was influenced by Scottish engineer Robert W. Thomson, who had made a pneumatic tire in 1845, Dunlop is credited with being the first to see and develop the potential in this innovation. In May, 1888, racing cyclist W. Hume, riding the first racing bicycle ever fitted with pneumatic tires, won all four prestigious Belfast Queens College races.

Although previously cyclists had not taken the "rubber hose" pneumatic tire seriously, now it would swiftly carry bicycles into their greatest period of popularity and refinement. This was indeed the beginning of a decade in which cycling would influence social, political, and industrial life, particularly in America.

Pneumatic tires had an immense effect upon the rideability of the safety bicycle. The new machines with air-filled tires and light wood rims were noticeably easier to pedal and much more comfortable to ride.

Young American women took to cycling with a passion. Withstanding the disapproval of their elders, they wore billowy bloomers on their rides into the countryside. Occasionally they would ride with their beaus far from the watchful gaze of chaperones.

As their numbers increased to tens of thousands, American cyclists became a major political force and their cries for better roads were heard from coast to

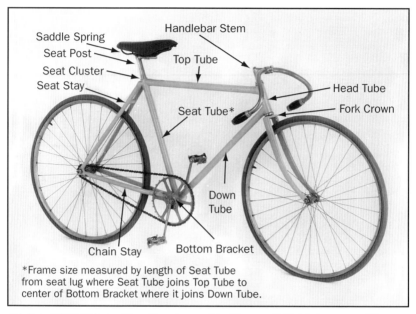

coast. Planks to placate cyclists became part of successful American political platforms and the cyclist's plight was a popular theme for political cartoons.

Fully accepted now as part of the American scene, bicycles were wheeled into the new photo studios to be included in family portraits. Bicycle songs were sung, and dishes, mugs, cigar boxes, ash trays, clocks, and other everyday items were decorated with pictures or representations of these popular vehicles.

Barbers complained that gentlemen were out riding their "wheels" as bicycles often were called, rather than coming in for a daily shave. Ministers noted vacancies in the pews on Sundays when cyclists were riding 100 mile "century" tours. Even makers of home pump organs were lamenting the sales lost to those using their money to buy bicycles.

Buying bicycles became an American obsession and makers were quick to introduce enough changes each year to entice customers to trade in the old model and ride the latest thing. It was the beginning of an annual planned obsolescence that many years later automobile makers also would use successfully to stimulate sales.

New American bicycle manufacturers sprung up like weeds until there were hundreds and competition for sales became intense. Department stores became centers for selling reduced-price bicycles and they cut deeply into established dealers' profits.

In 1892 bicycle makers in Toledo, Ohio, alone supplied 35,000 to 45,000 bicycles to department stores where they retailed for as little as $13.25 fully equipped. Soon alliances were formed between prominent makers and department store chains. Major American manufacturers began developing plans to export bicycles to Europe, an operation which became lucrative within the next few years.

Gimmicks were the rule of the day. Anything that would distinguish a bicycle from its competitors was tried. There were wood, aluminum, and bamboo bicycles, side-by-side companions and six person multicycles. But the most important innovation was the pneumatic tire. It not only made the ride more comfortable, resulting in women taking to the bicycle for the first time in large numbers, but it also permitted the overall lightening of the vehicle.

The first pneumatic tires were complicated, punctured easily, and held air for only a few hours. These problems led I. W. Boothroyd to devise a tire that was much simpler. By cementing the air tube to the inner side of the casing, he produced the "single tube" tire which could be more easily repaired using rubber cement solutions and plugs.

The single tube pneumatic tire received extensive commercial use beginning in 1892. Gradually its acceptance revolutionized the bicycle trade. Virtually all makers introduced a pneumatic tire safety. Even a few leftover ordinaries and high wheel safeties were equipped with them. The following table of usage in England, from *Bicyclist and Motorcyclist* magazine October, 1969, shows in percentages of bicycles sold the impact of pneumatic tires.

|           | 1890   | 1891   | 1894   |
|-----------|--------|--------|--------|
| Solid     | 98.60% | 29.10% | 0.04%  |
| Cushion   | 0.06%  | 54.20% | 3.30%  |
| Pneumatic | 1.20%  | 14.00% | 89.50% |

The pre-1900 period in American pneumatic tire bicycles was dominated by technological advances to save weight and improve drive mechanisms, by price wars, and by colorful promotions involving races, spectacular bicycle shows, and massive advertising programs.

Unfortunately the supply of bicycles exceeded the demand and saturated the market. The resulting price wars and expensive promotions depleted profits.

In 1899 the Pope Mfg. Co., Gormully and Jeffery, and 17 other principal makers with an annual bicycle production of 700,000 were consolidated in a trust called the American Bicycle Company. The syndicate was headed by A. G. Spalding.

Charges and countercharges between the combine and the independents filled the cycling press. Between 1900 and 1905 the number of American bicycle manufacturers shrunk from 312 to 101.

In 1902 the name of the American Bicycle Company was changed to the American Cycle Manufacturing Company which sold Columbia, Cleveland, Crescent, Crawford, Imperial, Monarch, Rambler, and Tribune bicycles and motorcycles. By 1904 these brands were being sold by the "eastern" and "western" divisions of the Pope Mfg. Co.

The demise of the bicycle in America has been chronicled by many. Don Berkebile in *Wheels and Wheeling* noted that after the formation of the trust there was a switch to other forms of recreation and a number of electric railways took over the sidepaths originally constructed for bicycle use. Robert Smith in *A Social History of the Bicycle* referred to LAW Secretary Abbott Basset's observation that after the trust's formation, bicycle salesmen were dismissed, advertising was curbed and as a result of the latter, cycling newspapers went out of business.

Most important though, the adventure seekers who had popularized the bicycle took to the automobile. The September 20, 1900 issue of *The Cycle Age and Trade Review* in a story on the Chicago Automobile Show commented that this exhibition illustrated the extent to which the American Bicycle Co. had entered the automobile field. In its display were products from four of its divisions. H. A. Lozier & Co., makers of the Cleveland bicycle, had a tricycle with an air-cooled engine as did the Western Wheel Works, producer of Crescent bicycles; the latter tricycle having a motor carried by the front wheel. The Indiana Bicycle Co., manufacturer of the Waverly bicycle, showed electric cars and the Gormully & Jeffery Co., makers of the Rambler bicycle, exhibited a water-cooled two cylinder automobile.

## THE PNEUMATIC TIRE SAFETY IN AMERICA 1892–1900

Overman cautiously explained in his 1892 Victor catalog that "owing to the speed which has been developed on racing tracks with specially light bicycles and special light pneumatic tires, there has sprung up a demand for an inflated tire for road bicycles. It is indeed a question whether pneumatic tires will finally come to be acknowledged as a permanent improvement in bicycle construction."

### The Victor

Following that disclaimer was a description of Victor's new inner tube pneumatic, commonly referred to as the "man hole" tire (Fig. 7-2). It was made in two parts. The outer covering was reinforced by canvas and arranged to receive the thrust on the road. The inner tube was made of pure rubber to hold the air and was so constructed that it could be taken out in case of puncture and repaired or replaced with a new tube. It was emphasized that this important tire feature was owned by Victor and could not be used by any other maker.

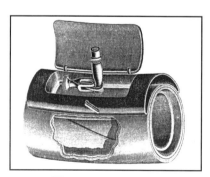

*Fig. 7–2.* Victor pneumatic tire with "manhole" rim.

*Fig. 7–3.* 1893 Victor Flyer.

Overman's 1893 catalog illustrations showed most Victor models fitted with 28" pneumatic tires at $15 extra. Model D, which if equipped with spring fork became Model E, was made lighter primarily by use of a lighter "Mannesmann" tubing which was drawn spiral by twisting strain rather than being drawn straight. A new crank hanger reduced the distance between the pedals, cranks fitted into tapered sockets made them adjustable for looseness, and light rubber mud guards replaced steel ones. Models B and C continued unchanged.

Victor, with its new Flyer (Fig. 7-3), joined the growing obsession to build lighter bicycles. Constructed in a manner similar to the model D, it featured

*Fig. 7–4.* 1894 Victor Racer.

Fig. 7–5. 1897 Victor Victoria.

slightly lighter tubing and was stripped of brake and mud guards. This type of bicycle was referred to as a "scorcher" and was increasingly popular with young bloods who wished to finish first in the popular century runs held by the LAW and other cycling clubs.

Overman ended an era in 1894 when he discontinued the famous Victor spring front fork. It had been available since 1887 with the introduction of his safety bicycles.

Two trade thrusts were dominant in 1894; lighter weight and higher frames, the latter in the belief that a long saddle tube, well extended to raise the saddle, resulted in poor handling.

The American bicycle industry achieved an important weight saving measure by developing wood rims which remain in use today on some track racing bicycles. They were not popular with British manufacturers.

Victor offered wood rims for the first time in 1894 on its 19 lb. racer (Fig. 7-4). All models were reduced in weight to levels comparable with high grade bicycles of today. The Model D weighed 33 lbs. and the Flyer 27 lbs.

Predicting that the single tube pneumatic tire used by Columbia and most other makers would someday be extinct, Victor continued to promote the advantages of its inner tube tire.

Prices were reduced in 1895 to $100. Wood rims with single tube tires were offered by Victor for the first time along with the traditional Victor inner tube tire. The line was limited to one gents' and one ladies' model offered in five frame sizes for men, two sizes for ladies. Handlebars were narrower, and saddles with less spring support were used.

In 1896 top tubes on all gents' models were parallel with the ground. The number of frame sizes was reduced to three, frame tube diameter was increased,

*Fig. 7–6.* 1897 Victor Victoria Tandem.

and crank tread was narrowed. Wood rims with 26" or 28" tires and a new aluminum chain helped save weight. A step that was an extension of the rear axle, coaster bars for the front fork, and a brake operating on the front wheel were offered.

Important to the 1896 line was Victor's first tandem. Priced at $150, it was designed to be ridden by men front and rear. Weighing 41 lbs. it could be steered by either the front or rear handlebar.

The 1897 Victor catalog detailed an enlarged 1⅛" diameter upper tube, ¾" lower rear fork and ⅝" upper rear fork. The front fork crown was smoother appearing. A Victor Road Racer with more rakish front fork angle was added and a new ladies' Victoria featured a shorter wheelbase, larger diameter tubing, and for the first time a top tube connecting the head with the base of the seat tube and running approximately parallel to the down tube (Fig. 7-5). This drop frame safety design has not changed materially to this day.

A Victoria tandem with a dropped frame and skirt guard at the front and the usual gent's frame at the rear with steering parts connected so each rider could steer was offered at $150 (Fig. 7-6). Weighing 41 lbs. it and other similar tandems designed to be ridden by a lady and a man, came to be called combination tandems.

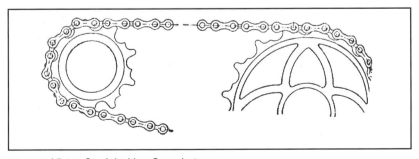

*Fig. 7–7.* Victor Straight Line Sprocket.

*Fig. 7–8. Victor Spinroller gear.*

Trying to counteract the new bevel gear shaft-driven chainless that had been announced by Columbia in October of 1897, Victor in 1898 emphasized that a chain was superior for driving the sprockets and so introduced a new "Straight Line Sprocket" which simply had a different cut of the sprocket teeth with space removed from between the teeth to allow it to shed mud and grit (Fig. 7-7). Maroon and green finishes were available on the top of the line Model 35 Victors and Victorias.

Not to be outdone though, Victor in 1899 introduced its version of the chainless which, unlike Columbia's bevel gear model and Iver Johnson's roller pin gear, made exclusive use of a spinroller gear.

The Victor spinroller consisted of two sets of intermeshing rotary roller teeth with one roller simply meeting and rolling against the other to transmit power from the cranks through a shaft inside the hollow rear fork to the rear gear where it meshed with the rear axle (Fig. 7-8). The spinroller shaft drive was a $25 option on both Victor and Victoria models. Wheel axles were made narrower, the rear by almost an inch, and the crank tread also was narrowed. Handlebars were made adjustable simply by turning the nut on the top of the bar in the manner of today's bicycles.

Overman's efforts were in vain, however. Several factors including the price wars forced the company to conclude the manufacture of bicycles in 1899.

### The Columbia

In tribute to the many club riders who were endeavoring to ride century runs, Pope called his new 1892 single-tube pneumatic tire safeties the Century Columbia (Fig. 7-9) and the Century Road Racer.

Guaranteed by the maker not to puncture due to faulty material or construction, the Columbia pneumatic was of the Boothroyd type with the outer casing and inner tube vulcanized together into a single tube of a sufficient thickness to wear well and resist puncture (Fig. 7-11). The 2" rear and ¾" front pneumatic tires were inflated to 50 or 60 lbs. pressure.

The $150 Road Racer was a Century stripped of brake, step, coaster bars, and lamp bracket and fitted with a light weight saddle. At 39 lbs. it was 4 lbs. lighter than the fully equipped Century.

The unchanged gents' and ladies' Columbia Light Roadsters were continued, fitted with cushion or solid tires or with optional pneumatic tires. The Columbia Racing Safety at $175 was available only with pneumatic tires.

*Fig. 7–9.* 1892 Century Columbia.

"Among all the intelligent classes of people, the bicycle is now accepted as a machine of importance and value. There is not a profession, nor a trade into which the safety bicycle has not been received and welcomed by these men and women who stand for whatever is progressive and recognize that which is helpful to them. From a social point of view, also, it takes a prominent rank among the inventions of the century." So began Pope's 1893 Columbia catalog!

He went on to explain that he was the first to introduce the bicycle into the regular army (at least one Volunteer Columbia ordinary exists with "U.S. Army"

*Fig. 7–10.* 1893 Columbia Light Roadster safety equipped with Babcock fire extinguisher and fireman's ax.

149

stamped into its nameplate) and that the Light Roadster safety he supplied to General Miles for service at Fort Sheridan had stood the test and had received

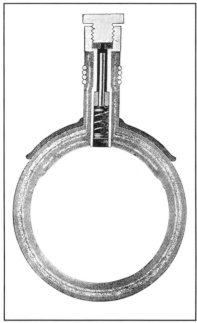

Miles' endorsement as a valuable military vehicle.

Suggesting that gents' Columbia Light Roadster safety Model 27 and ladies' safety Model 28 were best suited for use by soldiers, letter carriers, and telegraph and other messengers, he also encouraged adoption of the "wheel" by police officers and firemen.

For the latter he made exclusive arrangements with the Fire Extinguisher Mfg. Co. of Chicago to make available a Model 28 equipped with a Babcock fire extinguisher and fireman's axe (Fig. 7-10).

The 1893 Century Columbia Model 32 at $150 made an important step forward with a rear band brake operating on the hub much like an automobile brake of today (Fig. 7-12). For the first time, the tire itself was not used as a braking surface. Also the Model 32 was

*Fig. 7–11.* The Columbia "Boothroyd" type pneumatic tire.

equipped with the new elliptical shape front sprocket (Fig. 7-13).

The advantage claimed for the elliptical sprocket was that the higher gear was operative not only at the best position of the crank, but also at the best position of the rider's leg when the power was exerted to the most advantage and was the greatest. The catalog went on to explain that since the speed for the machine remained practically constant, the crank had to revolve at a varying velocity, the velocity being highest when the cranks were at the "dead" points and the power least, and lowest when they were at their best positions and the power greatest. The elliptical sprocket allowed a longer time to exert the propelling power and consequently caused an acceleration of the crank, or the pedal, around the dead points.

*Fig. 7–12.* Century Columbia band brake.

*Fig. 7–13.* 1893 Century Columbia elliptical sprocket.

I notice very little, if any, advantage in riding the Century Columbia Model 32. However, the elliptical sprocket concept has persisted and is offered today as an aftermarket accessory for ten-speed safeties.

In addition to the Model 32 Century gents', the 1893 line included the Model 32 Road Racer at $150, which was essentially a 33 lb. stripped Century; the $150 Model 30, a new gents' machine described as a light road bicycle and the gents' $130 Model 29, which was the 1892 Century carried over from the preceding year. The old Model 27 Light Roadster at $125 with pneumatic tires and a new

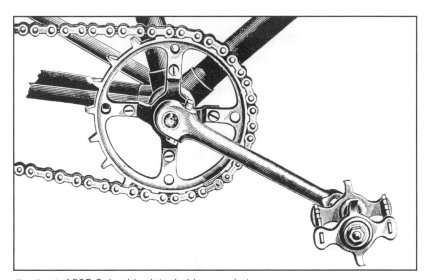

*Fig. 7–14.* 1895 Columbia detachable sprocket.

Fig. 7–15.
Narrow tread 1895
Columbia crank
hanger.

Ladies' Model 31 also were offered. Following the general lines of earlier ladies' Columbias, the $150 Model 31 featured 26" rear, 28" front hollow rims, tangential spokes, and pneumatic tires. The old ladies' Model 28, fitted with pneumatic tires for $125, also was continued as was the 26½ lb. racing safety for $160.

Pope guaranteed all Columbias to be free from imperfections in material or manufacture for one year. He offered to police officers and citizens who returned to its owner a stolen Columbia still in good condition a reward of $50 payable upon conviction and sentencing of the thief. "It is grand larceny to steal a bicycle; it is arrest and conviction to steal a Columbia," he stated.

With his 1894 Model 33 Columbia Racer, Pope offered wood rim wheels for the first time. In addition to his standard single tube tire, he made available the Hartford inner tube tire embodying patents issued to Thomas Jeffery. Pope manufactured these himself.

As was fashionable in the trade at the time, he also increased the number of frame sizes offering a $140 Model 31 with extra high frame. Light Roadster ladies' and gents', safeties which had evolved from Pope's solid tire safety in 1888, were discontinued.

Describing his bicycles as the "standard of the world," Pope in 1895 introduced a new nickel steel which had been developed for military use and was claimed to be stronger than any previous tubing stock.

Yielding to a raging price war brought on by the department stores' sales of cheaper lines, the manufacturer introduced the new Model 40 at $100. Offering 28" wood rims, 1½" single tube tires, detachable sprockets front and rear (Fig. 7-14), narrow 5½" tread (Fig. 7-15), and seamless nickel steel tubing, it and its companion Model 41 for ladies achieved a level of sophistication that would not be appreciably exceeded for the rest of the century.

Also important in 1895 was the addition of a tandem, Columbia's first since its ill-fated 1889–1890 solid tire model. The new tubing made it possible to build a tandem strong enough to carry two riders of more than average weight while the complete machine weighed only 38 lbs. It featured a double loop dropped front and gents' diamond rear frame with double steering, 28" wood rims, and 1¾" single-tube tires.

Remarking that after he instituted an inner tube option in 1894, the call for single tube tires increased from 40 to 90 percent, Pope nevertheless announced that he would offer in 1895 the Dunlop inner tube tire which he would manufacture himself. It had a new valve design and a molded cover.

Also for the first time that year, Pope added the Hartford bicycle line to his Columbia catalog. Four years later, the Hartford Cycle Co. was established by the Pope Mfg. Co. for the manufacture of a less expensive line of bicycles. Gents' and ladies' Pattern 1 and 2 models for $80, Pattern 3 and 4 for $60, and Pattern 5 and 6 for $50 were offered.

Columbias were sold at the unvarying price of $100 to all alike with no discounts and tandems at $150 and the 1896 line continued with no major changes except the addition of a double gents' Model 43 tandem. These prices were in effect at a time when a new Sears Roebuck buggy could be purchased for $27.75.

By now it was not fashionable to have brakes. They were standard only on the ladies' Model 40 and on the tandems. The brake was arranged so once removed there was no visible evidence of its having been attached. Detachable coasting foot rests automatically were fitted to the front fork when the brake was ordered as an option. Bicycles not equipped with brakes required that the rider use only backpedaling to slow the machine and in order to stop, to press the heel of his shoe against the tire.

In the 1896 catalog Pope described his testing department. There was a 100,000 lb. hydraulic machine for testing tension or compression. It was used to determine the force necessary to break any material and with it, Pope was able to learn the exact qualities of steel required in each part of the Columbia. Another device measured the amount of power needed to overcome friction at any bearing.

Before he released the 1897 Columbia bicycles to the public, Pope required that the prototypes be ridden 100 miles per day by 30 of his employees for nearly two months. Their suggested improvements were implemented and then followed by additional testing. Thus assured of the quality of his bicycles, the manufacturer took a major risk by guaranteeing the tires against defects for six months.

The new Columbias had frames of five percent nickel steel tubing with flush joints so that all tube junctures would be smooth. Within the tubes were long reinforcements and thimbles brazed together (Fig. 7-16).

There were crank shaft improvements and spokes were attached to studs which, it was claimed, prevented them from bending or twisting.

The wood rims, which now were on all Columbia models, were laminated from very stiff wood. As the grain of each layer was different, splitting, shrinking, and warping were discouraged in the laminated rim. Single piece wood rims of much less cost were common with many manufacturers, but were thought not to have the same advantages as the laminated ones.

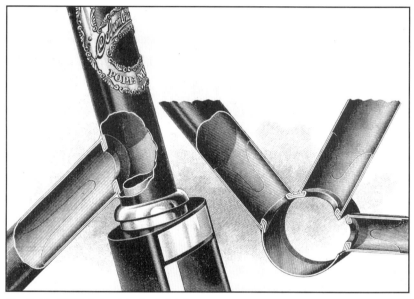

*Fig. 7–16.* 1897 Columbia flush joints.

In 1897 for the first time Pope offered a wood handlebar as an option on any model Columbia. It was slightly springier than the steel bar and was believed to reduce vibration transmitted to the hands.

Gents' and ladies' 23 lb. Model 45 and 46 Columbias were offered at $100 with barrel stud hubs and narrower wood or steel handlebars with vulcanite and cork grips.

The big news at Columbia in October, 1897 was the introduction of the shaft-drive chainless safety (Fig. 7-17). The shaft drive bevel gear chainless was based on a similar mechanism introduced in 1894 by the League Cycle Co. of Hartford, Connecticut, and later sold to Pope in 1897. The company was small and lacked the money to carry out an advertising campaign to convince the public of the merits of the chainless design. The chainless Acatene had been in production in Europe and had been used to set speed and distance records.

By 1897 Pope's sales were slowing due to extensive advertising by dozens of new competitors. A chainless was seen by him as a way of distinguishing his line. Within a year, however, most principle makers were offering this design.

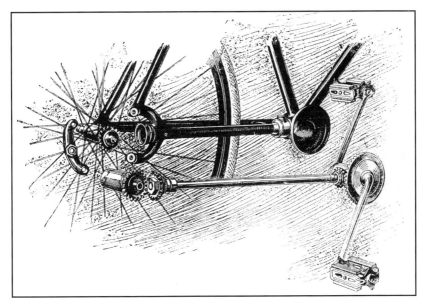

*Fig. 7–17.* 1897 bevel gear chainless mechanism.

Although their popularity declined after 1900, some were available in the United States until the 1920s.

Always more costly to produce, the chainless was less profitable to manufacture than the chain driven bicycle. In a day of price wars and high inventories, production cost was critical. It sold well in 1897 and 1898, but the public soon discovered that the flamboyant advertising claims of chainless pedaling ease simply were not true. Frames often became bent from hitting severe road irregularities, rendering the bicycle useless. The difficulty of removing the rear wheel and its attendant gear mechanism on the frequent occasions of a flat rear tire also contributed to the demise of the chainless. Nevertheless, Pope continued to advocate its merits.

In his 1898 catalog, he explained that the Columbia bevel gear chainless (Fig. 7-18) had no backlash and no chain slack at dead points and that the bevel gear was more durable and easier running than the chain because of the absence of exposure to grit and mud. He said the chainless was more secure to ride, especially for women who no longer had to worry about their clothing getting caught in a chain.

Those who purchased the chain safety could also buy a case that completely enclosed the chain. Such chain cases were popular on European bicycles.

Overshadowed by the excitement of the new chainless was the more important introduction of the Columbia New Departure brake which slowed and stopped the rear wheel upon exertion of a backpedaling motion on the pedals. No longer did stopping the bicycle depend upon a heel or a brake spoon pressing on a tire or a complicated series of rods actuating a leather strap on a drum.

The brake, which also allowed safe coasting with the feet securely on the pedals where they were kept in a fixed position as on today's coaster brake bicycles, was at first described as being especially valuable to women in descending steep grades or in an emergency. There still was a strange reluctance on the part of many riders, mostly "youngblood scorchers," to equip a bicycle with a brake. However the less daring could purchase a Columbia with the New Departure coaster brake. It was explained in the advertising that the brake hardware was so hidden no one would notice it.

The 1898 Columbia catalog was printed in English, French, German, and Spanish editions indicating the importance of the export market. A separate 32 page catalog was published on the chainless that suggested the maker's high expectations for that model.

In 1899 Pope emphasized low purchase price in his advertising for the first time. The reduced price chain-driven Model 49 retailed at $40 and the Hartford Vedettes at $25 and $26. His major promotional effort continued though to be focused on the chainless.

Pope's advertising in 1900, the first year in which Columbia was a division of the American Bicycle Company, finally emphasized the coaster brake. It noted that one could coast even on the level thus reducing by up to one third the amount of pedaling required.

Addressing his message to the fair sex, Pope noted in his 1900 advertising of the ladies' chainless that "A woman is as much entitled to the best bicycle as a man. Today women devote as much care and thought to their cycling costume as they give to their gown for other occasions. Select a bicycle which is in keeping with this idea," he suggested. The spacious opening between the seat and

*Fig. 7–18.* 1898 Columbia ladies' chainless.

down tube assured room for the skirt, and the lack of a chain to entangle it made the ladies' chainless the perfect machine in Pope's view.

### Gormully and Jeffery

Although its bicycles continued largely unchanged from 1891, America's third major maker, Gormully and Jeffery introduced a highly acclaimed version of the inner tube pneumatic tire in 1892 (Figs. 7-19 and 7-20).

The uniqueness of the G & J pneumatic tire was in the way it fastened to the rim. The edges of the casing were turned outward and engaged the inwardly turned edges of the rim. The inner tube, separate and inside the casing, when inflated pressed sideways the hooked edge of the casing locking the tire onto the rim. When the inner tube was deflated, a side pressure on one of the edges disengaged that part from the rim making the tire easy to remove. The G &J pneumatic closely approximated today's bicycle tire and was used extensively, even by the Pope Mfg. Co.

Because the series of refinements in Gormully and Jeffery's Ramblers and Ideals so closely paralleled what was being done by Overman and Pope, we will look at only the highlights from the 1892–1900 Gormully and Jeffery production period.

Gormully and Jeffery broke its tradition in 1892 when it introduced a Diamond Rambler without the company's much touted spring frame that had been part of the Rambler safety since the first solid tire one in 1888.

In addition to their unique pneumatic tire, they differed from Victor and Columbia in the method of joining frame tubes. Rather than flush joints that concealed reinforcements inside the tubes, Ramblers had exposed joints with one tube flared to embrace the other (Fig. 7-21). Joined by a method called lap brazing, the process involved spreading or lapping of the flared ends of one tube

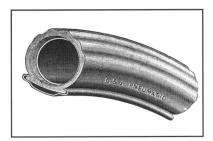

*Fig. 7–19.* G & J pneumatic tire mounted.

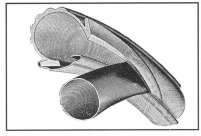

*Fig. 7–20.* G & J pneumatic tire construction detail.

partially around the outer surface of another after which both were firmly brazed together. Thus, they explained, the actual brazing was accomplished in full view of the operator and the element of chance played no part in the operation as necessarily was the case when flush joints and reinforcing lugs or thimbles hidden inside the tubes were used. All brazing on Ramblers was done by immersing the joint in molten brass, thus preventing both oxidation and over-heating of any of the metal. The surplus brass was carefully removed without the use of acid, according to the 1900 Rambler Catalog.

Gormully and Jeffery continued to offer children's Ideal Ramblers. In 1893 boy's and girl's models with 26" driving and 24" steering wheels and cushion tires sold for $50.

In 1894 there were improvements in Rambler lap jointing and the brake. The latter pivoted below the front fork crown and was actuated by pressing its side arms with the feet. Rambler's rather wide crank tread was narrowed to 5½".

By 1895 Gormully and Jeffery was including a one-year warranty against defects with the sale of all Ramblers. The catalog emphasized that the time had come when the bicycle was a neces-sity for business purposes, largely replacing the horse and buggy for med-ical, professional, and businessmen whose affairs carried them to the cen-ters of cities at some distance from their homes.

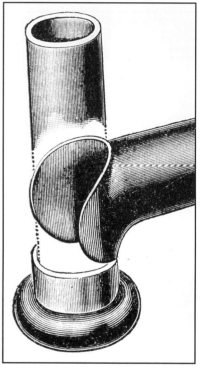

Fig. 7–21. 1893 Rambler joint.

A gents' Rambler Number 14 semi-racer (Fig. 7-22) was offered at 22 lbs. for $100 and surprisingly was described in the catalog as appropriate for women who favored rational dress. A Number 11 weighing 34½ lbs. was introduced for large and heavy men and single and double loop frame ladies' Models C and D were offered at $100. A dropped frame light-weight 20 lb. Model E (Fig. 7-23) was introduced for ladies "... slight of stature ... (who) ... are not satisfied to go slowly through the world, but wish to ride as fast as their compatriots of the male sex," according to the catalog.

A major addition to the 1895 line was the $150 32 lb. tandem (Fig. 7-24). "The expression 'a bicycle built for two' will be thoroughly understood and appreciated by sympathetic young couples who desire to ride together," the cat-alog said. Double gents' and racing tandems also were offered.

In 1895 Gormully and Jeffery offered wood rims specially shaped with an extra groove into which the G & J pneumatic tire locked (Fig. 7-25). With the wood rim, the outer locking edge served mainly to keep the tire in position.

*Fig. 7–22.* 1895 Rambler Number 14.

Gormully and Jeffery offered $40 in gold in 1896 to the cycling club whose members riding Ramblers fitted with G & J tires rode the largest number of

*Fig. 7–23.* 1895 Rambler Model E.

*Fig. 7–24.* 1895 Rambler double steering combination tandem.

aggregate miles from April to December and $1,000 to the person riding the fastest mile on a Rambler also during that time.

Over the next few years Gormully and Jeffery continued to emphasize its lap brazed joints with "fish mouth" outside reinforcements, its decreasing prices, and its fine finish with gold lining and filigree. An 1899 advertisement read "$40 is the 1899 price, the very lowest the Rambler price can go—this is bottom."

In 1900 Rambler tube joints were cut in a new rococo pattern (Fig. 7-26) edged in gold paint; black, olive, maroon, and black and red frame colors were offered. The following year, after becoming a division of the American Bicycle Co., a Rambler bevel gear chainless was added to the line.

## UNIQUE FEATURES, 1892–1900

Of the several hundred makers of bicycles in the period 1892–1900, many operated very small shops. They bought components from suppliers and assembled bicycles under their own name. Others were small high quality manufacturers who brought outstanding skill and advanced technology to their product.

With so many makers competing for cyclists' attention, many incorporated unique features into their machines to distinguish them from their competitors and to have something different to

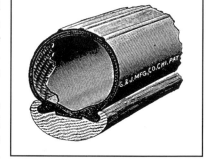

*Fig. 7–25.* 1895 Rambler clincher wooden rim.

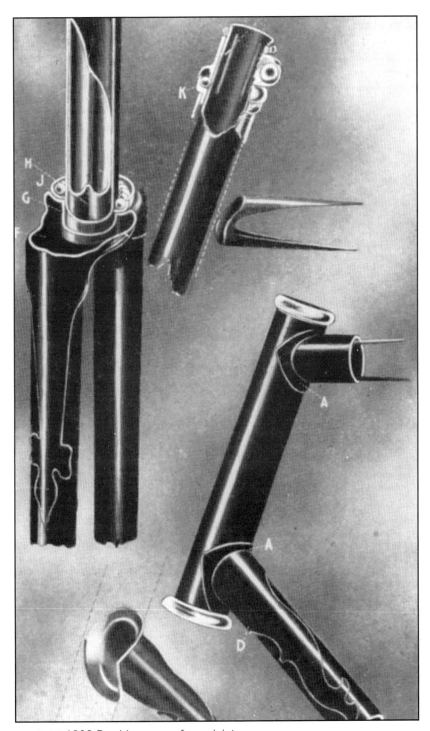

*Fig. 7–26.* 1900 Rambler rococo frame joints.

distinguish them from their competitors and to have something different to mention in their advertising.

Following is a selection of features that became strongly identified with particular brands.

### Curved Cranks

Patented April 17, 1894 by Ferdinand F. E. Ide, the curved crank on his Ide bicycles was designed to work like the commonly used rigid crank under normal use. Under heavy pressure, though, the curved spring steel Ide crank straightened out, thus making itself longer and providing the additional leverage of a long crank. Also it was claimed that this crank would not transmit jolts to the rider and would yield when the pedal struck an obstruction, thus preventing any excessive shock from being imparted to the machine. Ladies' and gents' and tandem Ides were manufactured from 1894 to 1898 by the Ide Mfg. Co., Peoria, Illinois.

### Racycle Crank

Patented by Franklin Burnham and Jefferson Alsup of Chicago in 1897, the Racycle crank (Fig. 7-27) had a hollow hub in which were ball bearings; locating the bearings in the crank allowed the chain to pull between them. It was claimed by the Miami Cycle Mfg. Co. of Middletown, Ohio, that the design reduced pressure on the bearings by 20 to 30 percent. Another distinctive feature of many Racycles was a large diameter front sprocket.

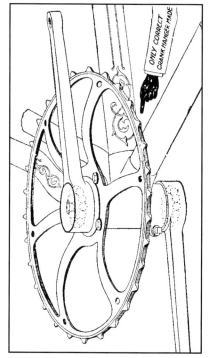

*Fig. 7–27.* Racycle with bearings in crank.

### Curved Seat Tube

Manufactured by the Keating Wheel Co., Holyoke, Massachusetts, from 1892 to 1898, Keating bicycles had a distinctive forward curve at the base of the seat tube, (Fig. 7-28) which was said to make the frame stronger. It also served as an easy way to identify a Keating bicycle.

### Truss Seat Tube

A feature of the American bicycle, made by the International Mfg. Co., Chicago, and the Fowler, made by the Fowler Cycle Co. also of Chicago, was a bifurcated seat tube (Fig. 7-29) that was claimed to be as strong and as rigid as the usual tube while being lighter. A youthful Ignaz Schwinn was employed by these companies prior to his striking out on his own to found Arnold, Schwinn & Co.

*Fig. 7–28.* 1896 Keating with curved seat tube.

### Spring Front Fork

The George N. Pierce Co. of Buffalo, N.Y., in its high grade models incorporated a distinctive spring front fork, the sides of which were formed of two leaves of spring steel. At the rear, the seat stays, chain stays, and crank hanger were free to move independently of the remainder of the frame. A short spring in the rear of the crank bracket reduced vibration at that point and acted in concert with a compression spring operating between the crown of the rear seat stay and the top of the seat tube (Fig. 7-30).

### Roller Sprocket

The Elmore roller sprocket in 1898 substituted free-turning discs for teeth claiming an easier running chain as the result (Fig. 7-31). Elmore bicycles were made in Elmore and Clyde, Ohio, from 1895 to 1898.

### The Spur Gear Chainless

Thomas A. Carroll of Philadelphia, Pennsylvania, patented a spur gear chainless which consisted of three sprockets, one attached to the crank axle, a second which meshed with the first and was attached to the reinforced chain stay, and a third smaller one fixed to the rear hub. The teeth were very small, keeping the amount of friction to a minimum. The gear ratio could easily be changed simply by switching to sprockets with different numbers of teeth. All could be encased to prevent interference from dirt and grit, and it was claimed the system was stronger than a chain. A racer and gents' and ladies' roadsters were offered. The Reading Cycle Co. of Reading, Pennsylvania, produced a similar model using a Gentry spur gear in 1898 (Figs. 7-32, 7-33). Spur gear safeties also were produced in Europe.

*Fig. 7–29.* 1896 American bicycle with divided seat tube.

### Chainless Front Drivers

Frank H. Bolte in 1892 patented a new frame design for his Telegram front driving chainless (Fig. 7-34) which was made by the Sercombe-Bolte Mfg. Co., Milwaukee, Wisconsin. Based on the British Crypto, the last geared front driver

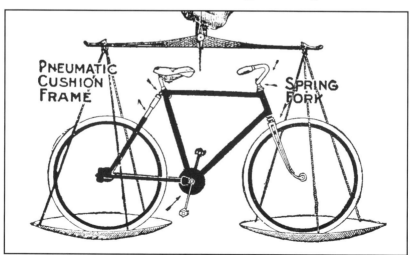

*Fig. 7–30.* 1902 Pierce cushion frame chainless.

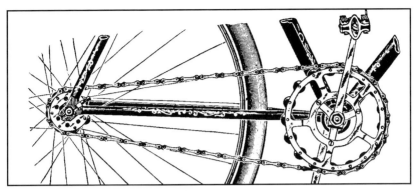

*Fig. 7–31.* 1898 Elmore roller sprocket.

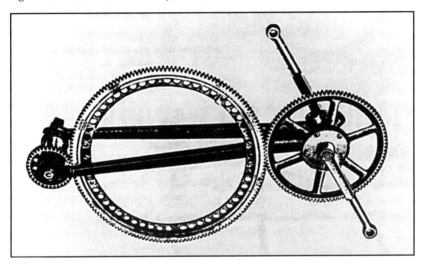

*Fig. 7–32.* 1898 Gentry spur gear.

*Fig. 7–33.* 1898 Reading Cycle Co. Vindex spur gear chainless.

*Fig. 7–34.* 1892 Telegram chainless.

*Fig. 7–35.* 1892 Mondamin chainless.

to survive (Fig. 1-2), the Telegram came in 28", 30", and 32" diameter drive wheels geared double to 56", 60", and 64". It was priced at $150 with pneumatic tires.

The 1892 Mondamin bicycle (Fig. 7-35), made by the Thos. Kane Co., of Chicago, was very similar to the Telegram except for frame differences. It was claimed to be easier to pedal than any chain wheel, steady at all speeds, free from headers, and safe on rough, wet, and slippery roads.

## WOOD FRAME BICYCLES

Wood frame bicycles began in America in 1888 with the solid tire Elliott Hickory (Fig. 6-39). Phineas York of Chicago in 1897 patented a bicycle frame and front fork constructed of 16 plies of laminated, second growth, hollowed out hickory (Fig. 7-36). In one continuous piece the laminations began at the crank hanger, continued on to form the head, then onward forming the top tube and finally bent downward and forward to make the seat tube. The bicycle was trimmed in carbonized steel stampings (Fig. 7-37). Manufactured under the name Old Hickory by Tonk Mfg. Co., Chicago, Illinois, the lightest model weighed 17½ lbs. and sold for $100. In 1897, Tonk produced what he claimed was the first American ladies' wood safety.

*Fig. 7–36.* 1898 Old Hickory.

Fig. 7–37. 1898 decorative stampings and curved laminated frame.

The Huseby, made by the Huseby Cycle Co., Milwaukee, Wisconsin, had frame, fork, and stays made of jointless rock elm tubing with aluminum connections. The handlebar was of rock elm as was the fork which was elliptical in section. The fork crown was steel. Hubs, spokes, and 28" rims were hickory. Parts were joined without screws or bolts and they were guaranteed never to loosen.

A similar wood bicycle was made by the Allwood Cycle Co., Canarsie Grove, Long Island, New York (Fig. 7-38). Frame, handlebar, and rims were made of solid, second growth hickory; the connections were of aluminum alloyed with nickel steel. The Allwood frame could easily be disassembled by unscrewing the copper rings from the threaded ends of the joints that held the frame together. When the rings were tightened they firmly grasped the wood frame rods making it as strong, it was claimed, as a steel bicycle. Gents' and ladies' models were offered at $50.

Still another similar machine was manufactured by the Seaman Machine Co., Milwaukee, Wisconsin. Its frame joints were more ornamental in shape than the Allwood's and it could not be disassembled.

One of the largest makers of wood safeties was the M. D. Stebbins Mfg. Co. of Springfield, Massachusetts, makers of the Chilion (Fig. 7-39). The Chilion's hickory frame was connected by aluminum-bronze lugs. The wood frame rods were of natural finish or were stained. The connections were burnished, giving the appearance of polished bronze (Fig. 7-40). Advantages claimed for the wood construction were the tubes would not buckle—buckling of steel frames when riders hit curbs or other road obstructions was a common problem at the time—it did not rust or tarnish; it was of a uniform color and did not show nicks and scratches. Further the natural springiness of the wood eliminated the need for special springs to assure a comfortable ride.

Ladies' and gents' bicycles made by the Elliott Hickory Wheel Co., Newton, Massachusetts, continued to be made in the pneumatic tire period, but on gents'

*Fig. 7–38.* c. 1896 Allwood ladies' Favorite.

models the use of wood was confined to the wheels whose felloes and spokes were constructed of second growth hickory. Hubs were of rock elm (Fig. 7-41). The mud guards and chain guard on ladies' models were wood and the 28" tires were attached to cold rolled steel rims which were screwed to the felloes. Elliott wheels were sold to other manufacturers including the Common Sense Bicycle Co. of Philadelphia, Pennsylvania, which made a bicycle of that same name.

*Fig. 7–39.* 1897 Chilion. *(courtesy of Henry Ford Museum)*

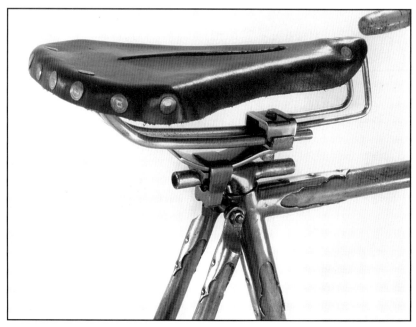

Fig. 7–40. 1897 Chilion frame joint. *(courtesy of Greenfield Village and Henry Ford Museum)*

Fig. 7–41. c. 1891 gents' Elliott Hickory. Note candle lamp.

*Fig. 7–42.* 1897 Bamboo. *(courtesy of Henry Ford Museum)*

Another unique bicycle was the Bamboo, made by the Bamboo Cycle Co., Ltd. of London (Fig. 7-42). It used hollow bamboo stalks for the frame rods, front fork, and stays and steel for joints and fork crown. Rims were wood. Ladies' and gents' bicycles and a tricycle were made. An American bamboo bicycle made in Milwaukee, Wisconsin, used bamboo stalks as jackets over small diameter steel rods. Splitting of the stalks was a problem common to all of these bicycles.

### ALUMINUM FRAME BICYCLES

Introduced about 1893 by the St. Louis Refrigerator and Wooden Gutter Co., St. Louis, Missouri. the Lu-Mi-Num bicycle frame was cast hollow in one piece (Fig. 7-43). Containing a small percentage of alloy, this bicycle evidenced a very early use of aluminum. The front fork was cast solid and all was polished, but not to a mirror finish.

Rights to the manufacture of the Lu-Mi-Num bicycle were purchased by M. M. Cycles, Sans Soudures en Lu-Mi-Num who manufactured it in Paris. It was sold in England by the Lu-Mi-Num Mfg. Co., Ltd. of London.

Lu-Mi-Num's 1895 ladies' and gents' models weighed 25 lbs. and sold for $125. At the 1895 Chicago Bicycle Show, a Lu-Mi-Num exhibit provided for testing the strength of the aluminum handlebar. Two heavy men were permitted to suspend their weight from either side to show that it would not bend or break. Samples of the aluminum used in making the bicycle were twisted and

*Fig. 7–43.* 1894 Lu-Mi-Num.

bent into every conceivable shape without fracturing. A gauge demonstrated the perfect alignment of the Lu-Mi-Num frame, which was claimed to be truer than any steel frame.

A chain case, integrally cast with the frame, gave extra strength to the 1896 model (Fig. 7-44). Today Lu-Mi-Num bicycles must be ridden with care to guard against fracturing due to the age and embrittlement of the aluminum.

*Fig. 7–44.* 1896 Lu-Mi-Num.

## UNIQUE FRAME DESIGNS
### The Dursley Pedersen

Patented in 1893 by Mikael Pedersen, a Dane who had moved to Dursley, England, the Dursley Pedersen was one of the most innovative designs ever to be created for a safety bicycle (Fig. 7-45). It used a triangulated frame of small diameter tubing rods which were soft soldered together and plated both inside and out.

Starting with the desire to make a more comfortable saddle, Pedersen developed an unusual hammock woven from 45 yards of silk cord and supported at the front by an adjustable leather strap and at the back by seven springs (Figs. 7-46, 7-47). The saddle required a totally new frame design. His first experimental model used hickory frame rods instead of steel tubes and weighed only 11½ lbs. complete.

*Fig. 7–45.* c. 1900 Dursley Pedersen with mudguards. *(courtesy American Bicycle Museum)*

The 1907 Dursley Pedersen catalog explained that the triangulated frame and fork were designed to afford the maximum strength with the minimum weight. This was based upon principles used in bridge construction where strength and lightness were desired.

The catalog went on to note that the tubes were in pairs throughout, each pair making in conjunction with the bottom bracket or other portion of the frame, a triangle. Thereby the frame imparted a great lateral stability to the machine and offered excellent resistance to pedal pressure. Four pairs of tubes, including the back stays, radiated from the ends of the crank bracket, making this part, subjected as it was to the greatest stress in riding, adequate to the strain.

The front fork was built of four tubes. The two in front were perfectly straight and capable of withstanding the strain of compression. The two behind were drawn back in the center to withstand a tensile stress. An open steel crown plate held all four fork tubes in position.

When Pedersen's first production model was exhibited at the Stanley Show in 1897, it created a mini-sensation. Always very expensive, the Dursley Pedersen

*Fig. 7–46.* Gents' Dursley Pedersen saddle.

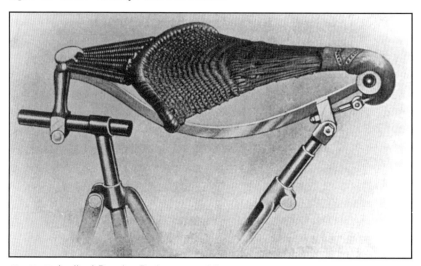

*Fig. 7–47.* Ladies' Dursley Pedersen saddle.

was luxuriously finished and practically custom built for the owner. Since saddle height adjustment was limited by the frame design, eight frame sizes were available chosen by the length of the rider's inside leg measure. The top of the line Royal was completely nickel plated or it could be painted the color of the buyer's choice.

In 1901 a folding model, intended for military use, was developed and a 28 lb. tandem, a 45 lb. triplet, and a 64 lb. quadruplet were built. A Pedersen three speed gear, shifted from the handlebar, was patented in 1902 and offered the following year. A similar two speed gear was introduced in 1904. Ladies' and gents' models were produced until 1914. Relatively plentiful in England, Dursley Pedersens are rare and desirable in the United States.

### The Upright

Distributed by Herbert Torrey of Boston, Massachusetts, the Upright bicycle of the mid 1890s (Fig. 7-48) was claimed to be the only one having the unqualified approval of all physicians. Its frame design forced the rider to sit in an upright position, a posture favored by most physicians at that time. The handlebar, which was of British design and was called the Whatton, curved around the back of the rider to provide a convenient pull when the rider was sitting perfectly upright.

It is not known how many Uprights were sold, but there is one in a private American collection.

*Fig. 7–48.* 1896 Upright.

## The Giraffe

S. MacCormack invented the Giraffe in 1893. It was introduced into the American market in 1894 by the John P. Lovell Arms Co. of Boston, Massachusetts, in response to strong demand by tall riders for high frames (Fig. 7-49). Its extreme height was made possible by shortening the seat tube and running the chain stay as a continuation of the down tube. This gave a very high position to the front sprocket, putting it in reach from the lofty saddle.

*Fig. 7–49.* 1894 Lovell Giraffe.

## The Rex

Bohn C. Hicks in 1896 patented the Rex which was manufactured by the Rex Cycle Co., Chicago, Illinois, and was first exhibited at the Chicago National Bicycle Show in 1897.

The Rex saddle was attached to a curved backbone which pivoted in front at a point midway on the down tube and curved over the rear driving wheel, terminating behind it where it was pivoted to a rear fork in which was a small third wheel (Fig. 7-50). A brace was attached to the third wheel's fork crown and to the hub of the drive wheel. Thus the backbone was free to move independently of the rest of the bicycle. This was supposed to smooth out the bumpy roads of the day. It was claimed that the Rex would not vibrate, would stand alone when dismounted, and would not slide out from under the rider on wet pavement. Tandem, (Fig. 7-51) gents', and ladies' models were offered.

*Fig. 7–50.* Rosemarie Wiedman riding a ladies' Rex.

*Fig. 7–51.* c. 1898 Rex Tandem. *(courtesy of Henry Ford Museum)*

## TANDEMS AND COMPANIONS

Tandem manufacturers in the 1890s were reluctant to build frames that would position the man ahead of the lady, but gents, who probably were depended upon to steer, complained that they couldn't see where they were going.

*Fig. 7–52.* Gary Woodward and an 1897 Tally-Ho tandem.

### The Tally-Ho

The Maumee Cycle Co. of Toledo, Ohio, responded to those who complained that their view was blocked when it marketed the Tally-Ho in 1897 (Fig. 7-52). A larger wheel in the rear and a high frame enabled the gent to be elevated 5½" higher than the lady. Based on the donkey back frames used on some pacing multicycles, the Tally-Ho eliminated the rear chain and seat stays entirely, thus reducing the wheelbase to 53" making it more maneuverable than other tandems.

A similar concept was tried by the Western Wheel Co., Chicago, Illinois, with its Crescent Model 30 "poop deck" tandem. To a standard combination tandem was added a "Lovell Diamond Giraffe type" rear frame with rear chain sprocket axle at the intersection of the seat tube and an auxiliary high-mounted down tube. Offered at $125, it was not a commercial success.

**The Companion**

Since the days of the solid tire side-by-side adult tricycle of the 1880s, romantics had cried for a companion bicycle upon which lady and gentleman could ride beside each other.

Albert H. Weaver of Hamilton, Ontario, Canada studied the problem and in 1895 patented a unique frame (Fig. 7-53) which would be manufactured with minor variations by The Punnett Cycle Mfg. Co., Rochester, New York, and the Fox Machine Co., Battle Creek, Michigan.

The Fox Flyer was the first to be exhibited and was shown at the January 4, 1897 Chicago National Bicycle Show. The Punnett Companion was shown two weeks later at the New York National Bicycle Show in Madison Square Garden.

*Fig. 7–53.* Don and Jane Adams, riding an 1896 Punnett Companion.

Fig. 7–54.
Mounting the
Punnett
Companion.

In 1895 the Monarch Bicycle Co. also announced plans to purchase manufacturing rights, but it is not known if it ever produced any companions.

Offered at $150, the companion featured a duplicated dropped frame connected by cross tubes and an extended rear axle with sprockets at each end driven by chains from front sprockets in the usual manner. At the center of the back cross tube was a socket in which either seat post could be secured enabling a single rider to sit in the middle and ride the companion alone by working the inside pedals.

The author has found in riding a Punnett Companion that the best mounting procedure is for the lighter rider to mount first and place the feet on the pedals while the other holds the bicycle upright and then, grasping the handlebar firmly, pedal mounts (Fig. 7-54). Since both handlebars steer through a connecting rod, it may be necessary to have the second rider simply keep the hands at the center of the bar near the stem thus minimizing any counterproductive steering effort he or she may be contributing. The companion is easy and fun to ride. Although it may tilt some, it may be ridden by two people with up to a 100 pound weight difference. Somehow in the act of balancing the bicycle, the riders compensate for the weight difference.

Weighing 45 lbs., the companion sold for $150. The Punnett was advertised as being ideal for giving a ride to a friend who did not know how to manage a bicycle. Major problems were the immense strain on the rear wood rim and spokes that could cause breakage, punctures, and a heavy pedaling effort due to pushing against the wind resistance of two persons.

The design was patented throughout the world and similar machines were manufactured in France and England.

### Pacing Multicycles

Paced racing, whereby the racer took pace immediately behind three, four, five, or six man pacing machines was very popular in America in the mid to late 1890s. The theory simply was to tuck behind the pacing bicycle to lessen wind resistance and to be pulled along in the partial vacuum created by the pacer in the same manner that a large truck passing a small car will momentarily pull the car along.

The racer would have two or three pacing machines on the track waiting to replace the one that was operating at the time. The change of pace, which required making the shortest possible move to a second machine while going at

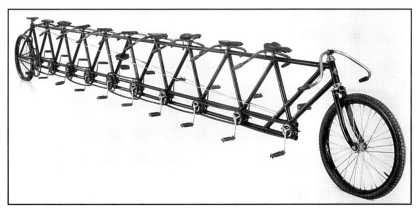

*Fig. 7–55.* 1896 Oriten. *(courtesy of Henry Ford Museum)*

top speed, was tricky and required great skill (Fig. 7-56). It was almost a certainty that if the racer lost his pace in these switches, he would lose the race. Later, motorcycles were used for pacing cyclists.

The pacing bicycles incorporated the finest components and were expensive to purchase. Frequently they were purchased by a group of men who would earn their living by shipping them by rail to races where they had a pacing contract. Occasionally multicycles were ridden for pleasure on the streets. Often they were used to promote a manufacturer's regular bicycle line.

The Waltham Mfg. Co., Boston, Massachusetts, which made a popular line of Orient pacing bicycles, in 1896 constructed a 10-person show model called the "Oriten" (Fig. 7-55). It appeared throughout the United States and Europe promoting the company. Today it is on exhibit at Henry Ford Museum in Dearborn, Michigan.

To shorten the wheelbase and get the last rider closer to the racer, some pacing bicycles had "donkey back" frames with the last crank operating directly off the rear wheel axle.

*Fig. 7–56.* Switching pace behind quints.

# Chapter 8:
# The Post-1900 Safeties: 1900-1970

Although a detailed examination of the post-1900 period is beyond the scope and emphasis of this book, there is enough enthusiasm among collectors for these "special interest" bicycles to make a discussion of the highlights worthwhile.

In America the automobile and motorcycle operated effectively on roads that gradually were improved to permit travelers to cover long distances. An American fascination with motorization made the bicycle unfashionable and impractical for adults who increasingly commuted long distances daily. The American bicycle largely became a toy for children soon after 1900.

Less affluence, shorter distances to cover, and a less fickle market preserved the bicycle as a suitable vehicle for adult transportation and enjoyment in Europe and many countries of the world where, as a vehicle of importance, it continued to be refined.

As described in C. F. Caunter's *History and Development of Cycles,* three types of British bicycles were made in the period 1900 to 1925. There were those produced in small numbers and assembled from purchased parts, those made by established manufacturers and sold in large quantities, and those known as deluxe bicycles which were finely made without regard to cost.

The great majority of British bicycles of the period were made by such familiar names as Bayliss and Thomas, Humber, BSA, Rudge-Whitworth, Raleigh, and Triumph.

By 1904 in America, the grand old names of Columbia, Tribune, Cleveland, Crawford, Rambler, Crescent, Monarch, and Imperial all were owned by the Pope Mfg. Co. With the exception of the Columbia, they were discontinued within a few years. Pope's interests, like those of his colleagues at Gormully and Jeffery, had shifted to making automobiles. In 1906 the manufacture of Pope bicycles was transferred to the old Lozier automobile factory in Westfield,

Massachusetts, where local citizens helped establish funds for a new larger factory, raising the money through local subscription.

That year the Pope Mfg. Co. began producing private brand bicycles for large national merchandising chains, a business which it continues to pursue to this day. In 1913 the famous Pope Mfg. Co. name was changed to the Westfield Mfg. Co., ending an era in which the name of Colonel Albert Pope had dominated the American bicycle scene.

A relatively new American company established in 1895 by Adolf Arnold and Ignaz Schwinn had weathered the stormy late 1890s and in 1900 had purchased the March-Davis Bicycle Company. Schwinn manufacturing operations were moved to the old March-Davis factory in west Chicago. In the late 1890s and during the post-1900 period many of the highest quality American bicycles were built by this firm.

American bicycles at best were not exciting from 1900 to 1925. The market for such fine English deluxe bicycles as the Dursley Pedersen, Golden Sunbeam, and Lea Francis did not exist here.

Most inventive American minds were no longer interested in experimenting with improvements for the bicycle. Whereas such innovations as the European "gradient" derailleur had been developed in 1899 and the derailleur gear, with a chain that shifted from one sprocket to another, much as we know it today, had been created about 1910, American developments of the period were linked to increasing the sale of bicycles to youngsters. Many manufacturers, to appeal to children, designed their bicycles to look like heavy motorcycles (Fig. 8-1).

*Fig. 8–1.* c. 1930 Van Cleve designed to look like a motorcycle. Its maker, W. F. Meyers of Dayton, Ohio purchased the Van Cleve name from the Wright brothers who had manufactured the St. Clair and Van Cleve during the period when they were developing their first airplane. *(courtesy of Henry Ford Museum)*

In 1902 Englishmen Henry Sturmey and James Archer produced the first Sturmey-Archer three-speed hub gear. It gave 25 percent above and 20 percent below direct drive and incorporated a freewheel for coasting in all gears. A hub brake was incorporated into the three-speed Sturmey-Archer gear in 1908.

Several other gears also were developed in England, the most elaborate being the Sunbeam bracket gear (Fig. 8-3) introduced in 1904. It was continually lubricated by being enclosed in a chain case containing oil.

In 1900 the Raleigh Cycle Co. of England introduced the substitution of light and strong steel stampings to hold the frame together. The innovation was incorporated in the 1901 Raleigh all-steel bicycle.

Double butted steel tubing, which was thickened where it had to be jointed to make a frame, was made mostly by the Reynolds Tubing Co., Ltd. and helped in the creation of stronger light frames. Improved British brakes of two types, the caliper, which squeezed the brake pads against the edges of the rim,

*Fig. 8–2.* The nameplate on the c. 1930 Van Cleve has the W.F. Meyers name under the log cabin. Nameplates on those made by the Wrights are the same except the Wright Cycle Co. is stamped in this location. *(courtesy of Greenfield Village and Henry Ford Museum)*

and the stirrup, which pushed the pads against the face of the rim, were developed during this period.

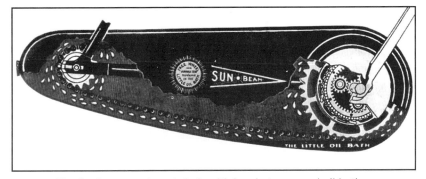

*Fig. 8–3.* The Sunbeam enclosed chain with bracket gear and oil bath.

Unique new machines, such as the British X frame Centaur and the German semi-recumbent Jaray, still were coming from the shops of European makers.

The lightweight bicycle had its beginning in England in 1926. Differing little in basics from earlier safeties, it used stronger and lighter steels with improved brazing, silver soldering, and welding to produce lighter, stiffer, and stronger bicycles. The more compact machines had shorter wheelbases with more upright steering heads, smaller wheels of 26" diameter, lighter tires of 1¼"

*Fig. 8–4.* The 1933 Schwinn advertisement introducing the balloon tire.

to 1⅜" width, and components such as handlebars and pedals made of light alloys.

Meanwhile, back in America, attention was being focused on how to popularize a tire that would be more satisfactory than the old single tube from the 1890s which remained in use on many American bicycles into the early 1930s.

In 1933 Schwinn introduced a new inner tube tire of over 2" cross sectional diameter that would make it longer wearing than the 1½" width previously used

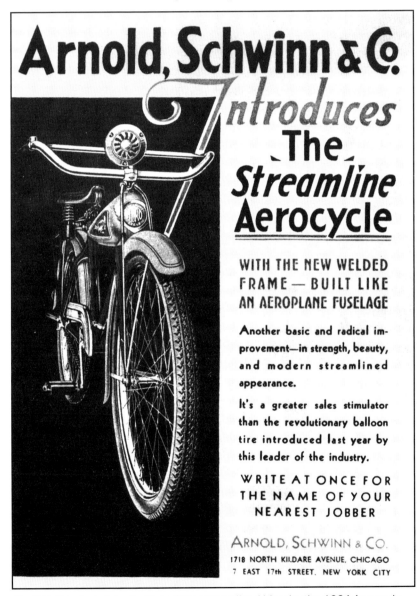

# Arnold, Schwinn & Co.

## *Introduces* The. *Streamline* Aerocycle

### WITH THE NEW WELDED FRAME — BUILT LIKE AN AEROPLANE FUSELAGE

Another basic and radical improvement—in strength, beauty, and modern streamlined appearance.

It's a greater sales stimulator than the revolutionary balloon tire introduced last year by this leader of the industry.

### WRITE AT ONCE FOR THE NAME OF YOUR NEAREST JOBBER

ARNOLD, SCHWINN & CO.
1718 NORTH KILDARE AVENUE, CHICAGO
7 EAST 17th STREET, NEW YORK CITY

*Fig. 8–5.* Schwinn's introduction of the streamlined bicycle, the 1934 Aerocycle.

(Fig. 8-4). These low pressure balloon tires were of the type that had been used on automobiles beginning some years earlier and had been well-publicized. Children loved them, especially when they had white sidewalls, and they became the standard of the American industry by 1935.

In 1934 Schwinn introduced the Streamline Aerocycle (Fig 8-5) which sold well to youngsters who liked its aircraft-inspired styling. By the end of that year, most manufacturers were preparing flamboyant new designs. Speedometers, headlights, tail and stop lights, enclosed frame tanks containing an electric horn and the attendant battery, luggage carriers, handlebar cross bars, knee action front forks, odometers, and even radios were piled onto the American bicycle to make it more appealing to the youth market.

The "balloon bombers" were immensely popular in America up to about 1960. By the late 1970s they had staged a comeback as a collectible. Enthusiasts had nostalgic memories of their bizarre styling and smooth ride and collectors saw them as suitable mounts for Whizzer and other motor bike conversions.

Although in 1938 Schwinn reintroduced the lightweight adult bicycle for American riders with its new Paramount, it wasn't until the mid 1950s, when British Raleighs and other imported lightweights started to become popular with American youngsters, that the high pressure, narrow tire, multi-speed bicycle gained a hold in the American market.

Following World War II, European families had a revival of interest in a more general use of the bicycle. The British Swift of 1926 was cited by Caunter in *The History and Development of Cycles* as a machine that marked the abandonment of the earlier heavily constructed lady's bicycle that had been influenced in its design by women's voluminous skirts and the roughness of the roads. Postwar racing bicycles likewise had advanced with the best weighing as little as 15 lbs. fully equipped.

According to Caunter, the hand-made deluxe models, which had existed until 1935 in England, had become too expensive to produce. Such bicycles as the 42 lb. 1949 Raleigh Superbe Tourist were the post-war equivalent of the deluxe bicycles. This particular model featured a hub dynamo and accumulator (generator and battery, to Americans) lighting system, oil-bath chaincase, front fork lock, and either a 3- or 4-speed hub gear.

New European forms continued to be introduced. For the World War II effort, BSA and others made finely crafted folding bicycles. In 1933 the interesting French Velocar horizontal bicycle was marketed. The 1950 Butler road racing bicycle with 10 speed derailleur gear using five different sprocket sizes on the rear hub and two different diameter chain wheels at the front set the pattern for most adult bicycles to this day.

Among the few unique American bicycles of the period were the c. 1935 Monark Silver King, a balloon tire bicycle with an aluminum alloy frame made by the Monark Battery Co., Chicago, Illinois, and the Bowden Streamliner

Fig. 8–6. Mid-fifties Bowden Streamliner. *(courtesy American Bicycle Museum)*

shown in Fig. 8-6, made by Bowden Industries, Kansas City, Missouri, with frame, fork, and mudguards of fiberglass.

Not a bicycle in the usual sense, but certainly unique and of interest, was the Ingo-Bike made from 1934 to 1937. It resembled a scooter and was propelled by a standing rider moving in rhythm with an eccentric rear wheel.

The 1960s and 1970s again were decades of standardization in American bicycles, but this time it was a world-wide standardization. American, British, French, Italian, and Japanese bicycles had interchanging components and name tags and looked and rode much alike.

Important however, during this period, was the American adult's return to cycling. Motivating forces may have been the ease of riding the sophisticated new machines which were so superior in pedaling ease to the earlier "balloon bombers", and interests in ecology and physical fitness. Whatever the reasons, American adults bought more bicycles than they had since the 1890s.

Perhaps it was the burgeoning interest in bicycles coupled with the sameness of them that caused Alex Moulton's unique 16" wheel English bicycle to be received so enthusiastically. Introduced in 1962, the Moulton was the first entirely new bicycle design in many years. Today it sports its own international owners club.

In the 1970s, the mountain bike had its beginning in places like Marin County, California. The sport of riding back country trails and hillsides led to bicycle racer Gary Fisher and many others developing rugged, multi-speed bicycles with very wide high-pressure tires, flat handlebars, and heavy-duty brakes. By 1983, ten percent of all bicycles sold in America were mountain bikes. By the mid 1990s, mountain bikes were outselling any other type at many bicycle outlets across the United States.

## SELECTED EXAMPLES POST-1900

### Golden Sunbeam

Perhaps the highest quality deluxe bicycle built in the 1900 to 1925 period was the Golden Sunbeam (Fig. 8-7). Introduced in 1900 by John Marston, it was a highly refined version of the standard safety of the period.

Unusual was the complete enclosure of the chain and sprockets in a sheet steel case. This not only gave protection from dirt, but also incorporated an oil reservoir called "The Little Oil Bath," in which the chain and two-speed gear, contained in the center of the pedal bracket, ran continuously (Fig. 8-3). Oilers were provided at all friction points and the pedals were fitted with needle roller bearings. The 26" wheels had stirrup brakes front and rear operating on Westwood steel rims through rods and bellcranks. Inner tube pneumatic tires were secured in place by the beaded edges of the rim. Rims were bright with enameled centers and gold lining. A handlebar lock was fitted and was useful if a thief quickly jumped on the bicycle and attempted to ride it off or if you were transporting it by train and wanted to keep the front fork from flopping about. Contained within one celluloid handlebar grip was a tire repair kit. The Golden Sunbeam was enameled in black with genuine gold leaf pin striping.

*Fig. 8–7.* c. 1907 Golden Sunbeam.

### Centaur X Frame

Actually a diamond frame modified to incorporate extra tubes for a cross bracing effect, the X frame was developed in England by Raleigh in 1896–97 and was further popularized with the introduction of the Centaur featherweight in 1901 (Fig. 8-8). The frame was alleged to assure a light, strong, and efficient bicycle. The principal distinctive feature of the early Centaur was the down tube which extended continuously in a straight line from the head to the rear axle similar to the early cross frame down tube. Reportedly the rigidity caused by the design was too much, making it a very hard riding machine due to excessive vibration.

In 1909 a modification to the X frame was made with the down sloping top tube changed to a conventional position. In 1910 the Centaur name was purchased by Humber who produced a Centaur bicycle until 1925. A later modifi-

*Fig. 8–8.* c. 1901 Centaur featherweight.

*Fig. 8–9.* A later style X frame built under license from Referee in the period 1900 to 1910.

cation to the X frame involved stopping the down tube at the seat tube and adding a compression spring to the seat stay and a pivot behind the crank to allow the rear wheel to move independent of the rest of the frame, thus cushioning the ride (Fig. 8-9).

### The Jaray Recumbent

Locating the rider in a low semi-sitting position seemed for many years to be a reasonable way to reduce wind resistance created by an upright bicycle rider.

German Paul Jaray, known as the "father of aerodynamic form," and a builder of zeppelins, in 1920 created a semi-recumbent bicycle (Fig. 8-10). The rider, seated directly over the rear wheel, drove levers to propel the machine. Pivoting at their upper ends, the levers had wires attached at their lower ends that ran to the rear axle where they drove the machine through a ratchet gear (Fig. 8-11).

*Fig. 8–10.* Don Adams riding a c. 1920 Jaray.

By selecting from the three pedal extensions on each lever, it was possible to vary the leverage thus creating the effect of three speeds.

*Fig. 8–11.* Pedal levers and rear hub drive mechanism of Jaray.

In addition to lessening wind resistance, the Jaray, built by GMBA of Stuttgart, Germany, featured a seat with a back rest that was designed to allow maximum use of the back muscles while pedaling. The Jaray, although fast on the level, was hard to balance and was a strain to pedal uphill. It saw limited use mostly in Switzerland and Holland.

**The Ingo-Bike**

Invented by Phillip and Prescott Huyssen in the early 1930s, the Ingo (Fig. 8-12) was more like a scooter than a bicycle, yet a good rider could propel it indefinitely without touching a foot to the ground, thus using it like a bicycle. Produced by the Ingersoll Division of the Borg Warner Corporation from 1934 to 1937, the Ingo-Bike required that the rider push off with his foot as he would with a scooter. Then, standing with both feet on the hardwood platform, he bent his knees slightly and pulled back on the handlebar flexing the spring steel frame in rhythm with the rotation of the rear wheel, which was mounted off center, to create an eccentric motion (Fig. 8-13).

Fig. 8–12. Early straight platform Ingo-Bike with rear in lowest position. *(courtesy of Henry Ford Museum)*

To demonstrate that it would work, one of the inventors rode one from Chicago to Miami in 12 days, doing 10 to 20 mph.

Describing its qualities, Ingo-Bike literature said: "Imagine yourself carried only by perpetual motion with just the gentle body lift you experience in horseback riding. The rhythmic motion brings you into new harmony with the world…."

Today Ingo-Bike races sometimes are held during field events at Wheelmen meets. Occasionally one is ridden on a 10 mile Wheelmen tour.

### The BSA Folding Bicycle

Designed to be folded into a compact unit the BSA folding bicycle was built for use by paratroopers during World War II (Fig. 8-14). Finished in a sand color camouflage for desert use or in olive drab, it was built to very high standards of workmanship with 26" pneumatic tires, roller chain, and caliper brakes front and rear.

In wartime use they were folded and attached to a parachute in bundles of five and then were dropped from aircraft. They were quickly unfolded by ground troops who used them for swift and silent movement.

*Fig. 8–13.* Bob George of the Southern Veteran Cycle Club of England riding a later Ingo-Bike with curved rear axle braces.

*Fig. 8–14.* c. 1943 BSA paratrooper bicycle. Note original rod pedals.

Those found today nearly always have survived in very good condition except frequently the original pedals, which were rods that slid through the crank hole flush with the edge of the crank when folded, have been replaced with normal pedals—this because the rod pedals are uncomfortable on the feet.

BSA also built folding bicycles for the South African War, 1899 to 1902, and World War I from 1914 to 1918.

### The Schwinn Black Phantom

Manufactured by Arnold, Schwinn and Co. in 1950, the Black Phantom was one of the highest quality American balloon tire bicycles (Fig. 8-15). Well made with heavy chrome plating on the mudguards and other bright parts and handsomely enameled in black with contrasting striping, the Black Phantom was an

Fig. 8–15. 1950 Schwinn Black Phantom. *(courtesy of Henry Ford Museum)*

attractive, smooth riding, and durable bicycle. Its sturdy frame permitted it to be ridden with abandon and to carry a second youngster on the handlebar when parents weren't looking. Like many American bicycles of the period, it had a spring suspension front fork, a built-in battery operated headlight, a frame case enclosing the horn and its battery, a rear fender luggage carrier and light, and a heavy saddle that was fitted with deep coil springs.

**The Moulton**

In 1959 renowned British designer Alex Moulton developed his Moulton bicycle, the first major redesign in many years. By 1962, he had developed a sprightly machine that was ridden by John Woodburn the 162 miles from Cardiff to London in six hours, 44 minutes—18 minutes faster than it had ever been done.

The Moulton used a compact and simple suspension system that gave a smooth ride despite the small 16" wheels. The low center of gravity created a lively response to the pedals and provided for carrying heavy loads with minimal effect on the handling. The F-shape frame and quickly adjustable seat and handlebar post made the Moulton equally suitable for men and women, youngsters and adults (Fig. 8-16).

Frame tubes were flat sided, oval and tapering. A simple compression spring worked just above the front fork crown. The rear suspension enabled the rear wheel to react to bumps independently of the rest of the frame through a rubber compression spring, or pad as Moulton called it, which was located directly in front of the rear wheel. The chain stay was pivoted to the end of the down tube and was braced to the extended top tube.

Standard, Deluxe, Safari, Speed Six, Continental, and Stowaway models were made by Moulton Bicycles Ltd. of Nottingham, England. Three- and four-speed hub gears, derailleur gears, alloy components, large carrier bags, and touring and high speed tires distinguished the various models. The Stowaway came apart midway on the down tube.

*Fig. 8–16.* 1967 Moulton. *Reprinted from* The Story of the Bicycle. *(courtesy of the author John Woodforde)*

*Fig. 8–17.* Triangular suspension assembly detail on later style 1970 Moulton Mark III. Note rubber ball upper right corner.

Moulton patents were purchased by Raleigh in 1967. In 1970 they introduced the 35 lb. Moulton Mark III which had a new rear suspension. A triangular assembly, which moved independently of the rest of the frame, was attached by a pivot back of the crank hanger and a rubber compression ball midway up the seat tube (Fig. 8-17). Deluxe, Stowaway, and Safari models were offered and a Junior model was added.

In May, 1983, Alex Moulton took over production of the third generation Moulton called the AM–7. Several high-quality variants of the AM–7 continue to come from his Bradford-on-Avon manufactory, including a mountain bike version that was introduced in 1988.

### ESTABLISHING AUTHENTICITY AND CONDITION

Compared to ordinaries and high wheel safeties, small wheel safeties have more individual parts and are more likely to have been modified to keep them in operating condition.

Solid and cushion tire models that are in poor condition and are missing components often are more costly to restore than ordinaries. However, they are rare and their value may be sufficient to warrant the machining of replacement parts and a full restoration.

Pneumatic tire safeties, unless they are of the unusual types, many of which are described in this book, are plentiful but costly to restore. Although service-able 28" single tube tires are available, they may need to be replaced frequently if allowed to slide on the rim, dislodging the valve. Collectors should view good original condition and completeness as more important with the pneumatic safeties than with any other category of antique bicycle.

The best way to determine whether a safety's components have been switched over the years is to study the guide to dating which follows.

In consulting the guide, you are very apt to find that newer saddles, handle-bars and wheels, coaster brakes, and modern pedals have been substituted for the originals on all types of safeties. Although spare parts are somewhat more likely to be located for safeties, especially for post-1900 models, generally parts like handlebars, forks, and 1890s saddles will be difficult to find.

Identifying the maker of a solid or cushion tire safety is difficult unless it is one of the common American makes described in this book, or has the original maker's name tag, decal, or stamping on it or has a unique feature.

There was a great deal of standardization throughout the safety period and there were large numbers of British bicycles imported to the United States. Often they were marked with long-since-removed decals rather than with metal plates. A lack of research material and a similarity among British bicycles can make them very hard to identify.

You should be aware that if you find a small metal tag wrapped around a tube on a safety bicycle it can be one of two things. It may be a bicycle or foot path license tag, which is rare and desirable and although it probably will not be for the same year that the bicycle was manufactured, it should be kept with the bicycle. Less frequently it could be a LAW membership tag. Each LAW member was assigned a number and given a small tag with that number stamped on it to attach to his bicycle. This was thought to be an assist in recovering stolen bicycles. Today if you find an LAW number tag and an appropriate LAW membership book with members listed by number, the previous owner can be identified.

Be sure to look for the bicycle's serial number which often is stamped on the bottom of the crank hanger or on the top of the seat tube facing the rear wheel. On some bicycles it is possible to check if numbers stamped on the front fork match those stamped on the frame. You should record any numbers found.

Check bearings, seat tubes, pedals, hubs, brakes, and handlebar stems for maker names which might give a clue to the manufacturer. Be prepared however, to find many makers represented on a safety, each of whom was a supplier of components to the maker.

Having attempted to identify the safety, examine it carefully for condition.

Stand back and look at it in side profile. Do the two opposing blades of the front fork line up or is one bent back? Does the angle of the front fork appear correct? In almost all cases the angle of the head tube and the front fork should match on pneumatic safeties. With some solid and cushion tire bicycles, however, this is not true.

Buckling of the top tube just back of the head tube, and the down tube near the head is common (Fig. 8-18). The hollow tubing is very difficult to straighten and unless the bicycle is unique and/or desirable, you should avoid purchasing it when this has happened.

*Fig. 8–18.* This bicycle has buckled top and down tubes which are difficult to repair.

Rear chain and seat stays should align correctly. If it is an early cross frame safety, that part of the seat tube above the down tube is apt to be bent and the bolted-on stay rods are apt to be missing or broken.

Check everywhere for deep pitting or metal fatigue cracks, especially at front and rear dropouts where the wheel axles enter the forks and stay rods. The seat posts also should be checked for fatigue cracks and incorrect bends.

Study the rims. Even if spokes are missing and are not properly tightened, the rims should be round enough so they can be used. Metal rims are difficult to reshape for roundness. It is possible to bring wood rims back into roundness with skillful spoking, but separation of laminations and joints is hard to correct and flat spots are nearly impossible to get rid of permanently. With difficulty, good condition wood rims can be found at flea markets and Wheelmen meets, but don't be surprised about having to buy an entire bicycle just for the needed wood rim. Be sure that the number of holes drilled in the rim is equal to the number in the hub to which it is to be spoked and that the front and rear rims match in cross section contour.

Check whether front and rear hub designs match. Especially on wood rim models, it is not unusual to find that the front wheel has been switched. This is a major problem if the front axle was unusual, such as some Columbia models that used a ball end spoke. Both spoke and hub are very difficult to find for ball end models.

If, based on the dating guide, you determine that the bicycle is American and was produced in the wood rim period, but it now has metal rims, it is likely they are substitutes for the originals. It was very common to switch to smaller steel rims when 28" single tube tires were discontinued in the mid-1930s.

Next examine the bicycle from the front. Is everything symmetrical? Check for fork blade bends and bends in the seat and chain stays and handlebar. Are the cranks straight or have they been bent inward by a fall? Does the pedal shaft form a right angle with the crank or is it bent? Is there substantial warping of the wood rims? When the warp is major, straightening usually does not last long. The same concern applies with wood frame bicycles.

Are there brackets on the handlebar where a brake lever should be or on the down tube where a shift lever was? Close examination can reveal that there are missing parts that are hard to replace.

Spin the front sprocket. Does the chain seat properly on the sprocket teeth or has wear caused the chain to run unevenly? Worn or missing chains, especially on solid tire safeties, are a major problem, but some sizes of new block chain are available. Modern chain will fit most post-1900 bicycles that had roller chain.

On later models with thin sprockets, check to see if the sprocket wheel is bent. This can best be done by looking straight down at the chain to see if it wobbles while the sprocket is turning.

If there are gears, check to see that they shift properly and that all the mechanism is complete. Also check the operation of coaster brakes on later models. It is not unusual for a mid-1890s safety to have had its original rear hub switched for a later coaster brake model.

If there is a great deal of lateral looseness in the cranks, bearing components inside the bottom bracket may be missing.

If it is a chainless, spin the pedals to check the gear operation. It should be smooth and quiet with no binding. A missing cover over the rear bevel gear can be expensive to make and almost impossible to find.

A heavy deposit of grease on all components can indicate that what is underneath is in good condition. Scrape a small section of a handlebar or crank to see if good original nickel plating remains.

## DATING GUIDE, AMERICAN SAFETIES 1887–1900

The precise dating of safeties is very difficult for numerous reasons. Each maker developed his own combination of available components. Many would keep a particular type on their machines long after others had switched to a newer variety.

For purposes of the following dating guide, I will use the Columbia, Victor, and Gormully and Jeffery lines as they were leaders in the trade. I will empha-

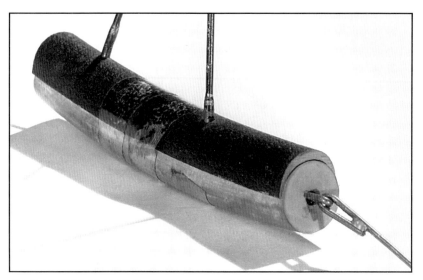

*Fig. 8–19.* Solid steel crescent shaped rim. Originally glued on, tiring used today has a drilled out core and is attached with wire as pictured. The loop in the foreground illustrates how the wire is connected. *(courtesy of Henry Ford Museum)*

size components such as handlebars that often were purchased from outside suppliers and therefore were fairly consistent year to year among most maker's bicycles because these components can be examined easily without having to disassemble the bicycle.

*Fig. 8–20.* Hollow steel rim, original solid tire still attached.

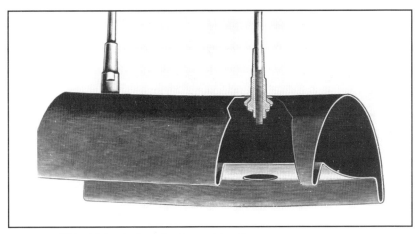

*Fig. 8–21.* Wider Victor hollow rim for cushion tire.

I have largely avoided relying on frame angles and jointing techniques, bearing systems, and other design component aspects with unique approaches as there is not enough consistency or broad application to be helpful in dating the bicycle.

For additional year-by-year analyses, a study of this book's sections on solid and pneumatic tire safeties could be helpful.

Even though components may be out of synchronization with the expected date of the safety, we do not recommend that you remove or switch them prior to thorough research on the specific options originally available.

*Fig. 8–22.* Original Victor cushion tire. *(courtesy of Greenfield Village and Henry Ford Museum)*

Fig. 8–23. Typical wood rim and single tube tire. *(courtesy of Greenfield Village and Henry Ford Museum)*

The first date listed in the guide in each case is the first year that a particular specification was offered by Columbia, Victor, or Gormully & Jeffery. Even among these three makers, exceptions to this guide may have occurred at time of manufacture. The second date is the last year the specification was offered by these companies. None of these dates necessarily applies to British machines or to any American brand other than those used in this guide.

**Handlebars, Grips, and Stems**

1887-95    Wide 25" to 30", measured edge-of-grip to edge-of-grip, fixed on stem. Elongated bakelite grips, spade grips

1893-1900  Cork handlebar grips

1895-1900  Stem clamp to permit adjusting angle of handlebar or reversing it. Bar narrowed to about 20".

1897       Handlebar narrowed to about 17". Wood handlebars first became standard equipment on some Columbias; available previous to this from aftermarket suppliers.

**Heads**

1888-91    Hinged head (See Fig. 6-8)

1887-1900  Socket steering head (see Fig. 6-10)

**Rims**

1888-93    Solid steel, about ⅞" and wider width; great diameter variation, 32" largest diameter (Fig. 8-19)

1887-96    Hollow steel rims, variation in width, Victor (Fig. 8-20), ⅝" front, ¾" rear rims

1891-94    Wider steel hollow rim for cushion tire of
                1⅛" to 1½" rear, ¾" front (Fig. 8-21)
1892-1900  Wider steel hollow rim for pneumatic tire of
                1⅝" to 2" with valve hole
1894-1900  Wood rim, 1⅜" x 28" typical
**Tires**
1887-91    Solid rubber wired, molded, or compressed on, narrow up to 1¼".
1891-94    Cushion tires (Fig. 8-22)
1892-1900  Pneumatic single tube tire (Fig. 8-23)
1892-97    Victor inner tube pneumatic with tube detachable through large
                opening in rim (Fig. 7-2)
1897-1930  British Westwood rim (Fig. 8-24)

*Fig. 8–24.* Westwood rim typical of British bicycle of late 1890s, early 1900s.
*(courtesy of Greenfield Village and Henry Ford Museum)*

*Fig. 8–25.* Lest we forget.... In one hundred years, even this bicycle will look quaint. Be aware that many of today's designs are worthy of careful preservation so that future enthusiasts need not go through the restoration procedures that are detailed in Chapters 11 and 12. This is artist George Retseck's conception of the bicycle to be used in the 1996 Olympics. *(courtesy of Bicycling magazine)*

# Chapter 9:
# The Adult Tricycle: 1819-1900

Although a thorough discussion of the evolution of the adult tricycle is beyond the scope of this book, it is important for the collector to be aware of the basic variations in these fascinating machines. (Fig. 9-1)

Illustrations of 1819 period European hobby horse tricycles (Fig. 9-2) show that they were ridden like a hobby horse or propelled by levers. Their production is thought to have been very limited.

American use of the tricycle began when two wheels were fitted to the boneshaker in the late 1860s as an assist for those learning to ride. The American firm of Pickering and Davis offered a bifurcated perch that would accept a rear axle to which were mounted two wheels (Fig. 9-3). The axle could be removed, and one of the rear wheels positioned between the forks to instantly convert it back to a boneshaker.

Topliff and Ely of Elyria, Ohio, developed a unique boneshaker tricycle in which the rear track could be altered from 2 inches to 2 feet from the saddle while in motion.

Boneshaker-type tricycles reportedly were unsteady and had a tendency to turn over when not ridden on the crown of the road.

The development of a practical adult tricycle began in 1876 when Englishman W. B. Blood introduced his Dublin with 40" rear driving wheel and two 24" front steering wheels. Light rods connected the treadles with cranks on the rear axle.

Later that same year, James Starley secured a patent on his Coventry Lever tricycle (Fig. 9-4), the product of adding a small second wheel to his unsuccessful ladies' Ariel bicycle.

The first commercially successful adult tricycle, the Coventry Lever, was noted for its instability in turning corners unless the driving wheel was on the outside of the curve.

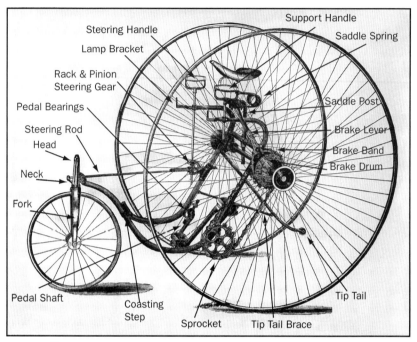

*Fig. 9–1.* The adult tricycle. 1884 Victor.

In 1878 the Coventry Lever was converted to chain drive and the steering tiller was replaced by rack and pinion steering connected to a spade grip steer-

*Fig. 9–2.* 1819 hobbyhorse tricycle.

*Fig. 9–3.* c. 1869 Pickering tricycle.

ing handle. In this form it was called the Coventry Rotary. A tandem Coventry Rotary (Fig. 9-5) was offered as was a convertible sociable (Fig. 9-6) on which the riders rode side-by-side. The sociable attachment could be removed to change it back to a single model.

James Starley's next machine, the 1877 Salvo, (Fig. 9-7) was equally signifi-cant. This front-steering tricycle with equal sized rear wheels and a loop frame

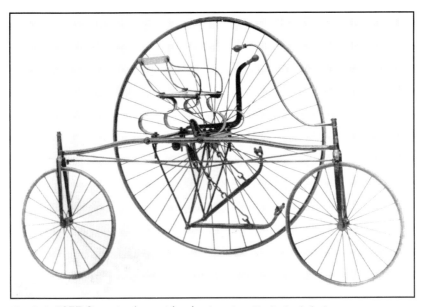

*Fig. 9–4.* 1877 Coventry Lever tricycle. *(courtesy Southeby & Co.)*

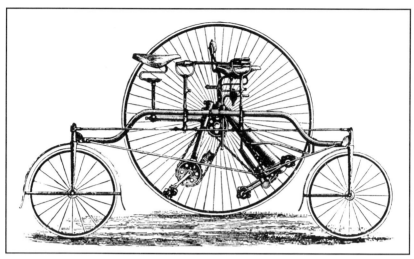

*Fig. 9–5.* 1879 Tandem Coventry Rotary.

introduced such important technical innovations as the differential gear, rack and pinion steering, and a band brake—all developed for tricycles, but important in the functioning of the first automobiles.

Of all the technological advances made by tricycle designers, probably the differential gear was most important. It was described in the November 11, 1898, *LAW Bulletin History of the Tricycle* as follows:

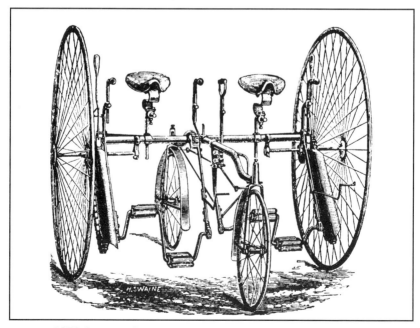

*Fig. 9–6.* 1879 Coventry Rotary convertible sociable.

Fig. 9–7. c. 1877 Starley Salvo. *(courtesy of Sotheby & Co.)*

"Earlier tricycles had all been single drivers, the rider's power being applied to a single wheel. But Mr. Starley now adopted a principle that had long been used in connection with steam carriages and traction engines. He firmly attached one wheel to one end of the axle while at a convenient distance near to the other end was attached a bevel wheel. The chain wheel, which was mounted on the axle carrying a pinion, was geared into this bevel wheel. The driving wheel, which fitted on this side of the machine, was also fitted with a bevel wheel. This, in its turn, was geared into the pinion on its opposite side.

"The result was that when running in a straight line, both wheels drove equally, but, in turning, more power was applied to the outer wheel and it ran the faster. This gave perfect double driving and, taken in connection with the chain and rotary action, revolutionized tricycle construction."

*Fig. 9–8.* Rack and pinion steering. *(courtesy of Henry Ford Museum)*

Numerous refinements in adult tricycles were made between 1877 and 1900. They will be discussed in categories based on tricycle frame designs.

### The Boneshaker Type

Used primarily by indoor riding schools beginning about 1867, boneshaker tricycles had rear axles about two feet long with wheels running free. They were not suitable for use on regular roads.

### The Loop Frame

Beginning with the 1877 Salvo, the loop frame tricycle was popular throughout the early adult tricycle period.

Attached at the rear axle, the tubular or flat frame came forward making a loop which generally was squared, but sometimes was rounded at the front. At one or both ends of the axle a tip tail usually was attached to prevent the machine from going over backward.

Loop frame tricycles were driven by pedals mounted on shafts running in bearings fixed to the frame. Single or double chains attached to the pedal shaft and drove sprockets at the rear wheels. Some unique examples substituted levers

Fig. 9–9.
Foot operated
drag brake on
early loop
frame
tricycle.

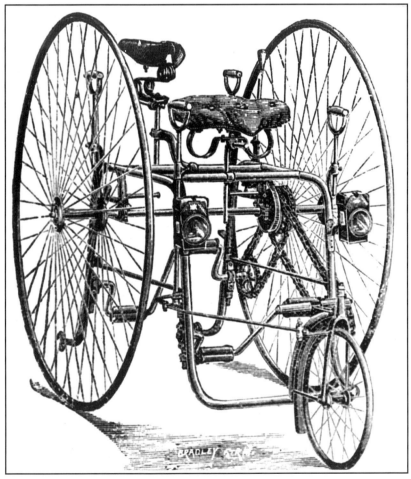

Fig. 9–10. 1884 Centaur loop frame tandem tricycle.

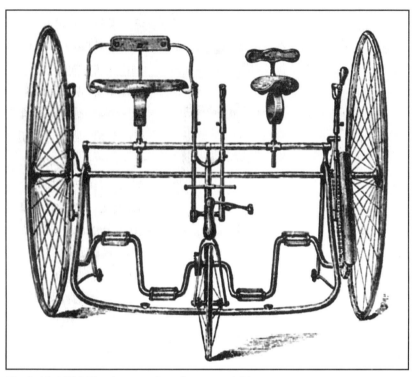

*Fig. 9–11.* 1884 Cheylesmore loop frame sociable.

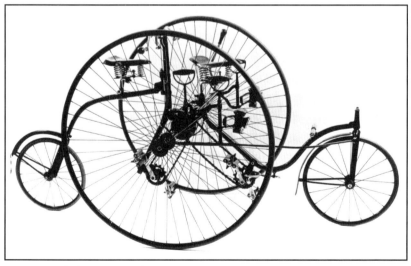

*Fig. 9–12.* 1886 tee frame Coventry Club with a tandem unit attached as a trailer.

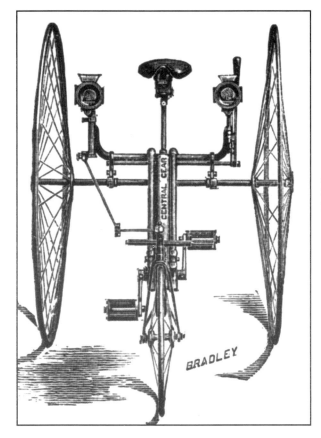

*Fig. 9–13.*
1884 Wanderer
tee frame tricycle.

for the chain. Remote rack and pinion steering operated by a spade handle connected by a rod to the front wheel was common (Fig. 9-8).

A second handle was used to support the rider's arm and was pulled on for
leverage when ascending a hill. Band brakes actuated from the saddle by a lever
were common in the mid 1880s. Some earlier loop frame tricycles used foot-
operated drag brakes (Fig. 9-9).

Tandem (Fig. 9-10) and side-by-side (Fig. 9-11) loop frame tricycles were
available.

**The Tee Frame**

Similar in most respects to the loop frame, the tee had a center-mounted
chain and sprocket for smoother running (Fig. 9-13) and the front was left somewhat more open for mounting and dismounting; dual brake bands were positioned at the center of the axle where they were the most effective. The weight
of this tricycle was somewhat lessened by the reduction of frame material.

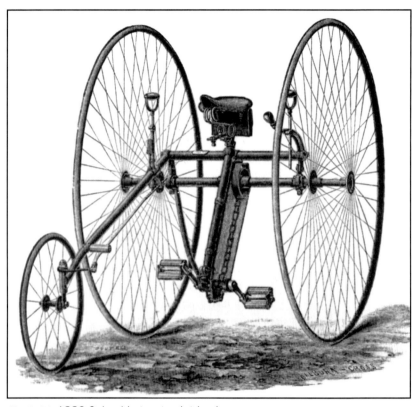

*Fig. 9–14.* 1886 Columbia two track tricycle.

Tee frame tricycles were produced in tandem form sometimes with the tandem portion attached at the rear as a trailer. It could be easily removed to convert it back to a single (Fig. 9-12).

**Two Track**

A further refinement of the tee frame simply involved locating the front steering wheel directly ahead of the right rear wheel (Fig. 9-14). The result was that the tricycle made two tracks instead of three making it easier to stay out of the deep ruts that were common to the roads of the day. Also the openness of the front helped facilitate mounting and dismounting. Tandem (Fig. 9-15) as well as single two track tricycles were produced.

**Humber Pattern**

The front-driving Humber, patented in 1877 and introduced to the public in 1880, was created by attaching the backbone, handlebar, and head of an ordinary to an axle with large wheels at each end. It was the first adult tricycle to have the drive chain at the center of the axle (Fig. 9-16). Both front wheels were driven by bicycle cranks and pedals. With the motion that of riding an ordinary,

*Fig. 9–15.* 1884 Royal Mail two track tandem tricycle.

the Humber pattern tricycles were popular with many manufacturers for several years and were offered in both single and tandem forms (Fig. 9-17).

**Hayfork Pattern**

Another variation of the front-driving tricycle was the hayfork frame design (Fig. 9-18) which simply eliminated the front cross member of the loop frame thus giving the frontal appearance of an inverted U or of the tines of a hayfork. The central frame tube going back to the rear wheel formed the handle of the hayfork.

Hayfork frame tricycles usually were single or double chain driven by a pedal shaft. Some, however, were cog or lever driven. The small rear wheel steered, usually by rack and pinion. Tandem and single models were produced.

**Cripper**

Front steering by a handlebar attached to a steering rod and front fork was the major design feature of the Cripper which was introduced in 1884 by the British Humber Co. The first Cripper in 1885 was ridden by British Five Mile

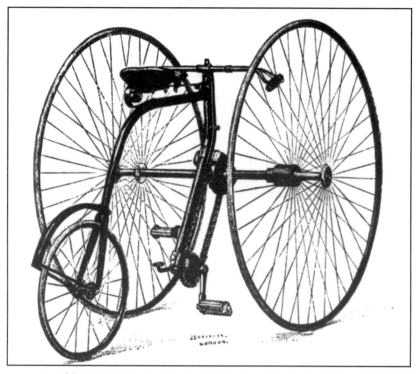

*Fig. 9–16.* 1884 Humber Regent Roadster.

Amateur Champion R. Cripper who subsequently won so many races on the machine that it came to be called the Cripper.

Perhaps more than any other, the Cripper foreshadowed the direct front steering configuration of the modern tricycle. Cripper type tricycles were produced in single and tandem models by many manufacturers (Fig. 9-19).

**Safeties**

A refinement of the Cripper type was the solid-tire tricycle, incorporating features of the solid tire safety bicycle frame, steering head, and curved front fork.

Although most riders lost interest in adult tricycles after 1890, they continued to be produced in sizable numbers in Europe until about 1900 and then in smaller numbers after the incorporation of pneumatic tires, improved brakes and tubing, variable gears, and other refinements that were being developed for safety bicycles (Fig. 9-20). A small number of adult tricycles is built to this day.

*Fig. 9–17.* c. 1885 Humber. *(courtesy of Sotheby & Co.)*

**Carriers**

As early as 1881, Bayliss Thomas of England had obtained a contract for supplying carrier tricycles to the post office; however, most such machines were produced later as adaptations of the late 1880s and 1890s safety tricycles.

The Tinkham Cycle Co. of New York, N.Y., was the largest American maker of carrier tricycles (Fig. 9-21). The vehicles were used primarily in large cities but were more popular in Europe than in America.

## Establishing Authenticity and Condition

Any original adult tricycle is a rare and desirable machine today. Relatively few were built and they were costly to purchase. Only a small number survive today, partly because they were heavy to transport and awkward to store.

They became quite popular in the mid-1800s, especially in England where one owner was Queen Victoria. In America they were ridden mainly by city dwellers who had access to paved roads.

The elegant finish and high cost of their machines gave American women tricyclists an element of prestige. Clubs were formed and riders dressed elaborately for their tours.

*Fig. 9–18.* 1884 Royal Rob Roy hayfork frame tricycle.

There are few known reproduction tricycles. Gary Woodward has made a two-track, a side-by-side companion, and a loop frame all with modern bearings (Fig. 9-22). In 1978 John Vanderpoel built a tandem based on the Rudge Crescent (Fig. 9-23).

The guides appearing in earlier chapters for establishing authenticity and condition for boneshakers, ordinaries, and safeties apply fully to the examination of corresponding period adult tricycles.

When examining a tricycle be certain that it is indeed an adult tricycle and not a much less valuable child's machine being sold at an adult tricycle price. Size and construction should be appropriate to the size and weight of an adult woman or small man. Although the diameters of the largest wheels vary, generally the early adult tricycles of the late 1870s and early 1880s had a large wheel or wheels of 45" to 50". Later mid-to-late 1880s solid tired adult tricycles usually had 35" to 45" diameter for their largest wheel. Of course, mid-1890s pneumatic tire tricycles had wheel diameters of 26" to 32".

There are many pieces in an adult tricycle that can be costly to duplicate and perhaps nearly impossible to make correctly if an identical machine cannot be located for copying. Typically adult tricycle restoration costs are high. Rebuilding the wheels of a tricycle, for example, is equivalent to rebuilding those

*Fig. 9–19.* 1889 cripper type Victor.

*Fig. 9–20.* c. 1907 Golden Sunbeam pneumatic tire tricycle.

of two ordinaries. However, the high value of these machines almost always will make their restoration worthwhile for historic and investment value as well as riding pleasure.

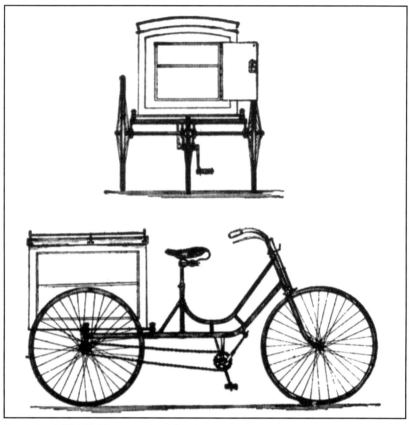

*Fig. 9–21.* 1898 Tinkham carrier tricycle.

### FURTHER RESEARCH

Catalogs published 1884 to 1890 for Victor, Columbia, and Gormully and Jeffery's American lines illustrate their adult tricycle offerings and are available to Wheelmen members through the club's catalog copying service.

Recent books that are useful references include *Bicycles and Tricycles of the Year 1886, King of the Road,* and *The Wheelmen* magazine, especially the tricycle number, Vol. 6, No. 1, Winter 1975.

Henry Ford Museum, The Bicycle Museum of America, the Smithsonian Museum of History and Technology, and Pedaling History, the Burgwardt Bicycle Museum, exhibit antique tricycles. The larger Wheelmen meets sometimes attract a few tricycles.

*Fig. 9–22.* Single and sociable loop frame reproduction tricycles built by Gary Woodward.

*Fig. 9–23.* John Vanderpoel with the Rudge Crescent reproduction tandem tricycle that he built.

*Fig. 9–24.* Doris Woodward on an 1884 Victor tricycle in her authentic black Victorian dress.

# Chapter 10:
# How to Find Them

The collector must be both a detective, following up every lead, and also a publicist, making it known to all his acquaintances that he is looking for old bicycles.

Among the many sources through which desirable antique bicycles have been found are old bicycle shops, especially those in small rural towns; pawn shops; garage sales in towns where there are few collectors; antique automobile and general flea markets; suggestions from water meter readers and others who get into basements; newspaper classified ads; Wheelmen-sponsored and general auctions; and of course, antique shops and dealers. Also at Wheelmen meets there are often bicycles that members have brought to sell.

Collectors have advertised successfully in small town newspapers and national antique journals for old bicycles. One collector made it a habit to visit small towns with which he was not familiar and spend time in the local bars, telling anyone who would listen of his interest in old bicycles. He located a Star and other desirable machines using this technique.

One rider who took a cross-country trip on his ordinary found that spectators along the route rushed to tell him where there were other bicycles like his. With his ordinary visible on the top of his car, another collector was told by a service station attendant where he could find others.

Another heard about and located an abandoned ordinary rusting in a ditch (Fig. 10-1). He dug it out and rides it today. I once owned a Star that was found stacked in a lumber pile in the loft of a barn. I also found an ordinary stashed in a horse stable on a deserted island.

Sometimes you can arrange for an antique dealer to be on the lookout for old bicycles, but if you do this, it is imperative that both parties understand the commitment. Even if there is no obligation to purchase the find, it is unlikely that the dealer will offer succeeding items if you turn down the first one.

Auctions can be risky places to purchase antique bicycles. Sometimes they are offered at antique automobile auctions where affluent car collectors run bicycle prices up on a whim. Many bicycles are past 100 years of age and can command exorbitant prices when sold by prestigious dealers and auction houses (Fig. 10-2).

*Fig. 10–1.* Colin Bohash examines remains of an ordinary that had been abandoned in a ditch.

The best clearinghouse for antique bicycles is the quarterly *Wheelmen Newsletter* in which members can place For Sale and Wanted ads free of charge.

Buying bicycles sight unseen can be risky, especially if you do not know the seller and the seller claims to have no knowledge of old bicycles. However, my experience with buying by mail from members of the Wheelmen has been satisfactory. Always be sure the seller is prepared to properly crate the bicycle for shipping.

## DETERMINING VALUE

Unless the bicycle you are purchasing is in excellent original condition or has been restored, the purchase price is only one element in the total investment.

Starting with a complete ordinary in good condition, a show restoration will be expensive when done by a professional restorer. The cost will rise sharply when parts are missing and must be reproduced and when the bicycle is more complicated than the usual ordinary.

Remember the complete and original bicycle with only surface rust and requiring such common repairs as new spokes and leather will not cost any more to restore, and indeed may be less costly, than the one that has been rebuilt incorrectly with such flaws as the wrong rims and handlebar.

*Fig. 10–2.* Bidding can become very heated when an antique bicycle is offered at auction.

Some machines may be serviceable and presentable though close examination may reveal they have been fabricated from the parts of one or more original bicycles. Avoid such bicycles unless the "marriage" of the components is minor. Even the wrong rear wheel will cause considerable expense by the time you make the hub, rim, and spokes.

### Price Levels

Unlike many collecting areas such as furniture and automobiles, antique bicycle collecting is such a recent phenomenon in America that price levels have not been established.

As with any antique, price is a function of supply and demand. Antique bicycle demand is greatest where there are the largest number of collectors. Prices asked by dealers in isolated areas may be several times less than those asked in states where there are large Wheelmen chapters.

Through the 1990s, collectors found a wide range of prices being paid for similar machines and little evidence of consistency in pricing.

Generally, the most costly types are the hobby horses, solid tire adult tricycles and high wheel safeties. The mid-cost range includes boneshakers, ordinaries, solid tire and cushion tire safeties, and unique pneumatic tire and special interest safeties. The least costly include standard 1890 to 1900 safeties and post-1900 special interest safeties that are not rare.

Hobby horses, quadricycles, and solid tire safety tandems are rare in American collections. High wheel safeties, adult tricycles, and cushion tire safeties are also hard to find. Boneshakers, ordinaries, early pneumatic tire safeties (1893 to 1896), tandems, chainless bikes, and ladies' and gents' chain driven safeties 1896 to 1900 are most common.

Foreign made bicycles and tricycles usually do not command a lesser price than American ones among American collectors.

The best way to keep current on prices is to read auction reports and watch for the sale advertisements in the quarterly *Wheelmen Newsletter.*

# Chapter 11:
# How To Make Them Safe To Ride

The importance of knowing the condition of an antique bicycle was dramatized to me during a tour when my riding companion suddenly plummeted to the ground. The backbone of the ordinary he was riding had split into two pieces at the neck.

On another occasion half of a two piece handlebar came off in a rider's hand as he was pulling on the bar while climbing a hill. Still another rider suffered an injurious fall when he sheared a crank from his ordinary's axle when applying power on a hill. Descending a hill was another rider's downfall; the front tire came off, immediately throwing him into an unavoidable header. Two broken arms were the result.

People may ride antique bicycles safely hundreds of miles a year. Indeed most avoid injurious accidents, but it is because they are always cautious in their riding and they do not ride an unsafe bicycle.

Almost any antique bicycle you buy will have fallen to the pavement repeatedly during its long life, bending and jarring handlebars, cranks, and forks. The rough roads over which they were ridden have taken their toll on spokes, fork ends, saddle posts, and other components. Weakened by deep rust from years of exposure to the elements, frames, forks, and handlebars sometimes succumb to the punishment by developing hairline fatigue cracks.

Given all these potential problems, it is essential that you examine every component of your antique bicycle for safety before riding it the first time and each time afterward.

## COMMON SAFETY PROBLEMS

Here are some safety problems to be on the lookout for; their importance cannot be overemphasized:

☞ If you suspect hairline cracks, sandblast the frame and forks and then examine the metal very closely, perhaps using a magnifying glass. Most auto paint shops can do sandblasting. If that is not available, wire brush all parts. However, cracks do not stand out as well from brushing as they do from sandblasting. Look especially closely at frame necks and heads, fork crowns, and ends where the axles go into the forks.

Do not sandblast handlebars or other parts that are to be plated. Rather, if they are rusted and are going to be replated, wire brush them to reveal cracks. If you locate cracks, have them repaired correctly before riding the bicycle.

☞ Closely examine steel rims inside and out for "rust through" (rust that has caused a hole), cracks, and evidence of weak welding joints. Hollow rims are especially prone to rust and should be checked very carefully. All types of steel rims can be duplicated and must be if the originals are not in safe riding condition.

☞ Examine spokes closely for serious rust, particularly at the point where they enter the rim, hub, or nipple. If the spoke has rusted enough so it is thinner at these points, it will break off when you attempt adjustment or when it is exposed to road shocks, possibly setting off a chain reaction of breaking spokes that will collapse the wheel (See Fig. 11-17).

After the spokes are adjusted and the rim is perfectly true, run a finger over the inside of the rim to see if any spokes have extended beyond the nipples. If they have, cut and file them off so the tire will be mounted on a perfectly smooth surface. Protruding spoke ends will puncture a tire immediately.

☞ I recommend if you are going to ride the bicycle that it have a functioning original equipment type brake.

☞ Every time you ride an antique bicycle, inspect the tires to be sure they are secured tightly to the rims. Today's collectors wire solid rubber tires to the rims rather than using glue as was customary in the original period of the ordinary. Frequently the tire will rotate on the rim wearing the rubber away and loosening the tire. Try to pull the tire back from the rim. If it is more than fractionally loose or if it is loose enough to make a thumping sound under the weight of being ridden, reattach it making it tighter. Nothing spells disaster and serious injury quicker than a tire coming off while the bicycle is being ridden. Be sure also that the width of the tire material is the same or slightly less than the width of the rim and that the joint in the tire is smooth. Use only the best quality rubber tiring material.

☞ Original molded-on cushion tires should be preserved whenever possible because of the rarity of machines so equipped and because this tiring cannot be duplicated. However, in most cases it would be unwise from a safety viewpoint to ride tours on original cushion tires unless they are soft and pliable and in like-new condition. You can replace the cushion tires with the wired-on solid rubber ones for purposes of riding the bicycle.

Single tube pneumatic tires are a problem. New ones are expensive. If a tire will hold air pressure even for a very brief time, a material called "bikefill," which is available at bicycle shops, can be injected into it. It sets up in a short time, permanently filling the inside of the tire with a solid but pliable material that is not very heavy. It does not work well if materials to stop leaks have previously been injected into the tire. Air pockets inside the tire may create soft spots which can be solidified by injecting the material directly into the spots with a hypodermic needle.

Another solution to the tire problem is to use 1¼" diameter solid rubber tiring which is available without tread in red and black (Fig. 11-1). It can be wired on to steel or wood rims and will make the bicycle rideable. Care should be exercised in making certain these tires are mounted tightly using the method for wiring on any solid rubber tire. Gluing a dummy tire valve into the valve hole will give the wheel a more authentic appearance. The biggest disadvantage of using solid rubber as a substitute for pneumatic tires is the heavy weight of the rubber. The advantages are moderate cost, immediate availability of the rubber, and immunity from blowouts.

Best of all is to find new old stock single tube tires or excellent used ones. If you are lucky enough to have such tires, be very cautious about installing and

*Fig. 11–1.* Dick Hammel inserting wire in 1¼" safety tiring.

maintaining them; it is likely the tire will have shrunk with age. If it is the correct diameter tire for the rim on which it is being installed, but will not fit, warm the tire to make it pliable enough to stretch over the rim. The most important thing to remember about all single tube tires is that they must be glued to the rim securely. Use good quality bicycle tire glue for use with modern sew-up tires available at all bicycle shops.

Never ride on a single tube tire that is not firmly glued to a properly prepared rim. If the glue bond between the rim and tire has broken, the tire will rotate on the rim as the bicycle is ridden. The valve will pull out, making the tire unusable. This can happen in riding just a few feet.

Few single tube tires will hold air over any extended time. If an antique bicycle is stored in an exhibit position with wheels on the floor, rather than by hanging it bottom side up from a ceiling, be certain to turn the wheels occasionally so the tires will not develop flat spots. Better still, try to locate stands that will hold front and rear tires off the floor while securing the bicycle from tipping over. Keep air pressure at a point where the tire can be flexed by squeezing it hard, but not so soft that the glue adhesive will be stressed. Of course be extremely cautious about avoiding broken glass and other puncturing objects. Puncturing objects usually ride around on the tread penetrating the rubber only when they are pressed into it by the road surface on the next revolution, so remove any puncturing object from the tread immediately before the tire completes its next revolution.

Many pre-1900 European safeties are fitted with steel rims that will take 28" and 26" clincher tires that may still be available new at bicycle shops that sell Raleigh bicycles.

Some pre-1900 American safeties are equipped with 28" "sprint" rims of 1" width. Modern sew up tires available at any bicycle shop will fit them. Sew-ups should not be used, however, with the more common 1¼" wide wood rims. They do not look correct and are apt to roll off the rim.

- Be aware that old pedal rubber usually has hardened with age and may not provide the foot with a firm grip on the pedal.
- Examine saddle leather carefully for rot and tears. If the saddle collapses, it is likely that you will fall. If the original saddle leather with an embossed maker's script is serviceable, it should be preserved. The leather can be softened by use of such products as "Lexol." Avoid treating a saddle leather with any material that will stain clothing when you ride the bicycle.
- Remove the chain, soak it in a degreaser such as "Gunk," and then wire brush it clean. Examine each link for loose and badly rusted pins. Be sure the screw or clip that holds the two ends of the chain together is complete and firmly in place when you ride. Soak the cleaned chain in heavy oil to lubricate each pivot point, then wipe it clean and check that each link moves freely. You may wish to have it re-blued. Keep the chain clean and

well oiled to minimize wear. A chain that binds can break easily and become lodged in the rear sprocket, causing a fall.

☞ Do not extend safety bicycle saddle posts outside the frame by more than three quarters of their total length or be sure at least 3" extends into the frame. Be especially cautious that this component is not cracked or badly bent.

☞ Do not ride any bicycle unless the ends of the handlebar are suitably capped either by the proper original grip or by a modern substitute. If you use a modern substitute, be sure the grip is the right diameter for the handlebar and glue it firmly in place. An epoxy glue works well. A fall onto a handlebar that is not capped can cause serious injury.

☞ A slippery or loose mounting step can be very dangerous. Wear soft soled shoes that will give your foot a good grip on the small step. The serrations or points on many ordinary steps often have worn smooth. On some steps, such as the adjustable Columbia, you can remove the step plate and hammer its points back out. If the step surface cannot be roughed up, be particularly careful that your foot does not slip off. If the step is being

*Fig. 11–2.*
Carl Wiedman demonstrates how your legs hit the handlebar when riding too small an ordinary.

renickeled, be sure to instruct the plater not to smooth off the serrations or points. Ordinary steps that are designed to be adjustable up and down on the backbone usually are tightly clamped in place by a nut and bolt; if the adjustable step gets bumped, it can loosen and unexpectedly come off when mounting or dismounting. Plagued by this problem, I have permanently attached my adjustable steps to backbones with small, barely noticeable set screws through the step bands on the side opposite the mounting surface. Be certain to have the step adjusted to the preferred height before pinning it in place.

☞ An ordinary or high wheel safety that is too large for a person cannot be ridden safely. See the wheel size chart on page 40. Likewise you cannot safely ride a machine that is so small that your knees do not clear the underside of the handlebars (Fig. 11-2). When the machine is too small, do not reverse the handlebar so it is turned up. Such an incorrect adjustment disturbs the riding balance and could make the handlebar very injurious in a fall.

☞ Be sure that Star drive straps are not frayed or cracked. Metal reinforcements riveted to each end of the leather straps are a good precaution.

☞ Be certain adult tricycles that originally had tip tails have them now and that they are firmly in place. These machines will tip over backward surprisingly easily.

☞ Wheel and pedal ball bearings usually should be replaced, bearing ways cleaned and reground if necessary, and a good commercial grease applied. Make sure there are not too many bearings. The general rule is to fill the bearing race with balls, then remove one.

## MAKING A NEW SADDLE

*(adapted with permission from* Wheelmen Bulletin No. 10, *by Carl Wiedman)*

Ordinary saddles are of two types: the suspension and the hammock. The suspension saddle is fitted to a metal pan that is bolted to the steel spring that attaches at the front to the neck of the backbone and at the rear to a clip that allows it to slide up and down on the backbone. In this way it is suspended above the backbone.

A thin leather is best to use for recovering saddle pans because of the ease with which it can be shaped. The pan is covered with a horsehair or other cushioning material and the leather is formed over it. The leather wraps around the edges of the pan so none of the metal is exposed.

Because of the specialized tools required in sewing the cover, it is best to have pan saddles recovered professionally. The same applies to the similar pan saddles that commonly were fitted to pneumatic tire safeties.

The hammock saddle, supported at the front by a spring clip at the neck of the backbone and at the back by a curved brace mounted to a spring fixed to the backbone, was used on most American ordinaries.

Hanging freely between the two attaching points, the hammock saddle was tensioned simply by moving the rear bracket backward and downward on the backbone. The hammock saddle should be kept tight so the rider will not bottom-out against the backbone when riding over bumps.

The following are four basic requirements for the shape of the hammock saddle if it is to look correct and be comfortable:

☞ The front should taper. Too much width here will cause chafing of your legs. About five inches overall width, half of it on the top surface and the rest rolled into side panels will make a comfortable saddle. These measurements are taken about 2" back from the forward end of the saddle.

☞ The leather should fit the rear bracket curve and have enough overhang so it can be curved over and completely cover the bracket in a smooth arc.

☞ The saddle should be sufficiently long, about 14", so the rider can shift his weight to the forward portion for ascending hills and for speed and to the back on rough surfaces when he wants to transfer weight to the rear wheel to help prevent a header.

☞ There should be sufficient leather to permit side panels that overhang about 1½" on each side of the forward portion of the saddle. They do away with the cutting edge of the saddle and were part of the original design of all saddles. The depth of the overhang varied among makers. Some even had side flaps sewn on that extended over the tire. Note Fig. 4-39 of an early Victor ordinary with saddle side panels extending to the backbone.

If the saddle meets all these requirements, it probably duplicates the original and can be used for a pattern.

1. When making a replacement hammock saddle, start by obtaining a good quality piece of 9 gauge cowhide. Leather shops sell top grain cowhide by the square foot or the pound. Make sure the pieces are smooth and free of scratches or blemishes.

   The leather will be flat and fairly rigid. When working with it, be certain your hands are very clean because the light colored face of the leather is very susceptible to staining from dirt or grease. It will pick up the ink if laid on newspaper. Stains will be almost impossible to remove.

2. Lay the leather on a clean flat surface and trace the pattern on the underside using a soft lead pencil (Fig. 11-3). This pattern is very important and should follow the shape of the original saddle as closely as possible.

   In most cases, the saddle on the bicycle is a replacement that, although it appears to be old, does not necessarily correspond to the original. Moreover it may be of a bad design and probably has stretched to too great a length. Be suspicious of the originality if it does not have a manufacturer's name embossed on it.

3. The next step is to cut out the saddle (Fig. 11-4). This is best done with a cutting tool that has a heavy cigar-shaped handle with razor sharp replaceable blades mounted at one end between the split halves of the handle.

These are inexpensive and available at hardware stores. Use a new blade and carefully follow the pencil line drawn on the leather. If you have a

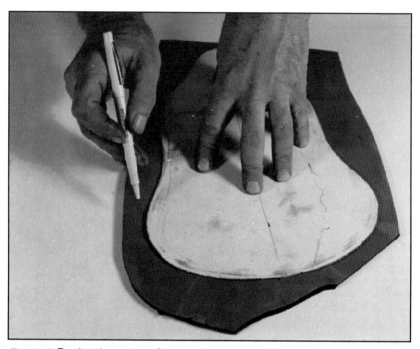

*Fig. 11-3.* Tracing the pattern for a replacement saddle.

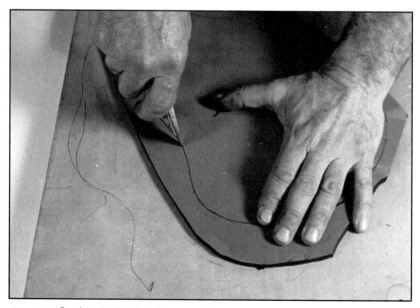

*Fig. 11-4.* Cutting the leather for a saddle.

steady hand it is not difficult to do this freehand; otherwise find some curved objects to trace—dishes and cups, for example. There are metal French curves available in most drafting supply houses that work well. Be sure to cut on the inside surface of the leather so if there is a slip, the side that will show will not be damaged.

4. Cut on a flat piece of heavy plywood. Try to bear down hard enough to cut through on the first pass. Also bear down on the curved object that is being traced so it does not slip. Once the cutting is done, any rough edges can be made smooth with a fine file or sandpaper. The same technique applies to cutting an elongated hole in the center of the saddle which provides ventilation and was common on most original ordinary saddles. The leather should be immersed in clean hot water for about 20 minutes until it is thoroughly saturated. At this stage it can be bent and formed, and any tooling, such as a groove around the saddle just inside the outer edge, can be cut. When dry the saddle will retain the form to which it has been shaped.

5. Start the shaping by forming the rear section over the curved bracket. Immediately after forming, punch the holes for the rivets in the moist leather. Use a sharp leather punch and make certain both it and your hands are clean.

6. After completing the punching, insert small plated nuts and bolts into the rivet holes to hold the leather to the bracket while it is drying. Next curve the sides down so that the front of the saddle will describe an arc matching the front bracket and the side panels will be bent down perpendicular

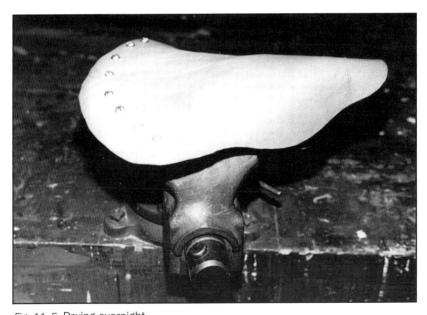

*Fig. 11–5.* Drying overnight.

to the seating surface. Squeeze the sides inward so the top of the saddle begins to get narrower just forward of the rear clamp. The more narrow the slope here, the deeper the flaps will drop and the more comfortable the saddle will be. When this forming is complete, the leather should be left to dry overnight (Fig. 11-5).

7. Now the leather can be stained. Use a good quality commercial leather stain. We think that most American ordinaries left their factories with a medium dark brown stain. Let the stain dry overnight. Then apply a clear leather polish. Do not use colored shoe polishes as they can stain clothing. After the staining is completed, the leather can be attached to the front bracket and the rear curved bracket with copper rivets available in most hardware stores.

8. Insert rivets with the heads on the outside surface of the leather. Next place the rivet head on a clean flat steel plate or flat section of a vise, insert a washer over the stem of the rivet and peen this end until it tightly overlaps the washer. This part of the job should be done carefully. A nail-set or center punch will help start the peening operation. An extra pair of hands is helpful for a short time to hold the assembly in place while it is being peened.

## WIRING ON SOLID RUBBER TIRES

*(adapted with permission from* Wheelmen Bulletin Nos. 4 *and* 25 *by Robert McNair and Carl Wiedman)*

The proper installation of solid rubber tires may be more important than any other consideration in the safe operation of the antique bicycle. Be advised that even if these installation recommendations are precisely followed, I am unable to guarantee that the tiring will not loosen or come off while the bicycle is being ridden. It is, however, the experience of seasoned riders that properly installed, solid tires will give several hundred miles of safe, comfortable service.

Because of the considerably greater number of rotations made by the small wheel, its tiring always will wear out more quickly than the large wheel. Most wear occurs inside the core of the tiring where it cannot be seen. As the wire rubs against the core it often enlarges it causing the tire to loosen and to have a softer feel. Also the tire joints may become soft with wear and make a thumping noise. Even when in need of replacement, the tire's exterior surface seldom will show much evidence of wear.

With the exception of cushion tire machines on which the original tiring should be preserved if at all possible, we strongly recommend replacement of old tire rubber on any solid tire machine intended to be ridden.

Begin the replacement procedure by obtaining the correct tiring material. Tiring materials have been produced specially for antique bicycles in the correct red color and in the proper consistency for smooth riding and maximum wear.

Two methods of mounting solid tires will be described, one using the tire machine that was popular in the 1880s, the other using a device developed by Wheelmen member Carl Wiedman.

### Mounting the Tire with an Original Tire Machine

Before beginning the tiring of the wheel, paint the inside of the rim. Be sure the inside rim surface is free from any protrusions and is perfectly smooth.

Then measure the width of the rim from edge to edge to determine the tire diameter needed. Never install tiring that is wider than the rim because it will not seat and the rim edges will shave the tiring, causing it to continually loosen. The tire must press against the bottom of the rim. Typically, Star rims have a flat base which requires that one side of the tiring be filed or buffed flat to assure a firm fit.

*Fig. 11–6.* Cut tire rubber longer than the circumference of the wheel.

1. Cut a length of rubber that will go completely around the rim with 2" extra for every 10" of wheel diameter (Fig. 11-6). Square off the ends of the rubber with a file or power grinder.
2. Buy 12 gauge wire from a hardware store. Soft iron wire is suitable, but check its solderability. Cut off and straighten a length of the wire that is 12" longer than the length you have cut the rubber and lay the wire out on the floor. Round the ends with a file. After applying to the wire a small amount of a lubricant that does not decompose rubber, such as castor oil, force the wire through the tiring. If you use pliers to push it through, do not nick the wire. It may help to grip the wire in a vise and push the rubber onto it. Push the wire entirely through the tire so it extends from both ends.

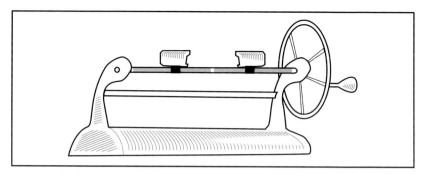

*Fig. 11–7.* Antique tire machine.

The tire machine consists of a stand with brackets that hold a long threaded column which can be turned by a handle at one end (Fig. 11-7). Each end of the threaded column has opposing threads and when clamping members are mounted on these threads, turning the handle causes them to move in opposite directions. By proper positioning and preparation, wires coming from opposite ends of the tire rubber can be clamped to these members and when the handle is turned the wire will be pulled from each end. When the tire is on the rim, and when the wires are positioned so they cross at the bracket member, turning the crank causes the wire and rubber to tighten. Then the entire wheel is given a single twist and the wire and tire are tight.

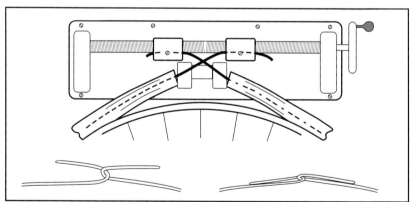

*Fig. 11–8.* With wires as shown, turn the crank to tighten tire into rim. Then twist the wheel to knot the wires and flatten the joint to slide it into the tire.

3. Begin by turning the crank until the jaws are about 2" apart and put the wires through the holes in the posts. Wrap the wire around the posts so it does not pull on the edges and break under the strain.
4. Practice with the small wheel first. Position the tire so the wires cross as shown in Fig. 11-8. Insert the spreader, start tightening, then work the tiring into the rim of the wheel.

5. The tire tightens quickly at this stage. Once tight enough so it cannot be pulled away from the rim, tie the knot. The side of the wheel whose wire is behind is twisted forward while the other side goes back. This requires a 180 degree twist of the entire wheel. It is necessary to pull one side of the wheel down to let the upper end of one wire slip forward as the spacer jaw turns with the wheel. With the wires looped around each other, cut them at the machine posts, but keep the ends down with your fingers so the knot cannot slip. During this procedure the spacer is kept in place. In tiring the big wheel, tie the knot by turning the tire machine instead of the wheel. This permits the installation of tires without removing the wheels from the bicycle.

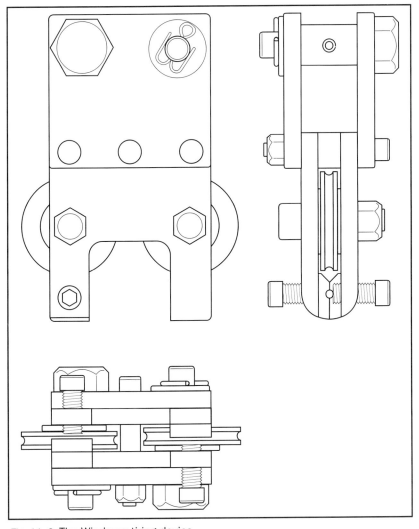

*Fig. 11–9.* The Wiedman tiring device.

6. Although the wheel is now free of the tire machine, keep the spreader jaws in. With pliers, squeeze the wire loops tight. Solder them, then cut the wires close to the end of the solder. Smooth the ends of the loops with a file so the knots can slide through the hole in the tire without catching. The soldering and filing are important because when they are omitted, the wire knot catches on the tire joint as the wire tries to move, forcing the tire joint open.

*Fig. 11–10.* Proper positioning of the wires.

7. To complete the installation, remove the spreader jaws and try to push the tire together at the joint using hands or a rubber hammer. If that doesn't work, riding the bicycle around the block usually will bring the joint together. Once the joint closes, it should never reopen if the tire was installed properly.

A preferred method of joining the wires is to scarf and braze the joint without twisting the wheel to form a loop. The resulting joint is smaller and does not create a bulge in the tire.

**Making and Using an Improved Tiring Device**

In *Wheelmen Bulletin 25* Carl Wiedman describes a new tiring device that he developed which is simpler to use than the other method. It has several advantages. Tires can be mounted easily with the wheels left on the bicycle. The wire is joined by silver soldering. This requires some knowledge and care, but eliminates the bulky knot within the tiring which can become a wear point with use. A properly soldered silver joint has strength equal to the wire itself, and has a great advantage over welding in that much less heat is required. Using this method, tires can be put on with inexpensive equipment. A common propane torch has adequate heat. The essentials of a good silver solder joint are cleanliness and proper fluxing. The new tiring device can easily be fabricated in a machine shop and should not be an expensive item. In addition, the device is small and portable, providing for simple field use in replacing tires. The device is shown in Figs. 11-9 through 11-16.

The device consists of the following structural members:

☛ A pair of shaped arms through which the wires are fed and which extend into the rim during the entire operation. These arms have a space between them, which is the area used later for the silver soldering operation. The arms have a slotted groove for the wire. Opposite this groove is a tightening screw for locking the wire once it has been properly tensioned around

*Fig. 11–11.* Beginning the tightening.

Fig. 11–12.
Finishing the tiring
using the clamp
screw.

the wheel. This locking clamp is important—there is so much tension on the wire that it would pull apart when heated for the silver soldering. The clamps are not released until this operation is completed, the material has cooled down, and the extension ends are cut off and filed.

☞ A pair of pulleys—the wires are fed through the clamping arms and around the pulley on the opposite side as shown.

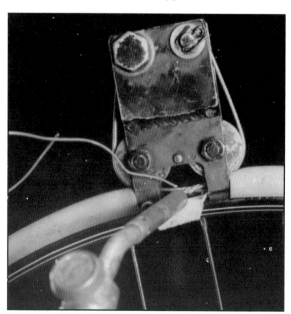

Fig. 11–13.
Soldering the crossed
wires. Asbestos scrap
prevents burning the
rim paint.

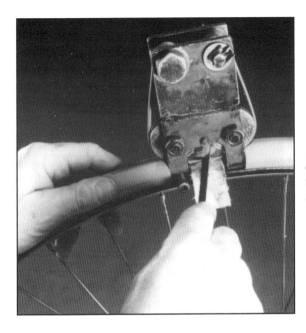

Fig. 11–14.
Cutting the ends
beyond the joint with
a hacksaw blade.

☛ A pair of tightening shafts for tensioning the wire. These turn freely in the assembly, and have a hexagonal head on one end for tightening with a ratchet wrench. Each shaft has a hole for attaching the wire ends before pulling them tight.

Rubber lengths are required that exceed the diameter of the rim in the same amount as with the old tiring machines.

Fig. 11–15.
The final smooth joint.

*Fig. 11–16.*
Carl Wiedman
removes the tiring
device.

1. In practice, position the wire ends as shown (Fig. 11-10). When the device is properly positioned in the rim, it holds the rubber apart for the entire operation to permit soldering after the wire is tensioned.
2. Tighten each side (Fig. 11-11). This operation should be done carefully as tremendous tension can be applied to the wire which will break if over-done.
3. After tightening on one side, clamp that wire end with the clamp screw before tightening the other side. By going back and forth a few times, you can apply proper force and the rubber will be seated (Fig. 11-12).
4. Put a piece of asbestos under the joint so the rim paint won't burn. Clean the joint with a solvent such as lighter fluid.
5. Silver solder the crossed wires (Fig. 11-13). If the surface is clean and you follow proper procedures, the silver solder will wet both wires when heated and flow among them. A bad joint is a very serious safety hazard.
6. Cut off the ends beyond the joint with a hack saw blade (Fig. 11-14) and file the rough cuts so the entire joint is smooth and won't cut the rubber (Fig. 11-15).
7. Finally, release the clamp screws and pull out the device (Fig. 11-16). If the rubber tiring length was properly sized, the tire should snap together, leaving a smooth joint line with no bulging.

## ADJUSTING AND SPOKING A WHEEL

Round, wobble-free wheels made with strong rims and spokes are critically important to the safety and enjoyment of an antique bicycle. If wheels are not properly tight, a collapsed wheel can easily result (Fig. 11-17). Should the wheel collapse, get a group of strong friends and try pulling it back into shape. Frequently an ordinary large wheel will spring back with a resounding snap. You should then check the spoke adjustment carefully.

In determining what needs to be done to the wheels, first examine them closely as follows:

On a direct spoke wheel, are the spokes rusted thin where they enter the threaded hub flange? If so, they simply will break off when twisted to true wheels and will have to be replaced. Check for the same problem where the spokes enter the nipple.

*Fig. 11–17.* A collapsed wheel.

Is the rim rusted through? If so, it cannot be used. If it is not round, but has flat spots that are very large, the tightening of spokes will not pull it back in shape. The wheel will have to be dismantled to reshape or replace the rim. See Appendix B for rim and spoke sources. Cracked wood rims can be replaced only by finding usable originals.

### Adjusting for Roundness

Check for roundness by steadying a piece of crayon against the edge of the fork and holding it at the outside edge of the rim while spinning the wheel. The crayon will mark the sections of the rim that are out of round. Loosen the spokes in the section of the rim that needs to be pushed further away from the axle, tighten the opposite spokes. Finish by again checking and adjusting for lateral wobble. Manipulate spokes as shown in Fig. 11-18 to adjust for flat spots.

If the hub is to be replated or if the spokes or rims need to be replaced, it is necessary to dismantle the wheel. Try to salvage as many spokes as possible by treating them with penetrating oil before removing them. All new spokes are costly and have to be hand made. Always replace double butted spokes with new ones that are double butted using the same gauges of wire as the originals. Search bicycle shops for new spokes for 28" rims. Some Schwinn tandem spokes will work. Such unique types as those with ball ends will have to be hand made. Be very cautious about breaking off the ends of spokes in the hub flanges. When that happens the spokes will have to be drilled out.

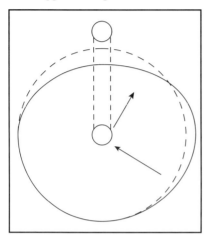

*Fig. 11–18.* Loosen spokes that need to be pushed away from axle, tighten those extending beyond the correct circumference.

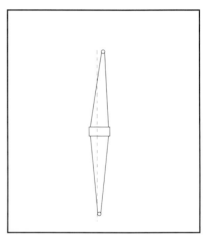

*Fig. 11–19.* Loosen the right spokes and tighten the left ones, to move the rim to the left.

**Adjusting for Wobble**

Assuming the rim is sound and spokes are in good condition, spin the wheel with it in the fork to check for wobble. Watching from in front of the wheel, you should notice no more than a minuscule wobble as it spins. If there is a wobble, hold a crayon at the right fork so it nearly touches the rim and spin the wheel. The crayon will mark those sections of the rim that are too far to the right side of the fork. To move the rim to the left, loosen the spokes in that section that are on the right side and tighten those on the left side (Fig. 11-19). Before loosening any spokes, treat them with penetrating oil until they turn freely. Grasp direct spokes near the hub flange using pliers wrapped in masking tape or the vise-grip tool described in this chapter. Twist gently counterclockwise to loosen. Use a good spoke grip available at bicycle stores for nippled spokes. Loosening spokes on one side one turn and tightening on the opposite side one turn will shift a 26" rim about ⅛" sideways.

**Rebuilding a Wheel**

Before dismantling the wheel, diagram how the spokes are laced. On ordinaries spokes may cross from one to seven times. To determine the right number of crosses, count the number of rim holes between similar spokes. You must record the cross pattern before taking the wheel apart. Also make note of which direction the spokes go through the hub flanges. It is helpful to take closeup photos of the spoking arrangement.

When everything is apart, refinish the rim inside and out. Use a washer in all the countersunk holes in wood rims. Then thread all the spokes into the hub flange or rim nipples with one turn. Follow the original lacing pattern. Next tighten all the spokes by the same amount, maybe six turns. Then work around the rim making all spokes as equally tight as possible. A medium tightness is preferable for ordinaries and safety rims. Wood rims particularly should not be pulled to an extreme tightness.

Finish the project by testing and adjusting for roundness and freedom from wobble. If it was done originally, the final touch on many antique bicycles is to tie the spokes where they cross with wire and a touch of solder. If the machine had a combination nickel and painted spoke, now is the time to paint the spokes from the last cross to the rim or in the pattern that was original to the bicycle.

**How To Make a Spoke Grip**

John Vanderpoel in the May, 1979 *Wheelmen* magazine described as follows how to make a useful grip for adjusting direct spokes.

"These grips are made in two styles: one has the slot for the spokes at a 90 degree angle to the grip handles. This style is ideal for the final truing of a wheel, but it does not permit a very large angular motion with each application of the grip. The other style has the spoke slot as nearly parallel to the handles as can be accomplished. Such a style permits the grip to be rotated a full revolution or more during the assembly of all large wheels and such small wheels as have but few spokes.

"Both styles of grip are fabricated by drilling a small pilot hole in a short, round piece of brass. I have found that a piece ⅜" inch diameter by ½" long is quite ideal. This piece is brazed or silver soldered between the jaws of the 5" Vise-Grip.

"It is advisable to grind off some of the teeth on the Vise-Grip either directly crosswise or on a long oblique before the brazing operation to ensure more surface contact. It is also mandatory to remove the small jaw-closing spring before brazing. If you don't, all temper will be taken from the spring and you will be forced both to open and close the jaws manually during every subsequent operation.

"After the cylinder is brazed or silver-soldered into both jaws, redrill the pilot hole to the correct size for the spoke to be gripped. I drill a hole about two thousandths smaller than the actual spoke size because the brass will distort and/or wear very rapidly to fit the spoke.

"The brass cylinder is now split lengthwise with as thin a hacksaw as one can find. Some burr filing may be advisable at this point. The final operation is to reconnect the spring.

"You now have an adjustable spoke grip of great power with the halves in perfect register. It is strong enough to easily twist off an old rusty spoke, but will not twist off a new one unless its operator has immensely strong hands."

# Chapter 12:
# How To Make Them Ready To Show

aving made the repairs to make your antique bicycle safe to ride, should you preserve it in its original condition, or should you restore it? *Preserved* condition is defined as keeping intact as much as possible the original paint, plating, leather, and rubber while making certain the machine is safe to ride. *Restored* is stripping the finish to bare metal in preparation for repainting, buffing plated parts to a mirror finish for renickeling, and replacing all unusable components with meticulously correct replicas of the originals, thus returning the machine to a like-new condition.

Although all antique bicycles must be rideable to qualify for judging at Wheelmen meets, describing a bicycle in that manner as opposed to preserved or restored is to say that on the *rideable* machine some parts have been redone, others have not, and that the intent has not been to make the machine as it was originally, but rather to make it rideable by whatever means possible that closely approximate the original.

In this book I will discuss only the preservation and restoration approaches. The decision of which to do can be based on two factors: what the bicycle is and its condition.

## PRESERVE OR RESTORE?

It is vital the collector appreciate that in a sense he does not own his antique bicycle in the same way that he owns the disposable objects which he uses every day. The collector has the role of a temporary custodian who is preserving the only historical record of the history of the bicycle that will exist for future generations.

It is most unusual to find good examples of early bicycles with their original finish intact. If this does in fact occur, do not refinish them, as this would destroy their value as historical documents. Likewise, substituting a new wheel for a serviceable but scruffy appearing original would be unthinkable. Every effort should be made to preserve the original qualities of the original machine, even when parts must be fabricated to replace missing original components.

If a collector owns a hobby horse or boneshaker with original paint that has been varnished and decorated with a commercial stripe, it probably is one of a handful of such examples in existence. Destroying the original appearance of the very few good remaining originals, hastens the day when there will be no completely original examples left for restorers and connoisseurs to study and appreciate.

As a rule, if the appearance of the antique bicycle gives any indication that its paint and plating is original and can be returned to presentable appearance using the cleaning and refurbishing techniques outlined in this chapter, then try to preserve it before starting to sandblast the old paint and plating. If the intention is to ride or show the bicycle, always replace any components such as rims that have been made unsafe by deterioration, but carefully preserve the original so it can be reinstalled. Remember that an ordinary with highly polished and carefully touched up original paint and with the soft glow of original nickel can be very attractive even if new rims and spokes have been fitted.

## CLEANING AND PRESERVING THE SAFETY

Begin by preparing the work area. Since many antique bicycle hobbyists work on their machines during the winter months—they are too busy riding during the summer—it is a good idea to have a work space indoors. Select a block of time allowing work on the project without long interruptions.

### Materials

Buy two plastic covered hooks sold at hardware stores and bike shops and screw them about 27" apart into the ceiling near the workbench. Next get the best lighting available. Two fluorescent shop lights hung parallel to each other on each side of the hooks work well. Keep the work area and your hands as clean as possible at all times.

Next assemble the needed materials.

Good quality cheesecloth
Medium and fine steel wool
Firm toothbrushes
Hand-held wire brush
Red sable, camel hair, or other fine quality brushes, ¾" and touch up sizes
Dust and pollen mask to wear during heavy sanding and spraying
Liquid bleach
Lacquer thinner
Armorall™ protectant
Flecto Varathane™ liquid plastic clear gloss or similar substitute
Clear spray Krylon™
Strypeeze™ or similar semi-paste paint remover

Penetrating oil
3 in 1™ or similar oil
Lexol™ or neatsfoot oil compound
Paste saddle soap
Leather dye
Clear shoe polish
Murphy™ oil soap
Pre-wax liquid cleaner such as Simoniz™
Spray and liquid degreaser such as Gunk™
1" wide rolls of coarse, medium, and fine emery cloth
Tack cloths
Pen knife
Putty knife
Electric drill
Buffing pads
Epoxy cement
Liquid chrome cleaner such as Simoniz
Cleaner-wax such as high gloss Turtle Wax™
Paste wax such as Simoniz Yellow
Happich Simichrome™ polish
Automotive touch up enamel
Workbench vise
Two 21" rubber straps with hooks at each end
Tire glue such as Tubasti™ rim cement
Liquid hand cleaner such as Goop™
Protective hand cream such as Protek™ by Dupont

## Inspection

Take the bicycle outdoors and examine it very closely under natural light. The importance of this was dramatized to me by a personal experience. What had appeared under artificial light to be a pattern of pitting on the neck of a chain driven high wheel safety was discovered, with the use of a magnifying glass and natural light, to be a maker's name. Later research revealed the bicycle to be a rare one with an interesting history.

Does the paint upon close examination have the smooth, rather thick appearance of an original baked on enamel with crisp edges on any paint chips or does it appear to have been painted over? If it has been overpainted, select an inconspicuous spot and brush on a thin coat of semi-paste paint remover, being careful it doesn't splash onto other areas of the bicycle. Let it stand for 30 seconds and clean it off with a water soaked paper towel. Repeat the procedure until the original finish is reached. The original enamel will not be easily affected by paint remover, but any striping will be, thus the necessity of using this procedure very carefully.

## Disassembly

If you find presentable original paint rather than rust, remove all the over-paint on frame, forks, and rims after disassembling the bicycle as outlined in this chapter. Let the paint remover do its work. Avoid using steel wool or any other abrasive material that will scratch the original paint and remove decals and striping. Even traces of decals and striping should be saved on preserved bicycles (Fig. 12-1).

1. Begin the disassembly by applying penetrating oil to all nuts and bolts. Then use a good quality wrench of the correct size. Avoid adjustable crescent wrenches if possible because they are apt to round the edges of the nut. Do not force frozen nuts as doing so may twist off the end of the bolt.

*Fig. 12–1.*
Traces of decals such as this one on a Beeston Humber ordinary should be saved on preserved bicycles. *(courtesy of Greenfield Village and Henry Ford Museum)*

Persistence with penetrating oil applying it over several days or weeks and with tapping that sets up vibrations and forces the oil to penetrate more deeply, nearly always will free even the most stubborn nut. Applying a little heat to the stubborn part, being careful not to burn any paint, also will help.

2. When disassembling a safety, first remove the chain guard and then the chain. The chain has a clasp or a threaded screw and nut at the break link. Put the chain in a shallow pan of "Gunk" or other degreaser for an hour or more, then lay it on the workbench and clean all four sides with a stiff wood handled wire brush.

3. Hang the bicycle by looping two 21" rubber straps, 1" wide with hooks at each end and available at hardware stores, under the top tube and through the triangle made by the down tube and the seat stays at the back of the bicycle. At the front, loop the strap under the top tube and forward of the handlebar. Given a normal height ceiling this should suspend the bicycle at the most convenient height.

4. Remove the rear wheel. Do not forget the fastener securing the coaster brake arm on later models. Reattach all washers and nuts so they will not get lost.

5. Remove the front wheel axle nuts and washers. Pull the front fork apart, being careful not to damage the original paint, and remove the front wheel.

6. Having thoroughly saturated the nuts or shaft ends with penetrating oil, attempt to remove the pedals. The cranks will be easier to clean if they are removed. Removal will also permit repacking of the crank bearings. However if doing so will cause damage to plated parts, and if the bearings are free and operating smoothly, leave them on. When removing crank keys, tap the threaded end only when the nut is on. Tapping directly on the threaded end will peen it over making it impossible to replace the nut without rethreading the key. The same applies to any threaded shafts.

7. Remove all attachments and store them in cardboard boxes. Observe how the pieces were assembled so the bicycle can be properly reassembled. The attachments that should be removed include brake lever, lamp bracket, bolted-on coaster bars, and bolted-on frame stays. Remove the name badge very carefully and secure the tiny screws to the back of it with masking tape. It is not necessary to remove the handlebar or spring suspension parts.

8. Beginning with the handlebar, start the cleaning of the plated parts. It will be easier to do if you return the bicycle frame to the floor and brace the front fork between your legs. Apply liquid chrome cleaner with fine steel wool and rub firmly straight back and forth across the tarnished and rusted surface. When the corrosion is gone, move to the next section. Start on the underside of the handlebar where errors will not be noticed. If a cop-

per color appears, this means the rubbing is too hard and is removing the nickel, revealing the copper underplating. Wash the piece frequently so as to gauge the effect of the work. Don't be concerned about the shine of the nickel at this point, but just with the removal of rust and tarnish. Where nickel is flaking, the cleaning is certain to expose copper or bare metal.

Fig. 12–2. The handlebar nickel looked like the fork crown plating and name badge on this Monarch chainless before it was cleaned.

Don't despair. With the later polishing of the plating, bare metal will tend to blend with the plated surface (Fig. 12-2).

9. As work progresses on the handlebar stem there will be areas hard to reach with steel wool. Use a firm toothbrush soaked in chrome cleaner. If there is a heavy deposit of grease, squeeze a degreaser such as Gunk on the toothbrush and scrub. Lay the name badge on a dowel-like surface such as a broom handle so as not to flatten it while scrubbing.

10. When all plated parts have been cleaned of corrosion, washed, and dried, wash the painted parts with a soft cloth using warm water and Murphy's oil soap. Be very gentle in areas where there are decals or striping. Cautiously use Gunk or another degreaser on painted parts that are heavily coated with grease. Remove the degreaser almost immediately to prevent a whitish streaking from developing.

11. Clean each nut by securing it in a padded vise and buffing each side and the top surface with steel wool and chrome cleaner. Likewise clean the ends of each bolt and the threads.

12. Begin cleaning the wheels by removing the tires. Start opposite the valve. Be sure the tire is largely off the rim by the time you reach the valve. Be cautious that there is not a nut screwed onto the valve that has to be removed before the valve will come out. Reach through the spokes and with chrome cleaner and steel wool remove corrosion from the hubs. Clean inside and outside flanges of the hubs with a firm toothbrush soaked in chrome cleaner. It is necessary to scrub hard in this area.

   Also use the toothbrush to clean the oiler caps. Next clean each spoke. If there is only grime and surface rust on a plated spoke, use the steel wool and chrome cleaner. If the spoke is not plated and is rusted use a fine emery cloth, sanding the spoke to the bare metal. Laying the wheel flat on the bench, go all around once cleaning each spoke. Mark the starting point by beginning at the spoke closest to the tire valve hole. Repeat the procedure for the inside surface of the spokes on the other side of the wheel. Then flip the wheel over and complete the procedure on the other side. The nipples probably will be brass. Polish each with steel wool making certain to clean all sides of it.

13. If the rim is painted metal, clean it as you would any other painted part. Be especially thorough in cleaning around the nipples. Tire cement that has hardened on to the rim often can be chipped off or softened with a cautious application of lacquer thinner. A wood rim often is finished in varnish that has become brittle and discolored. If this has happened and has created an unsightly appearance, try smoothing the original finish with a fine sandpaper. If this does not clean it and make it look presentable, you may want to remove at least the top coat of varnish with a paint remover and fine steel wool. Soaking the wood rim in an undiluted household bleach will help remove stains. Wear rubber gloves to protect yourself from contact with the bleach.

14. The next step is to clean the tires. With a fingernail brush, apply a liquid tire and rubber cleaner available at auto supply stores to remove the deep dirt and stains. Be sure to clean the tread thoroughly. Grease stains on red or white rubber sometimes can be removed with a cautious application of lacquer thinner. Yellowed white sidewalls can be whitened with automotive type whitewall cleaner or household bleach. Clean the pedal rubber and any other rubber components by the same method.

15. The painted parts are now ready to be polished. Using only a soft cheesecloth, apply an automotive pre-wax cleaner such as Simoniz to all the painted parts and rub it out. Again be cautious around striping and decals. Thoroughly clean out all chipped areas where the cleaner residue may have become lodged. Rub a little solvent into the chips to remove any grease.

Then, using a clean and soft small artist's brush, preferably one with red sable bristles, brush a good quality automotive enamel, such as that contained in touch-up tubes sold by auto dealers, into chipped areas, stopping at the edge of the chip. Let each coat dry, then apply another until the surface has been built up to where it is level with the original thickness of the paint. It is fortunate that most antique bicycles are black; avoid touching up those painted another color unless they can be matched perfectly.

17. After the painted surfaces have been touched up as well as possible and the paint has dried, polish the plated parts beginning again with the handlebar. Use only a soft cheesecloth with a fine polishing paste such as Simichrome. Apply the paste, rubbing firmly and then buff briskly with clean cheesecloth. Repeat until the polishing cloth is not blackened by the tarnish. If there is no peeling original nickel, an electric drill with a buffing pad can be used on the large plated surfaces, but this is not necessary. Polish all plated parts including spokes and nipples where applicable. Simichrome also will restore a luster to painted surfaces clouded and dulled by years of exposure to grease and oil. Use it also to polish bakelite handlebar grips.

18. If there are clouded and dulled painted parts that do not respond to buffing with Simichrome, spray clear gloss Krylon directly onto the painted surface. Make certain the surface is clean and that adjacent areas are covered so they will not be coated with overspray. Krylon will not discolor, is easily removable, can be waxed, and works well on plated parts. However, it is more easily scratched than Varathane. When all painted surfaces are polished as well as they can be, apply a cleaner wax such as Turtle Wax, rubbing it out thoroughly.

19. Cement the tires back on the rims, using a special bicycle tire cement available at bicycle shops. Inflate the tires hard after cementing them to press them tightly into the rim. Immediately remove any cement that spilled on the outside surface of the rim or if this proves difficult, wait until it has hardened.

20. Mount the wheels on the bicycle. If the rims are wood and have been stripped, clean them thoroughly with a tack cloth and apply three coats of a clear material such as glossy liquid Varathane using a clean soft artist's brush. Follow the Varathane directions closely. With the bicycle hanging, rotate the wheel to make refinishing easier.

21. If it was necessary to sand the spokes to the bare metal, coat them now with Varathane or Krylon to keep them from rusting. Also apply clear glossy Varathane or Krylon to any plated areas where bare metal has been exposed. Three coats are required. If wood or metal rims are painted, but the paint cannot be burnished to a shine, apply Varathane or Krylon directly over the cleaned and tack-clothed paint.

22. When the rims are dried, coat the tires with a substance such as Armorall following the directions closely. It will blacken the rubber and help soften and preserve it. Do not apply Armorall to the area that must be glued to the rim.
23. Completely assemble the bicycle, applying a light oil to all threads and the chain and a final heavy paste wax such as Simoniz to all surfaces.
24. Complete preserving the bicycle by cleaning the saddle leather with saddle soap and treating it with a softener such as Lexol. If the leather has unsightly chips or cracks, it can be dyed with a good quality shoe dye. Be sure to use one that will not rub off on clothes. Complete the saddle with a coat or two of clear shoe polish.
25. The bicycle should be thoroughly touched up and waxed at least once a year or each time it is transported to and from a meet.

## CLEANING AND PRESERVING THE ORDINARY

Generally the techniques used in working on the ordinary are the same as those used for the safety with a few exceptions:

☞ Hang the machine from rubber straps, one slung under the handlebar and the other through the rear saddle spring. This necessitates removing the rear saddle spring last.
☞ Leave the wheels on the bicycle. Do not finish the spokes by polishing to the bare metal and coating them as on the safety. Rather, it will be more authentic to repaint them if they are corroded.
☞ As indicated in the preceding chapter, do not try to salvage old solid rubber tires, but replace them with new for riding safety. Also replace pedal rubber unless the original is soft and complete.

## WOOD BICYCLES

Confronted with the cleaning and preserving of a hobby horse or wooden safety in good original finish, begin by washing with warm water and Murphy Oil Soap. Dry thoroughly and gently apply a liberal coat of Trewax™ or Butcher's Bowling Alley Wax™ rubbing gently with a soft cheese cloth. If rubbing the wax will remove quantities of flaking original paint, stop with just the oil soap washing. Do not apply Varathane, Tung Oil™ or any material other than the aforementioned waxes to the painted wood surface. Also do not scrub the surface with SOS™ pads or any other material.

Remove rust from iron components using the techniques described for cleaning plated parts, but use only Krylon or paste wax for coating the non-wood components.

By following these procedures you will preserve the valuable historical artifact using sound conservation techniques that will not damage the original finish, will be easily removable, and will protect the machine from further deterioration.

If there has been painting over the original paint, remove the overpaint using paint remover as described earlier in this chapter to determine if any original finish can be preserved. With hobby horses and other very early and rare machines, even traces of original finish are preferable to a repaint.

If you are refinishing a wood frame pneumatic safety, use the techniques described for refinishing wood rims. Complete the refinishing of the wood safety frame and rims by rubbing them with paste wax applied with very fine steel wool, followed by buffing with cheesecloth. This will cut the Varathane high gloss and give a smooth luster to the wood.

## PAINT AND PLATING

Pre-1900 bicycle factories didn't have paint sprayers. Often the elegant finish was applied by skilled artisans working with a brush. Working with great care and using the procedures that are about to be outlined, a collector can achieve a brushed finish that actually is superior to a sprayed one in smoothness, authenticity, and durability. The sense of satisfaction in doing a perfect job by this method is enormous.

### Preparing for Painting and Plating
1. If you decide that the original finish cannot be saved, complete all required repairs such as straightening bent parts, truing wheels, and making correct replicas of missing components. It is a good idea to take overall photos of the bicycle before you begin disassembly and close-up pictures of assemblies such as rod brakes for use in reassembling.
2. Completely disassemble the bicycle being certain not to misplace any parts.
3. If plating is beyond saving, consider the following treatment:
    Clamp the piece in a vise, protecting it against scratching with a sheet of brass, leather or cardboard between the vise surface and the component. Wire brush the part with a wire brush disc mounted on an electric drill. A bench mounted motorized brush will make the job faster and easier. Follow this with a thorough hand sanding with strips of emery cloth (80 grit or coarser) pulling back and forth as if polishing shoes. Wrapping the emery cloth around the curved surfaces during the sanding process will guard against creating flat spots. A great deal of elbow grease will be required to work the surface until it is smooth. Be cautious not to cut off too much of a section of a component that must fit securely into a mating piece. When the piece is as free of pits as possible, repeat the procedure with a finer grade emery cloth to remove the fine scratches left by the coarse sanding. Repeat the procedure one more time with a fine emery cloth and polish the surface until it is so shiny that it appears to have already been plated. A power buffer would be helpful at this point. If the bicycle is not to be a show one, coat the polished parts with clear Krylon or clear gloss Varathane.

Do not use aluminum paint on parts that originally were plated; it does not look authentic and is difficult to remove once applied.

Likewise, chrome on pre-1930 bicycles is not authentic; the plating would have been nickel. Instead, if you will be painting such components as handlebars, hubs, cranks, and pedals, use the same color as the bicycle frame.

4. If sending the parts to a plater, be absolutely certain that the plater is reputable. Many good-condition antique bicycles have been rendered nearly unrestorable by platers who have ground through the metal and have lost parts. Make a list of every piece being sent. Lay the pieces out and photograph them. When the finished plating is picked up, check it off piece by piece before leaving the shop. Unfortunately, to have a piece lost by a plater is not uncommon.

*Fig. 12–3.* Plating patience and workmanship is rewarded in Fred Schumacher's Columbia ordinary on which even the rims are plated.

Insist that the plater not plate threads. In cases such as the front fork of an ordinary, where usually only the crown is plated and the rest is painted, insist that the plater mask off portions that are not to be plated. It is hard to make paint stick to a plated surface. Also insist that the plater not grind off any script on parts such as the Columbia ordinary dust shield which contains the maker's name and patent dates. It is better to have a few pits near the script than to lose the script. Also caution the plater not to cut through thin metal parts. If the nickel is too thin and shows through or if it is peeling, return it to be redone. Such efforts will be reflected in the brilliant surface of a well-nickeled bicycle (Fig. 12-3).

5. Immediately upon receiving parts, especially spokes, back from the plater, heat them for at least 4 hours at 400 degrees in your kitchen oven to help prevent hydrogen embrittlement that can cause cracking and breaking. The heating will not discolor the nickel or soften tempered springs. As soon as the heated parts are cool, clean and wax them with a heavy paste wax.

Gun blue rather than plate tiny parts such as spring steel axle oiler caps and flat brake return springs as was done originally.

### Striping

Having decided upon the manner in which the plated parts are to be treated, begin preparations for painting the disassembled bicycle. Take the vehicle outdoors and check it closely for evidence of striping. Photograph close-up all striping details, even if there are only traces left. Keep these photos even if striping is not redone. They will be useful in the years ahead.

If striping is to be redone, and if the striping pattern is complicated, take the machine to the striper to have him make diagrams as a guide. If you make the diagrams yourself, take very accurate measurements of where the lining and other decoration was placed and try to trace any filigree as closely as possible. Where fancy filigree or decals are involved, they can be photographed and replicas made.

If the bicycle is not black, look for the original color where paint has been protected from fading such as under a chain guard bracket. Also check the rims carefully for original colors. Then take the piece to an auto supply shop to have a duplicate color custom mixed. Specify an enamel that does not set up quickly if you will be brushing the finish. Avoid metallic finishes. Automotive maroons, for example, often are metallic, but similar truck maroons sometimes are not.

### Removing Old Paint and Repainting

Having matched the paint and properly recorded all striping and decal details, now strip the old finish to the bare metal. Air holes drilled in the tubing must be plugged if the frame and fork are to be dipped for stripping. The best finish is achieved when the parts are sandblasted, a technique that removes the rust at the bottom of each pit. Auto body shops often are equipped for sandblasting. You must take great caution because of the thin walls in bicycle tubing.

1. Semi-paste paint remover usually is ineffective on any original baked-on enamel, but scraping the paint off with a pen knife, sharp putty knife, and a coarse wire brush usually works well. Be sure to protect your eyes from flying paint chips.

2. Having removed the paint to the bare metal, wire brush the surface to get all the corrosion out of every pit. Be very careful in clamping parts for wire brushing that you do not flatten the hollow tubes. Thoroughly clean the bare metal with a solvent such as Metal Prep™ that will remove grease and oil and, with clean hands, immediately apply a coat of lacquer primer.

3. When it is dry, examine the parts for pits, file marks and other imperfections. Then do the initial filling with a lacquer putty such as Dupont's Spot 'N Glaze™. Follow directions closely. If you cannot find such materials, multiple applications of lacquer primer will accomplish the same effect. What is happening is that the pit holes are being filled with lacquer primer and the sanding to the bare metal after each coat is removing the high spots, creating a smooth filled surface.

4. When the bare metal is perfectly smooth to the touch, apply two final coats of lacquer primer sanding each smooth, but not down to the bare metal.

If you are not matching the original color, black is the safest color to use. Buy a good quality black enamel, a ¾" artist's brush, and a small touch up brush, preferably with red sable bristles. The absolute cleanliness of the surface to be painted, the quality of the light, and the cleanliness and quality of the brushes are extremely important.

5. At this point be sure the work area is as clean as possible. Hang the bicycle frame so it can be worked on freely, and bathe it in good light. An exhaust fan or open window is helpful to get rid of lacquer fumes. Clean with a fresh tack cloth and apply the finish color coat immediately.

6. Before beginning to paint, soak the brush in the paint for several minutes so the bristles are thoroughly saturated. Starting with a brush well filled with paint, begin at the top tube and work down the frame doing the crank hanger last. First brush the paint on, then flow it, dragging the saturated brush from one end of the surface to the other. Watch all the time for runs. Work quickly, starting on the underside of the tube surfaces then repeat the procedure on the top before the underside has had a chance to dry. Do not go back over the surface after having gone the length of it with the final flow stroke. Move on to the next section promptly, painting the entire frame in one session.

7. The front fork is done next. The rims are done later. Always do the underside or side that doesn't show on any component first. In that way if the paint sets up too fast, any roughing of the surface will appear in an area

that doesn't show. Be careful not to rub against a part that has already been painted. To prevent dust contamination, leave the work area as soon as the painting is completed.

Allow at least 72 hours for the frame to dry; sometimes a week or more is required. This long drying time is needed because of the heavy coat of paint that has been applied. If the paint bubbles or raises, something such as grease or oil from the fingers has contaminated the surface. There is no choice but to start over. Remove the wet finish coat with paint thinner, allow it to dry, sand the lacquer primer back to the bare metal, being careful not to remove the fill; re-prime, and sand and apply the finish coat a second time.

8. If a second finish coat is needed to fully cover the primer, wait several days, sand the first coat with a fine sandpaper, rub with a tack cloth, and repeat the procedure. If the first heavy finish coat is not allowed to cure it will curl when sanded thus creating a rough surface that will require redoing by going back to the bare metal. Heavy runs also are apt to curl when sanded. If that happens sand only the affected section of the frame back to the primer before applying a new finish coat.

9. The rims and spokes are next. If the wheel is apart to have the hub renickeled, strip, fill, and sand the rim and paint it before putting the spokes back in. Be sure to paint the inner surface of the rim where the tire seats to guard against rusting. Also fill and sand each spoke until it is smooth. Avoid using as full a brush when painting spokes as they are likely to give problems with runs.

10. Allow all to dry and cure for a few days before reassembling the wheel.

Expect that the spokes will need to be touched up with a brush where they are threaded into the hub after the wheel is assembled. If new spokes have been made, sand their surface and prime before painting. If they are stainless steel, either paint or nickel them, whichever was correct for the machine. The polished stainless steel spoke finish is not authentic to any high wheel bicycle. If the bicycle has tangential spokes, determine if they originally were nickeled to where they cross. If this was the case, have the whole spoke nickeled and finish the painted portion after the wheel is assembled. Be sure to heat spokes as described earlier in this chapter if they have been nickel plated.

If the original nickel was preserved, the bare metal burnished, or the hub painted and the wheel was not taken apart, paint the rim with the wheel mounted on the bicycle.

1. First tightly mask all the nipples, go through the filling and sanding procedure, and clean with the tack cloth.

2. Brush the finish coat all around one side of the rim rotating the wheel as you go. Paint past the center of the rim; be careful of runs at each spoke.

3. Then flow a heavy coat all around the rim by dragging a saturated brush while rotating the wheel. Then immediately repeat the procedure on the other side.

On a pneumatic safety, apply a clear Varathane or Krylon coating to burnished spokes. On early safeties and ordinaries, painting the spokes is more authentic. Paint one side of five or six spokes, then finish the opposite side before moving on to the next section. Examine each spoke carefully to be certain no part has been missed.

If you are applying black or another color paint to wood rims, prepare the surface with a coat of sealer. When using other than black paint, always keep a supply of leftover paint tightly corked for future touching up. Allow all to dry and cure for several days before reassembling the bicycle and before striping it.

## PLANNING THE PROFESSIONAL RESTORATION

The preceding information has outlined how an antique bicycle can be preserved or restored by an owner with limited tools and only minimal outside help.

If you want a professional restoration, it is important to consider several points in making the decision.

☛ Is the investment value of the bicycle a major consideration or is it overweighed by the enjoyment and appreciation of the machine? Seldom does a professionally restored bicycle command a price that is higher than its unrestored counterpart by an amount that is enough to pay for restoration.

☛ Because of the problem of recovering the professional restoration cost, give considerable thought before contracting for the restoration of any that will not be permanently in your collection. At best, it most likely would take several years before the bicycle's appreciated value would allow for recovering the professional restoration cost.

☛ How much is invested in the bicycle now relative to its restored value? If a desirable vehicle such as a Kangaroo has been acquired at a low price but requires an expensive restoration, the investment would be well protected by the machine's high market value.

☛ How will the bicycle be used? If you enjoy showing your machines at Wheelmen judging events, a superior professional restoration will be a source of great satisfaction. However, the show bicycle with a perfect restoration will have to be meticulously maintained and very carefully ridden and transported or it will deteriorate rapidly.

Since most antique bicycle hobbyists enjoy having at least a few show machines in their collections, consider the following recommendations in selecting a professional restorer.

☛ Examine examples of the restorer's work and discuss quality, pricing, scheduling, and the correctness of restorations with Wheelmen members who have contracted with this person in the past. It is senseless to engage a professional restorer and then not demand absolute correctness in every detail. Operate on the basis that the bicycle will be restored only once and insist upon faultless accuracy and workmanship.

☞ Do not expect in advance an accurate cost estimate for labor. A warped axle, spokes that break off in a hub, and many other problems cannot be anticipated. However, insist that the restorer give you a written estimate of the total cost and that written reports on the status of the restoration be sent to you when one half and three fourths of the anticipated charge has been reached.

☞ If you wish to do part of the restoration yourself, work out in advance to the satisfaction of both, the exact responsibilities of each. By doing your own research, either by locating sister machines that can be borrowed for duplicating parts or by locating original catalog illustrations from which to copy, you can save considerable restoration time and expense. In fact, do not take the machine to the restorer until it has been thoroughly researched. If there are several missing parts and the machine is rare, the required research may take years, but it can be an enjoyable and most worthwhile aspect of the hobby. When the professional restorer does fabricate missing parts, insist they be duplicates of the originals. If the original oil cap was made of spring steel, the reproduction should be also.

☞ Remember that a good professional restorer will take a great deal of pride in his work. He will not take kindly to constant demands midway through the restoration to reduce costs. When you contract for a restoration, be prepared to spend what is legitimately required to complete it.

More important than the personal satisfaction gained from successfully campaigning a show bicycle, is the role that Wheelmen judging has in encouraging collectors to preserve and restore their bicycles authentically and correctly for future generations.

## JUDGING

Bicycles and tricycles are exhibited for judging at most national and large regional Wheelmen meets. Reproductions are excluded from judging but not from any other Wheelmen activities.

Usually the machines are exhibited and judged in the following classes:

☞ hobby horses and boneshakers
☞ ordinaries
☞ high wheel safeties
☞ solid and cushion tire safeties
☞ pneumatic tire safeties and tricycles
☞ solid tire adult tricycles
☞ juvenile bicycles and tricycles

First and second places often are awarded in each class. Judges often vote for a best of show entry and members sometimes vote for a popular choice award. Usually no distinction is made between preserved and restored bicycles. The judging criteria that I adapted for a Wheelmen concours at Greenfield Village in October, 1979 uses the condition in which the machine left the factory when it was new as the standard by which all entries are judged.

Although judging procedures vary from meet to meet, in that particular case judges were instructed as follows: All entries begin with 100 points. The frame is given 30 points. The running gear—chain, sprockets, hubs, wheels, rims, and handlebars—is worth 40 points. Ancillary components such as tires, handlebar grips, and saddle are worth 30 points. No points are added for accessories such as bells and lamps that would not have been installed at the factory. Points can be deducted, though, if incorrect or inappropriate accessories such as bulb horns on ordinaries or modern kick stands on pre-1900 safeties have been added.

Each of the previous elements were judged on the basis of authenticity, workmanship, and maintenance. Maintenance refers to how well it has been maintained since it was restored or, in the case of the preserved machine, since it was new.

Each machine was grouped with others in its class on the judging field (Fig. 12-4). Judges were instructed to first inspect each entry and then to complete the scoring on it before going on to the next one. Each machine was being scored against the standard, not against other machines entered. When a defect was located, the judges made a deduction at their discretion keeping in mind that a perfect frame is 30, perfect running gear is 40, and so on. All machines must be fully rideable to be eligible for judging.

A first place award required a minimum of 85 points. A second required a minimum of 75. That meant that if a category had only one entry and it scored 75 points, then only a second place could be awarded in that category. If there were several entries, but not one scored 75 points or more, no award was given in that category.

*Fig. 12–4.* Judging safeties at a Wheelmen meet.

Angela Werner enjoying the summer on a comfortable Hartford pneumatic safety made some ninety-five years earlier.

Michael Höhne

# Chapter 13:
# How To Get Ready for an Outing

A lthough Wheelmen meets are informal and are held only for members' enjoyment, there are certain preparations that may be made in advance of the first meet.

As a family oriented organization, The Wheelmen provides for equal participation by men, women, and children in all meet activities. If there is not an antique bicycle for every family member, riders on modern bicycles are allowed to participate in tours so long as they separate themselves somewhat from the antique machines. Reproduction high wheel bicycles are allowed to participate fully in all activities with the exception of judging.

Since nearly all Wheelmen gatherings involve tours, it is important to learn to ride well and safely and to get yourself in good enough physical condition to ride ten or more miles at one time.

Parades also frequently are part of a meet. Riding in close formations with other wheelmen requires proficiency in mounting and dismounting the antique bicycle. The Wheelmen require that all parade riders be in club uniform and that new members practice formations with the group prior to the parade. Most meets offer field events which give the opportunity to test riding skills in competition with other members. Finally it is necessary to prepare for transporting the bicycles to the meet and for securing them in some kind of exhibit stand while they are there.

## LEARNING TO RIDE WITH SAFETY AND GRACE

T he ultimate reason to build and own a bicycle is to ride it. Although the inventors of the various designs were more than pioneers, in that they had to figure out how to mount, balance, and control their machines with no help from anyone, today we have plenty of instruction available for a first ride. But these are so different from a modern bike that you may feel like a kid again.

**The Hobby Horse**

☛ Respect the antique value of the machine and refrain from rough handling or long distance riding.

☛ Adjust the saddle so you can straddle it easily and so that your knees are slightly bent when you settle into it. Adjust the elbow rest so you are only slightly bending forward when your elbows are firmly on it.

☛ Start with a walking motion, then refine it into a skating motion. Thrust first with one foot then with the other and coast slightly between steps, having your weight firmly on the saddle and elbow rest. Once you develop the rhythm you can advance quite rapidly and can take full advantage of the coast between each step.

**The Boneshaker**

☛ If the boneshaker is low enough to permit straddling the saddle, simply sit on the machine, then place your left foot on the pedal, push off with your right foot and start to pedal (Fig. 13-1).

☛ If the machine is too high to straddle the saddle, walk briskly on the left side and with your hands on the handlebar, thrust your right leg over the spring and vault onto the saddle. A safer way to mount a high boneshaker is to install a removable step on the frame as far forward of the rear wheel as is comfortable. Then walking to the left of the machine with both hands on the handlebar, put your left foot on the step, raise yourself to the step and swing your right leg over the spring, settling into the saddle.

☛ Place the arch rather than the ball of your foot on the boneshaker pedal. This is the opposite of what is recommended for riding any other bicycle.

☛ When riding on smooth paved roads be prepared for the iron tire to slip out from under you. Avoid sharp turns because of the tendency for the tire to sideslip and because of the interference with your leg caused by a sharp turn of the front wheel.

☛ If the boneshaker feels too large or too small, loosen the nuts holding the saddle in place and slide the saddle forward or back on the spring. Also on most boneshakers the pedal can be positioned in one of three holes in the crank to adjust to your leg length.

☛ When coasting, stretch your legs straight out, supporting them by the coaster bar forward of the head. If the boneshaker is not equipped with a coaster bar, hold your legs out to the sides while coasting.

☛ Do not depend on the brake to do anything more than slightly slow the machine. The only real braking effect is from backpedaling.

*Fig. 13–1.* Note position of shoe on pedal when mounting and riding the boneshaker.

### The Ordinary

*(Ordinary, Star, and Eagle riding instructions are based on articles by Charles Hetzel in* The Wheelmen *magazine).*

☛ Before learning to ride the ordinary it is desirable that you know how to ride a regular bicycle. Learning how to balance a bicycle using an ordinary would be unnecessarily dangerous and difficult. Preferably use a small ordinary to learn on. Under no circumstances should you learn on one that is so large that you cannot easily reach the pedals. Likewise, be sure the machine isn't so small that your knees will hit the handlebar.

Choose a spacious paved riding area away from cars and spectators. A slight downgrade might be helpful. Smooth grass is a suitable surface for the first Star or Eagle ride, but does not work for learning to ride the ordinary. Be sure the tires, handlebar, and grips are tight, the brake works, and that the saddle is tightened so it is free of sags. Also fix protruding saddle rivets and extraneous leather that will hamper you in mounting and dismounting. Polishing the saddle leather with clear shoe polish will make it more slippery and thus easier to slide on and off. Slide the rear saddle bracket as far back on the backbone as possible. If the step is adjustable, secure it in as high a position as is comfortable.

Check to be sure your shoestrings are tightly and closely tied. They can easily get caught in the crank, wind around the axle, and cause a spill. Clip your pant legs or fasten them with rubber bands so they will not catch anywhere on the bicycle.

1. Begin the first lesson by placing your left foot on the step, both hands on the handlebar, and push off raising your right foot as the machine begins to move. Practice this coasting from the step until you can easily balance and maneuver the machine (Fig. 13-2) .

2. To mount from the step, stand behind the ordinary, place both hands on the handlebar grips and your left foot firmly on the step. Swing the big wheel to make certain it clears your left foot. Hop along on your right foot

*Fig. 13–2.* The author demonstrates how to push off with the right foot and coast with the left foot on the step.

to develop forward momentum. When the bicycle is moving with you on the step, raise your right leg and place it around the right side of the saddle (Fig. 13-3). Reach from the step as far as is convenient, with weight thrown forward and to the left. Then carefully pull yourself the rest of the way into the saddle, tightly gripping the handlebar grips. Catch the right pedal with your right foot, being careful to keep your foot out of the spokes. Switch your left foot from the step to the left pedal. Carefully maintain balance and the forward momentum of the bicycle and then begin pedaling immediately, lightly at first, holding the machine steady until underway.

Robert McNair explained in the Wheelmen's *Learning to Ride the Ordinary* Bulletin, "It is perfectly normal to have altitude trepidations with your ordinary even though you have spent considerable time practicing mounting and dismounting. Sitting on it, while it remains still, is not the

*Fig. 13–3.* Coasting with your right leg around the saddle is the last stage of mounting.

Fig. 13–4.
Edward Berry, Jr.
demonstrates good
high speed cornering
form, back on the
saddle, elbows out,
leaning into the turn.

same as being on it while it is in motion. Should these fears exist at the time you are ready for your first ride, there is one way to eliminate them almost immediately before you place yourself in the position of riding in total fear of the machine. When attempting your first live ride, do not go all the way into the saddle when the right pedal comes up. Instead just coast a very short distance with your left foot on the step and your thigh across the seat. One or two short ventures in this position will remove any fear you may still harbor about climbing into the seat."

Once you are riding, remember that the pedals will revolve with the wheel. If you try to exert a strong back pedal force on the pedal, such as would be done on a coaster brake bicycle to work the brake, the ordinary may pivot forward in a header.

Hold the handlebar firmly enough at first so that applying pressure to the pedal does not cause the fork to turn in the same direction. Stay well back on the saddle while learning. Do not look straight down, but instead focus on the road ahead. Looking back also can throw a learner off balance. Always avoid potholes in the road, curbs, and other encumbrances that might cause a header. The ordinary tips forward extremely easily.

If you hear a noise that suggests tire or bearing trouble, or if you are approaching loose gravel or a steep downgrade, dismount and walk the bicycle. As you become more experienced with the ordinary, try to develop a relaxed grip on the handlebar and make a conscious effort to "ankle", which promotes smoother, more powerful pedaling. Ankling is similar to the rhythmic bending of the wrist when working a hand crank. At the top of the stroke your heel is downward, already pushing the pedal. At the bottom of the stroke the toe is down and the heel up.

3. To dismount, slow to a near halt, either by gingerly using the brake or by exerting a gentle backpedaling force on the pedals. Simultaneously push off with your hands and feet and spring evenly from the pedals. Keep hold of the handlebar and push away from the bicycle so as not to strike the backbone or rear wheel. You'll land on your toes directly behind the bicycle with arms straight and hands still on the handlebar. This is called the

*Fig. 13–5.* Centered on the berm and grouped in small clusters, these tourists are observing safety rules.

275

emergency dismount. It is the fastest and safest way to get off an ordinary and should be practiced time and again until it becomes automatic.

Another popular dismount that is somewhat more graceful and less jolting to the back is the step dismount which is simply the reverse of the step mount. Slide back on the saddle as far as possible and reach for the step with the left foot being careful to avoid the spokes and to keep clear of the tire as it turns side to side. When the top of the foot is firmly on the step, step back on it and spring lightly to the ground still holding the handlebar.

☞ In cornering, lean into the corner as you would on a safety, but at a somewhat greater inclination. Cornering at speed may be improved by leaning backward, shifting weight to the rear wheel (Fig. 13-4).

☞ Use the hand brake only to increase the effect of backpedaling. To backpedal, apply pressure to the pedal just as it bottoms and begins its rise. Sit back in the saddle as far as possible when backpedaling to counteract the tendency of the ordinary to pitch forward.

*Fig. 13–6.* David Gray coasts a hill, legs over the handlebars.

☞ Never coast hills when you cannot see the bottom or when there is traffic, a rough road, a sharp turn, or the possibility of traffic entering from the side. To coast, remove your feet from the pedals either by holding your legs out to the sides or by positioning your legs over the handlebar. In the latter position, if you pivot forward you will fall feet first with the bicycle to your back (Fig. 13-6). The over-the-handlebar coasting position is achieved by swinging your legs one at a time over the handlebar, and repositioning your hands on the handlebar. These procedures and other mounting and dismounting techniques and trick riding possibilities are discussed in the Summer 1970 issue of *The Wheelmen* magazine. They should be attempted only after you have become an experienced rider.

☞ Always observe the following basic safety rules:

1. Never follow close to a motorized vehicle. The benefits from the suction draft are not worth the great risk.
2. Always watch the road well ahead for surface holes, drain grates, and opening car doors. Perhaps the greatest danger is young children who are apt to ride their bicycles directly in front of your path. They do not have the skill to get out of the way.

*Fig. 13–7.* Roberta Fiene coasting on her Star.

3. Remember that in riding an ordinary you are creating a seldom-seen spectacle that will cause auto drivers to brake quickly for a better look and approaching traffic to sometimes waver while fascinated drivers stare at the bicycle.

4. Try to stay on lightly traveled secondary roads. Do not ride so close to the edge of the road that the draft of a passing vehicle might push you into the ridge between the edge of the pavement and the dirt, likely causing a fall (Fig. 13-5).

5. Never ride when visibility is poor.

6. Always follow every rule of the road. When riding in a group, leave spaces between clusters of riders and announce each approaching car. Never cross the highway center line.

### The Star

If there is a choice, learn to ride the Star before trying the Eagle as it does not require a pedal mount and can be practiced from a coasting position as with the ordinary.

Choose a small Star if possible and be certain that all the machine's safety points are in order. The brake, which must be depended upon for stopping as there is no backpedaling, and the drive straps are particularly important. Also replace the rubber pedal pads with soft new ones so your feet will not slip on the levers.

You are now ready to ride in the following steps.

1. Before mounting the Star, have the dismount procedure firmly in mind. Know just where the step is. While someone holds the Star, practice getting your foot on the step without it getting caught in the spokes. Then on the first ride, as the Star slows, reach back with the left foot putting your weight on the step and bring your right leg over the saddle. Jump to the ground landing on your toes to cushion the impact on your knees. You will find that your right hand has been released from the handlebar and you will be standing beside the Star holding it with your left hand.

   Another dismount is directly to the rear. With the Star slowed, quickly pull back on the handlebar as you vault from the saddle to the ground behind you. You will land clear of the big wheel, behind the Star holding both handlebar grips with the front wheel high in the air. An easier variation of this dismount is to place your left foot on the step or frame member just above the step and vault backward.

2. Begin mastering the Star by standing facing forward on the left side of the bicycle holding the handlebar at the grips. Place the ball of your left foot securely on the step. Develop forward momentum by hopping on your right foot. Rising to the step, lean as far forward as possible. Keep the machine steering straight ahead and on an even balance. Practice the sideways balance by coasting on the pedal on a modern coaster brake bicycle.

*Fig. 13–8.* James Woodward demonstrates the quick pullback on the handlebars to dismount.

Step to the ground as the Star slows and practice coasting again until you are perfectly comfortable with it.

3. Enlist a friend to hold the Star while you climb aboard. Adjust the saddle as far forward as possible. Once on it, lean forward over the handlebar and depress first one lever, then the other. Remember the pedals will not come around as with the rotary motion of the ordinary. Pick up your leg at the completion of the stroke in preparation for the next stroke. Have your friend hold the Star while you dismount.

*Fig. 13–9.* Eagle saddle normal riding position. *(courtesy of Greenfield Village and Henry Ford Museum)*

*Fig. 13–10.* Eagle saddle unstrung.

4. Having familiarized yourself with riding the Star in a controlled coasting position from the step, you are ready to complete the mount. With left foot securely on the step, and leaning forward over the handlebar, lift your right leg all the way over the saddle, pull up onto it, and begin pumping the levers immediately. Smooth grass is a suitable surface for the first Star or Eagle ride, but does not work for learning to ride the ordinary.

5. Remember that when on loose gravel or other surfaces that make you vulnerable to going over backward, you can land on your feet behind the machine by pulling back on the handlebar as in the rear dismount.

6. As you ride the Star, you will note that unlike the ordinary pedal crank, the ratchet drive has no distinct bottom to support your weight. Thus your hands and seat must take the full load.

Also note that levers can be used alternately or thrust simultaneously for an extra burst of speed. In hill climbing the power of the lever stroke can be increased by attaching the strap to the lever using the rearmost of two pins. Also, you can stand on the pedals, relieving your weight from the saddle. Lean forward and take short quick strokes at the bottom of the reach, which is the most powerful part of the stroke.

Readjust the saddle position rearward as you become more proficient with the Star. To coast simply cross your legs over the steering rod (Fig. 13-7).

**The Eagle**

Having become familiar with the fore, aft, and sideways balance of the Star, you are ready to try the Eagle. If you have not learned to ride the Star first, practice the sideways balance by riding the pedal of a coaster brake bicycle. Have a friend hold the Eagle while you mount and dismount so you can first learn how to ride it. Then follow this procedure to learn the mounting and dismounting.

1. Standing at the left of the Eagle, grasp the handlebar and run forward slowly. Step on the pedal with your left foot just as the pedal reaches its lowest point. Leap high from your right foot just as you place your left on the rising left pedal. Then ride the pedal up. The Eagle's forward momentum will carry you into a position to swing the right foot over the saddle and catch the pedals. Lean forward all the while. Have an assistant on the right side of the Eagle to catch you as you make your first few vaults into the saddle.

   As Charles Hetzel advised in his Winter 1972 *The Wheelmen* magazine article "Learning to Ride the Star and Eagle," "Be determined that you are going to make it into the saddle as you step and vault upward. If it appears that you are falling short of your goal and straddling the rear saddle support or big wheel is imminent, pull quickly back on the handlebar, lifting the front wheel off the ground and landing on your feet" (Fig. 13-8).

2. The pedal dismount is the easiest way off the Eagle. As the bicycle slows and either pedal reaches its lowest point, throw all of your weight on it

while at the same time bringing the other leg over the big wheel and jumping to the ground. As with the Star, you can exit directly to the rear by pulling back on the handlebar while springing backward, clearing the big wheel, and landing on your feet behind the bicycle with your hands on the handlebar and the small front wheel in the air.

3. As you become accustomed to the Eagle, adjust the saddle backward. Riding and handling is best with as little weight as possible on the front wheel. In climbing hills, the saddle can be unstrung and dropped without dismounting (Figs. 13-9, 13-10). This will put more weight on the pedals. To coast simply cross your legs over the steering rod. Additional Eagle mounts and dismounts are discussed in the Winter 1972 issue of *The Wheelmen* magazine.

**The Adult Tricycle**

What could be simpler than riding an adult tricycle? Actually the person whose riding habits have been developed on a bicycle can find it difficult to master the three wheeler. The leaning and turning that is employed to keep the two wheeler in balance, when applied to riding a tricycle, causes it to veer off course with a tendency to turn in the direction of the lean rather than following the line prescribed by the steering. The following procedures are recommended for mastering the adult tricycle.

☞ On the loop frame or two track tricycle, adjust the saddle high enough so your legs are only slightly bent at the knee when fully extended. Adjust the handles so you are bent slightly forward when your hands are grasping them. The saddle should be as far back as possible to keep your weight off the small front wheel, but not so far back that you are constantly rocking back on the tip tail. Adjust the nose of the saddle to be slightly higher than the rear portion.

☞ When riding the tricycle try to develop a swivel of the hips movement rather than a lean when negotiating turns. Practice turns, shifting your weight in different ways on the saddle until you reach the right combination for the machine.

☞ Avoid making sharp turns which, done without the correct lateral weight shift on the saddle, can cause a tip over. Sideways tip-overs on tricycles can be dangerous because you are surrounded by spinning spokes and you cannot easily extricate yourself from the machine.

☞ If the tricycle is not fitted with a chain guard, be sure to arrange your clothing so it will not get caught in the chain. At all times be very cautious to keep fingers and loose fitting clothing from getting caught in the spokes and chains.

☞ Pull up on the handles when you need leverage on the pedals. When climbing hills, rise from the saddle, pull up on the handles, and lean forward.

☞ Coasting is marvelous on an adult tricycle, but be sure the brake is in good working order. Switch your feet to the coasting position soon as the pedals rotate too fast to stay with. Make turns very smooth and gradual when descending hills and be certain that the tires are secure.

*Fig. 13–11.* Mid 1880s LAW uniform advertisement.

**Safeties**

Riding techniques discussed in the ordinary, Star, and Eagle sections apply to the riding of all high wheel safeties although preventing loose fitting pant legs from catching in the chains and levers can be even more critical when riding some high wheel safeties.

Solid and pneumatic tire safeties, although seemingly not any different from today's bicycles, do require getting used to. Observe the following suggestions for a safe and comfortable ride.

☞ Adjust the saddle high enough so your knee will be only slightly bent when the pedal is fully extended. The nose of the saddle should be slightly higher than the rear.

☞ Be sure tires are tightly glued or wired on and that handlebar grips, skirt guards and guard string, seat posts, pedals, cranks, and brake are secure. Remember, if brakes are fitted they will be only marginally effective so prepare for stops well in advance. To slow quickly in an emergency, hold the handlebar firmly and press your heel hard against the front tire. Always be on the lookout for objects in the road that will puncture the fragile tires and bend the forks and frame.

☞ To mount, stand directly behind the machine and with both hands on the handlebar, put your left foot on the step and push off with the right. When there is sufficient momentum, rise on the step and swing into the saddle.

☞ The wide handlebar, high frame, fixed drive, and rakishly angled front fork will make an early safety feel considerably different from a modern bicycle. If there is a spring suspension on the front fork, the steering is likely to feel vague. Perhaps most difficult to get accustomed to is the fixed drive with the pedals rotating with every rotation of the rear wheel.

☞ Do not forget that you are positioned higher than on a modern bicycle. Dismounting is by reaching back to the rear step and stepping off or by using a pedal dismount as on a modern bicycle, but with the difference that you must step off the pedal just before it reaches the lowest point if the bicycle has a direct drive.

☞ Do not attempt to keep your feet on the pedals during fast coasting. Place them on the coaster bars if the bicycle is so equipped or hold your legs out to the sides.

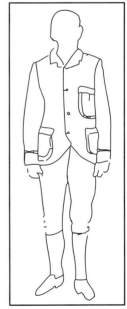

*Fig. 13–12.* The Wheelmen uniform.

## PREPARING FOR THE WHEELMEN TOUR

There are three categories of Wheelmen membership based on completion of sanctioned club tours.

Voting membership is accorded to those who successfully complete an official Wheelmen tour of ten miles on a hobby horse, boneshaker, high wheel safety, ordinary, solid tire adult tricycle, solid tire safety, or early pneumatic-tire safety.

Those who have not completed a ten mile tour are associate members and can participate in all club activities except voting. Ownership of an antique bicycle is not required; many members borrow one for the qualifying ride. Children who complete the ten mile tour are voting members. On tours, youngsters are the responsibility of their parents. Members often are surprised at the very young ages of those completing the ten miles. Also members in their 70s, whose good health in part may be due to their cycling, regularly ride ten and 100 mile tours on ordinaries.

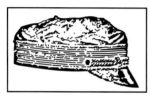

*Fig. 13–13.* Wheelmen cap.

Most meets offer a ten mile tour which usually is staged in a scenic area on lightly traveled roads with rest and refreshment stops and a sag wagon to pick up disabled bicycles or riders. Typically there will be 100 riders or more, most of whom will be riding ordinaries. They will separate into fast and average speed groups and a group riding slower machines such as boneshakers and adult tricycles.

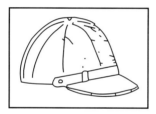

*Fig. 13–14.* Wheelmen cap.

Occasionally, special adult tricycle, boneshaker, or tandem tours will be offered. Members are encouraged in advance to bring a particular type of machine when this is planned.

In addition to checking the bicycle for safety before the tour begins, it always is a good idea to apply a few drops of light oil to the bearings. Bring a wrench and some tape along.

Century membership is accorded to members who ride any of the aforementioned classes of bicycles 100 miles in one day during the period between sun up and sun down. Century tours are offered at the Wheelmen annual meeting and at larger regional meets.

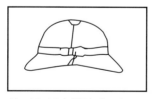

*Fig. 13–15.* LAW helmet.

To enter a century tour the bicycle must be in perfect mechanical condition. Equally important, you must condition yourself for the strain of 12 to 14 hours of continuous riding.

*Fig. 13–16.* LAW helmet.

One of the most enchanting spectacles of a Wheelmen meet is the moonlight ride during which only kerosene, candle, and carbide bicycle lamps are used.

## PARADES AND UNIFORMS

As much as anything else, parades have given The Wheelmen the national publicity that has helped the club grow and be of increasingly great service to collectors. Contributions for parade appearances are accepted and given to the state chapters or

*Fig. 13–17.* Wheelmen jacket.

*Fig. 13–18.* Wheelmen knee breeches.

national treasury for meet expenses, special projects, and the newsletter and magazine.

It is in parades that the truly national nature of most Wheelmen meets becomes apparent. Because The Wheelmen is the only American organization for collectors of early bicycles, members come from coast-to-coast to most major parades and meets, wearing the uniforms and carrying the pennants of their state chapters.

The tradition of a distinctive uniform goes back to the original LAW of the 1880s (Fig. 13-11). Today The Wheelmen has established a standard uniform pattern involving a cap, white shirt, ribbon tie, snug fitting knee breeches, long stockings, dark shoes, and an optional jacket (Fig. 13-12). Men, women, and children riding any machine up to a pneumatic tire safety wear this club uniform. Because the club has not yet contracted with a uniform supplier, each family is responsible for making its own uniforms.

According to the Wheelmen bulletin on uniforms, there were four principal uniform cap styles. Figures 13-13 and 13-14 were caps made of corduroy or cloth while Figs. 13-15 and 13-16 are helmets with corduroy covering. Figure 13-13 is typical of the cap worn today by most members of The Wheelmen. The deerstalker cap can be modified to resemble the LAW helmet. Approved safety helmets are required for field events.

A standard white shirt (long sleeved affords better protection in a fall) is prescribed for most chapter uniforms. A ribbon tie about 43" long, 2" wide and pointed at both ends is often worn tied with a simple loop knot. Make the tie

*Fig. 13–19.* Paul Knudson, foreground, showing the proper Wheelmen uniform.

from a hard finish cloth and be sure the color won't run if it gets wet. Bind the edges so it won't fray.

A dark belt, usually black and always the same color as the shoes, is worn in the knee breeches. Shoes should have a stiff composite sole rather than leather and should fit snugly to give a secure purchase on the tiny mounting steps. Shoes with the appearance of modern cycling shoes are ideal, but the soles have to be redone to get rid of the cleats.

Begin making the knee breeches (Fig. 13-18) by buying a pair of pants that have enough room in the seat so they won't split out with the stretching and bending you will do in mounting and dismounting. If you sew a rein-

Fig. 13–20. These cyclists are dressed in 1890s cycling apparel.

forcement into the seat of the breeches, avoid seams that would cause discomfort when riding.

Open the side seam all the way to the pocket to taper the legs for a snug fit. Before cutting the leg, put on the pants and long stockings and lift your foot to the bicycle step to see how far the pants are going to pull up. Your knee should not be exposed between the stocking and the end of the pants. When resewing the seams, be sure the legs fit snugly, but not so tightly as to prevent them from sliding up and down. To complete the making of the breeches, make three buttonholes on the outside edge at the bottom, positioning them one above the other. Sew on the buttons. When finished, the top one is right at the knee and there is no bagginess anywhere in the leg.

Fig. 13–21. Dorothy Conant on her Royal Salvo tricycle.

Reproductions of 1880s LAW buttons have been produced by The Wheelmen. Six small ones are needed for the breeches.

Try to find stockings that extend above the knee. If this is not possible, one method of preventing a gap between the stocking and the breeches is to sew a replacement girdle buckle on the inside of the pant leg at the bottom both on

*Fig. 13–22.* Bugler Robert McNair and Former National Commander Edwin Gerling flying the Illinois pennant lead a Wheelmen parade unit. *(courtesy of The Free Lance Star, Fredericksburg, VA)*

the front and back. Attach the stocking to the buckles. The added stitching will strengthen the knee area and the stocking and breeches will slide as a unit returning to normal position when the knee is not flexed. Another method is to use safety pins to attach the breeches and the top of the stockings. The disadvantage of this method of course is that the pins may tear the stockings.

The optional jacket (Fig. 13-17) gives a more formal appearance to the uniform. Jackets are close fitting and are suggestive of the military tunic. They should match the breeches in color and material and should use the larger reproduction LAW buttons on the front, the smaller ones on the sleeves. The complete uniform should look like the one worn by Paul Knudson in the foreground in Fig. 13-19.

The standard Wheelmen uniform does not apply to women riding adult tricycles or to anyone riding pneumatic tire safeties. Styles of the 1890s with knickers and baggy caps for the men and divided skirts, bloomers, "leg of mutton" sleeve jackets, high buttoned shoes, and natty hats for the women (Fig. 13-20) should be duplicated as closely as possible. The riding of tricycles in the 1880s (Fig. 13-21) and bicycles in the 1890s was seen by women as an opportunity to wear the latest styles. Summer 1971 and November 1979 issues of *The Wheelmen* magazine provide useful information on these costumes.

Once you have acquired the proper wearing apparel, you are ready to join the Wheelmen in a parade. It is advisable to arrive at the staging area early enough to practice some of the basic club formations and learn the simple bugle signals that are used. The Wheelmen has carried on the LAW tradition of communicating with the long ranks of riders by bugle signals. The bugler will usually ride at the head of the parade with the host captain and national commander (Fig. 13-22).

Because of the stop and start nature of most parades, numerous formations such as intersecting circles (Fig. 13-23) and interweaving lines are used. They provide a colorful and entertaining spectacle for viewers and enable riders to stay on the bicycles. The success of its appearance has won The Wheelmen participation in nearly all the nation's major parades.

A good way to ready yourself for the first parade is to practice figure eights on an ordinary on a two lane residential street. Learn to speed up and slow

*Fig. 13–23.* Practicing interweaving circles.

down smoothly and quickly. Practice to achieve a graceful and quick mounting and dismounting style with only a couple short hops of the right foot and concentrate on riding erect, steering with one hand on the handlebar, and dismounting on command.

Unusual bicycles, such as boneshakers, pacing multicycles, and even Ingo-Bikes, are crowd pleasing additions to Wheelmen parade appearances.

## FIELD EVENTS

As with all Wheelmen meet activities, field events offer every member of the family from the youngest to the oldest the opportunity to participate. In

*Fig. 13–24.* The hands off race. Note the rider on the right is wearing a modern cycling head protector. Currently, helmets are required on participatants in Wheelmen field events.

addition to being entertaining and fun, field events help riders develop their riding skill.

Perhaps the most exciting field events are the races. Hands off, slow, and speed races are held for ordinaries with classes for youngsters, women, and men.

*Fig. 13–25.* Youngsters get an early start on learning how to navigate the obstacle course run.

*Fig. 13–26.* The shoulder brace. These bicycles are stopped!

Separate Star, solid tire safety, pneumatic tire safety, tandem, adult tricycle, and Ingo-Bike races also are held.

The hands-off speed race for ordinaries begins from a running start. As they cross the starting line, all riders must have their hands off the handlebar (Fig. 13-24). Any rider whose hands return to the handlebar is disqualified by club spotters positioned around the track.

Surprisingly high speeds are attainable in the race due to the ease with which most ordinaries may be ridden hands off by keeping your knees close to the front fork.

The ordinary slow race tests your balancing ability under this most difficult riding circumstance. Organized in heats, three riders at a time begin from a running start. The last rider to reach the finish line while staying in his lane wins. At the hands of accomplished riders, some ordinaries can be held almost completely still.

Speed races usually are run on two mile oval tracks. The Wheelmen use a running start rather than the fixed start employed by the Southern Veteran Cycle Club of England. Track, bicycle, and rider safety is stressed. In a July 1972 *Wheelmen Bulletin,* Charles Hetzel established the following rules for antique bicycle racing:

There should be no racing on tracks of less than one-fourth mile circumference unless the race is a straight-line sprint. If the racing surface is paved, all loose cinders or other debris must be removed. The tires must be tight and there should be no loose spokes.

There must be no play in the handlebars, cranks, or pedals. Bearing cones must be adjusted so there is no play in the front wheel bearings, the rim must be sound, and the bicycle must be inspected for these points at every meet where it is raced. Shirt and pants must be of corduroy or material of equivalent weight or, at the option of the rider, he must wear knee and elbow pads. All riders must wear padded head protective gear or cycling helmets and should wear gloves.

All rules of the road are in force during a race. When overtaking another rider, the person intending to pass must give an adequate and audible warning of his intention. All passing is done to the left of the rider being overtaken. In turn the rider being passed must move to his right sufficiently so that the passing cyclist has adequate room to pass in safety. The passing rider shall allow ample room between himself and the rider just passed before cutting in, so as not to impede the progress of the rider just passed. No rider is to turn to look behind during the course of the race.

The obstacle course run (Fig. 13-25) utilizes a pattern of pylons laid out like a short ski slalom. Points are added to the rider's time for touching any pylon with the bicycle wheel. The rider with the shortest time wins.

The couple's race requires that three men stand at one end of a straight line that is divided into three lanes and three women at the other end. On signal the women mount, ride to the men, dismount, the men mount, and the first one back to the starting line wins for that couple.

Riding the plank involves riding onto and staying on a 1" flat wood plank about 3" wide and 5' or more long with the ends angle cut.

Most Wheelmen meets involve several public riding demonstrations. Step, standing start, and pedal ordinary mounts and step, pedal, emergency, and over-the-handlebar ordinary dismounts are shown. Mounting and dismounting such high wheel safeties as the Eagle and Star are shown and the driving mechanisms of such machines as the Facile and Kangaroo are demonstrated.

A highlight of the public demonstrations is trick riding. Skilled wheelmen show tricks handed down from the 1880s such as standing on the saddle, riding sidesaddle and with legs in the air, shoulder braces (Fig. 13-26), hands-off figure eights, and one-wheel riding of the Eagle.

During the winter months, The Wheelmen sponsor memorabilia meets usually at museums. Members show such diversified reminders of cycling's golden age as silver match safes enameled with a bicycle and rider and fine cycling prints. Tours of members' collections also are organized in winter months.

Periodically major special events are sponsored by The Wheelmen. In 1976 a 750 mile tour from Dearborn, Michigan, to Independence Hall in Philadelphia was held in observation of the American bicentennial and the 100th anniversary of the first showing of an ordinary in America. In 1980 The Wheelmen participated in the 100th anniversary of the founding of the LAW at observances in Newport, Rhode Island. Also that year the club sponsored a two week tour of England during which members visited museum and private bicycle collections and participated in a Southern Veteran Cycle Club of England antique bicycle tour. In more recent years the club has sponsored several trips to European antique bicycle meets.

Having familiarized yourself with the activities of The Wheelmen and readied the uniform or bicycling costume for participation in club activities, you will need to make plans for getting bicycles to and from meets and for exhibiting them securely while on display. Most members bring several machines to meets for both riding and show.

## GETTING AROUND

The simplest and preferable way to transport ordinaries and other antique bicycles and tricycles is by van. A 52" ordinary will go through the side door of a typical American van and will rest at an angle in the back without having to be taken apart. Larger wheel sizes will require that ordinaries be taken apart at the head or at the end of the front fork (Fig. 13-27). Avoid removing pedals, handlebars and other components any more frequently than necessary to reduce wear on parts and to help prevent loosening of parts.

Another good transporting method is to carry the bicycles in a small trailer. Small rental trailers will carry three fully assembled ordinaries. It is necessary to brace the wheels and to tie the bicycles firmly. Be certain they are not touching each other at any point.

A pickup truck also is serviceable but does not have the advantage of protection from the weather and curious onlookers.

Many wheelmen carry their bicycles on car roof racks with the large wheel placed on an inflated inner tube (Fig. 13-28).

### How To Build a Carrier

A final method is to construct a carrier for the back of the vehicle. It can be made to fit any size car or truck (Fig. 13-29). A bracket should be made to bolt to the frame under the bumper. Welded to the bracket is a piece of about 1⅞" tubing cut to a length of about 9". A slightly smaller diameter tubing of about 38" length then slides into the bracket tube about 5". By using mating tubes you can easily remove the carrier. The bracket tubes should not extend past the rear of the car body and should be set in a few inches from the rear bumper so they will not be hit and bent out of position.

To the bracket tube weld two or more pieces of 2" channel iron, one piece for each bicycle to be carried on the rack. The channel iron should be about 64" long which will permit a typical pneumatic tire tandem to be transported and

*Fig. 13–27.* Taking the ordinary apart at the end of the fork to transport it.

should be welded in place perpendicular to the bracket tubing each piece no less than 12" apart (Fig. 13-30). This will permit you to carry bicycles side-by-side without having to disassemble them.

An upright frame to which the bicycles are tied must be mounted firmly to the carrier. Make it detachable so as to allow access to the rear of the vehicle without having to remove the entire rack (Fig. 13-31). I prefer having the upright between the channel irons for ease of tying two bicycles (Fig. 13-32).

*Fig. 13–28.* An inner tube works equally well for an ordinary or safety and can be used on a car top carrier or a station wagon.

*Fig. 13–29.* Alex Pollack demonstrates that an ordinary can be transported with any size car.

Complete the carrier by painting it white so it will be visible at night for pedestrians and vehicles. Fix strips of reflectorized tape to the sides and back and add strips of adhesive foam tape to each inner side of the channel iron and the vertical frame to help guard against scratching the bicycles.

Secure the bicycles using heavy rubber straps in good condition that have hooks on each end. Stout rope tightly tied may be used. Be sure to tie the rims down to the channel iron so the bicycle cannot bounce out of the rack. A good case-hardened and rubber-covered chain and lock is necessary if the vehicle is

*Fig. 13–30.* The carrier with upright detached. Note bracket tubes under van bumper. That portion of the carrier tubes that slides into the brackets is a darker color and is nearer the van.

Fig. 13–31.
A method for
making the upright
detachable.

Fig. 13–32.
The carrier
installed with the
upright attached.
Note that it must
extend some
distance from the
bumper so
bicycles will not hit
the spare tire.

parked unattended. Remove a hub lamp or any other accessory that can easily be stolen. Use tin foil or plastic to completely enclose the saddle in the event of rain. Nothing is more uncomfortable than a wet saddle. Remember that the bicycle must not be covered with a material that will obscure rear vision, the tail lights, or license plate.

Although the rear mounted rack is convenient to use, it is vulnerable to being hit and carrying bicycles at the rear of a vehicle tends to get them very dirty.

**Exhibit Stands**

Once at the meet, you will exhibit the bicycles on the display area which may be grass or an indoor gym floor. The owner is responsible for providing his own display stands.

Transporting and exhibiting bicycles requires a lot of thought, care, and planning. Antique bicycles are damaged more from loading and unloading, transporting, and falling while on exhibit than by years of riding. It is especially critical that the bicycle be held securely when on exhibit at a meet because if one falls over it likely will start a chain reaction with the whole line of bicycles falling. Broken handlegrips, bent handlebars and cranks, chipped paint, and disappointed owners will result.

The most common stand for high wheel bicycles is a replica of an original one (Fig. 13-33). It is lightweight and separates into two pieces for ease in transporting, but you must be very cautious not to step on the center portion or it

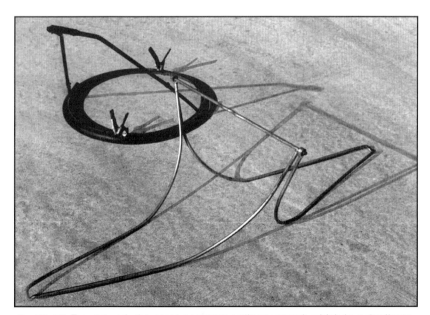

*Fig. 13–33.* Foreground, the most common ordinary stand, which is a duplicate of the original. Background, the author's favorite stand, which is made from a steel hoop.

will spring open, releasing the bicycle. When using it, always tie the rim to the stand at both ends.

The author's favorite stand is one made from a steel hoop about 1" thick and about 22" in diameter to which is welded a sturdy V shaped brace about 38" long. The wheel rests in two V-shaped channels and is supported by the brace. This stand is very sturdy and can be made with the base detachable for ease in transporting. Held by these stands, bicycles may be displayed very close to each other, which is an advantage is displaying them in a limited space.

Smaller versions of both these stands can be used for exhibiting safeties. Put the safety front wheel in the stand and there will not be the problem of the wheel moving about and knocking the bicycle over.

Two modern stands, available at bicycle shops, also may be used with many pneumatic tire antique bicycles. The one grasps the bicycle by the down tube and lifts the rear wheel. This rests the weight on the crank hanger and holds the rear wheel off the ground supported by two angled legs. The second unfolds in a scissor motion and grasps the rear axle. The hoop type is more stable than either of these, but the modern stands work well for indoor display. When using the modern stands the bicycles should be tied to them.

Always be on the lookout for hard to find original safety stands such as the one shown in Fig. 13-34.

*Fig. 13–34.* An original safety stand.

# Chapter 14:
# How To Form a Collection

There are as many ways to collect antique bicycles as there are collectors. The most common American collection approaches are the ones that will be discussed.

First are the rider-collectors. Their goal is to have a rideable bicycle, usually an ordinary, for everyone in the family. Often they will not restore the finish on their machines, but will keep them in safe condition. Most Wheelmen collections are in this category.

The second most popular collection is the one motivated by what appeals personally to the collector. If they happen to find a particular bicycle that is interesting to them they buy it, even though it may not necessarily fit into an overall collecting scheme. This collector is apt to emphasize ordinaries, but also have a few other types.

One of the most interesting and challenging collections is the one that traces the evolution of the bicycle. Relatively few machines are required to do this, but many of these are very difficult to find.

Some collections are organized around a single type of bicycle. One wheelman collects only solid tire safeties. An interesting collection also can be formed around a particular maker. Most bicycle variations from the ordinary on could be assembled in a collection of machines made by the Pope Manufacturing Company, for example.

A variation of the single type or maker collector is the one assembled by a person who owns an antique automobile that was built by a bicycle maker such as Pierce Arrow. That person might be interested only in Pierce bicycles and memorabilia.

A recent phenomenon, particularly on the American West Coast, are the nostalgia collectors whose interest is in the balloon tire bicycles they rode as a youth.

Increasingly, collectors are searching for the fascinating cycling memorabilia. Such items as prints, posters, snuff boxes, watches, books, steins, trophies, name badges, and toys that have a bicycle decoration or motif were popular from the hobby horse era until 1900. These are important reminders of the social impact of the bicycle (Fig. 14-1, 14-2).

Fig. 14–1. Cycling memorabilia ranges from buttons to this Stearns bicycle shipping box shown by Fred Fisk.

Fig. 14–2. This collector exhibits his bicycles with old bicycle signs and other memorabilia.

*Fig. 14–3.* This collector combines his bicycles with other antiques.

Be sure to exhibit the collection in a clean dry area. Fine prints should be framed using acid-free matting available at art shops.

Bicycles are most interesting when they are exhibited upright; however, hanging them bottom-side-up from hooks screwed into the ceiling and looped through the rims is satisfactory. One collector exhibits his bicycles with cycling signs and memorabilia (Fig. 14-2); another combines his with other antiques (Fig. 14-3).

Bicycles sitting upright should have their tires turned every few weeks to prevent flat spots. The nickel should be polished with Simichrome, paint should be touched up, light oil may be sprayed into hollow forks and backbones, and all should be waxed at least once a year.

Do not overlook insurance on antique bicycles and memorabilia. A standard homeowners policy probably will not be adequate. Antique bicycle collections qualify for fine arts policies which should be discussed with an insurance agent.

It is a good idea to keep a file on each bicycle, listing such data as purchase price and work that has been done along with photos and information documenting its authenticity. Also keep a photo of each bicycle in a secure place outside the home if your collection is insured.

Throughout the writing of this book I have looked forward to concluding with my idea of a dream collection. With the smallest possible number of machines, the collection would show the pre-1900 evolution of the bicycle and tricycle.

For whatever it is worth, here it is. Hopefully my reasoning in selecting these examples will be clear.

- c. 1818 hobbyhorse marked Denis Johnson, England.
- 1860 quadricycle marked Sawyer, England.
- 1866 boneshaker marked Michaux, France.
- 1871 Ariel ordinary, England.
- 1877 Coventry lever adult tricycle, England.
- 1878 Columbia ordinary, United States.
- 1878 Facile high wheel safety, England.
- 1880 Royal Salvo adult tricycle, England.
- 1882 Pony Star, United States.
- 1883 Kangaroo dwarf safety, England.
- 1886 Rover solid tire safety, England.
- 1887 New Mail Light Roadster ordinary, United States.
- 1887 Starley Psycho solid tire tandem, England.
- 1891 Columbia ladies' safety, United States.
- 1891 Victor cushion tire safety, United States.
- 1897 Van Cleve pneumatic tire safety, United States.

# Bibliography

Bartleet, Horace Wilton. *Bartleet's Bicycle Book*. London: Ed. J. Burrow & Co., Ltd., 1931.

Caunter, C.F. *Handbook of the Collection Illustrating Cycles*. London: Her Majesty's Stationery Office, 1958.

———— *The History and Development of Cycles*. London: Her Majesty's Stationery Office, 1972.

Dodge, Pryor. *The Bicycle*. Paris, New York: Flammarion Press. 1996.

Evans, David E. *The Ingenious Mr. Pedersen*. Dursley: Alan Sutton, 1978.

Fisk, Fred C. and Todd, Marlin W. *The Wright Brothers: From Bicycle to Biplane*. 1990.

Geist, Roland C. *Bicycle People*. Washington, DC: Acropolis Books, Ltd., 1978.

Griffin, Harry Hewitt. *Bicycles and Tricycles of the Year 1886*. London: L. Upcott Gill, 1886. Reprinted Yorkshire: The Scolar Press, Ltd., 1971.

Hillier, G. Lacy. *The Badminton Library of Sports and Pastimes, Cycling*. London: Longmans, Green & Co., 1889.

Humber, William. *Freewheeling: The Story of Bicycling in Canada*. Erin: Boston Mills Press, 1986.

Hurd, James and Pridmore, Jay. *The American Bicycle*. 1995.

Leonard, Irving A. *When Bikehood Was In Flower*. South Tamworth: Bearchamp Press, 1969.

Palmer, Arthur Judson. *Riding High*. New York: E.P. Dutton & Co., Inc., 1956.

Perry, David B. *Bike Culture: The Ultimate Guide to Human Powered Vehicles*. New York: Four Walls, Eight Windows.

Pratt, Charles E. *The American Bicycler: A Manual*. Boston: Rockwell & Churchill, 1880.

Ritchie, Andrew. *Major Taylor*. Bicycle Books, Inc. 1988.

———— *King of the Road*. London: Wildwood House Ltd., 1975.

Roberts, Derek. *The Invention of Bicycles and Motorcycles.* London: Usborne Pub. Ltd., 1975.

Sharp, Archibald. *Bicycles & Tricycles.* London: Longmans, Green & Co., 1896. Reprinted Cambridge: The MIT Press, 1977.

Smith, Robert A. *A Social History of the Bicycle.* New York: American Heritage Press, 1972.

Stevens, Thomas. *Around The World on a Bicycle, Vol. 1.* New York: Charles Scribner's Sons, 1887.

Sturmey, Henry. *Indispensable Bicyclist's Handbook.* Weymouth: H. A. Judd, 1879.

——— *Tricyclists' Indespensable Annual.* London: Iliffe & Son, 1884.

Taylor, Marshall W. *The Fastest Bicycle Rider in the World.* Brattleboro: Stephen Greene Press, 1972.

"Velox," *Velocipedes, Bicycles and Tricycles.* London: George Routledge & Sons, 1869, Reprinted Yorkshire: Scolar Press Ltd., 1971.

Williamson, Geoffrey. *Wheels Within Wheels.* London: The Chaucer Press, Ltd., 1966.

Anonymous. *Bicycling 1874, A Textbook for Early Riders.* London: Tinsley Bros., 1874. Reprinted London: David & Charles, Ltd., 1970.

Anonymous. *Fifty Years of Schwinn Built Bicycles.* Chicago: Arnold, Schwinn & Co., 1945.

## PERIODICALS

Periodicals used in research include *The Boneshaker* by the Southern Veteran Cycle Club, several issues.

*The LAW Bulletin & Good Roads,* by the League of American Wheelmen, several issues, 1897–1899.

*The Moulton Cyclist,* by the Moulton Bicycle Club, issues 2, 3 and 4, 1975.

*The Referee and Cycle Trade Journal by* the Referee Pub. Co., Chicago, April 9, 1896.

*Scientific American,* several issues, 1880s and 1890s.

*The Wheel & Cycling Trade Review* by F.P. Prial Co., New York, Feb. 2, 1894 and Oct. 23, 1896.

*The Wheelmen* magazine by The Wheelmen, several issues.

*The Wheelmen Bulletin,* several numbers.

Manufacturer's catalogs include Bronco, 1890; Columbia, 1879–1900; Dursley Pedersen, 1907; Eagle, 1889–1891; Elliott Hickory, 1892; Facile, 1885; Gormully & Jeffery, 1885–1890, 1893, 1895, 1900; Humber, 1886–1888; Lu-Mi-Num, 1894; New Mail, 1888, 1889; New Rapid, 1887; Otto, 1885; Reading, 1900; Rudge, 1885–1888; Singer, 1887; Springfield Roadster, 1887–1889; St. Nicholas, 1887, 1889; Star, 1886–1889; Union, 1891; Victor, 1884–1898; Warwick, 1889; White Flyer, 1890.

Distributor and dealer catalogs include H.B. Hart, 1884, 1885; E. L. Horsman, 1884; Llewellyn Johnson, 1886, 1890; George Rouse, 1885–1887; Rouse Hazard, 1889, 1892; A. G. Spalding, 1883, 1885; W. W. Stall, 1887, 1889; Stoddard Lovering, 1886; John Wilkinson, 1885.

In addition, more than 2000 advertisements and clippings from the period 1880 to 1900 were consulted.

# Appendix A:
# Directories

### DIRECTORY OF AMERICAN MUSEUMS EXCLUSIVELY DEVOTED TO BICYCLES

Pedaling History – the Burgwardt Bicycle Museum
  3943 North Buffalo Road    (716) 662 - 3853
  Orchard Park, NY 14127-1841  Fax: (716) 662 - 4594
  E-mail: bicyclemus@aol.com   Carl F. Burgwardt, Clarice H. Burgwardt

The Bicycle Museum of America, Chicago, Illinois 60611

### RESOURCES FOR BICYCLE INFORMATION
### EXHIBITING FEW, IF ANY, BICYCLES

American Bicycle and Cycling Museum
  Box 8533
  Santa Fe, New Mexico 87504

Bicycle Racing Hall of Fame
  166 West Main Street
  Somerville, New Jersey  08876

League of American Bicyclists
  190 W. Ostend Avenue, Suite 120
  Baltimore, MD

Mountain Bike Hall of Fame and Museum
  PO Box 845
  126 Elk Avenue
  Crested Butte, Colorado  81224

National Bicycle History Archive
  PO Box 28242
  Santa Ana, California  92799

## Directory of American Museums Exhibiting some Antique Bicycles

**Bicycle History Museum & Gift Shop**, Old Boise, Idaho 83702
**Carillon Park** (reproduction Wright Cycle Shop), Dayton, Ohio
**The Franklin Institute**, Philadelphia, Pennsylvania
**Greenfield Village** (original Wright Cycle Shop), Dearborn, Michigan
**Henry Ford Museum**, Dearborn, Michigan
**Museum Wharf, Boston**, Massachusetts
**San Antonio Museum of Transportation**, San Antonio, Texas
**Smithsonian Institution**, Museum of History and Technology, Wash., DC
**Three Oaks Spokes Bicycle Museum**, Three Oaks, MI

## Directory of Foreign Museums Exclusively Devoted to Bicycles

**Bicycle Culture Center**, Tokyo, Japan
**Christchurch Tricycle Museum**, Christchurch, England
**Edinburgh Royal Scottish Museum**, Edinburgh, Scotland
**Mark Hall Cycle Museum and Gardens**, Harlow, England
**Museum of Historical Cycling**, Camelford, England
**Oldenburger Fahrradmuseum**, Oldenburg, Germany
**National Bicycle Museum Velorama**, Nijmegen, The Netherlands

## Directory of Foreign Museums Exhibiting some Antique Bicycles

**Beaulieu National Motor Museum**, England
**Belfast Ulster Museum**, Belfast, Ireland
**Biggleswade Shuttleworth Collection at Old Warden Aerodrome**, UK
**Buisset Bicycle Museum**, Cadouin, France
**Castle Donnington**, The Donnington Collection, UK
**Chateau de Compiegne**, France
**Chedder Motor and Transport Museum**, UK
**Coventry Museum**, Coventry, England
**Falmignoul**, Belgium Museum of the Bicycle, Belgium
**Glasgow Museum of Transport**, Glasgow, Scotland
**Heidelberg Museum**, the Chapman Collection, Heidelberg, South Africa
**Henri Malarte Auto Musée**, Rochrtaille, France
**Horsham Museum**, Horsham, England

Lincoln Bicycle Museum, Lincoln, England

London Science Museum, London, England

Musée d'Art-Industrie, St. Etienne, France

St. Fagans Welsh Folk Museum, Wales

#### DIRECTORY OF ORGANIZATIONS AND PERIODICALS FOR ANTIQUE BICYCLE COLLECTORS

California *Balloon Bicycle* and *Whizzer News,* Box 765, Huntington Beach, California, 92648

Moulton Bicycle Club, *Moulton Cyclist,* David Sanders, 59 Sweetpool Lane, Hagley, West Midlands, DY8 2XA, England

The International Veteran Cycle Association, *The International Veteran Cyclist,* Treasurer Valerie Dalzell Pears, 22 Woodbank Road, Groff, Leicester, LE6 0BN, England

Southern Veteran Cycle Club of England, *The Boneshaker* and *News and Views.* Treasurer Douglas Marchant, 1 Pope's Grove, Shirley, Croydon, Surrey, CR 8AX, England

The Wheelmen, *The Wheelmen* magazine, *The Wheelmen Newsletter,* Treasurer, Mrs. Mary Peoples, 55 Bucknell Avenue, Trenton, New Jersey, 08619-2059

#### DIRECTORY OF RESTORATION INFORMATION

Wheelmen Bulletins available to members

| Number | Bulletin Title |
|---|---|
| 1 | Advice On Buying a High Wheel Bicycle |
| 2 | Learning to Ride the Ordinary |
| 3 | Restoration |
| 3a | Restoration Data Sheets |
| 4 | Mounting Tires on High Wheels |
| 5 | The Bicycle uniform from Head to Foot |
| 5a | Current Wheelmen State Uniforms |
| 6 | Bicycle Bugles and Bugling |
| 7 | Nickel, Bright, and Gun Blue Finishes |
| 8 | How to Organize a Wheelmen Meet |
| 8a | Sample Feature Story for Release 2 Weeks Before Event |
| 8b | Follow-up Sample Feature Story for Release 1 Week Before Event |
| 9 | Parade Riding |
| 10 | Making Leather Saddles for the Ordinary |
| 11 | Wood Finishing, Rim Straightening, and Bleaching |
| 12 | The Story of Bicycling in America |
| 13 | Research Your Antique Bicycles Before Restoring |
| 14 | Rules of the Road for OHWT and Century Tours |

## BOOKS

*The Restoration of Veteran Cycles,* F.R. Whitt, 1979, available from the Southern Veteran Cycle Club, 383 Wanstead Park Rd., llford, Essex, 161 3TT, England

*Collecting and Restoring Antique Bicycles,* G. Donald Adams, Pedaling History, 3943 North Buffalo Road, Orchard Park, NY 14127-1841, USA

# Appendix B:
# Resources & Services

At the time of publishing, the following sources of suppliers and restoration services are known to the publisher. The publisher makes no guarantee nor warranty for such services and these resources may change from time to time. Please also realize that these resources may not be able to handle nor accept an additional or increased volume of work as many of them do this as a hobby and do not wish to make full-time work of it. Please respect their wishes.

From time to time these resources may change and new ones become available. The publisher will maintain a current directory of these resources, which you may obtain by sending $1.00 and a self-addressed, stamped envelope to **Pedaling History–the Burgwardt Bicycle Museum, at 3943 North Buffalo Road; Orchard Park, NY 14127-1841; (716) 662-3853; e-mail: bicyclemus@aol.com** and requesting *The Antique Bicycle Restoration Resource List.*

Persons interested in being listed should register in writing with the museum to be included on this list, at no cost. The publisher may require references of unknown new resources.

Note: the numbers after each name in Resources correspond to each particular type of work listed in the Services section below.

### SERVICES
1. Restorations, complete and partial
2. Appraisals
3. Cleaning and preserving
4. Making - Pedals
5. Making - Spoke nipples (long for wood rims)
6. Machining

7. Making - Brake hardware
8. Making - Handlebar grips, ordinary double grips
9. Making - Handlebar grips, ordinary pear-shaped grips
10. Making - Handlebar grips, leather and cork
11. Making - Mudguards, chainguards (wood)
12. Plating (nickel)
13. Making - Rims (new duplicating original)
14. Saddle cutting template
15. Making - Saddle pans and hardware
16. Saddle leather work
17. Sandblasting or glass beading
18. Making - Spokes, single and double butted
19. Spoking and truing wheels
20. Making - Stands
21. Making - Steps
22. Tire Mounting
23. Making - Tire mounting device
24. Making - Tires, new single tube pneumatic
25. Making - Tires, wired-on $\frac{7}{16}$" to $1\frac{1}{2}$"
26. Making - Reproductions
27. Research
28. Illustration - Bicycle Specialties

**RESOURCES**

1. G. Donald Adams      2, 3, 27
   e-mail: da5210@aol.com

2. Carl Burgwardt      2, 3, 27
   Pedaling History—the Burgwardt Bicycle Museum
   3943 North Buffalo Road
   Orchard Park, NY  14127-1841
   e-mail: bicyclemus@aol.com

3. Coker Tire Company      24
   1317 Chestnut Street
   Chattanooga, TN  37402

4. Larry Davala      1, 2, 3, 4, 5, 6, 7, 9, 10, 11, 12, 14,
   18 D Evert Court      15, 16, 17, 18, 19, 20, 21, 22, 23,
   Princeton, NJ  08540-1718      25, 27

5.  Bill Gindele                                12
    National Metal Finishing Corp.
    175 Progress Ave.
    Springfield, MA 01104

6.  Richard Griffin                             10, 11
    3625 Emery Road
    Adrian, MI 49221-9519

7.  Richard Hammel                             22, 25
    970 Ray Street
    RR1, Box 17
    Huntington, IN 46750-1246

8.  Harper Machine Company                     24
    1329 Dunbar Avenue
    Dunbar, WV 25064

9.  Art Hart                                    9
    396 North Road
    Chester, NJ 07930-2327

10. Lowell Kennedy                             1, 3, 4, 6, 7, 8, 9, 10, 11, 13, 14,
    RR1, 19173 State Route 18 West             15, 16, 17, 18, 19, 20, 21, 22, 23,
    Defiance, OH 43512-9776                    25, 26

11. Memory Lane Classics                       26
    12551 Jefferson Street
    Perrysburg, OH 43551

12. George Retseck                             28
    310 Maple Avenue
    Doylestown, PA 18901
    e-mail: retillus@aol.com

13. Jesse Sarafin                             23
    163 Dorain Lane
    Rochester, NY 14626-1907

14. The Spillane Family                        1, 2, 4, 6, 7, 13, 17, 18, 21, 22, 25, 26
    85 Nortontown Rd.
    Madison, CT 06443-1937

15.  Universal Tire Company          24
     987 Stony Battery Road
     Lancaster, PA  17601

16.  Bill Warwood                    18
     104 W. Hiram
     Barberton, OH  44203

# Appendix C:
# 2100 American Brands

*Based on a compilation by Dr. Charles Hetzel.*
*Reprinted with the permission of The Wheelmen.*

ompiled from manufacturers' catalogs, advertisements, trade listings, and head badges found on bicycles, this directory includes the manufacturer (M) or distributor (D) for 2,100 brands of bicycle made in America between 1890 and 1918, the latest date of manufacture included in The Wheelmen's era of interest. The dates given in the last two columns are the earliest date that a name is known to have been used, and the latest use of that name; if only one date is given, it is the only year we are sure of. Where the same brand name is given two different date ranges, it is because we could not be certain that it was used continuously. Dates in italics are known to be the first year the bicycle was manufactured. Dates listed may not be the only years an entry was manufactured. The Wheelmen organization is continuing to refine and expand the directory as new information becomes available, and the Publisher, too, welcomes your contributions to this list.

Note that company names were often inconsistently presented to the public, so that, for example, "R. J. Middleton & Sons Hardware & Bicycle Manufacturing Company of Chicago" might appear in a catalog listing, but the bicycle's small head badge might read "Middleton Cyc. Wks. Cicero". It is hard to ascertain at this late date whether it is the same company, although it very well may be since Cicero is a suburb of Chicago. And of course company names might change over the years but remain essentially the same operation, or a different company might take over a name. Model names might be used discontinuously by the same or different companies, and it was not uncommon for a brand name to be used by two or more companies in the same year.

Despite the difficulties, this listing of 2,100 American bicycle brand names (including a few from Canada) is by far the most comprehensive ever published.

| Bicycle Brand | Manufacturer or Distributor | Company | City | ST | Date of First Notice |
|---|---|---|---|---|---|
| 310 Special | M | G. Hilsendegen | Detroit | MI | 1896 |
| 410 | M | Winnie Mach. Works | Chicago | IL | 1898 |
| 999 | M | Cuba Bicycle Works | Cuba | NY | 1898 |
| Abelard | D | Hibbard, Spencer & Bartlett Co. | Chicago | IL | 1896 |
| Acme | M | Acme Cycle Co. | Elkhart | IN | 1896 1898 |
| Acme Crown | D | Sears, Roebuck & Co. | Chicago | IL | 1898 |
| Acme Jewel | D | Sears, Roebuck & Co. | Chicago | IL | 1898 |
| Acme King | D | Sears, Roebuck & Co. | Chicago | IL | 1898 |
| Acme Prince | D | Sears, Roebuck & Co. | Chicago | IL | 1898 |
| Acme Princess | D | Sears, Roebuck & Co. | Chicago | IL | 1898 |
| Acme Queen | D | Sears, Roebuck & Co. | Chicago | IL | 1898 |
| Acme Wonder | D | Sears, Roebuck & Co. | Chicago | IL | 1902 1907 |
| Acorn | M | Gleason & Schaff | Chicago | IL | 1896 |
| Adelbert | D | Geo. Worthington & Co. | Cleveland | OH | 1896 |
| Adlake | M | Adams & Westlake | Chicago | IL | 1896 1900 |
| | | Consolidated with J. Lonn & Sons, and D. Bradley Co. in 1898 to form Great Western Mfg. Co. | | | |
| Adlake | D | James Bailey | Portland | ME | 1902 |
| Admiral | M | Chicago Wheel Works | Chicago | IL | 1896 |
| Admiral | M | March-Davis Cycle Mfg. Co. | Chicago | IL | 1896 1898 |
| Adonis | M | Hitchings Cycle Co. | St. Louis | MO | 1896 |
| | | Model - Adonis A-1 | | | |
| Advance | M | Advance Bic. Co. | Cincinnati | OH | 1896 1898 |
| Aeolus | M | Spooner-Peterson Co. | Chicago | IL | 1892 |
| Aerial | M | Aerial Cycle Mfg. Co. | Goshen | IN | 1895 |
| Aerolite | M | J. Thornton, Jr. | New York | NY | 1892 |
| Aetna | M | Elbridge Cycle Co. | Elbridge | NY | 1896 |
| Aetna | M | Marion Cycle Co. | Marion | IN | 1897 1899 |
| | | Model - Juvenile | | | |
| Ajax | D | Hibbard,Spenser, & Bartlett & Co. | Chicago | IL | ---- |
| Ajax | M | U.S. Cycle Mfg. Co. | Philadelphia | PA | 1892 1896 |
| Ak-Sar-Ben | M | Ak-Sar-Ben Cycle Works | Kearney | NE | 1896 1898 |
| Akron | M | Allen, Williams, & Allen | Akron | OH | 1896 |
| Akron Beauty | M | Ranney Cycle Co. | Akron | OH | 1896 |
| Akron Flyer | M | Ranney Cycle Co. | Akron | OH | 1896 |
| Akron, Jr. | M | Ranney Cycle Co. | Akron | OH | 1896 |
| Al-Ard | M | Goddard & Allen Co. | Beloit | WI | 1902 |
| Al-Ki | M | Stephen Ballard Rubber Co. | New York | NY | 1896 |
| Albany | D | R. H. Robe | Albany | NY | 1896 |
| Albert Lea Special | M | Lindsay Bros. | Milwaukee | WI | 1896 |
| Albia | M | Albia Cycle Co. | Albia | IA | 1898 |
| Albion | M | The Albion Co. | Louisville | KY | ---- |
| | | Model - Special | | | |
| Albion | M | Mead & Prentiss Mfg. | Chicago | IL | 1899 |
| Alcazar | M | Speeder Cycle Co. | New Castle | IN | 1896 1898 |
| Aldamar | M | Eastern Cycle Mfg. Co. | Amesbury | MA | 1897 |
| Alert | | | London | ON | |
| Alert | M | Packer Cycle Co. | Reading | PA | 1895 1898 |
| Alert | M | John Deere Plow Co. | Kansas City | MO | 1896 |
| Alix | D | Morgan & Co. | Ft. Wayne | IN | 1896 |
| Allen | M | Allen Mfg. Co. | Michigan City | IN | 1896 |
| Allen | M | Sensitive Governor Co. | Indianapolis | IN | 1896 1898 |

| Bicycle Brand | Manufacturer or Distributor | Company | City | ST | Date of First Notice |
|---|---|---|---|---|---|
| Allwood | M | Allwood Cycle Co. | Carnarsie Grv. | NY | 1896 |
| Alpha | M | E. T. Harris | Chicago | IL | 1896 |
| Alpine | M | Alpine Cycle Co. | Cincinnati | OH | 1898 |
| Alton | M | H. Scherer & Co. | Detroit | MI | 1900 |
| Alva Special | M | Lindsay Bros. | Milwaukee | WI | 1896 |
| America | M | Peerless Mfg. Co. | Cleveland | OH | 1892 |
| America | M | International Mfg. Co. | Chicago | IL | 1895 1896 |
| | | Models - Special, Tandem, Truss Frame | | | |
| America | M | Great Western Mfg. Co. | LaPorte | IN | 1900 |
| American | M | American Sewing Mach. Co. | Philadelphia | PA | 1895 1897 |
| | | Models - Special, Traveler | | | |
| American | M | American Harrow | Detroit | MI | 1900 |
| American Beauty | M | National Sewing Mach. Co. | Belvidere | IL | 1896 1898 |
| American Eagle | D | Bicycle Headquarters | Chicago | IL | 1896 |
| American Excelsior | M | H. A. Smith Co. | Newark | NJ | 1896 |
| American Express | D | Latta Bros. | Friendship | NY | 1892 |
| American Geared Ordinary | M | Aerial Cycle Co. | Goshen | IN | 1891 |
| American Ideal | M | Gormully & Jeffery | Chicago | IL | 1885 1892 |
| American King of Scorchers | D | McIntosh & Huntington Co. | Cleveland | OH | 1896 |
| American League Favorite | M | Worden Hickory Frame Cycle.Wrks | Syracuse | NY | 1893 1898 |
| American Ormonde | D | American Ormonde Cycle Co. | New York | NY | 1892 |
| American Pilot | D | Latta Bros. | Friendship | NY | 1892 |
| American Premier | M | A. G. Spalding & Bros. | | | 1891 |
| American Queen of Scorchers | D | McIntosh & Huntington | Cleveland | OH | 1896 |
| American Rover | D | Prince Wells | Louisville | KY | 1896 |
| American Safety | M | Gormully & Jeffery | Chicago | IL | 1885 1892 |
| American Scorcher | M | T. A. Anderson & Co. | Lancaster | PA | 1892 1898 |
| American Standard | M | Geo. A. Clark & Co. | Utica | NY | 1896 1898 |
| American Standard | M | George A. Clark & Co. | Utica | NY | 1896 1898 |
| American Star | M | Lindsay Bros. | Milwaukee | WI | 1896 |
| American Traveler | M | American Sewing Mach. Co. | Philadelphia | PA | 1895 1897 |
| Americus | M | Lindsay Bros. | Milwaukee | WI | 1895 1896 |
| Ames | M | Ames, Mfg. Co. | Chicopee | MA | 1886 1898 |
| Amesbury | M | Amesbury Carriage Co. | Amesbury | MA | 1896 |
| Amherst | M | Loegler & Ladd | Buffalo | NY | 1898 |
| Amity | M | Wm. Beattie | Cohoes | NY | 1898 |
| Amos | M | Amos Mfg. Co. | Chicago | IL | 1898 |
| Anderson | M | Anderson Cycle & Mfg. Co. | Detroit | MI | 1896 1898 |
| Anderson Special | M | Anderson Bic. Works | Cincinnati | OH | 1898 |
| Anderson Transit | M | Albert & J. M. Anderson | Boston | MA | 1896 |
| Andrae | M | Julius Andrae Cycle Works | Milwaukee | WI | 1895 1900 |
| | | Models by number | | | |
| Anis | M | | Cherry Creek | NY | c. 1890 |
| Anita | D | A. R. Maines | Los Angeles | CA | 1896 1898 |
| Ann Arbor | M | Lindsay Bros. | Milwaukee | WI | 1896 |
| Antelope | D | Hibbard, Spencer & Bartlett Co. | Chicago | IL | 1896 1897 |
| Apollo | M | Apollo Cycle Co. | Chicago | IL | 1895 1896 |
| Apple Blossom | M | Whipple & Becker | Chicago | IL | 1896 |
| Aquena Ladies and Gents | M | Aquilla Wheel Mfg. Co. | Louisville | KY | 1898 |
| | | a tandem | | | |
| Aquilla | M | Aquilla Wheel Mfg. Co. | Louisville | KY | 1898 |
| | | Model - Tandem | | | |

| Bicycle Brand | Manufacturer or Distributor | Company | City | ST | Date of First Notice |
|---|---|---|---|---|---|
| Arab | M | Bailey Mfg. Co. | Chicago | IL | 1896 |
| Arabia | M | Ames & Frost Co. | Chicago | IL | 1898 |
| Arabian | M | Ames & Frost Co. | Chicago | IL | 1898 |
| Arcade | D | Krapp & Spalding Co. | Sioux City | IA | 1896 |
| Arena | M | The Western News Co. | Chicago | IL | 1897 1898 |
| Argentine | M | Ames & Frost Co. | Chicago | IL | 1898 |
| Argonaut | D | Mead Cycle Co. | Chicago. | IL | ---- |
| Argyle | M | Sieg & Walpole Mfg. Co. | Kenosha | WI | 1896 |
| Ariel | M | Ariel Cycle Co. | Goshen | IN | 1892 1898 |
| Ariston | M | Ariston Mfg. Co. | Westboro | MA | 1895 1898 |
| Arlington | D | Cash Buyers' Union | Chicago | IL | 1896 |
| Armor | D | Matlack, Coleman & Co. | Philadelphia | PA | 1896 |
| Arms | M | Lyman H. Arms | Chicago | IL | 1898 |
| Army & Navy | D | F. J. Werneth & Co. | Baltimore | MD | 1896 |
| Arrow | M | Century Cycle Co. | Chicago | IL | 1892 1893 |
| | | Century Cyc. Mfg. Co., 1894-95; Arrow Cyc. Mfg. Co., 1896, appears to be company evolution. | | | |
| Arrowanna | D | Galveston Cycle Co. | Galveston | TX | 1896 |
| Art's Special #10 | M | J. Ingalls & Son | Dodge Center | MN | 1898 |
| Asbury | D | Bicycle Headquarters | Chicago | IL | 1896 |
| Ashland | M | Ashland Cycle Co. | Chicago | IL | 1896 1898 |
| | | Model - Anderson Special. | | | |
| Atalanta | M | Patee Cycle Co. | Peoria | IL | 1896 1898 |
| Athlete | M | Rochester Cycle Mfg. Co. | Rochester | NY | 1896 |
| Athletic | M | Lindsay Bros. | Milwaukee | WI | 1896 |
| Athol | M | Skinner & Co. | Hamilton | ON | 1896 |
| Atlanta | D | VanCamp Hardware & Iron Co. | Indianapolis | IN | 1894 |
| Atlas | M | Farnsworth & Wilson Machine Co. | Amsterdam | NY | 1896 |
| Atlas | M | W. S. Demorest Co. | Chicago | IL | 1896 |
| Attica Special | M | Attica Cycle Works | Attica | NY | 1898 |
| Auburn | M | James J. Carr | Auburn | NY | 1898 |
| Auburn Special | M | Auburn Cycle Co. | Chicago | IL | 1896 1898 |
| Aurora | M | A. J. Hobbs | Aurora | IL | 1896 |
| Austin | M | Austin Bic. Works | Austin | IL | 1895 1898 |
| Austin | M | H. K. Austin | Reading | MA | 1898 |
| Autocrat | M | Driscoll & Fletcher | Buffalo | NY | 1898 |
| Auxiliary | | | | | 1892 |
| Avalanche | M | W. H. Jackson | Philadelphia | PA | 1892 |
| Avalon | | | | | |
| Avery | M | Avery Planter Co. | Kansas City | MO | 1896 1898 |
| | | Models - A, B, C | | | |
| Axtel | M | Timms Mfg. Co. | Seymour | IN | 1898 |
| Axtell | M | National Bic. Co. | Indianapolis | IN | 1892 |
| | | 30" wheels, $100.00. | | | |
| Aztec | M | F. S. Waters Co. | Chicago | IL | 1898 |
| B | M | Stephen Ballard Rubber Co. | New York | NY | 1896 |
| B & A | M | James Cycle Co. | Chicago | IL | 1893 |
| Bach | M | Garden City Cycle Works | Chicago | IL | 1896 |
| Badger | M | Badger Cycle Co. | Madison | WI | 1894 1898 |
| Baker | M | Myron C. Baker | Chicago | IL | 1898 |
| Ball | M | Ball Cycle Co. | Muncie | IN | 1898 |
| Ballard | M | Stephen Ballard Rubber Co. | New York | NY | 1896 |

| Bicycle Brand | Manufacturer or Distributor | | Company | City | ST | Date of First Notice |
|---|---|---|---|---|---|---|
| Bamboo | M | | Myers Mfg. Co. | New York | NY | 1895 |
| Bamboo | M | | Bamboo Cycle Co. | Milwaukee | WI | 1898 |
| Bangor | M | | Bangor Bicycle Co. | Bangor | ME | 1898 |
| Banker | D | | Excelsior Supply Co. | Chicago | IL | 1896 |
| Banner | M | | East Side Cycle Co. | Buffalo | NY | 1895 1896 |
| Banner | M | | Hughes & Browne | Chicago | IL | 1899 |
| Bantam | M | | Hill Cycle Co. | Chicago | IL | 1895 |
| Barden | M | | Barden Cycle Co. | Boston | MA | 1898 |
| Barker | M | | S. G. Barker & Son | Scranton | PA | 1898 |
| Barnes | M | | Barnes Cycle Co. | Syracuse | NY | 1896 1899 |
| Baron | M | | A. Featherstone & Co. | Chicago | IL | 1895 1898 |
| Baroness | M | | A. Featherstone & Co. | Chicago | IL | 1895 1898 |
| Batavia | D | | W. S. Winchell | Batavia | IL | 1896 |
| | | | Models - B. Belle, B. Special | | | |
| Batten | M | | W. W. Batten | Millville | NJ | 1898 |
| | | | Models - Special and Roadster | | | |
| Bay State | M | | Ramsdell & Rawson | Worcester | MA | 1892 1896 |
| | | | Rawson Mfg. Co. 1897-98 | | | |
| Baylor Special | M | | Henry D. Baylor | Boston | MA | 1898 |
| Bayvelgear | M | | Bayvelgear Cycle Co. | New York | NY | 1896 1898 |
| | | | Chainless | | | |
| Beacon | M | | Beacoa Cycle Co. | Westboro | MA | 1892 1895 |
| | | | Cole & Gerald Mfg. Co. 1896 | | | |
| Beauty | M | | S. A. Haines Co. | Indianapolis | IN | 1896 |
| Beck | D | | Beck & Corbitt | St. Louis | MO | 1896 |
| Bee | M | | Niagara Top Co. | Buffalo | NY | 1896 |
| Beebe | M | | Beebe Mfg. Co. | Racine | WI | 1898 |
| Bell | M | | Bell Cycle Mfg. Co. | Chicago | IL | 1898 |
| Bell | M | | Thaddeus H. Bell, Jr. | Port Chester | NY | 1898 |
| Belle Meade | D | | J. C. Combs | Nashville | TN | 1896 |
| Belleville Flyer | M | | Belleville Cycle Co. | Belleville | NJ | 1898 |
| Bellis | M | | Bellis Cycle Co. | Indianapolis | IN | 1895 1898 |
| Bellvue | M | | National Sewing Mach. Co. | Belvidere | IL | 1896 |
| Bellvue | M | | Sieg & Walpole Mfg. Co. | Kenosha | WI | 1896 |
| Belmont | M | | Sweeting Cycle Co. | Philadelphia | PA | 1891 1895 |
| | | | McLear & Kendall Co., Phila. 1896-98 | | | |
| Belsize | D | | Hibbard Spencer & Bartlett Co. | Chicago | IL | 1892 |
| Belvidere | M | | National Sewing Mach. Co. | Belvidere | IL | 1894 1898 |
| Ben Hur | M | | Central Cycle Mfg. Co. | Indianapolis | IN | 1892 1898 |
| Bennett | M | | Belleville Cycle Co. | Belleville | NJ | 1898 |
| Berkley | M | | W. W. Whitten Cycle Co. | Providence | RI | 1896 |
| Berkshire | M | | Bridgeport Cycle Co. | Bridgeport | CT | 1896 |
| Berkshire Special | M | | Berkshire Cycle Co. | North Adams | MA | 1896 |
| Berlo | M | | Berlo Cycle Mfg. Co. | Boston | MA | 1898 |
| Berwick | M | | Lindsay Bros. | Milwaukee | WI | ---- |
| Bethel | M | | J. A. Klahr | Bethel | PA | 1898 |
| Beverly | M | | Stokes Mach. Works | Kenosha | WI | 1896 1898 |
| Beverly | M | | Lillian, Harper & Co. | Beverly | MA | 1898 |
| Bicycle | M | | Miami Cycle Mfg. Co. | Middletown | OH | 1896 |
| Big Four | M | | Anderson Bic. Wheel Co. | Anderson | IN | 1898 |
| Bijou | D | | S. A. Haines Co. | Indianapolis | IN | 1896 |
| Binghamton | D | | Edward L. Rose & Co. | Binghamton | NY | 1896 |

| Bicycle Brand | Manufacturer or Distributor | Company | City | ST | Date of First Notice |
|---|---|---|---|---|---|
| Birmingham | M | Loosely Cycle Co. | Birmingham | AL | 1896 1898 |
| Bismarck | M | Horn Cycle Co. | Chicago | IL | 1896 1898 |
| Bison | D | Gibson & Prentiss Cycle Co. Seyfang & Prentiss, 1896-98 | Buffalo | NY | 1895 |
| Bison | D | Seyfang & Prentiss | Buffalo | NY | 1896 1898 |
| Black Beauty | M | D. P. N. Mfg. Co. | New York | NY | ---- |
| Black Diamond | M | Searls Mfg. Co. | Newark | NJ | 1892 1898 |
| Black Hawk | M | Western Wheel Works | Chicago | IL | 1892 1893 |
| Blankenheim | M | Charles Blankenheim | Chicago | IL | 1898 |
| Blight Special | M | Harry Blight | Cleveland | OH | 1898 |
| Bliss | M | Charles E. Graham | Chicago | IL | 1898 |
| Blitz | M | C. B. Metzger | Grand Rapids | MI | 1898 |
| Blizzard | D | Hibbard, Spencer, & Bartlett Co. | Chicago | IL | 1896 |
| Bloomington | D | Harber Bros. | Bloomington | IL | 1892 |
| Blue Bird | M | W. A. Beau & Co. | New Haven | CT | 1898 |
| Blue Grass | M | Fred J. Meyers Mfg. Co. | Hamilton | OH | 1896 1898 |
| Bluff City | M | Lindsay Bros. | Milwaukee | WI | 1896 1898 |
| Bohemian | D | Wm. H. Yergey | Philadelphia | PA | 1896 |
| Bolte | M | Bolte Mfg. Co. | Milwaukee | WI | 1895 1896 |
| Bostedo | M | Bostedo Co. | Chicago | IL | 1896 |
| Boston Special | M | F. X. Mueller & Co. | Buffalo | NY | 1896 |
| Bowley Special | M | Lindsay Bros. | Milwaukee | WI | 1896 |
| Boyd | M | Worcester Cycle Mfg. Co. | Worcester | MA | 1896 1898 |
| Bradley Chainless | M | Bradley Chainless Bicycle Co. | Albany | NY | 1893 |
| Bradley Special | M | Bradley Mfg. Co. | Newark | NJ | 1898 |
| Braithwaite Scorcher | M | Braithwaite Cycle Supply Co. | Williamsburg | VA | 1896 |
| Brandywine | D | F. M. Dampman Cycle Co. | Philadelphia | PA | 1895 1896 |
| Brantford | M | Gould Bic. Co. | Brantford | ON | 1896 |
| Bray Bros. Special | M | Bray Bros. | Cedar Rapids | IA | 1898 |
| Brazeless | M | T. H. Bolte | Kearney | NE | 1898 |
| Breeze | M | Albert & J. M. Anderson | Boston | MA | 1896 |
| Brewster | M | Brewster Mfg. Co. | Holly | MI | 1896 |
| Bridgeport Special | M | Bridgeport Cycle Co. | Bridgeport | CT | 1896 |
| Brightbill | M | David Brightbill Models - Special and Hustler | Lebanon | PA | 1898 |
| Brighton | D | J. E. Poorman | Cincinnati | OH | 1894 1895 |
| Brighton Special | M | Darlow Bros. Model - Flyer | Cambridge | MA | 1898 |
| Brilliant | M | Lindsay Bros. | Milwaukee | WI | 1896 |
| Bristol | M | Charles F. Netzow Mfg. Co. | Milwaukee | WI | 1899 |
| Broadway | M | Lindsay Bros. | Milwaukee | WI | 1896 |
| Brockton | M | Brockton Cycle Co. Model - Special | Brockton | | 1898 |
| Broncho | M | White Cycle Co. | Westboro | MA | 1890 |
| Broncho | M | Livingston Cycle Co. Chainless | Westboro | MA | 1891 1892 |
| Broncho Light Roadster | M | Knight Cycle Co. | St. Louis | MO | 1888 1890 |
| Brookes | D | Wm. Trafford | Philadelphia | PA | 1892 |
| Brookside | M | Hay & Willetts Mfg. Co. | Indianapolis | IN | 1896 |
| Brown | M | Brown Bros. | South Bend | IN | 1898 |
| Brownie | M | Eclipse Bic. Works | Beaver Falls | PA | 1892 1893 |
| Brownie | M | Eclipse Bic. Works | Indianapolis | IN | 1894 1896 |

| Bicycle Brand | Manufacturer or Distributor | Company | City | ST | Date of First Notice |
|---|---|---|---|---|---|
| Brownie | M | Razoux & Handy<br>Chas. L. Razoux, 1897-98 | Boston | MA | 1896 |
| Bruce | M | Lindsay Bros. | Milwaukee | WI | 1896 |
| Bryan | M | S. E. Folk | Bryan | OH | 1898 |
| Buck Racer | M | Plymouth Cycle Mfg. Co. | Plymouth | IN | 1894 1896 |
| Buckeye | M | Peerless Mfg. Co.<br>Model - Buckeye, Jr. | Cleveland | OH | 1892 1896 |
| Buckeye | M | F. J. Meyers Mfg. Co. | Hamilton | OH | 1896 |
| Buckingham | M | H. A. Smith & Co. | Newark | NJ | 1892 |
| Buffalo | M | Buffalo Cycle Works | Buffalo | NY | 1892 1896 |
| Buffalo Diamond | M | Buffalo Cycle Works | Buffalo | NY | 1896 |
| Buffalo King | D | Wm. Hengerer Co.<br>Manufactured by Pierce. | Buffalo | NY | 1898 1900 |
| Buffalo Queen | D | Wm. Hengerer Co.<br>Manufactured by Pierce. | Buffalo | NY | 1898 1900 |
| Bullock | M | H. Channon Co. | Chicago | IL | 1896 |
| Bur | M | Becker Bros. | Chicago | IL | 1898 |
| Burlington | M | Burlington Cycle Co. | Chicago | IL | 1896 |
| Burlington | M | Prugh | Burlington | IA | 1896 |
| Burt | M | M.H. Burt Cycle Mfg. Co. | Wichita | KS | 1898 |
| Butler Record Racer | M | Butler Co. | Butler | IN | 1896 |
| C. L. | | Charles L. Legg | Chicago | IL | 1898 |
| C & S Special | M | Ohio Bic. Co. | Coldwater | OH | 1898 |
| C & W | M | Cone & Witt | Jackson | MI | 1896 |
| Cadet | D | E.H. Shattuck | Lowell | MA | 1896 |
| Cadillac | D | Geo. Hilsendegen | Detroit | MI | 1896 |
| Caeser | M | St. Louis Cycle Co. | St. Louis | MO | 1896 |
| Caffrey | M | Chas. S. Caffrey Co. | Camden | NJ | 1898 |
| California | M | Walters & Davis Mach. Works | San Francisco | CA | 1896 |
| Calumet | M | Julius Andrae & Sons Co. | Milwaukee | WI | 1896 |
| Calumet | M | Calumet Cycle Co. | Chicago | IL | 1898 |
| Cambridge | M | Kankakee Mfg. Co. | Kankakee | IL | 1896 1898 |
| Cameron | M | Cameron Wheel Co. | Brockton | MA | 1896 1898 |
| Campbell | M | Campbell Mfg. Co. | Providence | RI | 1895 1896 |
| Campbell Special | M | W. A. Campbell Co. | Chicago | IL | 1898 |
| Canadian | M | Gould Bic. Co.<br>Canada | Brantford | ON | 1896 |
| Cannon Ball | M | Black Rock Cycle Works | Titusville | PA | 1898 |
| Canton Special | M | T. S. Culp | Canton | OH | 1896 |
| Capital | M | Emblem Bicycle Co. | Angola | NY | |
| Capital | M | H. S. Owen Mfg. Co. | Washington | DC | 1892 1898 |
| Captain | D | Wall & Boyer | Philadelphia | PA | 1892 |
| Captor | M | F. B. Catlin | Winsted | CT | 1896 1898 |
| Caribou | M | Bangor Bicycle Co. | Bangor | ME | 1898 |
| Carlisle | M | Carlisle Mfg. Co. | Chicago | IL | 1897 1900 |
| | | Model - Chainless (Sager Roller Gear, $75) and Tandem ($70) | | | |
| Carr Special | M | F. S. Carr Co. | Springfield | MA | 1895 |
| Carr Special | M | A. M. Carr Bic. Works | Wichita | KS | 1896 |
| Carriage Cycle | M | Ohio Bic. Mfg. Co. | Marion | OH | 1898 |
| Carrier | M | Harry E. Stahl | Trenton | NJ | 1898 |
| Carroll Chainless | M | Carroll Chainless Bic. Co. | Philadelphia | PA | 1895 1899 |
| Cartaret | M | Elizabeth Cycle Mfg. Co. | Elizabeth | NJ | 1896 1898 |

| Bicycle Brand | Manufacturer or Distributor | Company | City | ST | Date of First Notice |
|---|---|---|---|---|---|
| Carthage Clipper | M | Wheeler Co. | Carthage | MO | 1898 |
| Carthage Star | M | Peebles Cycle Co. | Carthage | MO | 1898 |
| Casco | D | James Bailey | Portland | ME | 1902 |
| Cataract | D | Warman-Schub Cycle House | Chicago | IL | 1895 |
| | | C.H. Schub Cyc. House, 1893 and again in 1898 | | | |
| Catford | M | Premier Cycle Co. | New York | NY | 1892 |
| Catlin | M | F. B. Catlin | Winsted | CT | 1896 |
| Cattaragus | | | | NY | |
| Cavalier | D | Morley Bros. | Saginaw | MI | 1896 |
| Cayuga | M | Iroquois Cycle Mfg. Co. | Buffalo | NY | 1896 |
| Celtic | D | C. J. Dale | Chicago | IL | 1896 |
| Centaur | M | St. Nicholas Mfg. Co. | Chicago | IL | 1892 |
| Centaur | M | Golden States & Miner's Iron Works | San Francisco | CA | 1896 1898 |
| Centaur | M | Centaur Bic. Co. | Boston | MA | 1898 |
| Central | M | Central Mfg. Co. | Indianapolis | IN | 1894 1895 |
| Central | M | Central Cycle Mfg. Co. | Indianapolis | IN | 1895 |
| Central City | M | Lindsay Bros. | Milwaukee | WI | 1896 |
| Central Special | M | Central Cycle Co. | Kansas City | MO | 1896 |
| Centuria | M | E. P. Wolf | Chicago | IL | 1898 |
| Centurion | D | H. B. Shattuck & Son | Boston | MA | 1896 |
| Century | D | Henry Keidal & Co. | Baltimore | MD | 1896 |
| Chainless Telegram | M | Telegram Cycle Mfg. Co. | Milwaukee | WI | 1896 |
| | | Model of the Telegram | | | |
| Challenge | M | Gormully & Jeffery | Chicago | IL | 1896 1898 |
| Champion | M | Heil Brothers | Buffalo | NY | |
| Champion | M | Famous Mfg. Co. | Chicago | IL | 1896 1898 |
| | | Model - Lady Champion | | | |
| Champion | M | Champion Machine | Philadelphia | PA | 1897 |
| | | Model - Champion Flyer | | | |
| Champion | M | The Western News Co. | Chicago | IL | 1897 1898 |
| Chancellor | M | Shephard Mfg. Co. | St. Louis | MO | 1896 |
| Charter Oak | D | A. H. Pomeroy | Hartford | CT | 1896 |
| Chautaugua | M | Kastler Cycle Co. | Chicago | IL | 1898 |
| Chautauqua | | The Larkin Co. | Buffalo | NY | |
| Cherub | D | VanCamp Hardware & Iron Co. | Indianapolis | IN | 1894 |
| Cheves | M | J. L. Cheves | Macon | GA | 1898 |
| Chicago | M | C. P. Warner and Bro. | Chicago | IL | 1896 1898 |
| Chicago | M | Arnold, Schwinn & Co. | Chicago | IL | 1898 |
| Chicago Flyer | M | Winnie Mach. Works | Chicago | IL | 1898 |
| Chicago Triumph | D | J. B. Rich Cycle Co. | Philadelphia | PA | 1892 1893 |
| Chicopee | M | Chicopee Falls Wheel Co. | Chicopee | MA | 1898 |
| Chief | M | Chief Cycle Mfg. Co. | Milwaukee | WI | 1896 1898 |
| Chief | M | Lockport Bic. Co. | Lockport | NY | 1898 |
| Chieftain | D | Wm. H. Cole & Son | Baltimore | MD | 1896 |
| Chilion | M | M. D. Stebbins Mfg. Co. | Springfield | MA | 1897 1898 |
| Chirocycle | M | Benjamin M. Pearne | Oxford | NY | 1898 |
| | | for invalids | | | |
| Chispa | D | Farwell, Ozmun, Kirk, & Co. | St. Paul | MN | 1896 |
| Christy | M | Derby Cycle Co. | Jackson | MI | 1898 |
| Chronicle | D | Harbridge & Whitbeck | Chicago | IL | 1896 |
| Cinch | M | Western Wheel Works | Chicago | IL | 1892 1893 |
| | | Models by number, $35-$50 | | | |

| Bicycle Brand | Manufacturer or Distributor | Company | City | ST | Date of First Notice |
|---|---|---|---|---|---|
| Cincinnatus | D | Sears, Roebuck & Co. | Chicago | IL | 1898 |
| Cinderella | | | | | 1892 |
| Circle | M | Circle Cycle Co. | New York | NY | 1898 |
| Clark | M | Geo. W. Clark Co. | Jacksonville | | 1898 |
| | | Models - Flyer and Special | | | |
| Clark Special | M | J. P. Clark, Boston | Boston | MA | 1898 |
| Classic | D | Louis Rosenfeld & Co. | New York | NY | 1896 |
| Cleopatra | M | N. A. Dolleris | Somerville | MA | 1898 |
| Cleveland | M | H. A. Lozier & Co. | Cleveland | OH | 1892 1899 |
| | | Lozier Mfg. Co., Toledo, Ohio, 1895-98 | | | |
| Cleveland | M | American Bicycle Co. | Cleveland | OH | 1901 |
| | | Cleveland Sales Department | | | |
| Cleveland | M | American Cycle Mfg. Co. | New York | NY | 1902 |
| | | Eastern Sales Department | | | |
| Cleveland | M | American Cycle Mfg. Co. | Hartford | CT | 1903 |
| | | Eastern Sales Department | | | |
| Cleveland | M | Pope Mfg. Co., Eastern Department | Hartford | CT | 1904 1909 |
| Clifton | D | Gray & Johnson | Cincinnati | OH | 1896 |
| Climax | M | Climax Cycle Mfg. Co. | Chicago | IL | 1892 1898 |
| Clinton | M | H. R. Olmstead & Co. | Syracuse | NY | 1896 1898 |
| Clipper | M | Gormully & Jeffery | Chicago | IL | ---- |
| Clipper | M | Grand Rapids Bic. Co. | Grand Rapids | MI | 1892 1898 |
| Clipper | M | American Bicycle Co. | Chicago | IL | 1900 |
| | | Gormully & Jeffery Sales Department | | | |
| Close | D | Close Cycle Co. | Olean | NY | 1896 1898 |
| Clover Leaf | M | Whipple & Becker | Chicago | IL | 1896 1897 |
| | | Becker & Becker, 1898 | | | |
| Clover Leaf | M | Orrville Buggy Co. | Orrville | OH | 1897 |
| Clymer | M | Berlin Mach. Works | Beloit | WI | 1896 1898 |
| Coaster | D | A. A. Bennett | Cincinnati | OH | 1892 |
| Cocheco | | Dover | | NH | |
| Coleman | M | H. D. Coleman, Jr. | New Orleans | LA | 1896 1898 |
| Collmer | M | Collmer Bros. | South Bend | IN | 1896 1901 |
| Colonial | M | John McClave & Son | New York | NY | 1896 |
| Colonial Dame | M | John McClave & Son | New York | NY | 1896 |
| Colton | M | Colton Cycle Co. | Toledo | OH | 1896 |
| Columbia | M | Pope Mfg. Co. | Boston | MA | 1879 1900 |
| | | Models - Standard, Light Roadster, Expert, Volunteer, Century, Racer, and others. | | | |
| Columbia | M | Pope Mfg. Co. | Hartford | CT | 1888 1899 |
| Columbia | M | American Bicycle Co. | Hartford | CT | 1900 1901 |
| | | Pope Sales Department | | | |
| Columbia | M | American Cycle Mfg. Co. | Hartford | CT | 1902 1903 |
| | | Eastern Sales Dept., Columbia Factory | | | |
| Columbia | M | Pope Mfg. Co. | Hartford | CT | 1904 1915 |
| Columbia | M | Westfield Mfg. Co. | Westfield | MA | 1916 1918 |
| Columbus | M | Demorest Mfg. Co. | Williamsport | PA | 1894 1896 |
| Columbus | M | Columbus Bic. Co. | Columbus | OH | 1895 1897 |
| | | Models - Royal Flush | | | |
| Comanche | D | L. C. Jacquish | Chicago | IL | 1896 |
| Combination, Jr. | M | Western Wheel Works | Chicago | IL | ---- |
| | | Models by number | | | |
| Comet | M | St. Louis Cycle Co. | St. Louis | MO | 1892 1896 |

| Bicycle Brand | Manufacturer or Distributor | Company | City | ST | Date of First Notice | |
|---|---|---|---|---|---|---|
| Comet | M | Grand Rapids Bic. Mfg. Co. | Grand Rapids | MI | 1896 | |
| Comet | M | Gormully & Jeffery | Chicago | IL | 1898 | |
| Comet | M | Henry J. Savoy | Paincourtville | | 1898 | |
| Commercial Flyer | D | New York Sporting Goods Co. | New York | NY | ---- | |
| Commodore | M | Gladiator Cycle Works | Chicago | IL | 1897 | |
| Common Sense | M | Common Sense Bic. Mfg. Co. | Philadelphia | PA | 1892 | |
| Competition | M | R. C. Wall Mfg. Co. | Philadelphia | PA | 1896 | |
| Competitor | M | J. T. Walck | Chicago | IL | 1898 | |
| Concord | M | Sieg & Walpole Mfg. Co. | Kenosha | WI | 1896 | |
| Condor | M | Bredder-Allen Cycle Mfg. Co. | Patterson | NJ | 1895 | 1896 |
| Conqueror | M | Copeland Cycle Mfg. Co. | Evansville | IN | 1896 | 1898 |
| Conquest | D | Geo. R. Bidwell Cycle Co. | New York | NY | 1892 | |
| Conroy | M | Conroy Mfg. Co. | New York | NY | 1898 | |
| Constellation | M | Midland Cycle Co. | Kansas City | MO | 1896 | |
| Cook | M | Cook Cutlery Co. | Homer | MI | 1898 | |
| Coomes Special | M | C. W. Coomes & Co. | Malden | MA | 1898 | |
| Coppins Special | M | Lindsay Bros. | Milwaukee | WI | 1896 | |
| Cornell | M | Lindsay Bros. | Milwaukee | WI | 1896 | |
| Coronado | M | El Dorado Cycle Co. | Chicago | IL | 1896 | |
| Coronet | M | Crown Mfg. Co. | New Bedford | MA | 1896 | |
| Corp | M | Corp. Bros. | Providence | RI | 1898 | |
| Cortland | M | Hitchcock Mfg. Co. Models - Ladies' Cortland | Cortland | NY | 1895 | 1896 |
| Cortland | M | H. G. Wadsworth | Wellington | OH | 1898 | |
| Cossack | D | Mead Cycle Co. | Chicago | IL | ---- | |
| Countess | M | Bernard T. Parsons | Camden | NJ | 1898 | |
| Courier | D | Hibbard, Spencer & Bartlett Co. | Chicago | IL | 1892 | 1896 |
| Crackajack | M | Union Cycle Mfg. Co. | Boston | MA | 1895 | 1896 |
| Crackajack II | M | Union Cycle Mfg. Co. 2nd year of brand | Boston | MA | 1897 | |
| Crackajack III | M | Union Cycle Mfg. Co. 3rd year of brand | Boston | MA | 1898 | |
| Crawford | M | Crawford Mfg. Co. | Hagerstown | MD | 1895 | 1899 |
| Crawford | M | American Bicycle Co. Crawford Factory | Hagerstown | MD | 1901 | 1902 |
| Crawford | M | American Cycle Co. Eastern Sales Department | Hartford | CT | 1903 | |
| Crawford | M | Pope Mfg. Co., Eastern Department | Hartford | CT | 1904 | |
| Credenda | M | Overman Wheel Co. | Chicopee Falls | MA | | |
| Credenda | M | Lamb Mfg. Co. Manufactured for A. G. Spalding & Bros., NY | Chicopee Falls | MA | 1895 | 1898 |
| Creole | M | S. M. Sloan | Galva | IL | 1896 | 1898 |
| Crescent | M | Western Wheel Works Models by numbers; also Chainless | Chicago | IL | 1891 | 1900 |
| Crescent | M | American Bicycle Co. Crescent Sales Department | Chicago | IL | 1901 | |
| Crescent | M | American Cycle Mfg. Co. Eastern Sales Department | New York | NY | 1902 | |
| Crescent | M | Pope Mfg. Co., Western Department | Chicago | IL | 1904 | 1905 |
| Crescent Sylph | M | Rouse, Duryea Cycle Co. Model of Sylph | Peoria | IL | 1892 | |
| Cribb | M | Cribb Carriage Co. | Milwaukee | WI | ---- | |
| Criterion | M | Sweeting Cycle Co. | Philadelphia | PA | 1892 | |

| Bicycle Brand | Manufacturer or Distributor | Company | City | ST | Date of First Notice |
|---|---|---|---|---|---|
| Crone | M | F. G. Crone | Pottsville | PA | 1898 |
| Crookston | M | J. F. Hawkins Co. | Crookston | MN | 1898 |
| Crow | M | Henry Sears Co. | Chicago | IL | 1896 |
| Crowley's Special | M | Edward Crowley | Springfield | MA | 1898 |
| Crown | M | Crown Cycle Co. Model - Ladies | LaPorte | IN | 1896 1897 |
| Crown | M | Relay Mfg. Co. | Reading | PA | 1896 |
| Crown | M | Great Western Mfg. Co. | Chicago | IL | 1900 |
| Crown | M | Great Western Mfg. Co. | LaPorte | IN | 1900 1918 |
| Crown Jewel | M | Long Island Rubber & Cycle Co. | | | 1898 |
| Crusader | M | Indiana Bic. Co. | Indianapolis | IN | 1890 1898 |
| Crusader | M | Harvard Cycle Co. | Harvard | IL | 1898 |
| Crypto | D | Mclntosh-Huntington Co. Geared Ordinary | | | 1885 |
| Cuba | D | Fred Town & Co. Cuba Bic. Works 1897-98 Models - Roadster, Ladies' Pride, Road Racer, Racer, Special Road Racer | | NY | 1896 |
| Cuba | M | Cuba Bicycle Works | Cuba | NY | 1897 1898 |
| Cullman | M | Cullman Wheel Co. | Chicago | IL | 1895 1898 |
| Culp | M | T. S. Culp Models - Special, Special Companion | Canton | OH | 1898 |
| Cumberland | M | Shad Bolt Mfg. Co. | Brooklyn | NY | 1896 1898 |
| Curry | M | Curry Cycles | Chicago | IL | ---- |
| Curtis | M | Curtis Mach. Works | Chicago | IL | 1895 1896 |
| Cycle Cart | M | W. M. Frisbie | New Haven | CT | 1898 |
| Cycloe | D | E. K. Tryon & Co. | Philadelphia | PA | 1893 1896 |
| Cycloid | M | Cycloid Cycle Co. | Grand Rapids | MI | 1898 |
| Cyclone | M | Lindsay Bros. | Milwaukee | WI | 1892 1896 |
| Cyclone | M | Cyclone Wheel Co. | Chicago | IL | 1898 |
| Cyclonia | M | Lighton Mach. Co. | Syracuse | NY | 1896 |
| Cygnet | M | Porter & Gilmore | New York | NY | 1896 |
| Cygnet | D | Cygnet Cycle Co. | Williamsport | PA | 1897 |
| Cygnet | M | Stoddard Mfg. Co. | Dayton | OH | 1897 |
| Czar | M | Czar Cycle Co. | Chicago | IL | 1895 1898 |
| Czarina | M | Czar Cycle Co. | Chicago | IL | 1895 1898 |
| D & C | M | Duffie & Christman | Chicago | IL | 1898 |
| D & D | M | Electric & Mach. Co. | El Paso | TX | 1898 |
| D & H, The | M | Budd Bros. Mfg. Co. | Glens Falls | NY | ---- |
| D & W | M | Derbyshire & Warne | Philadelphia | PA | 1898 |
| Dainty | M | Waltham Mfg. Co. | Waltham | MA | 1896 1898 |
| Daisy | M | Indiana Bic. Mfg. Co. | Indianapolis | IN | 1892 1896 |
| Daisy | M | Niagara Top Co. | Buffalo | NY | 1896 |
| Daisy Belle | M | Gilbert & Chester Co. | Elizabeth | NJ | 1896 |
| Dalsimer | M | Sylvan Dalsimer & Sons | Philadelphia | PA | 1898 |
| Damascus | M | Nash Mfg. Co. | Dixon | IL | 1896 |
| Damon | M | Mackay Cycle Co. | Chicago | IL | 1898 |
| Dampman | D | F. M. Dampman Cycle Co. | Philadelphia | PA | 1895 1896 |
| Dandy | M | Emblem Bicycle Co. | Angola | NY | ---- |
| Dandy | M | Indiana Bic. Mfg. Co. $40 in 1889 | Indianapolis | IN | 1889 1892 |
| Dark Horse | M | Schulenberg Cycle Co. | Detroit | MI | 1895 |
| Darling | M | Darling Cycle Co. | Cleveland | OH | 1898 |

| Bicycle Brand | Manufacturer or Distributor | Company | City | ST | Date of First Notice |
|---|---|---|---|---|---|
| Dart | M | Smith National Cycle Mfg. Co. | Washington | DC | 1892 1894 |
| | | Smith-Dart Cyc. Mfg. Co., New York, 1895-98. Ladies bicycle introduced in 1893 | | | |
| Dart | M | Smith Wheel Mfg. Co. | New York | NY | 1893 1894 |
| Dart | M | Smith-Dart Cycle Mfg. Co. | New York | NY | 1895 1898 |
| Dart | M | Carlisle Mfg. Co. | Chicago | IL | 1900 |
| Dashaway | D | Lathrop-Rhoades Co. | Des Moines | IA | 1896 |
| Dauntless | M | Toledo Bic. Works | Toledo | OH | 1892 1896 |
| | | Dauntless Bic. Co. in 1896 | | | |
| Davidson | M | Davidson & Sons | Chicago | IL | 1896 |
| Davis | M | March-Davis Cycle Mfg. Co. | Chicago | IL | 1895 1898 |
| Dawson | | | NY | | |
| Day | M | Day Mfg. Co. | Lakeview | NY | 1898 1903 |
| Daycycles | M | Day Mfg. Co. | Idlewood | NY | 1898 |
| Dayton | M | Davis Sewing Machine Co. | Dayton | OH | 1895 1918 |
| | | Models by number | | | |
| De La Belle | M | Phillip H. DeLaunty | Chicago | IL | 1898 |
| De Soto | D | Magee & Smith | St. Louis | MO | 1895 1896 |
| Dearborn | D | C. H. Sterner & Co. | Chicago | IL | 1896 1898 |
| | | Fort Dearborn Cyc. Mfg. Co. in 1898 | | | |
| Decker | M | Decker Cycle Co. | Worcester | MA | 1895 1896 |
| Deere | M | Deere, Wells & Co. | Council Bluffs | IA | 1896 1898 |
| Deerwell | M | Deere, Wells & Co. | Council Bluffs | IA | 1898 |
| Defender | M | Bolte Mfg. Co. | Milwaukee | WI | 1896 |
| Defender | M | Defender Cycle Works | Chicago | IL | 1896 |
| Defender | M | Koster & Co. | Erie | PA | 1896 1898 |
| Defender | M | Defender Cycle Co. | New York | NY | 1898 |
| Defiance | M | Monarch Cycle Co. | Chicago | IL | 1895 1898 |
| Defiance | M | Clark, Holgate & Co. | Defiance | OH | 1896 1900 |
| | | Became Defiance Mfg. Co. in 1897 and was sold to a Toledo firm in 1900 | | | |
| Defiance | M | Monarch Cycle Mfg. Co. | Chicago | IL | 1897 1899 |
| Delay' S Special | M | Joseph Delay | Chicago | IL | 1898 |
| Delker | M | Delker Cycle Mfg. Co. | Owensboro | KY | 1896 1898 |
| | | Models - D. Special, Lady D., Racer | | | |
| Delmonico | M | Miller & Roemle | Cincinnati | OH | 1898 |
| Delmonte | M | El Dorado Cycle Co. | Chicago | IL | 1896 |
| Demon | M | E. C. Meachem Arms Co. | St. Louis | MO | 1895 |
| Demorest | M | Demorest Mfg. Co. | Williamsport | PA | 1894 1898 |
| Denver | M | Denver Cycle Mfg. Co. | Denver | CO | 1894 1898 |
| Derby | M | Derby Cycle Mfg. Co. | Jackson | MI | 1892 1896 |
| Derby | M | Derby Cycle Co. | Chicago | IL | 1893 |
| Derby | M | G. Lombardi | Derby | CT | 1898 |
| Despatch | M | John Deere Plow Co. | Kansas City | MO | 1896 |
| Destiny | M | Sieg & Walpole Mfg. Co. | Kenosha | WI | 1896 |
| Detroit | M | Baulch Cycle Mfg. Co. | Detroit | MI | 1895 |
| | | Models - Fairy, Junior, Queen, and Scorcher | | | |
| Detroit Special | M | Lindsay Bros. | Milwaukee | WI | 1896 |
| Devore | D | L. M. Devore & Co. | Freeport | IL | 1896 |
| Dewitt | M | DeWitt Wire Cloth Co. | Philadelphia | PA | 1898 |
| Diadem | M | Wa-fa-no Cycle Mfg. Co. | Buffalo | NY | 1898 |
| Diamond | M | Indiana Bic. Mfg. Co. | Indianapolis | IN | 1889 |
| | | $125.00 | | | |

| Bicycle Brand | Manufacturer or Distributor | Company | City | ST | Date of First Notice |
|---|---|---|---|---|---|
| Diana | M | Cortland Wagon Co. | Cortland | NY | 1894 1896 |
| Diana | M | El Dorado Cycle Co. | Chicago | IL | 1896 |
| Dickenson Special | M | Buffalo Cycle Works | Buffalo | NY | |
| Dictator No. 1 | M | Lindsay Bros. | Milwaukee | WI | 1892 1896 |
| Director | M | Curtis Mach. Works | Chicago | IL | 1896 |
| Directum | D | Fred F. Dudley | Boston | MA | 1896 |
| Dirego | M | Puritan Cycle Mfg. Co. | Portland | ME | 1896 |
| Dirigo | M | T. B. Davis Arms Co. | Portland | ME | 1896 |
| Dixie | M | Lindsay Bros. | Milwaukee | WI | 1896 |
| Dixon | M | Elmore Mfg. Co. | Elmore | OH | 1894 1896 |
| | | Also in Clyde, Ohio | | | |
| Dodge | M | Dodge Cycle Co. | Syracuse | NY | 1896 |
| Dodson | M | Dodson Cycle Co. | Chicago | IL | 1896 1898 |
| Dolly Varden | M | Van Camp Hdw. & Iron Co. | Indianapolis | IN | 1896 |
| Domestic | M | Domestic Sewing Machine Co. | Chicago | IL | 1896 1898 |
| Donna | D | U.S. Bic. Co. | | NY | 1896 |
| Donna | D | U.S. Bicycle Co. | New York | NY | 1896 |
| Dorset | M | Cyclone Combination Cycle | Jamestown | NY | 1894 1896 |
| Double Diamond | M | Donnelly & Deward | Chicago | IL | 1896 |
| Douglas | M | Frank Douglas | Chicago | IL | 1896 |
| Druid | M | Maryland Mfg. & Construction Co. | Baltimore | MD | 1898 |
| Duchess | M | A. Featherstone & Co. | Chicago | IL | 1893 1898 |
| Duchess Richmond | M | Lindsay Bros. | Milwaukee | WI | 1896 |
| Duckworth | M | James Duckworth | Springfield | MA | ---- |
| Dueber | M | Dueber Watch Case Mfg. Co. | Canton | OH | 1898 |
| Duke | M | A. Featherstone & Co. | Chicago | IL | 1893 1898 |
| Duke | M | Lindsay Bros. | Milwaukee | WI | 1896 |
| Duley Special | M | Duley Cycle Co. | Rosendale | WI | 1898 |
| Dundore | M | Dundore Cycle Co. | Reading | PA | 1896 |
| Dunkirk | M | Jacob Bernhard | Dunkirk | NY | 1898 |
| Dunlop | M | E. C. Meacham Arms Co. | St Louis | MO | 1893 |
| Duplex | M | Ohio Bic. Mfg. Co. | Marion | OH | 1898 |
| Duquesne | M | Duquesne Mfg. Co. | Pittsburgh | PA | 1898 |
| | | Models - Standard and Special | | | |
| Duquesne Special | M | Duquesne Mfg. Co. | Pittsburgh | PA | 1897 1898 |
| Duquid | | | | NY | |
| Duryea Freak | M | Marion Cycle Co. | Marion | IN | 1896 |
| Dyer Folding Bicycle | M | Dyer Folding Bic. Co. | Danbury | CT | 1897 |
| E. Howard | M | E. Howard Watch & Clock Co. | Boston | MA | 1896 |
| Eagle | M | Eagle Bic. Co. | Torrington | CT | 1888 1900 |
| | | Models - Altair, Eagle Safety, Club Special | | | |
| Earlham | M | Richmond Bic. Co. | Richmond | IN | 1896 |
| Early Special | M | T. H. Early & Co. | Providence | RI | 1898 |
| Eastburn | M | Pitsville Cycle Works | Philadelphia | PA | 1898 |
| Eastern | M | Eastern Cycle Mfg. Co. | Amesbury | MA | 1897 |
| Echo | D | H. B. Shattuck & Son | Boston | MA | ---- |
| Eckstein | M | Lindsay Bros. | Milwaukee | WI | 1896 |
| Eclipse | | Jas. M. Antes, Jr. | Elmira | NY | |
| Eclipse | M | Eclipse Bicycle Co. | Elmira | NY | 1892 1899 |
| Eclipse | M | Standard Cycle Co. | Buffalo | NY | 1892 |
| Eclipse | M | The Eclipse Bicycle Co. | Indianapolis | IN | 1894 |

| Bicycle Brand | Manufacturer or Distributor | Company | City | ST | Date of First Notice | |
|---|---|---|---|---|---|---|
| Eclipse | M | Eclipse Bic. Works | Beaver Falls | PA | 1895 | |
| | | Located in Elmira, NY, from 1896-98 | | | | |
| Edgemere | D | Sears, Roebuck & Co. | Chicago | IL | 1902 | |
| Edwards | M | Edwards Cycle Co. | Chicago | IL | 1898 | |
| El Dorado | M | El Dorado Cycle Co. | Chicago | IL | 1896 | |
| | | Models - Belle and Gem | | | | |
| El Gabilau | M | Logan Cycle Co. | Hollister | CA | 1898 | |
| El Mahdi | M | Carlisle Mfg. Co. | Chicago | IL | 1900 | |
| | | $35.00 | | | | |
| Eldredge | M | National Sewing Mach. Co. | Belvidere | IL | 1894 | 1898 |
| Eldredge | M | National Sewing Machine Co. | Belvedere | IL | 1894 | 1900 |
| Electric | M | St. Nicholas Mfg. Co. | Chicago | IL | 1889 | 1892 |
| Electric | M | Lindsay Bros. | Milwaukee | WI | 1896 | |
| Electric | M | Rochester Cycle Mfg. Co. | Rochester | NY | 1896 | |
| Electric City | M | Electric City Cycle Co. | Buffalo | NY | 1895 | |
| | | Richardson & Riper Cyc. Co. in 1896, and Riper Cyc. Co. in 1898 | | | | |
| Electric City | M | Richardson & Riper Cycle Co. | Buffalo | NY | 1896 | |
| Electric City | M | Riper Cycle Co. | Buffalo | NY | 1898 | |
| Elfin | D | Frazier & Jones Co. | Syracuse | NY | 1897 | 1900 |
| Elgin | M | C. H. Woodruff Co. | Elgin | IL | 1896 | 1898 |
| | | Models - Lady E., Racer, Swell Special | | | | |
| Elgin | M | Elgin Cycle Co. | Elgin | IL | 1896 | 1898 |
| | | Models - King, Prince, Princess, Queen, Giant, Tornado, Tandem | | | | |
| Elgin Favorite | M | Elgin Sewing Mach. Co. | Elgin | IL | 1896 | 1898 |
| | | Models - Timer and Diamond | | | | |
| Elgin King | M | Elgin Cycle Co. | Elgin | IL | 1896 | 1908 |
| Elgin Queen | M | Elgin Cycle Co. | Elgin | IL | 1896 | 1908 |
| Eli | M | Bloomington Mfg. Co. | Bloomington | IL | 1892 | |
| Eliot | M | S. D. Balkam & Co. | Boston | MA | 1898 | |
| | | Model - Special | | | | |
| Elite | M | Denver Cycle Co. | Denver | CO | 1896 | |
| Elite | M | T. Riley | Boston | MA | 1898 | |
| Elk | M | Goldberg & Pollack | Chicago | IL | 1896 | |
| | | Goldberg Bic. Co. 1898. Models - Elk Tandem | | | | |
| Elk | M | Koster & Co. | Erie | PA | 1896 | |
| Elk | M | Lindsay Bros. | Milwaukee | WI | 1896 | |
| Elk | M | Black Rock Cycle Works | Titusville | PA | 1898 | |
| Elkhart | M | Elkhart Cycle Co. | Elkhart | IN | 1895 | 1896 |
| Elliott | M | Elliott Hickory Cycle Co. | Newton | MA | 1892 | |
| Elliptic | M | Freeport Bic. Co. | Freeport | IL | 1893 | |
| | | Elliptical sprocket | | | | |
| Elm City | M | Jesse W. Starr | Westville | CT | 1896 | |
| Elmira | D | Payne Engine Co. | New York | NY | 1896 | |
| Elmira Clipper | M | Clipper Chilled Plow Co. | Elmira | NY | 1898 | |
| Elmore | M | Elmore Mfg. Co. | Elmore | OH | 1895 | |
| | | Also Clyde, Ohio in 1896-98 | | | | |
| Elroy | M | Williams Bros. | Chicago | IL | 1898 | |
| Elyria | M | Fay Mfg. Co. | Elyria | OH | 1896 | |
| Emblem | M | W. G. Shack | Buffalo | NY | 1895 | 1896 |
| Emblem | M | Emblem Bicycle Co. | Angola | NY | 1899 | 1939 |
| Embree | M | Embree Cycle Co. | Philadelphia | PA | 1896 | |
| Emerson | D | W. S. Emerson & Co. | Philadelphia | PA | 1895 | 1896 |
| Emory | M | | Syracuse | NY | ---- | |

| Bicycle Brand | Manufacturer or Distributor | | Company | City | ST | Date of First Notice |
|---|---|---|---|---|---|---|
| Emperor | M | | Standard Cycle Co. | Buffalo | NY | 1892 |
| Emperor | M | | Hitchcock Mfg. Co. | Cortland | NY | 1896 |
| Empire | M | | Chicago Sewing Mach. Co. | Chicago | IL | 1892 |
| Empire | M | | Empire Cycle Co. | Addison | NY | 1892 1899 |
| | | | Originally Empire State Cyc. Co. until 1895, changed name and moved from original location in Oneonta, NY, to Syracuse. Moved to Addison in 1899. | | | |
| Empire | M | | Empire State Cycle Co | Oneonta | NY | 1892 1895 |
| Empire | M | | Hitchcock Mfg. Co. | Cortland | NY | 1894 1895 |
| Empire | M | | Empire Bic. Mfg. Co. | New York | NY | 1896 |
| Empire Special | M | | Hollely Cycle Mfg. Co. | Buffalo | NY | 1898 |
| Empire State 999 | M | | Empire State Cycle Co. | Buffalo | NY | 1895 1896 |
| | | | See under Empire brand above for company evolution | | | |
| Empress | M | | Standard Cycle Co. | Buffalo | NY | 1892 |
| Empress | M | | Hitchcock Mfg. Co. | Cortland | NY | 1896 |
| Enchantress | | | | | | 1892 |
| Enfield | M | | Enfield Cycle Co. | Thompsonville | MA | 1898 |
| Englewood | M | | Indiana Bic. Mfg. Co. | Indianapolis | IN | 1892 |
| Ensign | M | | Snell Cycle Fittings Co. | Toledo | OH | 1899 |
| Enterprise | M | | Charles Kaufman | Marion | OH | 1898 |
| Enterprise | M | | Enterprise Mach. Works | Newton | PA | 1898 |
| Enterprise | M | | Enterprise Mach. Works | Richmond | VA | 1898 |
| Envoy | M | | Buffalo Tricycle Co. | Buffalo | NY | 1892 1894 |
| | | | Became Buffalo Cyc. Co. from 1895-98 | | | |
| Envoy | M | | Buffalo Cycle Co. | Buffalo | NY | 1895 1898 |
| Epoch | M | | Eddy Mfg. Co. | Greenfield | MA | 1896 |
| Equator | M | | Kabaker & Debo | Chicago | IL | 1898 |
| Ericson | M | | Jacon Wallerius & Co. | Cambridge | MA | 1898 |
| Erie | M | | Queen City Cycle Co. | Buffalo | NY | 1895 1898 |
| Erwin | M | | Erwin Mfg. Co. | Greenbush | NY | 1898 |
| Escort | M | | Western Wheel Works | Chicago | IL | 1892 1893 |
| | | | Models by number | | | |
| Escort | M | | Lindsay Bros. | Milwaukee | WI | 1896 |
| Essex | D | | Porter & Gilmour | New York | NY | 1894 1895 |
| Essex | D | | Porter & Gillman | New York | NY | 1895 |
| Essex | M | | Eastern Cycle Mfg. Co. | Amesbury | MA | 1897 |
| Euclid | D | | F. G. Brookshank | Riverton | NJ | 1895 1896 |
| | | | M - Sociable | | | |
| Eureka | M | | The Eureka Co. | Rockfall | NY | 1896 |
| Evans | M | | T. S. Evans Mfg. Co. | New Albany | IN | 1896 |
| Evans & Dodge | M | | Canadian Typograph Co. Canada | Windsor | ON | 1896 |
| Evans Special | M | | Queen City Cycle Livery Co. | Cincinnati | OH | 1898 |
| Everett | D | | Knight-Campbell Music Co. | Denver | CO | 1896 |
| Excel | M | | John P. Lovell Arms Co. | Boston | MA | 1894 1898 |
| Excelsior | M | | H.A. Smith & Co. | Newark | NJ | 1896 |
| Excelsior | M | | Mayo Damper Co. | Pottstown | PA | 1896 |
| Excelsior | M | | Gleason & Schaff | Chicago | IL | 1898 |
| Explorer | M | | Empire State Cycle Co. | Oneonta | NY | 1898 |
| Export | D | | Fred H. Hungus | New York | NY | 1896 |
| Express | M | | E. C. Meacham Arms Co. | St Louis | MO | 1892 1893 |
| Express | M | | Latta Brothers | Friendship | NY | 1892 1900 |

| Bicycle Brand | Manufacturer or Distributor | | Company | City | ST | Date of First Notice |
|---|---|---|---|---|---|---|
| Express | M | | Meacham Arms Co. | St. Louis | MO | 1892 |
| Extra Bulletin | M | | J. C. Shuler | Janesville | WI | 1896 |
| F.F.V. | M | | Virgina Cycle Co. | Chicago | IL | 1896 |
| | | | Though listed as manufacturer of the brand above, this brand may well be the Fast Flying Virginian also, and not a separate brand | | | |
| F.F.V. - (Fast Flying Virginian) | M | | Maryland Mfg. & Construction Co. | Baltimore | MD | 1898 |
| F & R | M | | Ross, Burgin, & Hartzell | Holyoke | MA | 1898 |
| Fairbanks | M | | The Fairbanks Co. | New York | NY | 1897 |
| Fairmount | M | | Fairmount Cycle Co. Chainless | Philadelphia | PA | 1898 |
| Fairy | M | | Fay Mfg. Co. | Elyria | OH | 1896 |
| Falcon | M | | The Yost Mfg. Co. | Toledo | OH | 1893 1898 |
| Falcon | M | | Yost Mfg. Co. | Toledo | OH | 1895 1898 |
| Falcon Junior | M | | The Yost Mfg. Co. | Toledo | OH | 1893 1894 |
| Falconess | M | | The Yost Mfg. Co. | Toledo | OH | 1893 1894 |
| Fall Brook | M | | Senate Wheel Co. | Corning | NY | 1898 |
| Falls City | D | | Prince Wells | Louisville | KY | 1896 |
| Famous | M | | Famous Cycle Works Formerly Viaduct Bic. Repair Works | Indianapolis | IN | 1893 |
| Famous | M | | Lindsay Bros. | Milwaukee | WI | 1896 |
| Famous | M | | Cherry Cycle Co. | Toledo | OH | 1898 |
| Famous | M | | Famous Cycle Co. | Chicago | IL | 1898 |
| Famous Fox | M | | Fox Mach. Co. | Grand Rapids | MI | 1896 |
| Fanning | M | | Fanning Cycle Mfg. Co. | Chicago | IL | 1898 |
| Farmer's & Mechanic's Friend | M | | F. J. Werneth & Co. | Baltimore | MD | 1896 |
| Farragut | M | | Geo. W. Phelan Cycle Co. | Chicago | IL | 1898 |
| Fashion | M | | Indiana Bic. Co. Models by number | Indianapolis | IN | 1891 |
| Fashion | M | | Fay Mfg. Co. | Elyria | OH | 1892 |
| Fast Mail | M | | Lindsay Bros. | Milwaukee | WI | 1896 1898 |
| Faulhefer | M | | Frank Faulhefer | Boston | MA | 1898 |
| Faultless | M | | E.H. Corson Corson Cyc. Mfg. Co. in 1898 | Nashua | NH | 1896 1898 |
| Favorite | M | | Allwood Cycle Co. | Carnarsie Grv. | NY | 1896 |
| Favorite | M | | Lindsay Bros. | Milwaukee | WI | 1896 |
| Favorite | M | | Sharpless & Watts | Philadelphia | PA | 1896 1898 |
| Favorite | M | | Toledo Metal Wheel Co. | Toledo | OH | 1898 |
| Fawn | M | | Miami Cycle Mfg. Co. | Middletown | OH | 1896 |
| Fay | M | | The Fay Mfg. Co. | Elyria | OH | 1899 |
| Fay | M | | Pope Mfg. Co. | Hartford | CT | 1905 1915 |
| Fay Juvenile | M | | Columbia Mfg. Co. | Hagerstown | MD | ---- |
| Featherstone | M | | A. Featherstone & Co. | Chicago | IL | 1893 1899 |
| Fenton | M | | Fenton Metallic Co. | Jamestown | NY | 1894 1898 |
| Fenway | M | | Everett Cycle Co. | Everett | MA | 1897 |
| Ferris | M | | Hunt, Helm, & Ferris | Harvard | IL | 1896 1898 |
| Ferris | M | | Union Cycle Mfg. Co. | Minneapolis | MN | 1898 |
| Field | D | | Marshall, Field & Co. | Chicago | IL | 1896 |
| Field Racer | M | | Lindsay Bros. | Milwaukee | WI | 1896 |
| Fischer | M | | Fischer Bros. | Saginaw | MI | 1898 |
| Fisher Special | M | | John W. Fisher | Waco | TX | 1896 |
| Fisher's Flyer | M | | Fisher Carriage Co. | Cincinnati | OH | 1896 |
| Fitchburg | M | | Iver-Johnson Arms & Cycle Co. | Fitchburg | MA | 1896 1898 |

| Bicycle Brand | Manufacturer or Distributor | Company | City | ST | Date of First Notice |
|---|---|---|---|---|---|
| Flash | M | Fay Mfg. Co. | Elyria | OH | 1892 1896 |
| Fleetwing | M | Buffalo Tricycle Co. Buffalo Cyc. Co., 1894-98 | Buffalo | NY | 1892 1893 |
| Fleetwing | M | Buffalo Cycle Co. | Buffalo | NY | 1894 1898 |
| Fleetwood | M | Anderson & Harris Carriage Co. | Elmwood Place | OH | 1896 |
| Fleetwood | M | U. S. Bic. Co. | | NY | 1898 |
| Fleetwood | M | U. S. Bicycle Co. | New York | NY | 1898 |
| Fleur De Lis | M | Tobias & Watson | Perth Amboy | NJ | 1898 |
| Flier Model B | M | Illinois Cycle Works Only model listed | Chicago | IL | 1893 |
| Flora | M | John Sherry | Pensacola | FL | 1896 |
| Flour City | M | Frederick Roach | Minneapolis | MN | 1896 1898 |
| Flower City | D | Hamilton & Matthews | Rochester | NY | 1896 |
| Fly | M | A. J. Street Cycle Co. Price- $100 | Chicago | IL | 1891 1892 |
| Flyer | M | Burke Cycle Co. | Chicago | IL | 1896 |
| Flyer | M | Relay Mfg. Co. | Reading | PA | 1896 1898 |
| Flying Jib | M | A. Featherstone & Co. | Chicago | IL | 1895 1896 |
| Flying Merkel | M | The Miami Cycle & Mfg. Co. | Middletown | OH | 1915 |
| Flying Yankee | M | Eastern Cycle Mfg. Co. | Amesbury | MA | 1896 1897 |
| Folding Bicycle | M | Folding Bic. Co. | Bridgeport | CT | 1896 1898 |
| Foley's Special | M | James Foley & Co. | Chicago | IL | 1898 |
| Forest | M | Forest Cycle Co. | Springfield | MA | 1898 |
| Forest City | M | Geo. Worthington Co. | Cleveland | OH | 1892 |
| Forward | M | Lindsay Bros. | Milwaukee | WI | 1896 |
| Fowler | M | Hill Cycle Mfg. Co. | Chicago | IL | 1893 1895 |
| Fowler | M | Fowler Cycle Co. | Washington | DC | 1896 1898 |
| Fowler | M | Fowler Cycle Works | Chicago | IL | 1896 1900 |
| Fox | M | Fox Machine Co. | Grand Rapids | MI | 1895 1899 |
| Fox | M | W. S. Holmes & Sons | Lansing | MI | 1898 |
| Franklin | M | National Sewing Mach. Co. Model - Franklin, Jr | Belvidere | IL | 1894 1898 |
| Franklin | M | G. A. Phillips | Chicago | IL | 1898 |
| Frazier | M | W. S. Frazier & Co. Included a musical wheel | Aurora | IL | 1895 1898 |
| Freeman | D | Avery Planter Co. | Kansas City | MO | 1896 |
| Friend | M | Hull Bros. | Gasport | NY | 1898 |
| Frontenac | M | Syracuse Specialty Mfg. Co. | Syracuse | NY | 1896 |
| Frontenace | M | Frontenace Mfg. Co. | Syracuse | NY | 1898 |
| Fullworth | D | Lathrop-Rhoads Co. | Des Moines | IA | 1896 |
| Furniss | M | William E. Furniss | Cambridge | MA | 1898 |
| G & J | M | Gormully &Jeffery | Chicago | IL | 1898 |
| G & M | M | Gardener & Morgan | Chicago | IL | 1898 |
| Gales | M | Schoverling, Daly & Gales | New York | NY | 1890 1896 |
| Garden City | M | Willand & Vle Mfg. Co. Canada | St. Catherines | ON | 1896 |
| Gardner | M | Curtis Mach. Works | Chicago | IL | 1896 |
| Garfield | M | Stillwell & Walters | Chicago | IL | 1896 1898 |
| Garland | M | Climax Cycle Co. Garland Cyc. Mfg. Co., Arlington Hgts., 1898 | Chicago | IL | 1896 |
| Garland | M | Peninsular Cycle Co. | Grand Rapids | MI | 1896 1898 |

| Bicycle Brand | Manufacturer or Distributor | Company | City | ST | Date of First Notice | |
|---|---|---|---|---|---|---|
| Gazelle | M | Crawford Mfg. Co. | Hagerstown | MD | 1892 | 1896 |
| | | Models - Standard, Combination | | | | |
| Gazette | M | Columbia Carriage & Cycle Co. | Milwaukee | WI | 1895 | 1896 |
| Gem | M | Lindsay Bros. | Milwaukee | WI | 1892 | 1896 |
| Gendron | M | Gendron Iron Wheel Co. | Toledo | OH | 1891 | 1900 |
| Gendron | M | Gendron Wheel Co. | Toledo | OH | 1897 | 1918 |
| | | till 1937 | | | | |
| General | M | Cream City Cycle Co. | Milwaukee | WI | 1898 | |
| Genesee | D | C. J. Connolly | Rochester | NY | 1896 | |
| Geneva | M | Geneva Cycle Co. | Geneva | OH | 1895 | 1899 |
| | | Model - Geneva Special | | | | |
| Georgia Special | M | Georgia Bic. Co. | Atlanta | GA | 1898 | |
| Geraffe | D | W. Hoffman | Chicago | IL | 1896 | |
| Ghost | M | Warwick Cycle Mfg. Co. | Springfield | MA | 1892 | |
| Ghost | M | Kankakee Mfg. Co. | Kankakee | IL | 1898 | |
| Giant | M | Lozier & Yost Bicycle Mfg. Co. | Toledo, | OH | 1890 | |
| Giant | M | H. A. Lozier & Co. | Cleveland | OH | 1891 | 1892 |
| | | Models - Giantess and Little Giant (Factory Toledo) | | | | |
| Giant #4 | M | H. A. Lozier & Co. | Cleveland | OH | 1889 | 1890 |
| Giantess | M | H. A. Lozier & Co. | Cleveland | OH | 1891 | |
| | | (Factory Toledo) | | | | |
| Gilbert | M | Gilbert & Chester Co. | Elizabeth | NJ | 1896 | |
| Gilchester | M | Gilbert & Chester Co. | Elizabeth | NJ | 1896 | 1898 |
| Gildolph | M | Rudolph & Gill | Philadelphia | PA | 1898 | |
| Girard | D | Supplee Hdw. Co. | Philadelphia | PA | 1896 | |
| Girder Star | D | Montgomery Ward & Co. | Chicago | IL | 1892 | |
| Gladiator | M | Gladiator Cycle Works | Chicago | IL | 1896 | 1898 |
| Gladstone | M | James Cycle Mfg. Co. | Chicago | IL | 1895 | 1898 |
| | | Located in White Cloud, MI, in 1898 | | | | |
| Glen Oak | M | F. A. Henning Cycle Co. | Peoria | IL | 1896 | |
| Glendon | M | Loegler & Ladd | Buffalo | NY | 1898 | |
| Glide | M | W. F. Horton | Hicksville | OH | 1896 | 1898 |
| Glideaway | D | Kingman & Co. | | | 1893 | |
| Globe | M | Globe Cycle Works | Buffalo | NY | 1895 | 1898 |
| Globe Trotter | M | John A. Kling | Chicago | IL | 1898 | |
| Glyde | M | W. F. Horton | Hicksville | OH | 1896 | |
| Go Fast | D | Farwell, Ozmun, Kirk, & Co. | St. Paul | MN | 1896 | |
| Goddess Of Liberty | M | Rockaway Mfg. Co. | New York | NY | 1892 | |
| Golconda | M | E. E. Harris | Perrysville | IN. | 1898 | |
| Golden Crown | M | Folmer & Schwing Mfg. Co. | New York | NY | 1898 | |
| Golden Eagle | M | Bernard T. Parsons | Camden | NJ | 1898 | |
| Goold | M | Goold Bic. Co. | Brantford | ON | 1896 | |
| Gordon | M | Gordon M. Richardson | Chicago | IL | 1896 | |
| Goshen | M | Walker & Stutz Co. | Goshen | IN | 1896 | 1898 |
| Goshen Special | M | Lindsay Bros. | Milwaukee | WI | 1896 | |
| Gotham | M | Schoverling, Daly & Gales | New York | NY | 1892 | 1896 |
| Gould | M | J. W. Gould | Syracuse | NY | 1898 | |
| Graham | M | Charles E. Graham | Chicago | IL | 1898 | |
| Grampian | M | Galletts Felice | Williamsport | PA | 1898 | |
| Grand Central | M | New York Cycle Co. | New York | NY | 1898 | |
| Grand Keating | M | Keating Wheel Co. | Middletown | CT | 1898 | |
| Grant | M | Climax Cycle Co. | Chicago | IL | 1896 | |

| Bicycle Brand | Manufacturer or Distributor | Company | City | ST | Date of First Notice | |
|---|---|---|---|---|---|---|
| Graphic | M | Graphic Cycle Co. | New York | NY | 1898 | |
| Gray | M | Gray Cycle Mfg. Co. | Gloucester | MA | ---- | |
| Gray Fox | M | Fox Mach. Co. | Grand Rapids | MI | 1896 | |
| Great Eastern | M | Eastern Cycle Mfg. Co. | Amesbury | MA | 1897 | |
| Great Scott | M | Scott Paper Co. | Philadelphia | PA | 1898 | |
| Grenadier | M | Champion Machine Co. | Philadelphia | PA | 1898 | |
| Greyhound | M | Emblem Bicycle Co. | Angola | NY | ---- | |
| Greyhound | M | Brown Bros. Mfg. Co. | Chicago | IL | 1892 | 1896 |
| Greyhound | M | Central Machine Works | Toronto | ON | 1896 | |
| Greyhound | M | Cole & Gerald Co. | East Brookfield | MA | 1896 | 1897 |
| | | The Greyhound Bic. Mfg. Co., 1898 | | | | |
| Guernsey | M | Kankakee Mfg. Co. | Kankakee | IL | 1896 | 1898 |
| Guide | M | Fay Mfg. Co. | Elyria | OH | 1892 | |
| Guide | M | F. X. Mueller Co. | Buffalo | NY | 1896 | |
| Gump | D | A. W. Gump & Co. | Dayton | OH | ---- | |
| | | Probably America's first large discounter | | | | |
| Gunning | M | Elgin Sewing Mach. Co. | Elgin | IL | 1896 | 1898 |
| Gypsie | D | Hibbard, Spencer & Bartlett Co. | Chicago | IL | 1892 | |
| | | Ladies' | | | | |
| Gypsy | D | Hibbard, Spencer & Bartlett Co. | Chicago | IL | 1892 | 1896 |
| | | Men's | | | | |
| Gypsy Queen | M | Congress Cycle Co. | Hartford, City | IN | 1896 | |
| Hackney | M | Hackney Bic. Co. | Cleveland | OH | 1896 | |
| Hadley | D | C. J. Connolly | Rochester | NY | 1896 | |
| Hall's Special | M | Spencer Hall. | Racine | WI | 1898 | |
| Halladay | M | Marion Cycle Co. | Marion | IN | 1892 | 1900 |
| | | Model - Halladay-Temple | | | | |
| Hamilton | M | Hamilton Cycle Co. | Hamilton | OH | 1896 | |
| Hamilton | M | Hamilton-Kenwood Cycle Co. | Grand Rapids | MI | 1897 | |
| Hampden | M | Sieg & Walpole Mfg. Co. | Kenosha | WI | 1896 | |
| Hanauer | M | Charles Hanauer & Bro. | Cincinnati | OH | 1896 | 1898 |
| | | Models - Model, Special, Mascot | | | | |
| Hansen (The) | M | Thorvald Hansen | Boston | MA | 1898 | |
| Hardy Jarless Bicycle. | M | Hardy Cycle Co. | New York | NY | 1896 | |
| Hare | M | Lindsay Bros. | Milwaukee | WI | 1896 | |
| Harger | M | Harger Convertible Bic. Co. | Chicago | IL | 1898 | |
| | | Convertible Tandem only | | | | |
| Harley Davidson | M | Harley Davidson | | | 1917 | 1921 |
| Harper | M | L. W. Harper | McHugh | MN | 1894 | |
| | | a unicycle | | | | |
| Hart | M | W. D. Hart | Oatfield | OH | 1898 | |
| | | Models - Special, Roadster | | | | |
| Hartford | M | Hartford Cycle Co. | Hartford | CT | 1895 | 1899 |
| | | Subsidiary of the Pope Mfg. Co | | | | |
| Hartford | M | American Bicycle Co. | | | 1900 | 1901 |
| | | Pope Sales Department | | | | |
| Hartford | M | American Cycle Mfg. Co. | Hartford | CT | 1902 | 1903 |
| | | Eastern Sales Dept., Columbia Factory | | | | |
| Hartford | M | Hartford Cycle Co. * | Hartford | CT | 1904 | 1915 |
| Hartford | M | Westfield Mfg. Co. | Westfield | MA | 1916 | |
| Harvard | M | Washburne Cycle Co. | Boston | MA | 1892 | |
| Harvard | M | Knapp & Spaulding Co. | Sioux City | IA | 1896 | |
| Hawkeye | M | Lindsay Bros. | Milwaukee | WI | 1896 | |

| Bicycle Brand | Manufacturer or Distributor | Company | City | ST | Date of First Notice |
|---|---|---|---|---|---|
| Hawley-King Roadster | M | Lindsay Bros. | Milwaukee | WI | 1896 |
| Hawthorne | D | Montgomery Ward & Co. | Chicago | IL | 1895 1898 |
| Hawthorne | M | The Thorn Mfg. Co. | Washington | DC | 1896 |
| Hearsey | M | H. F. Hearsey & Co. | Indianapolis | IN | 1896 |
| Hearsey | M | H. T. Hearsey Cycle Co. | Indianapolis | IN | 1896 |
| Hecla | D | A. G. Spalding & Bros. | New York | NY | 1892 |
| Hector | D | O. J. Faxon & Co. | Boston | MA | 1893 1896 |
| Heinz | M | Heinz & Munschauer Cycle Works | Buffalo | NY | 1897 1898 |
| Heloise | D | Hibbard, Spencer & Bartlett Co. | Chicago | IL | 1896 |
| Helwig's Special | M | Charles Helwig & Co. | Jenkintown | PA | 1898 |
| Hendee | M | Hendee & Nelson Mfg. Co. |  |  | 1895 1896 |
|  |  | Models - Silver Queen and Silver King |  |  |  |
| Henley | M | Henley Bic. Works | Richmond | IN | 1895 1898 |
|  |  | Models - Special, Roadster, Diamond, Lady Henley |  |  |  |
| Hennecke Special | M | Lindsay Bros. | Milwaukee | WI | 1896 |
| Herald | D | VanCamp Hardware and Iron Co. | Indianapolis | IN | 1894 |
| Herald | M | Herald Cycle Co. | New York | NY | 1895 1896 |
| Hercules | M | McIntosh-Huntington Co. | Cleveland | OH | 1895 1898 |
| Hercules | M | Glenn Curtiss | Hammondsport | NY | 1899 |
| Herman Special | M | Erie Cycle Co. | Erie | PA | 1898 |
| Hero | M | Union Mfg. Co. | Toledo | OH | 1892 1898 |
|  |  | The 1892 and 93 models were sold by Montgomery Ward & Co. |  |  |  |
| Herold | M | Bolte Mfg. Co. | Milwaukee | WI | 1896 |
| Hiawatha | M | Central Cycle Mfg. Co. | Indianapolis | IN | 1896 1898 |
| Hiawatha | M | E. J. Davis | Winona | MN | 1898 |
| Hickok | M | Hickok Mfg. Co. | Harrisburg | PA | 1898 |
| Hickory | M | Elliott Hickory Cycle Co. | Newton | MA | 1892 |
| Hickory | M | Hickory Wheel Co. | Newton | MA | 1893 1895 |
|  |  | Newton /South Farmington, MA |  |  |  |
| High Art | M | R. H. Wolff & Co. | New York | NY | ---- |
| High Grade | M | Leiter & Beazle | Navarre | OH | 1898 |
| High Speed | M | High Speed Cycle Co. | Chicago | IL | 1898 |
| Hildick | M | A. Edmund Hildick Co. | New York | NY | 1898 |
| Hilsendegen Special | M | H. T. Hearsey & Co. | Indianapolis | IN | 1896 |
| Hodge Spring Wheel | M | Hodge Bic-Works | Turner | IL | 1896 |
| Hoefler | M | William C . Hoefler | Geneva | NY | 1896 1898 |
| Hoffman | M | Hoffman Bicycle Co. | Cleveland | OH | 1896 1899 |
| Holbrook | M | Holbrook Cycle Mfg. Co. | Germantown | PA | 1895 1898 |
| Holton Special | M | W. B. Holton Mfg. Co. | Indianapolis | IN | 1898 |
|  |  | Model - Twentieth Century |  |  |  |
| Home | M | Home Bic. Co. | Chicago | IL | 1896 |
| Hoosier | M | Columbus Brass & Iron Co. | Columbus | IN | 1896 1898 |
| Hoosier Belle | D | Morgan & Co. | Ft. Wayne | IN | 1896 |
| Hornet | M | King "B" Cycle Co. | Chicago | IL | 1896 |
| Horseman |  |  |  |  | 1888 |
| Horsman | D | E. J. Horsman | New York | NY | 1892 1896 |
| Horton | M | Horton Mfg. Co. | Reading | MA | 1898 |
| Howard | M | E. Howard Watch & Clock Co. | Boston | MA | 1896 1897 |
| Howard Special | M | Mrs. Medora H. Howard | Chicago | IL | 1898 |
| Howe Special | D | Howe Scale Co. | San Francisco | CA | 1896 1898 |
| Hub King | D | John K. Hastings | Boston | MA | 1896 |
| Hub Model | M | Lindsay Bros. | Milwaukee | WI | 1896 |

| Bicycle Brand | Manufacturer or Distributor | Company | City | ST | Date of First Notice |
|---|---|---|---|---|---|
| Hub Queen | D | John K. Hastings | Boston | MA | 1896 |
| Hudson | M | Bean-Chamberlain Mfg. Co. | Hudson | MI | 1896 1902 |
| | | Models - Racer, Special, Lady Hudson | | | |
| Hudson | M | Miami Cycle Mfg. Co. | Middletown | OH | 1896 |
| | | Model - Lady Hudson | | | |
| Hudsonia | M | Miami Cycle & Mfg. Co. | Middletown | OH | 1914 |
| Hudsonian | M | Miami Cycle & Mfg. Co. | Middletown | OH | 1912 |
| Hughes | M | Frank L. Hughes | Rochester | NY | 1896 |
| Humber | M | Humber Co. of America | Westboro | MA | 1895 1898 |
| Humboldt | M | Humboldt Park Cycle Co. | Chicago | IL | 1896 |
| Hummer | M | Foley & Williams Mfg. Co. | Chicago | IL | 1896 1898 |
| Humming Bird | M | Bettys & Mabbett | Rochester | NY | 1896 1898 |
| Hunter | M | Hunter Arms Co. | Fulton | NY | 1895 1898 |
| Huron | M | Henderson Bic. Co. | Goderich | ON | 1896 |
| Huron | M | Horn Cycle Co. | Chicago | IL | 1898 |
| Hurricane | D | S. A. Haines Co. | Indianapolis | IN | 1896 |
| Huseby | M | Huseby Cycle Mfg. Co. | Milwaukee | WI | 1898 |
| Hussar | M | Champion Mach. Co. | Philadelphia | PA | 1898 |
| Hustler | M | Fox Mach. Co. | Grand Rapids | MI | 1893 1896 |
| Hy-Lo | D | Louis Rosenfeld & Co. | New York | NY | 1896 |
| Hyde | M | New London Bic. Co. | New London | CT | 1898 |
| Hydro-Cycle | D | McIntosh-Huntington Co. | Cleveland | OH | ---- |
| Hygeia | D | G. W. Pessy | Hammontown | NJ | 1895 |
| Ide | M | F. D. Ide Mfg. Co. | Peoria | IL | 1894 1898 |
| | | Models - Special, Lady Ide | | | |
| Ide | M | F. F. Ide Mfg. Co. | Peoria | IL | 1894 1898 |
| Ideal | M | Hotelling Bros. | Chicago | IL | 1896 |
| Ideal | M | Shelby Cycle Co. | Shelby | OH | 1896 1898 |
| Ideal | M | American Bicycle Co. | Chicago | IL | 1901 |
| | | Rambler Sales Department | | | |
| Ideal | M | American Cycle Mfg. Co. | Chicago | IL | 1903 |
| | | Western Sales Department | | | |
| Ideal | M | Pope Mfg. Co. | Chicago | IL | 1904 |
| | | Western Department | | | |
| Ideal | M | Pope Mfg. Co. | Hartford | CT | 1908 |
| Idlehour | M | Clark Mfg. Co. | Buffalo | NY | 1896 |
| Ilion | M | Remington Arms Co. | Ilion | NY | 1896 1898 |
| Illinois | M | John H. Miller | Chicago | IL | 1898 |
| Illinois Special | M | Illinois Watch Case Co. | Elgin | IL | 1898 |
| Imperial | M | Ames & Frost Co. | Chicago | IL | 1892 1900 |
| | | Models by letter | | | |
| Imperial | M | American Bicycle Co. | Chicago | IL | 1901 1902 |
| | | Cleveland Sales Dept. | | | |
| Imperial | M | Pope Mfg. Co. | Chicago | IL | 1904 1914 |
| | | Western Department | | | |
| Improved America | M | International Mfg. Co. | Chicago | IL | 1896 |
| Independence. | M | M. E. Griswold Co. | Chicago | IL | 1898 |
| Independent | D | E. T. Harris | Chicago | IL | 1896 |
| Indian | M | Hendee Manufacturing Co. | Springfield | MA | ---- |
| Indiana | M | Lindsay Bros. | Milwaukee | WI | 1896 |
| Indianapolis | D | Wheelmen's Co. | Indianapolis | IN | 1896 |
| Industrial | M | Industrial Cycle Mfg. Co. | Springfield | MA | 1898 |

| Bicycle Brand | Manufacturer or Distributor | Company | City | ST | Date of First Notice | |
|---|---|---|---|---|---|---|
| Ingall's | M | Lindsay Bros. | Milwaukee | WI | 1896 | |
| Ingomar | D | A. Treadway & Sons Hardware Co. | Dubuque | IA | 1896 | |
| Inter-Ocean | D | C. H. Sterner & Co. | Chicago | IL | 1896 | |
| Invincible | M | Bretz & Curtis Mfg. Co. | Philadelphia | PA | 1892 | |
| Invincible | M | Standard Cycle Co. | Buffalo | NY | 1892 | |
| Iowa | D | Baker & Son. | Fayette | IA | 1896 | |
| Iris | M | Stephen Ballard Rubber Co. | New York | NY | 1896 | |
| Iroquois | M | Stover Bic. Mfg. Co. | Freeport | IL. | 1891 | 1892 |
| Iroquois | M | Iroquois Cycle Mfg. Co. | Buffalo | NY | 1896 | 1898 |
| Iroquois | M | Iroquois Cycle Works | Chicago | IL | 1896 | 1898 |
| Iroquois | M | Lindsay Bros. | Milwaukee | WI | 1896 | |
| Irving | D | Charles H. Childs & Co. | Utica | NY | 1896 | |
| Irwell | M | Sweeting Cycle Co. | Philadelphia | PA | 1892 | |
| Isabella | M | Illinois Cycle Works | Chicago | IL | 1893 | 1896 |
| Ivanhoe | M | Morris Cycle Co. | New Castle | OH | 1892 | 1898 |
| Ivel | D | A. G. Spalding & Bros. | New York | NY | 1892 | |
| Ivel | D | Spalding & Bros. | New York | NY | 1892 | |
| Iver Johnson | M | Iver Johnson's Arms & Cycle Works Models by number | Fitchburg | MA | 1896 | 1918 |
| Izzer | M | Lindsay Bros. | Milwaukee | WI | 1896 | |
| James | M | James Cycle Co. | Chicago | IL | 1892 | 1896 |
| Jefferson | M | Graham Cycle Mfg. Co. | Chattanooga | TN | 1896 | |
| Jefferson (The) | D | Mercher & Co. | Richmond | VA | 1896 | |
| Jersey | M | Elizabeth Cycle Mfg. Co. Models - J. Belle, J. Boy, J. Flyer | Elizabeth | NJ | 1896 | 1898 |
| Jersey | M | New Jersey Stamping Works | | | 1896 | |
| Jewel | M | Geo. Worthington Co. | Cleveland | OH | 1892 | |
| Jewel | D | Charles Cogan Cycle Co. | Chicago | IL | 1896 | |
| Johnson Special | M | Johnson Cycle Works | Buffalo | NY | 1895 | 1898 |
| Joliet | M | Joliet Wheel Co. | Joliet | IL | 1892 | |
| Jones | M | Jones Cycle Co. | Portland | IN | 1895 | |
| Jordan Special | M | L. Jordan Model - Model C | Chicago | IL | 1896 | 1898 |
| Josephine | M | Colfax Mfg. Co. | South Bend | IN | 1896 | |
| Josephine | M | Jenkins Cycle Co. | Chicago | IL | 1896 | 1898 |
| Josephine | D | Sears, Roebuck & Co. | Chicago | IL | 1902 | 1908 |
| Joy's Special | M | E. W. Joy | Wapello | IA | 1898 | |
| Joyslin | D | J. C. Joyslin Cycle Co. | Minneapolis | MN | 1896 | |
| Jubilee | | (Advertised with Dayton Bicycles) | | | | |
| Julian | | Fred W. Hubbard | Wellsville | NY | ---- | |
| Juliet | M | Ralph Temple Cycle Co. | Chicago | IL | ---- | |
| Juniata | M | H. H. Lane Mfg. Co. | Huntington | PA | 1896 | |
| Junior | M | Western Wheel Works 1893-1894 | Chicago | IL | 1891 | 1892 |
| Juno | M | Western Wheel Works Price - $70. Models by number | Chicago | IL | 1891 | 1893 |
| Jupiter | M | Clarke Cycle Co. | Chicago | IL | 1896 | 1898 |
| Juvenile | M | Hero Cycle Co. | Chicago | IL | 1898 | |
| Juvenile | M | Tricycle Mfg. Co. | Springfield | OH | 1898 | |
| Juvenile Williams | M | Fay Mfg. Co. | Elyria | OH | 1898 | |
| K | M | Herbert M. Kenyon | Ashoway | RI | 1898 | |

| Bicycle Brand | Manufacturer or Distributor | Company | City | ST | Date of First Notice |
|---|---|---|---|---|---|
| K & B Diamond | M | Keefe & Becannon | | NY | 1891 1892 |
| K. M. | M | Kelly, Maus & Co. | Chicago | IL | 1896 |
| Kalkaska | M | Elmer F. Johnson Cycle Works | Kalkaska | MI | 1898 |
| Kangaroo | D | A. G. Spalding & Bros. | New York | NY | 1892 |
| Kankakee | M | Kankakee Mfg. Co. | Kankakee | IL | 1896 1898 |
| Kansas | | | | | 1888 |
| Kathrina | M | Hampshire Cycle Mfg. Co. | | | 1896 1898 |
| | | Located in Northampton, MA, in 1898 | | | |
| Kaufman's White Flyer | M | Charles Kaufman | Marion | OH | 1898 |
| Kearney | M | Kearney Cycle Co. | Kearney | NE | 1895 1898 |
| | | Models - Kearney Special, Kearney Doublet, Lady Kearney | | | |
| Keating | M | Keating Wheel Co. | Holyoke | MA | 1892 1898 |
| Keating | M | Keating Wheel Co. | Middletown | CT | 1897 1898 |
| Keene Special | M | Wilkens Toy Co. | Keene | NH | 1898 |
| Kemp Special | M | Kemp, Atwood & Co. | Paxton | IL | 1896 |
| Kenilworth | M | Sieg & Walpole Mfg. Co. | Kenosha | WI | 1896 |
| Kenmore | D | Thorsen & Cassady Co. | Chicago | IL | 1896 |
| Kennebee Special | D | Mead Cycle Co. | Chicago | IL | ---- |
| Kennedy Special | M | Lindsay Bros. | Milwaukee | WI | 1896 |
| Keno | M | Hollingsworth & Co. | Philadelphia | PA | 1898 |
| Kensington | M | Martin & Gibson Mfg. Co. | Buffalo | NY | 1896 1898 |
| Kenton | D | Harbison & Gathright | Louisville | KY | 1896 |
| Kentucky | M | V. C. Razor Cycle Co. | Saltlick | KY | 1898 |
| Kenwood | M | Kenwood Mfg. Co. | Chicago | IL | 1892 1908 |
| Kerr | D | Beck & Corbitt | St. Louis | MO | 1896 |
| Keydic | M | Ohio Cycle Co. | | | ---- |
| Keystone | M | Williamsport Bic. Mfg. Co. | Williamsport | PA | 1895 1896 |
| Kid Mershon | M | Mershon Cycle Works | Philadelphia | | |
| Kim Juvenile | D | N.Y. Sporting Goods Co. | | NY | ---- |
| Kim Juvenile | D | New York Sporting Goods Co. | New York | NY | 1910 1911 |
| Kimball | M | Phillips Mfg. Co. | New York | NY | 1895 1898 |
| King | M | King Wheel Co. | | NY | 1885 1887 |
| | | Geared Ordinary | | | |
| King "B" | M | King B Cycle Co. | Chicago | IL | 1896 |
| King Bee | M | Hill Cycle Co. | Chicago | IL | 1895 1896 |
| King Chainless | M | A. Featherstone & Co. | Chicago | IL | ---- |
| King Errant | M | Knight Cycle Co. | St. Louis | MO | 1896 |
| King of Diamonds | D | Capitol Cycle Co. | Washington | DC | 1892 1896 |
| King of Racers | M | Kirkwood, Miller & Co. | Peoria | IL | 1892 1893 |
| King of Scorchers | D | McIntosh-Huntington Co. | Cleveland | OH | ---- |
| King of the Road | M | Indiana Bic. Mfg. Co. | Indianapolis | IN | 1892 |
| King of Trumps | M | Ralph Temple Cycle Co. | Chicago | IL | 1896 1898 |
| King Phillip | M | J. l. Gallagher | Boston | MA | 1898 |
| Kingdom | D | T. B. Raye & Co. | Detroit | MI | 1896 |
| Kingman | M | Kingman & Co. | Peoria | IL. | 1895 1896 |
| Kinnear's Special | M | George C. Kinnear | Boston | MA | 1898 |
| Kirkwood | M | Kirkwood, Miller & Co. | Peoria | IL | 1892 1893 |
| Kit Carson | D | Consumers' Supply Co. | Chicago | IL | 1896 |
| Kite | D | Kirkwood, Miller & Co. | Peoria | IL | |
| | | English make | | | |
| Kittaning | M | Kittaning Cycle Mfg. Co. | Kittaning | PA | 1898 |
| Kitten | M | Premier Cycle Co. | New York | NY | 1892 |

| Bicycle Brand | Manufacturer or Distributor | Company | City | ST | Date of First Notice |
|---|---|---|---|---|---|
| Kling | M | John A. Kling | Chicago | IL | 1898 |
| Klondike | M | Springfield Cycle Co. | Springfield | MA | 1898 |
| Klondyke | M | National Cycle Mfg. Co. | Bay City | MI | 1898 |
| Knickerbocker | M | Knickerbocker Cycle Mfg. | New York | NY | 1896 |
| Knight | M | Knight Cycle Co. | St. Louis | MO | 1895 1898 |
| | | Models - Racer, Errant, Special, Scorcher, Plumed Knight, Templar | | | |
| Knights | M | George L. Knights | Amesbury | MA | 1898 |
| Knox | D | A. Dean & Son | Galesburg | IL | 1896 |
| Koehler's Special | M | Jacob Koehler | Rochester | NY | ---- |
| Kohinor | M | Premier Cycle Co. | New York | NY | 1892 |
| Kohler Bros. | M | Kohler Bros. | Chicago | IL | 1898 |
| Konigslow | M | Otto Konigslow Bicycles | Cleveland | OH | 1900 1901 |
| | | Models - Standard, Chainless | | | |
| Konwark | M | Moore Carving Mach. Co. | Minneapolis | MN | 1898 |
| Koopman | M | Alfred T. Koopman | Chicago | IL | 1898 |
| Korker | M | Star Mfg. & Supply Co. | Chicago | IL | 1896 |
| Kosmos | D | Dunham, Carrigan, & Hayden | San Francisco | CA | 1896 |
| Kowalski | M | John Kowalski | Apollo | PA | 1898 |
| Kraft Special | M | Kraft Cycle Co. | St. Louis | MO | 1898 |
| Krafve | M | J. A. Alsten | Worcester | MA | 1898 |
| Kreuser Special | D | Gross Park Cycle Co. | Chicago | IL | 1896 |
| L.A.W. | M | Waltham Mfg. Co. | Waltham | MA | 1896 |
| L & B | M | L & B Cycle Mfg. Co. | Cleveland | OH | 1898 |
| L.C.W. | M | Lineville Carriage Works | Lineville | IA | 1898 |
| L & M Special | M | Long & Martin | Chicago | IL | 1898 |
| La Belle | M | LaBelle Bic. Co. | Holyoke | MA | 1892 1898 |
| La Clede | D | Beck & Corbitt | St. Louis | MO | 1896 |
| La Crosse | M | Lindsay Bros. | Milwaukee | WI | 1896 |
| Ladie Grace | M | Albia Cycle Co. | Albia | IA | 1898 |
| Ladies Bloomer-Brownie | M | Razoux & Handy | Boston | MA | 1895 |
| Ladies' Pride | M | Peru Cycle Exchange | Peru | IN | 1896 |
| Lady D | M | Harry Wilson | Doniphan | NE | 1898 |
| Lady Jay | M | Jones Cycle Co. | Portland | IN | 1898 |
| Lady Julia | D | A. Treadway & Sons Hardware Co. | Dubuque | IA | 1896 |
| Lady Somerset | D | John K. Hastings | Boston | MA | 1896 |
| Lake | M | Lake Cycle Mfg. Co. | Milwaukee | WI | 1898 |
| Lakeside | D | Lockwood-Taylor Hardware Co. | Cleveland | OH | 1896 |
| Lamasco | M | Single Center Springs Co. | Evansville | IN | 1896 |
| Lambert Special | M | Black Rock Cycle Works | Titusville | PA | 1898 |
| Langley | M | Sieg & Walpole Mfg. Co. | Kenosha | WI | 1896 |
| Larchmont | M | Peerless Rubber Mfg. Co. | New York | NY | 1896 |
| Lark | M | Ellicott Mfg. Co. | Tonawanda | NY | 1898 |
| Latest | M | Demorest Mfg. Co. | Williamsport | PA | 1896 |
| Laurel | D | S. D. Morrill & Co. | Amesbury | MA | 1896 1898 |
| Laurel | M | Bown Mach. Works | Battle Creek | MI | 1898 |
| Laurel Special | M | Rapp Bros. | Chicago | IL | 1898 |
| | | Built to order | | | |
| Le Clair | M | Bignall & Keeler Mfg. Co. | Edwardsville | IL | 1896 1898 |
| Le Jeal | M | Le Jeal Cycle Works | Erie | PA | 1898 |
| Leader | M | Fay Mfg. Co. | Elyria | OH | 1892 |
| Leader | M | U. S. Bic. Co. | New York | NY | 1896 1898 |
| Leader | M | U. S. Bicycle Co. | New York | NY | 1896 1898 |

| Bicycle Brand | Manufacturer or Distributor | Company | City | ST | Date of First Notice |
|---|---|---|---|---|---|
| League | M | League Cycle Co. | Hartford | CT | 1892 1898 |
| | | Model - Chainless, 1895 | | | |
| Lebanon | M | Kalbach & Son | Lebanon | PA | 1898 |
| Lebanon Eagle | M | Eagle Cycle Mfg. Co. | Lebanon | PA | 1898 |
| Lee | D | Lee-Clark-Andreesen Hardware Co. | Omaha | NE | 1896 |
| Legal Tender | M | Ohio Bic. Mfg. Co. | Marion | OH | 1898 |
| Lehigh | M | Crandall Mach. Co. | Groton | NY | ---- |
| Lehigh | M | Crandall Machine Co. | Groton | NY | ---- |
| Lehigh | M | Weatherby Bic. Mfg. Co. | Weatherby | PA | 1895 |
| Lelair | M | N. O. Nelson Mfg. Co. | St. Louis | MO | 1896 |
| Lenape | M | Pollock & Ruos | Doylestown | PA | 1898 |
| Lennox | M | Richmond Bic. Co. | Richmond | IN | 1896 |
| Lenox | D | Syndicate Trading Co. | | NY | 1896 |
| | | Model - Lady Lenox | | | |
| Leon | M | Curtis Mach. Works | Chicago | IL | 1895 1896 |
| Leonard | M | C. L. Leonard | Silver Lake | IN | 1896 |
| Leroy | | | Buffalo | NY | ---- |
| Leroy | M | Leroy Cycle Works | Philadelphia | PA | 1898 |
| Lexington | M | Sieg & Walpole Mfg. Co. | Kenosha | WI | 1896 |
| Lexington | M | Boston Wheel Works | Boston | MA | 1898 |
| Liberty | M | Liberty Cycle Co. | Bridgeport | CT | 1891 1898 |
| Liberty | M | Rockaway Mfg. Co. | New York | NY | 1892 |
| Light | M | Light Cycle Co. | Pottstown | PA | 1895 1900 |
| | | Models - Model A, Model B, Racer, Chainless | | | |
| Lightning | M | Indiana Bic. Mfg. Co. | Indianapolis | IN | 1892 |
| Lightning | M | O. G. Eggen Cycle Co. | Chicago | IL | 1896 1898 |
| Lightning Double Diamond | M | Western Wheel Works | Chicago | IL | 1892 |
| Lightning Flyer | M | Climax Cycle Co. | Chicago | IL | 1896 |
| Lightning Messenger | M | Sercombe & Bolte Mfg.Co. | Milwaukee | WI | 1892 |
| Lighton | M | Lighton Mach. Co. | Syracuse | NY | 1896 |
| Lily | D | Little Rock Tent & Awning Co. | Little Rock | AR | 1896 |
| Limited | M | Lindsay Bros. | Milwaukee | WI | 1896 |
| Lincoln | M | Climax Cycle Co. | Chicago | IL | 1896 |
| Lincoln | M | Frank W. Swett Mfg. Co. | Chicago | IL | 1898 |
| Lindsay | M | Lindsay Bros. | Milwaukee | WI | 1895 1898 |
| Lindsay | M | Lindsay Bic. Mfg. Co. | Lafayette | IN | 1896 1898 |
| Lititz | M | John G. Zook | Lititz | PA | 1895 1898 |
| Little Giant | M | J. S. Medary Saddlery Co. | LaCrosse | WI | 1896 |
| Little Jewel | D | Hibbard, Spencer & Bartlett Co. | Chicago | IL | 1892 1898 |
| Little Joe | D | Speedwell Cycle Co. | Baltimore | MD | 1896 |
| | | Little Joe Wiesenfield Co. in 1898 | | | |
| Little Nemo | D | N. Y. Sporting Goods Co. | | NY | ---- |
| Little Princess | M | Gendron Wheel Co. | Toledo | OH | 1896 |
| Little Scorcher | M | Gendron Wheel Co. | Toledo | OH | 1896 |
| Little Traveller | M | Luburg Mfg. Co. | Philadelphia | PA | 1892 |
| Lloyd | M | Roots & Co. | Indianapolis | IN | 1894 |
| Lloyd (The) | M | George E. Lloyd & Co. | Chicago | IL | 1898 |
| Lockport | M | Korf & Bunce | Lockport | NY | 1892 |
| Lohmann Special | M | D. N. Lohmann | Canajoharie | NY | 1896 |
| London Triumph | M | J. B. Rich Cycle Co. | Philadelphia | PA | 1892 |
| Lone Star | M | Crasten & Patterson | Chicago | IL | 1898 |
| Loomis Lightweight | M | Gilbert J. Loomis | Westfield | MA | 1895 1900 |

| Bicycle Brand | Manufacturer or Distributor | Company | City | ST | Date of First Notice |
|---|---|---|---|---|---|
| Looseley | M | Looseley Cycle Co. | Birmingham | AL | 1896 1898 |
| Lorenzo | M | Lawrence Bros. Cycle Mfg. Co. | Kansas City | MO | 1898 |
| Lorraine | M | Colonial Cycle Mfg. Co. | Philadelphia | PA | 1898 |
| Lotte Special | M | Anderson Bic. Wheel Co. | Anderson | IN | 1898 |
| Lovell | M | John P. Lovell Arms Co. | Boston | MA | 1891 1900 |
| | | (1889) Models - Excel, Diamond Frame, Special | | | |
| Lovell | M | Iver Johnson Sporting Goods Co. | Boston | MA | 1903 1909 |
| Loyal | M | Wesson-Nivisson Mfg. Co. | Cortland | NY | 1895 1898 |
| | | The Wesson Mfg. Co. in 1898 | | | |
| Loyal | M | Koster & Co. | Erie | PA | 1896 |
| Lu-Mi-Num | M | St. Louis Wooden Gutter Co. | St. Louis | MO | 1893 1898 |
| | | full company name is: St. Louis Refrigerator & Wooden Gutter Co. | | | |
| Lu-Mi-Num | M | St Louis Aluminum Casting Co. | St Louis | MO | 1898 |
| Luberg Special | M | Luburg Mfg. Co. | Philadelphia | PA | 1892 |
| Lucas | M | Ott & Henley | Toledo | OH | 1898 |
| Lucile | M | Lathrop-Rhoads Co. | Des Moines | IA | 1896 |
| Luthy | M | Luthy & Co. | Peoria | IL | 1892 1898 |
| Lycoming | M | Williamsport Bic. Mfg. Co. | Williamsport | PA | 1896 |
| Lyndhurst | M | McKee & Harrington | Lyndhurst | NY | 1892 1900 |
| | | Models - Lady Lyndhurst. Featured triple front fork | | | |
| M & C | M | Madden & Clark | Boston | MA | 1898 |
| Madelia | M | Lindsay Bros. | Milwaukee | WI | 1896 |
| Madison | M | D. D. Warner Co. | Madison | WI | 1896 1898 |
| Madonna | D | U. S. Bicycle Co. | New York | NY | 1896 |
| Magic | M | Moore Mfg. & Foundry Co. | Milwaukee | WI | 1896 |
| Magic | M | Tonawanda Cycle Co. | Tonawanda | NY | 1896 |
| Magnet | M | Ames & Frost Co. | Chicago | IL | 1896 |
| Magnet | M | Home Bic. Co. | Chicago | IL | 1896 |
| Magnet | M | Magnet Cycle Co. | Chicago | IL | 1898 |
| | | Model - Tandem | | | |
| Magnetic | | Walbridge & Co. | Buffalo | NY | |
| Maid Marian | M | McDaniel & Merrihew Cycle Co. | Wilmington | DE | 1896 |
| Maid Marion | M | Marion Cycle Co. | Marion | OH | 1893 |
| Maid of the Mist | M | Buffalo Wheel Co. | Buffalo | NY | 1896 |
| Majestic | M | Hurlbut Bros. & Co. | New York | NY | 1892 1898 |
| Mammouth Bicycle | | Ruben Woods | Syracuse | NY | ---- |
| Manhattan | M | Indiana Bic. Mfg. Co. | Indianapolis | IN | 1892 |
| Manhattan | M | Lindsay Bros. | Milwaukee | WI | 1896 |
| Manhattan | M | Schoverling, Daly & Gales | New York | NY | 1896 |
| Mann Special | M | J. W. Mann | Bloomsburg | PA | 1895 |
| Manson | M | Manson Cycle Co. | Chicago | IL | 1895 1900 |
| Maple Leaf | M | Brewster Mfg. Co. | Holly | MI | 1896 |
| Marble City | M | Coolidge Cycle Co. | Rutland | VT | 1898 |
| March | M | March-Davis Cycle Co. | Chicago | IL | 1892 1898 |
| March Daisy | M | A. R. March Mfg. Co. | Chicago | IL | 1896 |
| March Hare | M | A. R. March Mfg. Co. | Chicago | IL | 1896 |
| March-Davis | M | March-Davis Cycle Co. | Chicago | IL | 1895 1898 |
| Marion | M | Marion Cycle Co. | Marion | IN | 1893 |
| Mark Guy | M | Vigilant Cycle Co. | New York | NY | 1895 |
| Markey | M | J. M. Markey | Crosskill Mills | PA | 1898 |
| Maroon | M | H. T. Hearsey & Co. | Indianapolis | IN | 1896 |
| Marquette | M | Sniffen & Co. | Chicago | IL | 1896 |

| Bicycle Brand | Manufacturer or Distributor | Company | City | ST | Date of First Notice |
|---|---|---|---|---|---|
| Marquis | M | Toledo Metal Wheel Co. | Toledo | OH | 1896 |
| Marquise | M | Toledo Metal Wheel Co. | Toledo | OH | 1896 |
| Marr | M | W. L. Marr Cycle Co. | Saginaw | MI | 1898 |
| Marsh Up To Date | M | B. J. Marsh | Norton | KS | 1898 |
| Marvel | M | H. Von der Linden | Poughkeepsie | NY | 1895 1898 |
| Marvel | M | Von der Linden | Poughkeepsie | NY | 1895 1898 |
| Marvel | M | William H. Cole | Baltimore | MD | 1896 |
| Mascot | M | Globe Cycle Works | Buffalo | NY | 1895 1898 |
| Mascot | M | Charles Hanauer & Bros. | Cincinnati | OH | 1896 |
| Mascot | M | Ralph Temple Cycle Co. | Chicago | IL | 1896 |
| Massasoit | M | Horace Partridge Co. | Boston | MA | 1896 |
| Massey-Harris | M | Massey-Harris Co. Canada | Toronto | ON | 1896 |
| Matchless | M | Baulch Cycle Mfg. Co. | Detroit | MI | 1895 1898 |
| Matern | M | W. J. Matern | Bloomington | IL | 1896 |
| Maurer Roadster | M | J. C. Maurer | Chicago | IL | ---- |
| Maxim | M | Maxim Cycle Co. | Nashville | TN | 1898 |
| May Belle | M | Imperial Mfg. Co. | Buffalo | NY | 1898 |
| Mayer Special | | | Buffalo | NY | ---- |
| Mayflower | M | Imperial Cycle Co. | Buffalo | NY | 1898 |
| Mayo | M | Mayo-Bechtel & Co. Also Mayo Damper Co. | Pottstown | PA | 1896 1900 |
| Maywood | D | Cash Buyer's Union | Chicago | IL | 1896 |
| McCune | M | McCune Cycle Co. Everett Cyc. Co. 1895–96 | Everett | MA | 1892 1896 |
| Meacham | M | E. C. Meacham Arms Co. Models - Diamond Safety | St Louis | MO | 1892 1893 |
| Mechanic | M | Swartz Metal Refining Co. | Chicago | IL | 1896 |
| Medina | M | Medina Cycle Mfg. Co. | Medina | NY | 1896 |
| Medinah | M | Vanderkloot & Talbot | Chicago | IL | 1898 |
| Mercury | M | Winton Bic. Co. Model - Mercury Diamond | Cleveland | OH | 1892 |
| Mercury | M | Mercury Cycle Co. | Buffalo | NY | 1896 1898 |
| Mercury Racer | M | C. C. & W. B. Rossburg | New Britain | CT | 1895 |
| Meridian | M | Eddy Mfg. Co. | Greenfield | MA | 1896 |
| Merit | M | Strubel Bros. | Detroit | MI | 1896 |
| Mermaid | D | Kingman & Co. | | | |
| Messenger | M | Temple Cycle Co. | Chicago | IL | 1896 1898 |
| Meteor | M | Banker & Cambell Co. | New York | NY | 1891 1896 |
| Meteor | M | Meteor Cycle Co. | Chicago | IL | 1896 1898 |
| Meteor | M | Schreiber, Conchar, & Westphal Co. | Dubuque | IA | 1896 |
| Meteor | M | Allen Mfg. Co. | Michigan City | IN | 1898 |
| Metropole | D | Hill & Lyster | Philadelphia | PA | 1896 |
| Mexico Special | M | H. H. Dobson Cycle Co. | Mexico | NY | 1898 |
| Meyer Special | M | A & F Meyer Co. | Buffalo | NY | |
| Miami | M | Miami Cycle Mfg. Co. Model - Miami Two Speed | Middletown | OH | 1896 1916 |
| Michigan | M | James Cycle Mfg. Co. | White Cloud | MI | 1898 |
| Michigan Hickory | M | Michigan Wheel Co. | Lansing | MI | 1896 1898 |
| Middlesex | M | Marlboro Rubber Co. | Marlboro | MA | 1895 |
| Middletown | M | Worcester Cycle Mfg. Co. | Middletown | CT | ---- |
| Middy | M | A. Featherstone & Co. | Chicago | IL | 1895 1898 |

| Bicycle Brand | Manufacturer or Distributor | Company | City | ST | Date of First Notice |
|---|---|---|---|---|---|
| Midget | M | A. Featherstone & Co. | Chicago | IL | 1895 1896 |
| Midland | M | Lindsay Bros. | Milwaukee | WI | 1892 1896 |
| Midway | M | Nicholas & Whetsel | Midway | KS | 1896 |
| Mikado | M | Midland Cycle Co. | Kansas City | MO | 1896 |
| Miles Special | M | H. Miles | Cleveland | OH | 1898 |
| Milwaukee | M | A. D. Meiselbach | Milwaukee | WI | 1896 |
| Milwaukee Special | M | Fred Weil | Milwaukee | WI | 1898 |
| Milwaukee (The) | M | Benzemaker Bros. | Milwaukee | WI | 1896 |
| Minerva | M | Lindsay Bros. | Milwaukee | WI | 1896 |
| Minneapolis | M | S. F. Heath Cycle Co. | Minneapolis | MN | 1896 |
| Minnehaha | M | Central Cycle Co. | Indianapolis | IN | 1891 1896 |
| Minnehaha | M | Bird & Spencer | Minneapolis | MN | 1896 |
| Minneola | M | Sieg & Walpole Mfg. Co. | Kenosha | WI | 1896 |
| Miracle | M | Eddy Mfg. Co. | Greenfield | MA | 1896 |
| Mirage | M | J. I. Gallagher | Boston | MA | 1898 |
| Model | M | Lindsay Bros. | Milwaukee | WI | 1896 |
| Modern | M | Piqua Cycle & Edge Tool Works | Piqua | OH | 1898 |
| Moffatt | M | Moffatt Cycle Co. | Chicago | IL | 1892 |
| Mohawic | M | Lindsay Bros. | Milwaukee | WI | 1896 |
| Mohawk | M | Iroquois Cycle Mfg. Co. | Buffalo | NY | 1896 |
| Mohawk Chief | M | Smeallie Bros. | Amsterdam | NY | 1896 1898 |
| Moline | M | John Deere Plow Co. | Kansas City | MO | 1896 |
| | | Models - King, Flyer, Leader, Queen, Scorcher, Special | | | |
| Moline Special | M | Deere, Wells & Co. | Council Bluffs | IA | 1898 |
| Monarch | M | Monarch Cycle Co. | Chicago | IL | 1892 1899 |
| | | Models - Road Racer, Roadster, Lady's | | | |
| Monarch | M | Standard Cycle Co. | Buffalo | NY | 1892 |
| Monarch | M | American Bicycle Co. | Chicago | IL | 1900 1901 |
| | | Monarch Sales Department | | | |
| Monarch | M | American Cycle Mfg. Co. | Chicago | IL | 1902 |
| Monarch | M | Pope Mfg. Co., Western Department | Chicago | IL | 1904 |
| Monitor | M | Lindsay Bros. | Milwaukee | WI | 1896 |
| Monitor | M | Meilink Mfg. Co. | Toledo | OH | 1898 |
| Monnot | M | Charles D. Monnott & Sons | Canton | OH | 1896 1898 |
| Monogram | M | Lawrence Bros. Cycle Mfg. Co. | Kansas City | MO | 1898 |
| Monogram | M | Wa-Fa-No Cycle Mfg. Co. | Buffalo | NY | 1898 |
| Monroe | M | C. J. Connolly | Rochester | NY | 1896 |
| Montrose | M | Mead Cycle Co. | Chicago | IL | 1910 1912 |
| Moore | M | Moore Mfg. & Foundry Co. | Milwaukee | WI | 1896 1898 |
| Moosic | M | Holmes-Knox Co. | Oneonta | NY | 1896 |
| Morado | M | Unique Mfg. Co. | Beaver Falls | PA | ---- |
| Morris | M | Morris Cycle Co. | Chicago | IL | 1898 |
| Motor | M | Motor Cycle Co. | Cleveland | OH | 1895 |
| Mozart | M | Mozart Cycle Co. | Chicago | IL | 1898 |
| Mt. Shasta | M | J. C. Wright | Corning | CA | 1898 |
| Muncie | M | Ball Bicycle Co. | Muncie | IN | 1898 |
| Munger | M | Munger Cycle Mfg. Co. | Indianapolis | IN | 1894 1898 |
| | | Burner Mfg. Co. in 1898 | | | |
| Murray Special | M | E. Murray & Son | Chicago | IL | 1898 |
| Murray Special | M | Robert Murray | Olney | IL | 1898 |
| My Own | M | F. S. Beavis | Peoria | IL | ---- |
| Mystic | M | Mystic Cycle Works | Mukwonago | WI | 1895 1898 |

| Bicycle Brand | Manufacturer or Distributor | Company | City | ST | Date of First Notice |
|---|---|---|---|---|---|
| Mystic | M | Glens Falls Cycle Co. | Glens Falls | NY | 1896 1898 |
| Nancy Hanks | M | Sunol Bic. Co. | Chicago | IL | 1896 |
| Napoleon | M | Jenkins Cycle Co. | Chicago | IL | 1896 1898 |
| Napoleon | D | Sears, Roebuck & Co. | Chicago | IL | 1902 1907 |
| Narragansett | M | Whitten-Godding Cycle Co. | Providence | RI | 1892 |
| Narrow Tread | M | Miami Cycle & Mfg. Co. | Middletown | OH | 1896 |
| Nashua | M | E. H. Corson | Nashua | NH | 1896 1898 |
| Nassau | D | N. Y. Sporting Goods Co. | New York | NY | ---- |
| Nassau | D | New York Sporting Goods Co. | New York | NY | ---- |
| National | M | St Nicholas Mfg. Co. | Chicago | IL | 1889 1896 |
| National | M | National Cycle Mfg. Co. | Bay City | MI | 1895 1900 |
| Naumkeag | M | Naumkeag Mfg. Co. | Salem | MA | 1898 |
| Nellie Bly | M | | | | 1891 |
| Nelson Special | M | O. P. Nelson | Chicago | IL | 1898 |
| Neversink | M | Metropolitan Cycle Co. | Reading | PA | 1893 |
| New America | M | International Mfg. Co. | Chicago | IL | 1896 |
| New Barnes | M | Lucien Barnes & Co. | Buffalo | NY | 1896 |
| New Clipper | M | Grand Rapids Cycle Co. | Grand Rapids | MI | 1895 1896 |
| New Cripper | M | Hazzard, Spencer & Bartlett & Co. | Chicago | IL | 1896 |
| New Era | M | New Era Bic. Co. Bolte Cyc. Mfg. Co. in 1896 | Chicago | IL | 1892 |
| New Haven | M | New Haven Chair Co. | New Haven | CT | 1896 1898 |
| New Home | M | Powell & Co. | Philadelphia | PA | 1893 |
| New Howe | M | Amos Shirley | New York | NY | 1895 |
| New Kensington | M | New Kensington Mfg. Co. | New Kensington | PA | 1898 |
| New Mail | D | William Read & Sons (1887) Model - Scorcher | Boston | MA | 1889 1896 |
| New Model | M | Henry J. Savoy | Paincourtville | LA | 1898 |
| New Monarch | M | American Bicycle Co. Monarch Cyc. Co. | Chicago | IL | 1892 |
| New Rapid | D | Clark Cycle Co. | Baltimore | MD | ---- |
| New State | D | Salt Lake Hardware Co. | Salt Lake City | UT | 1896 |
| New York | M | New York Cycle Co. | New York | NY | 1892 1898 |
| New York | M | Lindsay Bros. | Milwaukee | WI | 1896 |
| New Yorker | M | New York Cycle Co. | New York | NY | 1896 1898 |
| Newark | M | Sutherland & Co. | Chicago | IL | 1898 |
| Newport | M | Snyder & Fisher | Little Falls | NY | 1896 |
| Newport | M | Mead Cycle Co. | Chicago | IL | 1898 |
| Newton | M | Elizabeth Cycle Mfg. Co. | Elizabeth | NJ | 1898 |
| Newton Challenge | M | R. H. Hodgson Made about 12 in 1879. Sold the company in 1880. Mentioned in the American Bicycler. | Newton U. Falls | MA | 1879 1880 |
| Niagara | M | Buffalo Wheel Co. Models - Roadster and Racer | Buffalo | NY | 1892 1898 |
| Niantic | M | Olympic Cycle Mfg. Co. | New York | NY | 1896 |
| Nichol | M | Nichol & Co. | Chicago | IL | 1896 |
| Nicol | M | Nicol & Co. | Chicago | IL | 1896 1898 |
| Nile | M | Mason & Mason Co. | Chicago | IL | 1896 |
| Nile | D | F. M. Prescott | New York | NY | 1899 |
| Nilsson | M | Nilsson Cycle Co. | Chicago | IL | 1896 |
| Nisbe | M | Central Cycle Co. | Chicago | IL | 1898 |
| Noble | M | Hector Mfg. Co. | Chicago | IL | 1898 |

| Bicycle Brand | Manufacturer or Distributor | Company | City | ST | Date of First Notice | |
|---|---|---|---|---|---|---|
| Nock | M | George W. Nock | Philadelphia | PA | 1897 | 1900 |
| Nomad | M | Houghton & Dutton | Boston | MA | 1892 | 1893 |
| Nonesuch | M | Roxborough Cycle Mfg. Co. | Roxborough | PA | 1896 | |
| Nonotuck | M | Hampshire Cycle Mfg. Co. | Northampton | MA | 1896 | 1898 |
| Nonpariel | M | Nonpariel Cycle Co. | Chicago | IL | 1896 | 1898 |
| Norman | M | Norman Wheel Co. | Philadelphia | PA | 1893 | 1898 |
| North King | M | Northway & Kingsbury | Rochester | NY | 1898 | |
| North Star | M | Eddy Mfg. Co. | Greenfield | MA | 1896 | |
| Northampton | M | Northampton Cycle Co. | Northampton | MA | 1896 | 1898 |
| Northern Spy | M | Adams & Hart | Grand Rapids | MI | 1896 | |
| Northland | M | Lindsay Bros. | Milwaukee | WI | 1896 | |
| Northwest | M | Anderson Cycle & Mfg. Co. | Bay City | MI | 1896 | |
| Norwood | M | H. F. Schlueter Cycle Mfg. Co. | Cincinnati | OH | 1895 | 1898 |
| Norwood Belmont | M | H. F. Schlueter Cycle Mfg. Co. | Cincinnati | OH | 1898 | |
| Novelty | M | Wheeler Novelty Co. | Chicago | IL | 1898 | |
| Noxal | M | Phila. Baby Carriage Factory, Inc. | Philadelphia | PA | 1898 | |
| Nugget | M | Dodson Cycle Co. | Chicago | IL | 1898 | |
| Nutmeg | M | W. M. Frisbie | New Haven | CT | 1898 | |
| Nyack | M | | Nyack | NY | 1888 | 1901 |
| O.K. | M | Industrial Cycle Mfg. Co. | Springfield | MA | 1898 | |
| O. T. | | | Otis | NY | ---- | |
| O. T. Bicycle | M | Hill Cycle Co. Otis Trow | Warren | PA | 1897 | |
| Oak | M | J. C. Monroe | Chicago | IL | 1896 | |
| Oak Flyer | M | C. J. Schoening | Oak Park | IL | 1898 | |
| Oak Harbor Special | M | Lindsay Bros. | Milwaukee | WI | 1896 | |
| Oakwood | D | Cash Buyer's Union | Chicago | IL | 1896 | |
| Occident | M | C. E. Seifert | Lincoln | NE | 1896 | |
| Oconto | M | Gross Park Cycle Co. | Baltimore | MD | 1896 | |
| Odd Fellow | M | W. M. Rees Cycle Co. | Depew | NY | 1896 | 1898 |
| Ohio | M | Columbus Buggy Co. | Columbus | OH | 1896 | |
| Ohio Diamond | M | Columbus Cycle Co. | Columbus | OH | ---- | |
| Ohio Model | M | Lindsay Bros. | Milwaukee | WI | 1896 | |
| OK | M | Otto Konigslow | Cleveland | OH | 1898 | |
| Old Hickory | M | Old Hickory Cycle Co. | Chicago | IL | 1897 | 1898 |
| Old Powder House | M | Churchill, Kelsey, & Co. | Somerville | MA | 1898 | |
| Olive | M | Olive Wheel Co. | Syracuse | NY | 1898 | |
| Olivette | M | Olive Wheel Co. Ladies | Syracuse | NY | 1898 | |
| Olympia | M | Olympic Cycle Mfg. Co. | New York | NY | 1896 | 1898 |
| Olympic | M | B. V. Covert | Lockport | NY | 1896 | 1898 |
| Olympic | M | Olympic Cycle Mfg. Co. | New York | NY | 1896 | |
| Olympus | M | Olympic Cycle Mfg. Co. | New York | NY | 1896 | |
| Omaha | D | Lee-Clarke-Andreeson Hrdware Co. | Omaha | NE | 1896 | |
| Omega | M | Bettys & Mabbett | Rochester | NY | 1896 | |
| Oneida | M | El Dorado Cycle Co. | Chicago | IL | 1896 | |
| Oneida | M | Iroquois Cycle Co. | Buffalo | NY | 1896 | |
| Oneita | M | Utica Cycle Co. | Utica | NY | 1898 | |
| Onondaga | M | H. R. Olmstead & Son | Syracuse | NY | 1896 | 1898 |
| Ontario | M | C. B. Rice Co. Oswego Tool Co., 1898 | Oswego | NY | 1895 | 1898 |
| Ontario | M | Oswego Tool Co. | Oswego | NY | 1898 | |

| Bicycle Brand | Manufacturer or Distributor | Company | City | ST | Date of First Notice |
|---|---|---|---|---|---|
| Onward | M | Lindsay Bros. | Milwaukee | WI | 1896 |
| Opal | M | Barden Cycle Co. | Boston | MA | 1898 |
| Oquaga | M | Oquaga Cycle Co. | Deposit | NY | 1898 |
| Orient | M | Waltham Mfg. Co. | Boston | MA | 1895 1902 |
| | | Models - Roadster, Leader, Chainless | | | |
| Oriental | M | Waltham Mfg. Co. | Boston | MA | 1895 1898 |
| Orinoco | M | Columbus Brass & Iron Co. | Columbus | IN | 1896 1898 |
| Oriole | M | Lindsay Bros. | Milwaukee | WI | 1896 |
| | | Model - Flyer | | | |
| Orion | M | Lindsay Bros. | Milwaukee | WI | 1892 1896 |
| Ormonde | D | American Ormonde Cycle Co. | New York | NY | 1892 |
| Orrville Buggy | M | Orrville Buggy Co. | Orrville | OH | 1897 |
| Osborne | M | Anderson Cycle Mfg. Co. | Detroit | MI | 1895 1898 |
| Osgood Special | M | Lindsay Bros. | Milwaukee | WI | 1896 |
| Oshkosh Chief | M | Sopor Furniture Co. | Oshkosh | WI | 1896 |
| Oskaloosa | M | Thomas & Caldwell | Oskaloosa | IA | 1896 1898 |
| Osmun | M | Frank W. Osmun | Chicago | IL | 1898 |
| Ostrich | M | L. H. Schmertman | Chicago | IL | 1896 |
| Otis | M | Otis Bic. Co. | Chicago | IL | 1898 |
| | | Models - A, Special | | | |
| Ottawa | M | Olds & Co. | Ottawa | IL | 1898 |
| Otto | M | East Otto Bicycle Co. | East Otto | NY | |
| Otto | M | Western Wheel Works | Chicago | IL | 1892 |
| Ottumwa | M | Lindsay Bros. | Milwaukee | WI | 1896 |
| Ouida | M | Toledo Bic. Co. | Toledo | OH | 1896 |
| Our Defender | M | Olive Wheel Co. | Syracuse | NY | ---- |
| Our Diamond | M | C. W. Hackett Hardware Co. | St. Paul | MN | 1896 |
| Our Leader | M | Otis Bic. Co. | Chicago | IL | 1898 |
| Our Little One | M | Fay Mfg. Co. | Elyria | OH | 1898 |
| Our Pet | M | Western Wheel Works | Chicago | IL | 1892 |
| Our Pride | M | Brown Bros. | South Bend | IN | 1898 |
| Our Special | M | Beard, Goodville & Co. | Port Huron | MI | 1896 |
| Our Special | M | Western Wheel Works | Chicago | IL | 1896 |
| Our Special | M | J. F. Hawkins & Co. | Crookston | MN | 1898 |
| Our Special | M | William Roberts & Son | Connersville | IN | 1898 |
| Our Wee-No-Wah | M | R. D. Cone & Co. | Winona | MN | 1896 |
| Ourish | M | Frank Ourish | Boston | MA | 1898 |
| Outing | M | Outing Mfg. Co. | Indianapolis | IN | 1896 1900 |
| | | Originally Hay & Willets Mfg. Co. | | | |
| Overland | M | Rouse, Hazzard & Co. | Peoria | IL | 1892 1900 |
| | | Also tandem | | | |
| Overlook | M | William G. Seavey | Boston | MA | 1898 |
| Owen Black Beauty | M | Owen Mfg. Co. | New London | CT | 1896 1898 |
| Owl | M | Owl Cycle Co. | Boston | MA | 1892 |
| Oxford | M | Oxford Cycle Co. | Chicago | IL | 1892 1893 |
| Oxford | M | St. Nicholas Mfg. Co. | | | 1896 1898 |
| P & G Special | M | Porter & Gilmour | New York | NY | 1895 1896 |
| Pacemaker | M | Kenyon Mfg. Co. | Des Moines | IA | 1892 1894 |
| | | The Pacemaker Bicyc. Co. 1895-98 | | | |
| Pacemaker | M | Bernard T. Parsons | Camden | NJ | 1898 |
| Pacer | D | Cunningham & Co. | Boston | MA | 1892 |
| | | Probably an English import. Model - Pacer, Jr. | | | |

| Bicycle Brand | Manufacturer or Distributor | Company | City | ST | Date of First Notice |
|---|---|---|---|---|---|
| Pacific | M | Pacific Bicyc. Co. | Los Angeles | CA | 1895 1898 |
| Pacific | M | North Pacific Bicyc. Co. | Portland | OR | 1896 |
| Packer | M | Packer Cycle Co. | Reading | PA | 1895 1900 |
| | | Models - Standard, Racer, Ladies | | | |
| Page | M | Page Steel Wheel Co. | Toledo | OH | 1892 |
| Pallas | M | Central Cycle Co. | Kansas City | MO | 1896 |
| Palmer | M | Palmer Mfg. Co. | New York | NY | ---- |
| Palo Alto | M | A. A. Pillsbury & Co. | Palo Alto | CA | 1896 1898 |
| Pan-American | M | George N. Pierce | Buffalo | NY | 1901 |
| Parade | M | Dean & Rogers | Taunton | MA | 1892 |
| Paragon | M | Stover Bicyc. Mfg. Co. | Freeport | IL | 1892 |
| | | Model - Ladies Freeport | | | |
| Paramount | M | H. T. Hearsey & Co. | Indianapolis | IN | 1896 |
| Paris | M | Scott Bicyc. Works | Paris | IL | 1896 1898 |
| Park City | M | Bridgeport Cycle Co. | Bridgeport | CT | 1896 |
| Parole | | | | | 1892 |
| Parthenia | D | A. Treadway & Sons Hardware Co. | Dubuque | IA | 1896 |
| Patee | M | Peoria Rubber & Mfg. Co. | Peoria | IL | 1896 1898 |
| | | Patee Cyc. Mfg. Co. Indianapolis 1899-1900. Patee was a partner in the Peoria firm who split off and formed his own company, taking the name with him. | | | |
| Pathfinder | M | National American Cycle Co. | Akron | OH | ---- |
| Pathfinder | M | Indiana Bicyc. Mfg. Co. | Indianapolis | IN | 1892 1898 |
| | | $60.00 | | | |
| Pathfinder | M | Grand Rapids Bicycle Mfg. Co. | Grand Rapids | MI | 1896 |
| Pathfinder | M | Snyder & Fisher | Little Falls | NY | 1896 |
| Pathfinder | M | Mead Cycle Co. | Chicago | IL | 1918 |
| Patriot | M | Newburg Cycle Co. | Newburg | NY | 1896 1898 |
| Patrol | M | Peerless Mfg. Co. | Cleveland | OH | 1898 |
| Paul Revere | M | Revere Wheel Co. | Boston | MA | 1896 |
| | | Model - Special | | | |
| Pearl | M | J. C. Maurer | Chicago | IL | 1896 |
| Peer | M | A. Featherstone & Co. | Chicago | IL | 1893 |
| Peer | M | A & F Meyer Co. | Buffalo | NY | 1896 |
| Peerless | M | Peerless Mfg. Co. | Cleveland | OH | 1895 1898 |
| Peerless | M | St. Nicholas Mfg. Co. | Chicago | IL | 1896 1898 |
| Peerless | M | M. H. Burt Cycle Mfg. Co. | Wichita | KS | 1898 |
| Peerless | D | Sears, Roebuck & Co. | Chicago | IL | 1907 |
| Pegasus | M | M. H. Burt Cycle Mfg. Co. | Wichita | KS | 1898 |
| Peninsular | M | Lansing Cycle Co. | Lansing | MI | 1895 |
| Penn | M | Powell & Co. | Philadelphia | PA | 1893 |
| Penn York | | Elmira | NY | | |
| Pennant | M | Acme Mfg. Co. | Reading | PA | 1896 1899 |
| | | Later became a part of The American Bicyc. Co. | | | |
| Pennant | M | Eddy Mfg. Co. | Greenfield | MA | 1896 |
| Penryn Hygeinis | M | Keystone Match & Mach. Co. | Lebanon | PA | 1898 |
| Peoria | M | Peoria Cycle & Mfg. Co. | Peoria | IL | 1892 1898 |
| Peregrine | M | Von Lougorke & Detmold | New York | NY | 1892 |
| Perfect | D | U.S. Bicyc. Co. | | NY | 1896 |
| Perfect | M | U. S. Bicycle Co. | New York | NY | 1896 |
| Perfection | M | Sieg, Walpole Mfg. Co. | Chicago | IL | 1895 |
| Perrigo | M | Illinois Bicyc. Works | Chicago | IL | 1898 |

| Bicycle Brand | Manufacturer or Distributor | Company | City | ST | Date of First Notice |
|---|---|---|---|---|---|
| Perry | M | Perry Cycle Co. | Chicago | IL | 1898 |
| Peruvian | D | Peru Cycle Exchange | Peru | IN | 1896 |
| Pet | M | Western Wheel Works Price, $20.00 | Chicago | IL | 1891 1894 |
| Pet | M | Lindsay Bros. | Milwaukee | WI | 1896 |
| Pet | M | Harry Wilson | Doniphan | NE | 1898 |
| Petite | M | Wyeth Hdw. & Mfg. Co. | St. Joseph | MO | 1896 |
| Peytonia | M | J. H. Fall & Co. | Nashville | TN | 1896 |
| Phantom | M | Irving Hamilton & Co. | New York | NY | ---- |
| Phantom | M | Campbell & Co. | Providence | RI | 1892 |
| Phantom | M | Henry Sears Co. | Chicago | IL | 1896 |
| Phantom | M | Tonawanda Cycle Co. | Tonawanda | NY | 1896 |
| Phantom | M | Charles Haufman | Marion | OH | 1898 |
| Philadelphia | M | Philadelphia Bic. Mfg. Co. | Philadelphia | PA | 1898 |
| Phillipian | M | C. A. Phillips & Son | Providence | RI | 1896 1898 |
| Phillips | M | Phillips Mfg. Co. | New York | NY | 1896 |
| Phoenix | M | Stover Bic. Mfg. Co. | Freeport | IL | 1892 1898 |
| Pickwick | M | VanCamp Hdwe. & Iron Co. | Indianapolis | IN | 1896 |
| Pierce | M | George N. Pierce & Co. (1891) (1935) Model - Special | Buffalo | NY | 1890 1918 |
| Pierson Lever Bicycle | M | William B. Pierson | Chicago | IL | 1895 |
| Pilgrim | M | Warwick Cycle Mfg. Co. | Springfield | MA | 1892 |
| Pilgrim | M | E. T. Harris | Chicago | IL | 1896 |
| Pilgrim | M | S. A. Haines Co. | Indianapolis | IN | 1896 |
| Pilot | M | Indiana Bic. Co. | Indianapolis | IN | ---- |
| Pilot | M | Latta Bros. | Friendship | NY | 1892 |
| Pilot | M | El Dorado Cycle Co. | Chicago | IL | 1896 |
| Pinafore | M | VanCamp Hdwe. & Iron Co. | Indianapolis | IN | 1896 |
| Pinny-Herr Special | M | Lindsay Bros. | Milwaukee | WI | 1896 |
| Pinta | M | Charles A. Trask | Jackson | MI | 1898 |
| Pioneer | M | Standard Cycle Co. | Buffalo | NY | 1892 |
| Piqua Scorcher | M | G. F. Snauffer | Piqua | OH | 1898 |
| Pirate | M | Chicago Tube Co. | Chicago | IL | 1898 |
| Pittsburg | M | Missouri Cycle Co. Models - Special, Belle | Kansas City | MO | 1896 |
| Planet | M | Standard Mfg. Co. | Indianapolis | IN | 1892 |
| Planet | M | McLean & Bulley | Toronto | ON | 1896 |
| Planet, Jr. | M | Lindsay Bros. | Milwaukee | WI | 1896 |
| Playford | M | Minnie Mach. Works | Chicago | IL | 1898 |
| Plumed Knight | M | Knight Cycle Co. | St. Louis | MO | 1896 |
| Plymouth | M | Lindsay, Bros. | Milwaukee | WI | 1896 |
| Plymouth | M | Plymouth Cycle Co. | Plymouth | IN | 1896 |
| Po Ambo | M | Tobias & Watson | Perth Amboy | NJ | 1898 |
| Pointer | M | Pointer Cycle Mfg. Co. | Chicago | IL | 1898 |
| Pomona | M | El Dorado Cycle Co. | Chicago | IL | 1896 |
| Pontiac | M | Lindsay Bros. | Milwaukee | WI | 1896 |
| Poorman | M | J. E. Poorman | Cincinnati | OH | 1894 1895 |
| Popular | M | P. Tattersfield | Philadelphia | PA | 1892 |
| Porter | M | G. M. Porter & Co. | Boston | MA | 1898 |
| Postal | M | Maryland Mfg. & Construction | Baltimore | MD | 1896 1898 |
| Potomac | M | Potomac Cycle Co. | Chicago | IL | 1898 |
| Powow | M | S. D. Morrill & Co. | Amesbury | MA | 1898 |

| Bicycle Brand | Manufacturer or Distributor | Company | City | ST | Date of First Notice |
|---|---|---|---|---|---|
| Prairie King | M | M. E. Griswold Co. | Chicago | IL | 1898 |
| Prairie Queen | M | Congress Cycle Co. | Hartford City | IN | 1896 |
| Premier | M | Premier Cycle Co. | New York | NY | 1892 1898 |
| | | Models - Popular Premier, Youth's Premier, Special Premier, Universal Premier, Standard Premier | | | |
| Prentiss | M | L. A. Prentiss Co. | Chicago | IL | 1896 |
| President | M | Devany, Hopkins, & Co. | San Francisco | CA | 1896 |
| Prince | M | John Wilkinson Co. | Chicago | IL | 1892 |
| | | Models - Princess, Jr | | | |
| Prince | M | A. Featherstone & Co. | Chicago | IL | 1893 1898 |
| Prince | M | Edward Parkinson | Providence | RI | 1898 |
| Prince | M | Mead Cycle Co. | Chicago | IL | 1912 1918 |
| Prince Regent | M | Bicycle Supply Co. | Philadelphia | PA | 1898 |
| Princess | | D. P. Harris Hardware | New York | NY | ---- |
| Princess | M | John Wilkinson Co. | Chicago | IL | 1892 |
| | | Model - Princess, Jr | | | |
| Princess | M | A. Featherstone & Co. | Chicago | IL | 1893 1898 |
| Princess | M | Edward Parkinson | Providence | RI | 1898 |
| Princess | M | M. H. Burt Cycle Mfg. Co. | Wichita | KS | 1898 |
| Princess | M | Mead Cycle Co. | Chicago | IL | 1912 1918 |
| Princeton | M | Empire Cycle Co. | Syracuse | NY | 1898 |
| Priscilla | M | Lindsay Bros. | Milwaukee | WI | 1896 |
| Progress | M | Ames & Frost Co. | Chicago | IL | 1898 |
| Prospect | | Watterling Bros. | Prospect | OH | 1896 |
| Psycho | D | Capitol Cycle Co. | Washington | DC | 1892 |
| Pulaski | M | Pulaski Cycle Co. | Chicago | IL | 1898 |
| Punnett Companion | M | Punnett Cycle Mfg. Co. | Rochester | NY | 1895 1896 |
| | | Model - Companion, a side-by-side tandem | | | |
| Puritan | M | Puritan Cycle Works | Portland | ME | 1895 1898 |
| Puritan | M | O. J. Faxon & Co. | Boston | MA | 1896 |
| Purity | M | Purity Cycle Co. | Philadelphia | PA | 1898 |
| Putnam | M | M. S. Meade & Prentiss | Chicago | IL | ---- |
| Pyramid | M | Soudan Mfg. Co. | Chicago | IL | 1896 1898 |
| Quadrant | M | Quadrant Cycle Co. | Chicago | IL | 1895 |
| Quaker | M | Penn Mfg. Co. | Erie | PA | 1898 1900 |
| Quaker City | M | Sharpless & Watts | Philadelphia | PA | 1896 |
| Queen | M | J. S. Medary Saddlery Co. | LaCrosse | WI | 1896 |
| Queen "B" | M | King "B" Cycle Co. | Chicago | IL | 1896 |
| Queen Belle | M | Lindsay Bros. | Milwaukee | WI | 1896 |
| Queen City | M | George N. Pierce Co. | Buffalo | NY | 1892 1898 |
| Queen Esther | M | Swartz Metal Refining Co. | Chicago | IL | 1896 |
| Queen Mab | D | Hibbard, Spencer & Bartlett | Chicago | IL | 1896 |
| Queen of Racers | M | Kirkwood, Miller & Co. | Peoria | IL | 1892 1893 |
| Queen of Scorchers | M | Hulbert Bros. & Co. | New York | NY | 1892 |
| Queen of Trumps | M | Ralph Temple Cycle Co. | Chicago | IL | 1896 1898 |
| Queenly | M | T. B. Raye & Co. | Detroit | MI | 1896 |
| Query | M | Avery Planter Co. | Kansas City | MO | 1896 |
| Quigley | D | VanCamp Hardware and Iron Co. | Indianapolis | IN | 1894 |
| Quimby | D | Capitol Cycle Co. | Washington | DC | 1892 |
| Quincy | M | Quincy Cycle Co. | Quincy | MA | 1896 |
| Quinton | M | Bretz & Curtis Mfg. Co. | Philadelphia | PA | ---- |
| R. L. Cooley | M | R. L. Cooley | Batavia | NY | ---- |

| Bicycle Brand | Manufacturer or Distributor | Company | City | ST | Date of First Notice |
|---|---|---|---|---|---|
| R & P | M | Robinson & Price Safety. Price, $140.00 | Philadelphia | PA | 1891 1892 |
| Raceland | D | Marshall & Ball | Newark | NJ | 1896 |
| Racine | M | Lindsay Bros. | Milwaukee | WI | 1896 |
| Racycle | M | Miami Cycle Mfg. Co. | Middletown | OH | 1894 1918 |
| | | Models - Standard, Chainless, Bullis Ball Gear, Special Racycle | | | |
| Raglan | M | Janssen & VanVleek | New York | NY | 1892 |
| Rainbow | M | Allen-Kramer Cycle Mfg. Co. | Dansville | NY | 1896 |
| Rainbow | M | Cline Cycle Mfg. Co. | Chicago | IL | 1896 1898 |
| Rainier | M | A. J. Williams | Seattle | WA | 1898 |
| Raleigh | M | Raleigh Mfg. Co. | Reading | PA | 1895 |
| Rambler | M | Gormully & Jeffery 1900+ | Chicago (1879) | IL | 1885 |
| Rambler | M | American Bicycle Co. Rambler Sales Department | Chicago | IL | 1901 |
| Rambler | M | American Cycle Mfg. Co. Western Sales Department | Chicago | IL | 1903 |
| Rambler | M | Pope Mfg. Co. | Chicago | IL | 1904 |
| Rambler | M | Pope Mfg. Co. | Hartford | CT | 1908 |
| Randall | M | Randall Cycle Co. Models - Roadster and Special | Ft. Wayne | IN | 1896 |
| Randolph | D | Western News Co. | Chicago | IL | 1896 |
| Ranger | M | Electric Mach. Co. | El Paso | TX | 1896 |
| Ranger | M | Mead & Prentiss Mfg. | Chicago | IL | 1899 |
| Ranger | M | Mead Cycle Co. (1925) | Chicago | IL | 1910 1918 |
| Raola | D | VanCamp Hardware and Iron Co. | Indianapolis | IN | 1894 |
| Rapid | M | Indiana Bic. Mfg. Co. | Indianapolis | IN | 1892 |
| Rapid Transit | M | Wilson Brothers | Boston | MA | 1895 |
| Rapid Transit | M | Waltham Mfg. Co. | Waltham | MA | 1896 1898 |
| Raven | M | Southern Wheel Works | Owensboro | KY | 1896 |
| Raven | M | William W. Marshall | Beverly | MA | 1898 |
| Ray | M | Greyhound Bic. Mfg. Co. | Boston | MA | 1896 |
| Ray-O-Cycle | M | Miami Cycle & Motor Co | | | ---- |
| Raymond | M | Raymond Skate & Bic. Co. | Boston | MA | 1898 |
| Reading | M | Reading Standard Mfg. Co. | Reading | PA | 1895 1900 |
| | | Models - Royal Reading, Reading Standard, Reliable Reading | | | |
| Reading Standard | M | Great Western Mfg. Co. | LaPorte | IN | ---- |
| Rebecca | M | W. M. Rees Cycle Co. | Depew | NY | 1898 |
| Record | M | W. G. Ribble Co. | Indianapolis | IN | 1892 1895 |
| Record | M | St. Nicholas Mfg. Co. | Chicago | IL | 1896 |
| Record | M | The Butler Co. | Butler | IN | 1896 1898 |
| Recreation | M | A. B. Ellis Mfg. Co. | | | ---- |
| Recruit | M | Winslow Skate Mfg. Co. | Worcester | MA | 1892 |
| Red Bird | M | Goold Bic. Co. Canada | Brantford | ON | 1896 1897 |
| Red Cloud | D | William Read & Sons | Boston | MA | ---- |
| Red Cross | M | Indianapolis Cycle Co. | Indianapolis | IN | 1899 |
| Red Diamond | M | F. D. Owen Mfg. Co. | Washington | DC | 1898 |
| Red Fox | M | Fox Mach. Co. | Grand Rapids | MI | 1896 |
| Red Head | D | Sears, Roebuck & Co. | Chicago | IL | 1907 1908 |
| Red Jacket | M | Ellicott Mfg. Co. | Tonawanda | NY | 1898 |

| Bicycle Brand | Manufacturer or Distributor | | Company | City | ST | Date of First Notice | |
|---|---|---|---|---|---|---|---|
| Red Star | M | | Lindsay Bros. | Milwaukee | WI | 1896 | |
| Redlinger Special | M | | Matt Redlinger | Freeport | IL | ---- | |
| Reese | M | | Sephaniah Reese Mach. & Tl. Wrks. | Plymouth | PA | 1898 | |
| | | | full company name is: Sephaniah Reese Machine & Tool Works | | | | |
| Reeves | M | | Lindsay Bros. | Milwaukee | WI | 1896 | |
| Referee | M | | Bretz & Curtis Mfg. Co. | Philadelphia | PA | 1892 | |
| Referee | M | | Tesch Cycle Co. | Chicago | IL | 1896 | 1898 |
| Regal | D | | Marshall Wells Hdw. Co. | Duluth | MN | 1896 | |
| Regena | M | | Wadman Cycle Co. | Utica | NY | 1901 | |
| Regent | M | | Derby Cycle Co. | Chicago | IL | 1892 | |
| Regent | M | | U. S. Cycle Co. | New York | NY | 1896 | |
| Reindeer | M | | Famous Mfg. Co. | Chicago | IL | 1896 | |
| Reindeer | M | | North Chicago Mfg. Co. | Chicago | IL | 1896 | |
| Reindeer | M | | Whitten Cycle Mfg. Co. | Providence | RI | 1896 | |
| Reiter Special | M | | Lindsay Bros. | Milwaukee | WI | 1896 | |
| Relay | M | | Relay Mfg. Co. | Reading | PA | 1894 | 1898 |
| Reliable | M | | Jordan & Sanders | St. Louis | MO | 1896 | |
| Reliable | M | | Lindsay Bros. | Milwaukee | WI | 1896 | |
| Reliable | M | | Louis Erhardt & Co. | Atchinson | KS | 1896 | |
| Reliance | M | | Standard Cycle Co. | Buffalo | NY | 1892 | |
| Reliance | M | | Gendron Wheel Co. | Toledo | OH | 1895 | 1900 |
| Reliant | M | | Latta Bros. | Friendship | NY | 1898 | |
| Remington | M | | Remington Arms Co. | Ilion | NY | 1892 | 1900 |
| | | | Models by number | | | | |
| Rensselear | M | | Erwin Mfg. Co. | Greenbush | NY | 1898 | |
| Renton Special | | | | Elmira | NY | ---- | |
| Rentz | M | | Rentz Cycle Mfg. Co. | Wells | MN | 1898 | |
| Republic | M | | Diamond Cycle Co. | Philadelphia | PA | 1898 | |
| Revere | M | | Sieg & Walpole Mfg. Co. | Kenosha | WI | 1896 | |
| Reward | M | | William H. Cole & Son | Baltimore | MD | 1896 | |
| Rex | M | | Rex Cycle Co. | Chicago | IL | 1892 | 1898 |
| Rex | M | | VanCamp Hdw. & Iron Co. | Indianapolis | IN | 1896 | |
| Rex | M | | Hicks Patents Controlling Co. | Philadelphia | PA | 1899 | |
| Rhodes | M | | Rhodes & Co. | Kalamazoo | MI | 1898 | |
| Rialto | M | | Continental Cycle Co. | Chicago | IL | 1895 | 1896 |
| Richards | M | | C. W. Coomes & Co. | Malden | MA | 1898 | |
| Richmond | M | | J. Henry Brown | Richmond | VA | 1896 | |
| Richmond | M | | Richmond Bicycle Co. | Richmond | IN | 1896 | 1898 |
| | | | Models - Duke Richmond, Lady Richmond, Lady R., Cashier Frame | | | | |
| Richmond Flyer | M | | N. Leonard | Richmond | VA | 1895 | |
| Richmond Special | M | | Perkins and Richmond | Grand Rapids | MI | 1895 | 1898 |
| Rick | M | | T. A. Rick Bicycle Co. | Buffalo | NY | 1896 | 1918 |
| Riddle | M | | V. G. Riddle | Mechanicsburg | OH | 1898 | |
| Rinaldo | M | | Midland Cycle Co. | Kansas City | MO | 1896 | |
| Ripley | M | | Capitol Cycle Co. | Washington | DC | 1892 | |
| Rival | M | | Western Wheel Works | Chicago | IL | 1892 | |
| | | | Model - Juvenile Rival | | | | |
| Rival | M | | Gendron Wheel Co. | Toledo | OH | 1896 | |
| Rival | M | | VanCamp Hdw. & Iron Co. | Indianapolis | IN | 1896 | |
| Riverside | M | | Stafford Bros. | Cambridge | MA | 1898 | |
| Road King | M | | A. Featherstone & Co. | Chicago | IL | 1892 | 1898 |
| Road Queen | M | | A. Featherstone & Co. | Chicago | IL | 1892 | 1898 |

| Bicycle Brand | Manufacturer or Distributor | Company | City | ST | Date of First Notice |
|---|---|---|---|---|---|
| Roamer | | D. P. H. Mfg. Co. | New York | NY | ---- |
| Roamer | M | D. P. Harris Hardware & Mfg. Co. | New York | NY | ---- |
| Roanoke | D | M. S. Mead & Prentiss | Chicago | IL | ---- |
| Roanoke | M | Mead & Prentiss Mfg. | Chicago | IL | 1899 |
| Rob Roy | M | Western Wheel Works | Chicago | IL | 1891 1893 |
| | | Models by number. Prices-$50, 65, 70, 85 | | | |
| Robert E. Lee | M | J. E. Stonebraker & Bros. | Fredericksburg | VA | 1896 1898 |
| Robert Jay | M | Jones Cycle Co. | Chicago | IL | 1898 |
| Robin Hood | M | McDaniel & Merrihew Cycle Co. | Wilmington | DE | 1896 |
| Rochester | M | Rochester Cycle Mfg. Co. | Rochester | NY | 1892 1900 |
| | | Models - Chainless, Special, Model G, Athlete, Independent, Peerless (1892). Prices respectively- $60, 50, 40, 35, 30 | | | |
| Rochester | M | Lawrence Bros. Cycle Mfg. Co. | Kansas City | MO | 1898 |
| Rock | M | Rock Cycle Mfg. Co. | Chicago | IL | 1898 |
| Rocket | M | Rocket Cycle Co. | Chicago | IL | 1892 |
| Rocket | M | Charles A. Trask | Jackson | MI | 1896 1898 |
| Rockford | M | Rockford Watch Co. | Rockford | IL | 1896 |
| Rogers | M | Rogers Mfg. Co. | Mitchell | SD | 1896 |
| Rolland | M | Climax Cycle Co. | Chicago | IL | 1896 |
| Roman | M | Central Cycle Mfg. Co. | Indianapolis | IN | 1896 |
| Romeo | M | Temple Cycle Co. | Chicago | IL | 1896 |
| Romona | M | VanCamp Hdw. & Iron Co. | Indianapolis | IN | 1896 |
| Rosalind | M | VanCamp Hdw. & Iron Co. | Indianapolis | IN | 1896 |
| Rose | M | Rosengren Bros. | Chicago | IL | 1898 |
| Rose Special | M | Edward L. Rose & Co. | Binghampton | NY | 1896 |
| Roslindale | M | Roslindale Cycle Co. | Boston | MA | 1898 |
| Roth | | | Erie | PA | ---- |
| Roulette | M | Roulette Cycle Co. | New York | NY | 1892 1895 |
| Rouse | M | George W. Rouse Co. | Peoria | IL | ---- |
| Rover | M | Humber-Rover Cycle Co. | Chicago | IL | 1892 |
| Roxana | M | VanCamp Hdw. & Iron Co. | Indianapolis | IN | 1896 |
| Royal | M | Marshall Cycle Works | Marshall | MI | 1892 |
| | | Royal Cyc. Works, Marshall, MI 1893-98. Models - Royal Lady, Royal Limited, Red Head, Jester | | | |
| Royal | M | Mead Cycle Co. | Chicago | IL | 1910 1912 |
| Royal And Hare | M | David Kelly | Chicago | IL | 1898 |
| Royal Blue Diamond | M | F. D. Owen Mfg. Co. | Washington | DC | 1898 |
| Royal Flush | M | F. A. E. Hamilton | Beverly | MA | 1898 |
| | | Also a model of the Columbus brand | | | |
| Royal Flyer | | Kruitibaum | Buffalo | NY | ---- |
| Royal Mail | D | William Read & Sons | Baltimore | MD | 1892 |
| | | English import | | | |
| Royal Middy | M | A. Featherstone & Co. | Chicago | IL | 1893 |
| Royal Salvo | D | Howard A. Smith & Co. | | | 1888 |
| Rubey | M | Penhard Mfg. Co. | Louisville | KY | 1892 1896 |
| Ruby | D | Penhard Mfg. Co. | Louisville | KY | 1895 1898 |
| Ruby Rims | D | E. H. Shattuck | Lowell | MA | 1896 |
| Rudge | D | Rouse, Hazzard & Co. | Peoria | IL | 1893 |
| Rudolph's Popular Bicycle | M | Rudolph Mfg. Co. | Chicago | IL | 1895 |
| Rugby | M | Toledo Metal Wheel Co. | Toledo | OH | 1896 |
| Rummel | M | A. J. Rummel Arms Co. | Toledo | OH | 1898 |
| Rumsey | M | Mohawk Cycle Co. | Indianapolis | IN | 1898 |

| Bicycle Brand | Manufacturer or Distributor | Company | City | ST | Date of First Notice |
|---|---|---|---|---|---|
| Runabout | D | Louis Rosenfeld & Co. | New York | NY | 1896 |
| Rush | M | Western Wheel Works | Chicago | IL | 1891 1892 |
| | | Hard tire, $100. Pneumatic tire, $115 | | | |
| Russel | M | William T. Russell | Chicago | IL | 1898 |
| Russet Flyer | M | Syracuse Specialty Co. | Syracuse | NY | 1896 |
| Rutland | M | Coolidge & Morse | Rutland | VT | 1896 |
| | | Coolidge Cy. Co. in 1898 | | | |
| S & B | M | Studley & Barclay | Grand Rapids | MI | 1896 1898 |
| | | Became Studley & Jarvis in 1898. Models - #1, #2, #3 | | | |
| S & B | M | Slocum & Bartholomew | Geneva | OH | 1898 |
| S. D. & G. | M | Schoverling, Daly & Gales | New York | NY | 1896 |
| S & F Special | M | Snyder & Fisher Bike Works | Little Falls | NY | ---- |
| Sagamore | M | Porter & Gilmour | New York | NY | 1896 |
| Saginaw | M | Lindsay Bros. | Milwaukee | WI | 1896 |
| Salem | M | R. H. Robson | Salem | MA | 1896 1898 |
| Sampson | M | Sieg & Walpole Mfg. Co. | Kenosha | WI | 1896 |
| Samson | D | Capitol Cycle Co. | Washington | DC | 1892 |
| Sandburg | M | Lindsay Bros. | Milwaukee | WI | 1896 |
| Sandow | M | Sandow Cycle Co. | | | 1896 |
| Sanger Racer | M | Telegram Cycle Mfg. Co. | Milwaukee | WI | 1895 1896 |
| Santa Barbara | M | C. R. Jordall | Santa Barbara | CA | 1895 |
| Saracen | M | Waltham Mfg. Co. | New York | NY | 1896 1898 |
| Saturn | M | George T. Simpson | Buffalo | NY | |
| | | 507 E. General St. | | | |
| Saturn | M | A. M . Kleinschmidt | Indianapolis | IN | 1896 |
| Savoy | M | Charles H. Childs & Co. | Utica | NY | 1896 |
| Schack | M | W. G. Schack | Buffalo | NY | 1895 1896 |
| Scorcher | M | Bretz & Curtis Mfg. Co. | Philadelphia | PA | 1892 |
| Scorcher | M | Elmore Mfg. Co. | Elmore & Clyde | OH | 1896 |
| | | Model - Scorcher Junior | | | |
| Scorcher | M | St. Nicholas Mfg. Co. | Chicago | IL | 1896 1898 |
| Scorcher, Jr. | M | King "B" Cycle Co. | Chicago | IL | 1896 |
| Scotia | M | Scott Paper Co. | Philadelphia | PA | 1898 |
| Seaman | M | Seaman Mach. Co. | Milwaukee | WI | 1898 |
| Sears | M | Henry Sears Co. | Chicago | IL | 1895 |
| | | Model - Phantom | | | |
| Secure | M | Woodruff & Little Cycle Co. | Towanda | PA | 1982 |
| Seguranca | M | Lyman H. Arms | Chicago | IL | 1898 |
| Seminole | M | Brown-Lewis Cycle Co. | Chicago | IL | 1898 1899 |
| Seminole | M | Pope Mfg. Co. | Westfield | MA | 1915 |
| Senate | M | Senate Wheel Co. | Corning | NY | 1898 |
| Senator | M | The Congress Cycle Co. | Hartford City | IN | 1896 |
| Seneca | M | Queen City Cycle Co. | Buffalo | NY | 1895 1896 |
| Seneca | M | Seneca Mfg. Co. | Chicago | IL | 1898 |
| Sentinel | M | Mead Cycle Co. | Chicago | IL | 1898 |
| Sentinel | M | Mead Cycle Co. | Chicago | IL | 1910 1914 |
| Seuberth | M | Seuberth-Leach Mfg. Co. | Elgin | IL | 1898 |
| | | Models - Special and Jewel | | | |
| Shadow | M | | | | 1892 |
| Shamrock | M | Gerwing, Hilton, Kennedy Cycle Co. | Denver | CO | 1896 1898 |
| Shane's Flyer | M | Lindsay Bros. | Milwaukee | WI | 1896 |

# Appendix C: 2,100 American Brands before 1918

| Bicycle Brand | Manufacturer or Distributor | Company | City | ST | Date of First Notice |
|---|---|---|---|---|---|
| Shawnee | M | Sephaniah Reese Mach. & Tl. Wrks. | Plymouth | PA | 1898 |
| | | full name of company is: Sephaniah Reese Machine & Tool Works | | | |
| Sheboygan | M | Jenkins Mach. Co. | Sheboygan | WI | 1896 |
| Shelby | M | Shelby Cycle Mfg. Co. | Shelby | OH | ---- |
| Shenandoah | M | Fleming & Dobyne Mfg. Co. | Harvard | IL | 1896 |
| | | Became Rollins and Dobyne in 1898. Model - Shenandoah Belle | | | |
| Sheridan | M | George E. Lloyd & Co. | Chicago | IL | 1896 |
| Sheridan | M | Anderson Bic. Wheel Co. | Anderson | IN | 1898 |
| Sherman | M | Sherman Cycle Co. | Chicago | IL | 1896 1900 |
| | | Models by number | | | |
| Sherwood | M | Sieg & Walpole Mfg. Co. | Springfield | OH | 1896 |
| Shirk | M | G. M. Shirk Mfg. Co. | Chicago | IL | 1896 1898 |
| Shugers | M | Shugers Bic. Mfg. Co. | Coldwater | MI | 1896 |
| Sickle's Flyer | M | J. B. Sickles Saddlery Co. | St. Louis | MO | 1896 |
| Sieg Special | M | Charles H. Sieg Mfg., Co. | Chicago | IL | 1898 |
| Signal | M | Gendron Wheel Co. | Toledo | OH | 1898 |
| Silver King | M | Geo. M. Hendee Mfg. Co. | Springfield | MA | 1895 |
| | | Hendee & Nelson Mfg. Co. in 1896. Model - Silver Queen. Hendee also licensed Monarch Cyc. Co. of Chicago to manufacture this same bicycle | | | |
| Silver Star | M | Co-operative Cycle Co. | Toledo | OH | 1898 |
| Silver State | M | W. F. Althoff | Denver | CO | 1896 1898 |
| Silver State Special | M | Carl A. Hallin | Denver | CO | 1898 |
| Singer | D | Singer & Co. | Boston | MA | 1896 |
| Sir Julien | D | A. Treadway & Sons Hardware Co. | Dubuque | IA | 1896 |
| Sligh | M | Sligh Furniture Co. | Grand Rapids | MI | 1896 |
| Sloan | M | S. M. Sloan | Galva | IL | 1898 |
| Smalley | M | Marble Cycle Mfg. Co. | Plymouth | IN | 1893 1895 |
| Smalley | M | Marble Cycle Mfg. Co. | Plymouth | IN | 1895 |
| | | Plymouth Cyc. Mfg. Co. in 1896. Model - Superb Smalley | | | |
| Smart | M | Smart Treadle Co. | Carbondale | IL | 1896 |
| Smith Special | M | T. B. Smith Cycle Co. | Chicago | IL | 1896 |
| Snell | M | Snell Cycle Fittings Co. | Toledo | OH | 1895 1903 |
| | | Snell Cyc. Mfg. Co. 1899-1900 | | | |
| Snider | M | W. D. Snider Mfg. Co. | Paterson | NJ | 1896 |
| Snow | M | Snow Cycle Mfg. Co. | Minneapolis | MN | 1898 |
| | | Models - Special, Roadster, Tandem | | | |
| Snowflake | M | Hirsch Aluminum Co. | Chicago | IL | 1892 |
| Something New In Bicycles | M | Phillips Mfg. Co. | New York | NY | 1895 1896 |
| Sorrento | M | Ames & Frost Co. | Chicago | IL | 1898 |
| Soudan | M | Soudan Mfg. Co. | Chicago | IL | 1895 1898 |
| | | Moved to Elkhart, IN, in 1899 | | | |
| South Road | M | James Cycle Co. | Chicago | IL | 1893 |
| Southern | M | Woodworth Cycle Co. | Waco | TX | 1898 |
| | | Models - A and B | | | |
| Southern Express | M | Stoffner & Sloan | Chattanooga | TN | 1895 1898 |
| Southern Gem | M | R. C. Whayne | Louisville | KY | 1895 1898 |
| Souvenir | M | Grand Rapids Cycle Mfg. Co. | Grand Rapids | MI | 1896 1898 |
| | | The Souvenir Cyc. Co. in 1898 | | | |
| Sovereign | M | King "B" Cycle Co. | Chicago | IL | 1896 |
| Spalding | | | | NY | ---- |
| Spalding | M | American Bicycle Co. | New York | NY | ---- |
| | | East-Spalding Sales Department | | | |

| Bicycle Brand | Manufacturer or Distributor | Company | City | ST | Date of First Notice |
|---|---|---|---|---|---|
| Spalding | M | Lamb Mfg. Co. | Chicopee Falls | MA | 1892 1899 |
| | | Manufactured for A.G. Spalding & Bros. of New York. | | | |
| Spark | M | Spark Cycle Mfg. Co. | Goshen | IN | 1895 1896 |
| Spark | M | Canton Cycle Co. | Canton | OH | 1898 |
| | | Models - Special & Roadster | | | |
| Spartacus | M | Gladiator Cycle Works | Chicago | IL | 1897 |
| Spartan | M | J. V. Farwell Co. | Chicago | IL | 1896 |
| Spartan | M | Ohio Cycle Co. | Bellevue | OH | 1896 |
| Special | M | Lindsay Bros. | Milwaukee | WI | 1896 |
| Special | M | John Brandner | Chicago | IL | 1898 |
| Special | M | Kaestner & Co. | Chicago | IL | 1898 |
| Special Union | M | Union Cycle Mfg. Co. | Boston | MA | 1896 1898 |
| Spectre | M | Henry Sears Co. | Chicago | IL | 1896 |
| Speed | M | Prince Well | Louisville | KY | 1896 |
| Speeder | M | Speeder Cycle Mfg. Co. | New Castle | IN | 1895 1898 |
| Speedwell | M | Emblem Bicycle Co. | Angola | NY | ---- |
| Speedwell | M | Speedwell Bic. Mfg. Co. | Boston | MA | 1891 1892 |
| Speedy | M | Speedy Cycle Co. | Chicago | IL | 1892 |
| Speirs | M | Speirs Mfg. Co. | Boston | MA | 1896 1898 |
| Spencer | M | Inter-mountain Wheel Co. | Salt Lake City | UT | 1896 |
| Sphinx | M | Heinz & Munschauer Works | Buffalo | NY | 1897 |
| Spinaway | M | Keystone Cycle Co. | Reading | PA | 1898 |
| Spinroller | M | Spinroller Co. | Rochester | NY | 1899 1900 |
| Splendid | M | Parsons Mfg. Co. | Chicago | IL | 1896 1898 |
| Sport | M | J. W. Grady Co. | Worcester | MA | ---- |
| Spring City | M | Spring City Cycle Works | Spring City | PA | 1898 |
| Springfield | M | Springfield Bic. Mfg. Co. | Boston | MA | 1892 1894 |
| | | Moved to Springfield, MA, in 1895 | | | |
| Springfield | M | Thomas Mfg. Co. | Springfield | OH | 1896 |
| Springfield Roadster | M | Springfield Bicycle Co. | Boston | MA | 1889 1894 |
| Sprinter | M | Luburg Mfg. Co. | Philadelphia | PA | 1892 |
| Sprite | M | Tonawanda Cycle Co. | Tonawanda | NY | 1893 1896 |
| St. Clair | M | Steger's Wheel Co. | East St. Louis | MO | 1898 |
| St. Clair | M | Wright Cycle Co. | Dayton | OH | 1898 |
| St. Joseph | M | Colfax Mfg. Co. | South Bend | IN | 1896 |
| St. Joseph Special | M | Wyeth Mfg. Co. | Geneva | OH | ---- |
| St. Louis | M | St. Louis Cycle Co. | St. Louis | MO | 1892 1896 |
| St. Louis Special | M | Pequequot Bros. | St. Louis | MI | 1898 |
| St. Nicholas | M | St. Nicholas Mfg. Co. | Chicago | IL | 1892 |
| Stafford | M | E. H. Stafford&Bros. | Chicago | IL | ---- |
| Stag | M | Seyfang & Prentiss | Buffalo | NY | 1896 |
| Staidness | M | Toronto Cycle Co. | Toronto | ON | 1896 |
| | | Canada | | | |
| Stall Special | M | W. W. Stall | Boston | MA | 1892 |
| Standard | M | Standard Mfg. Co. | Martinsburg | WV | 1892 |
| Standard | M | Brewster Mfg. Co. | Holly | MI | 1896 |
| Standard | M | George Hasbrook Co. | | NY | 1896 |
| Standard | M | Standard Bic. Mfg. Co. | Chicago | IL | 1896 1898 |
| Standard Marine Bicycle | M | Marine Bic. Co. | Portsmouth | NH | ---- |
| Stanley | M | Stanley Cycle Mfg. Co. | New York | NY | 1896 1898 |

| Bicycle Brand | Manufacturer or Distributor | Company | City | ST | Date of First Notice |
|---|---|---|---|---|---|
| Star | M | H. B. Smith Machine Co. | Smithville | NJ | 1881 1896 |
| | | Models - Rover Star - 1892, 30" front and 39" rear wheel. Later pneumatic tire safeties. | | | |
| Star | M | Climax Cycle Co. | Chicago | IL | 1896 |
| Star | M | Lindsay Bros. | Milwaukee | WI | 1896 |
| Stearns | M | E. C. Stearns & Co. | Syracuse | NY | 1893 1899 |
| Stearns | M | American Bicycle Co. | Chicago | IL | 1901 |
| | | Crescent Sales Department | | | |
| Steelton | M | Keidel Henry & Co. | Baltimore | MD | 1896 |
| Stella | M | McIntosh-Huntington Co. | Cleveland | OH | 1892 1896 |
| Stephens | M | Charles H. Stephens Cycle Co. | Chicago | IL | 1895 1898 |
| Sterling | M | C. F. Stokes Mfg. Co. | Chicago | IL | 1892 |
| | | Stokes Mfg. Co. 1893. Sterling Cyc. Works 1895-1900 | | | |
| Sterling | M | Sterling Cycle Co. | Chicago | IL | 1894 1899 |
| Sterling | M | Pope Mfg. Co. | Hartford | CT | 1909 |
| Sterner | M | C. H. Sterner & Co. | Chicago | IL | 1896 |
| Stevens Special | M | Lindsay Bros. | Milwaukee | WI | 1896 |
| Stever | M | A. E. & H. H. Stever | Owosso | MI | 1898 |
| Stockman | M | Lindsay Bros. | Milwaukee | WI | 1896 |
| Stockton | M | Stockton Cycle Co. | Stockton | NJ | 1896 |
| Stokes | M | Stokes Mach. Works | Kenosha | WI | 1896 1898 |
| Stormer | M | Acme Mfg. Co. | Reading | PA | 1891 1899 |
| Straight | M | Straight Mfg. Co. | Jamestown | NY | ---- |
| Straight Line | M | Charles E. Drumbor | S. Bethlehem | PA | 1898 |
| Strong Safety | M | Strong & Green Cycle Co. | Philadelphia | PA | 1892 |
| Strubel Bros. Special | M | Strubel Bros. | Detroit | MI | 1896 |
| Student | D | George R. Bidwell Cycle Co. | New York | NY | 1892 |
| Stull | M | Curtis Mach. Works | Chicago | IL | 1896 |
| Sturmer | | | | | ---- |
| Suburban | M | Maryland Mfg. and Constr. Co. | Baltimore | MD | 1896 1898 |
| Success | M | J. S. Medary Saddlery Co. | La Crosse | WI | 1896 |
| Sultan | M | El Dorado Cycle Co. | Chicago | IL | 1896 |
| Sultana | M | El Dorado Cycle Co. | Chicago | IL | 1896 |
| Summit | M | Colton Cycle Co. | Toledo | OH | 1898 |
| Sunbeam | M | Julius Andrae & Son Co. | Milwaukee | WI | 1896 |
| | | Started in 1891 | | | |
| Sunflower | M | Nicholas & Whetsel | Pittsburg | KS | 1898 |
| Sunlight | M | Fred C. A. Gianetto | Brookline | MA | 1898 |
| | | Model - Special | | | |
| Sunlight Ladies | D | Soper Furniture Co. | Oshkosh | WI | 1896 |
| Sunol | M | McIntosh-Huntington Co. | Cleveland | OH | 1892 1898 |
| Sunshine | M | Cline Cycle Mfg. Co. | Chicago | IL | 1896 1898 |
| Superb | M | Ralph Temple Cycle Co. | Chicago | IL | 1896 1898 |
| Superba | M | Barnes Cycle Co. | Syracuse | NY | 1896 |
| Superba | M | Ralph Temple Cycle Co. | Chicago | IL | 1896 1898 |
| Superior | M | Keating Wheel Co. | Westfield | MA | 1892 |
| Superior | M | March-Davis Cycle Co. | Chicago | IL | 1896 |
| Superior | M | Superior Cycle Co. | West Superior | WI | 1898 |
| Supplee | M | Supplee Hdw. Co. | Philadelphia | PA | 1896 |
| | | Models - Standard and Special | | | |
| Supreme | D | Minnie E. Ranney | Providence | RI | 1896 |
| | | A ladies' bicycle | | | |

| Bicycle Brand | Manufacturer or Distributor | Company | City | ST | Date of First Notice |
|---|---|---|---|---|---|
| Survio | M | G. N. Hatch & Co. | Boston | MA | 1898 |
| Susquehanna | M | Bloomsburg Cycle Works | Bloomsburg | PA | 1898 |
| Swan | M | George W. Swan | Chicago | IL | 1896 1898 |
| | | Model - Lady Swan | | | |
| Sweepstakes | M | Bristol & Gales | Chicago | IL | 1895 |
| Sweepstakes | M | Lindsay Bros. | Milwaukee | WI | 1896 |
| Sweeting Diamond | M | Sweeting Cycle Co. | Philadelphia | PA | 1891 1892 |
| | | Price, $110 | | | |
| Swell Newport | M | Snyder & Fisher Bike Works | Little Falls | NY | 1896 |
| Swell Special | M | H. A. Lozier & Co. | Cleveland | OH | 1896 |
| Swiftsure | M | Copeland Cycle Mfg. Co. | Evansville | IN | 1896 1898 |
| Sylph | M | Rouse-Duryea Cycle Co. | Peoria | IL | 1892 1893 |
| Sylph | M | Rouse, Hazzard & Co. | Peoria | IL | 1893 1900 |
| Sylvan | M | John Deere Plow Co. | Kansas City | MO | 1896 |
| Syndicate | M | Lindsay Bros. | Milwaukee | WI | 1896 |
| Syracuse | M | Syracuse Cycle Co. | Syracuse | NY | 1894 1898 |
| Syrian | M | Brown-Lewis Cycle Co. | Chicago | IL | 1898 1899 |
| Tacoma | M | Richmond Bic. Co. | Richmond | IN | 1898 |
| Talisman | M | Midland Cycle Co. | Kansas City | MO | 1896 |
| Tally-Ho | M | Tally-Ho Mfg. Co. | Toledo | OH | 1896 |
| | | Maumee Cyc. Co. Maumee Ohio 1897-98. Tandem model only | | | |
| Tanner Special | M | M. Tanner | Medina | NY | 1898 |
| Taylor's Art | M | Kankakee Mfg. Co. | Buffalo | NY | 1896 1898 |
| Telegram | M | Telegram Cycle Mfg. Co. | Milwaukee | WI | 1895 1896 |
| Telephone | M | Kirkwood, Miller & Co. | Peoria | IL | 1892 |
| Telephone | M | F. H. Henning Cycle Co. | Peoria | IL | 1896 1898 |
| Templar | D | VanCamp Hardware & Iron Co. | Indianapolis | IN | 1894 |
| Temple | M | Marion Cycle Co. | Marion | IN | 1896 |
| Temple | M | Ralph Temple Cycle Co. | Chicago | IL | 1898 |
| | | Models - Scorcher, Special, Lady Temple | | | |
| Tennessee Belle | M | Stoffner & Sloan | Chattanooga | TN | 1896 1898 |
| Tenny | M | J. W. Dillon | Chicago | IL | 1896 1898 |
| Terrell Special | M | Lindsay Bros. | Milwaukee | WI | 1896 |
| Thiel | M | J. L. Riley & Co. | Greenville | PA | 1896 |
| Thiem | M | Northwestern Mach. & Cycle Works | St. Paul | MN | 1896 |
| Thistle | M | Fulton Mach. Works | Chicago | IL | 1892 1898 |
| Thomas | M | Thomas Mfg. Co. | Springfield | OH | 1896 1898 |
| | | Models - Thomas Special and Racer | | | |
| Thorp | M | Thorp Cycle Co. | Philadelphia | PA | 1896 1898 |
| | | Models - Special, Superior, Changeable Gear, Tandem | | | |
| Thorsen | M | Thorsen & Cassady Co. | Chicago | IL | 1896 |
| Tidd-Rugg | M | Tidd-Rugg Cycle Co. | St Louis | MO | 1896 |
| Tiger | M | Stover Bic. Mfg. Co. | Freeport | IL | 1891 1892 |
| Tiger | M | Stoddard Mfg. Co. | Dayton | OH | 1895 1898 |
| | | Models - Regular and Combination Tandem as well as standard bicycle | | | |
| Tiger | M | Eddy Mfg. Co. | Greenfield | MA | 1896 |
| Tigress | M | Stoddard Mfg. Co. | Chicago | IL | 1895 1898 |
| Timekeeper | M | Lindsay Bros. | Milwaukee | WI | 1896 |
| Timms | M | Timms Mfg. Co. | Seymour | IN | 1896 1898 |
| Tinkham | M | Tinkham Cycle Co. | New York | NY | ---- |
| Titania | M | Aerial Cycle Mfg. Co. | Goshen | IN | 1892 |

| Bicycle Brand | Manufacturer or Distributor | Company | City | ST | Date of First Notice |
|---|---|---|---|---|---|
| Tivy | M | Tivy Cycle Mfg. Co. | Williamsport | PA | 1898 |
| Tobasco | M | H. T. Hearsey & Co. | Indianapolis | IN | 1896 |
| Toledo | M | Toledo Cycle Co. Colton Cyc. Co. | Toledo | OH | 1893 1898 |
| Toledo | M | Lindsay Bros. | Milwaukee | WI | 1896 |
| Tornado | M | Hibbard, Bartlett & Spencer | Chicago | IL | 1896 |
| Tourist | M | Tourist Bicycle Co. | Syracuse | NY | 1896 |
| Tourist Special | M | Tourist Bicycle Co. | Syracuse | NY | 1896 |
| Townsend | M | Frank H. Townsend | Winchendon | MA | 1898 |
| Trafford | M | William Trafford | Philadelphia | PA | 1896 1898 |
| Transfer | M | S. C. Haines & Co. | Boston | MA | 1898 |
| Transit Special | M | Albert & J. M. Anderson | Boston | MA | 1896 |
| Traveler | M | American Sewing Mach. Co. | Philadelphia | PA | 1896 |
| Traveler | M | Traveler Cycle Co. | Boston | MA | 1898 |
| Traveller | M | Luburg Mfg. Co. | Philadelphia | PA | 1892 |

Models - Advance Traveller, American Traveller, Little Traveller, Rapid Traveller, Junior Traveller

| Bicycle Brand | | Company | City | ST | |
|---|---|---|---|---|---|
| Tremont | M | W. W. Stall | Boston | MA | 1892 |
| Tremont | M | Sieg & Walpole Mfg. Co. | Kenosha | WI | 1896 |
| Trent | M | Harry E. Stahl | Trenton | NJ | 1898 |
| Trenton | M | Eastern Wheel Works | New York | NY | 1898 |
| Triangle | M | Peerless Mfg. Co. | Cleveland | OH | 1895 |
| Tribune | M | Black Mfg. Co. | Erie | PA | 1894 1899 |

Models - Tribune Freak, Tribune Blue Streak

| | | | | | |
|---|---|---|---|---|---|
| Tribune | M | American Bicycle Co. Featherstone Sales Department | Chicago | IL | 1901 |
| Tribune | M | American Cycle Mfg. Co. Eastern Sales Department | Hartford | CT | 1903 |
| Trilby | M | Brewster Mfg. Co. | Holly | MI | 1896 |
| Trilby | M | Ott & Henley | Toledo | OH | 1898 |
| Trinity | M | Trinity Cycle Mfg. Co. | Worcester | MA | 1897 |
| Trinity | M | Trinity Cycle Co. | Keene | NH | 1898 |
| Triumph | M | Peerless Mfg. Co. | Cleveland | OH | 1891 1897 |
| Triumph | M | Lindsay Bros. | Milwaukee | WI | 1896 |
| Triumph | M | Specialty Mfg. Co. | Indianapolis | IN | 1896 |
| Trojan | M | Lindsay Bros. | Milwaukee | WI | 1896 |
| Truman | M | Charles Truman & Co. In 1898 became Truman Bic. Co. | Toledo | OH | 1896 1897 |
| Trusty | M | Lindsay Bros. | Milwaukee | WI | 1896 |
| Truth | M | Koster & Co. | Erie | PA | 1896 |
| Tucker Special | M | A. P. Tucker | Cincinnati | OH | 1898 |
| Turner | D | Turner & Co. | Chicago | IL | 1896 |
| Turtle | M | Ariel Cycle Mfg. Co. | Goshen | IN | ---- |
| Tuscarora | M | Iroquois Cycle Mfg. Co. | Buffalo | NY | 1896 1898 |
| Tuxedo | M | Hulbert Bros. & Co. | New York | NY | 1892 |
| Tuxedo | M | Indiana Bic. Mfg. Co. | Indianapolis | IN | 1892 |
| Twentieth Century | M | Auburn Cycle Co. | Chicago | IL | 1896 1898 |
| Twentieth Century | M | Erie Cycle Co. | Erie | PA | 1896 |
| Twins | M | U. S. Cycle Co. | Philadelphia | PA | 1892 |
| Two Speed | M | Two Speed Bic. Co. | Chicago | IL | 1895 |
| Two Ten | M | Union Cycle Mfg. Co. | Highlandville | MA | 1892 |
| Tygard | M | James W. Tygard Co. | Pittsburgh | PA | 1898 |

| Bicycle Brand | Manufacturer or Distributor | Company | City | ST | Date of First Notice |
|---|---|---|---|---|---|
| Typhoon | M | Fay Mfg. Co. | Elyria | OH | 1892 |
| U. P. Flyer | M | A. F. Brown | Calumet | MI | 1898 |
| U. S. | M | U. S. Bic. Co. | New York | NY | 1896 1898 |
| U. S. | M | U. S. Bicycle Co. | New York | NY | 1896 1898 |
| Umpire | M | Norman Wheel Co. | Philadelphia | PA | 1893 |
| Union | M | Union Cycle Mfg. Co. | Highlandville | MA | 1891 1900 |
| | | Model - Union Special Tandem Factory Highlandville, MA | | | |
| Union | M | Stokes Mfg. Co. | Chicago | IL | 1893 |
| Union | M | Union Mfg. Co. | Toledo | OH | 1896 |
| Unique | M | Unique Mfg. Co. | Beaver Falls | PA | ---- |
| Unique | M | Buffalo Tricycle Co. | Buffalo | NY | 1892 1893 |
| United States | M | Chicago Stamping Co. | Chicago | IL | 1896 1898 |
| Universal | M | | | | 1891 |
| | | 30" wheels | | | |
| Valentine | M | Wilson Mfg. Co. | Toledo | OH | 1898 |
| Valiant | M | Supplee Hdw. Co. | Philadelphia | PA | 1896 |
| Valid | M | F. F. Ide Mfg. Co. | Peoria | IL | 1894 |
| Valkyrie | M | Powell & Clement Co. | Cincinnati | OH | 1895 |
| Vallamont | M | Galletts Felice | Williamsport | PA | 1898 |
| Vamoose | M | Bridgeport Cycle Co. | Bridgeport | CT | 1895 1896 |
| Van Cleve | M | Wright Cycle Co. | Dayton | OH | 1898 |
| Vanderburgh | M | Evansville Cycle Works | Evansville | IN | 1896 |
| Vanguard | M | Vanguard Cycle Co. | Indianapolis | IN | 1896 1897 |
| | | Sensitive Governor Co. in 1898 | | | |
| Varsity | M | St. Nicholas Mfg. Co. | Chicago | IL | 1896 1898 |
| Vassar | M | Lindsay Bros. | Milwaukee | WI | 1896 |
| Vassar | M | St. Nicholas Mfg. Co. | Chicago | IL | 1898 |
| Vedettes | M | Pope Mfg. Co. | Hartford | CT | 1898 1899 |
| Vedettes | M | American Bicycle Co. | Hartford | CT | 1901 |
| | | Pope Sales Department | | | |
| Vedettes | M | American Cycle Mfg. Co. | Hartford | CT | 1902 1903 |
| | | Eastern Sales Dept., Columbia Factory | | | |
| Vedettes | M | Pope Mfg. Co. | Hartford | CT | 1904 1905 |
| Velo-King | M | E. C. Brown Co. | Rochester | NY | c. 1930 |
| Velocity | M | McKee & Harrington | New York | NY | |
| Velocity | M | R. H. Hodgson | Newton U. Falls | MA | 1897 1880 |
| | | Manufactured 12 in 1879. Sold to McKee & Harrington, NY, in 1880 | | | |
| Velox | M | Western Cycle Co. | Salt Lake City | UT | 1898 |
| Vendex | M | Erwin Mfg. Co. | Greenbush | NY | 1898 |
| | | Models - #1, #2, #3 | | | |
| Venus | M | Hitchings Cycle Co. | St. Louis | MO | 1892 1896 |
| Venus | M | Aquilla Wheel Mfg. Co. | Louisville | KY | 1898 |
| Vermont | M | Coolidge & Morse | Rutland | VT | 1896 1898 |
| | | Coolidge Cyc. Co. in 1898 | | | |
| Viator | M | Moore Cycle Fittings Co. | Harrison | NJ | 1898 |
| Viatrix | M | Moore Cycle Fittings Co. | Harrison | NJ | 1898 |
| Victor | M | Overman Wheel Co. | Chicopee Falls | MA | 1885 1899 |
| | | (1884) Model - Victor, Jr | | | |
| Victor | M | Indiana Bicycle Co. | Indianapolis | IN | 1899 |
| Victoria | M | Overman Wheel Co. | Chicopee Falls | MA | 1892 1898 |
| | | Ladies bicycle | | | |
| Victory | M | Bretz & Curtis Cycle Co. | Philadelphia | PA | 1892 |
| | | Model - Special | | | |

| Bicycle Brand | Manufacturer or Distributor | Company | City | ST | Date of First Notice |
|---|---|---|---|---|---|
| Victula | M | Collman Bros. | South Bend | IN | 1896 |
| Vidette | M | Bernard T. Parsons | Camden | NJ | 1898 |
| Vigilant | M | Black Mfg. Co. Model - Vigilant Special | Erie | PA | 1896 |
| Viking | M | John Shirley Cycle Co. | Philadelphia | PA | 1892 |
| Viking | M | Union Mfg. Co. | Toledo | OH | 1896 1898 |
| Vim | M | Vim Bicycle Co. | Buffalo | NY | ---- |
| Vindex | M | Reading Cycle Mfg. Co. | Reading | PA | 1898 |
| Vineyard | M | Winslow Skate Mfg. Co. | Worcester | MA | 1892 |
| Violet | M | | | | 1892 |
| Virginia | M | Edward Ebert | Chicago | IL | 1898 |
| Virginia Belle | M | Enterprise Mach. Works | Richmond | VA | 1898 |
| Virginia Swell | M | Enterprise Mach. Works | Richmond | VA | 1898 |
| Vogue | M | The Thomas Mfg. Co. | Springfield | OH | 1896 |
| Volant | M | Springfield Bic. Mfg. Co. | Boston | MA | 1892 |
| Volant | M | Maumee Cycle Co. | Toledo | OH | 1896 1898 |
| Volcano | M | Hagmann & Hammerly | Chicago | IL | 1898 |
| Volunteer | M | Marshall Wells Hdwe. Co. | Duluth | MN | 1896 |
| Vulcan | M | Whitten-Godding Cycle Co. Whitten Cycle Mfg. Co. 1896 | Providence | RI | 1892 1895 |
| W. J. L. Special | M | W. J. Loomis | Carson City | MI | 1896 |
| W. L. Louis | M | Spring City Bic. Works | Royersford | PA | 1898 |
| W & O | M | Willey & Oakley Model - Special | Bay Shore | NY | 1898 |
| W. S. C. H. | M | Warman-Schub Cycle House | Chicago | IL | 1896 |
| W & S Charlotte | M | Watts & Smith | Charlotte | MI | 1896 |
| Wabash | D | Thorsen & Cassady Co. Went bankrupt in 1897. | Chicago | IL | 1895 1897 |
| Wagner Special | M | Bird Cycle Co. | St. Paul | MN | 1896 1898 |
| Waldo | D | Clark Bros. | Kansas City | MO | 1896 |
| Wall's Special | M | R. C. Wall Mfg. Co. | Philadelphia | PA | 1896 1898 |
| Walsh Special | M | Lindsay Bros. | Milwaukee | WI | 1896 |
| Waltham | M | Waltham Mfg. Co. | Waltham | MA | 1902 |
| Waltham Comet | M | American Waltham Mfg. Co. | Waltham | MA | 1896 1898 |
| Walton | M | E. S. Lippincott & Co. | Philadelphia | PA | 1897 1898 |
| Walworth | M | Norman Cycle Co. | St. Louis | MO | 1898 |
| Wanderer | D | Wanderer Cycle Co. | Toronto | ON | 1892 1896 |
| "War" Cycle | M | Nilsson Cycle Co. | | | ---- |
| Warner | M | C. P. Warner & Bro. | Chicago | IL | 1898 |
| Warner Special | M | D. D. Warner Co. | Madison | WI | 1896 1898 |
| Warren | M | Warren Mach. Co. | Boston | MA | 1896 1898 |
| Warwick | M | Warwick Cycle Mfg. Co. Model-Perfection | Springfield | MA | 1889 1898 |
| Washington | M | Ohio Cycle Co. | Cleveland | OH | 1896 |
| Washington | M | Standard Cycle Co. | Chicago | IL | 1896 |
| Washington | | C. H. Meibohm | Buffalo | NY | 1898 |
| Wasp | M | King"B" Cycle Co. | Chicago | IL | 1896 |
| Waverley | M | Indiana Bicycle Co. | Indianapolis | IN | 1894 1899 |
| Waverly | M | Indiana Bic. Co. Models - Belle, 26 Belle, Scorcher | Indianapolis | IN | 1895 1898 |
| Wayne | M | Anderson Cycle Mfg. Co. | Detroit | MI | 1896 1898 |
| Weatherby | M | Weatherby Bic. Mfg. Co. | Weatherby | PA | 1896 |

| Bicycle Brand | Manufacturer or Distributor | Company | City | ST | Date of First Notice |
|---|---|---|---|---|---|
| Webster | M | Webster Mfg. Co. | Paterson | NJ | 1896 1898 |
| Wellesley | M | Lindsay Bros. | Milwaukee | WI | 1896 |
| Wellington | M | Stokes Mfg. Co. Climax Cyc. Co. 1896 | Chicago | IL | 1895 |
| Western Union | M | Western Union Bic. Co. | Chicago | IL | 1896 |
| Western Wonder | M | Moffatt Cycle Co. | Chicago | IL | 1892 |
| Westfield | M | H. A. Lozier & Co. | Cleveland | OH | 1896 1898 |
| Westfield | M | American Cycle Mfg. Co. Eastern Sales Department | Hartford | CT | 1903 |
| Westfield | M | Pope Mfg. Co., Eastern Department | Hartford | CT | 1904 1909 |
| Westland | M | John Deere Plow Co. | Kansas City | MO | 1896 |
| Weymouth | M | W. F. Sylvester | E. Weymouth | MA | 1898 |
| Wheel In White | M | Grand Rapids Bic. Mfg. Co. | Grand Rapids | MI | 1896 |
| Wheeler | M | Defiance Bic. Co. Model - Lady Wheeler | Defiance | OH | 1896 1898 |
| Wheloc | M | Cole Mach. Co. | Camden | NJ | 1898 |
| Whipple | M | Whipple Cycle Co. | Chicago | IL | 1898 |
| Whirlwind | D | Bigelow & Douse | Boston | MA | 1892 |
| Whistler | D | William Read & Sons | Baltimore | MD | ---- |
| Whistler | D | VanCamp Hardware and Iron Co. | Indianapolis | IN | 1894 |
| Whitaker Chainless | M | Whitaker Chainless Bic. Co. | Caledonia | MI | 1895 |
| White | M | White Sewing Machine Co. Model - White Diamond | Cleveland | OH | 1892 1900 |
| White City | M | Warman-Schub Cycle House | Chicago | IL | 1895 1898 |
| White Cloud | D | William Read & Sons | Boston | MA | ---- |
| White Diamond | M | F. D. Owen Mfg. Co. | Washington | DC | 1898 |
| White Fawn | M | Miami Cycle & Mfg. Co. | Middletown | OH | 1896 |
| White Flyer | M | White Cycle Co. | Westboro | MA | 1889 1892 |
| White Flyer | M | Barnes Cycle Co. | Syracuse | NY | 1896 |
| White Fox | M | Fox Mach. Co. | Grand Rapids | MI | 1896 |
| White Head Racer | M | Union Cycle Mfg. Co. | Boston | MA | 1896 1898 |
| White Star | D | Montgomery Ward & Co. | Chicago | IL | 1895 1896 |
| White Wings | D | VanCamp Hardware and Iron Co. | Indianapolis | IN | 1894 |
| Whiteside | M | J. Whiteside Cycle Mfg. Co. | Philadelphia | PA | 1898 |
| Whitman Patriot | M | Whitman Saddle Co. | New York | NY | ---- |
| Whitten | M | Whitten Cycle Mfg. Co. | Providence | RI | 1895 1896 |
| Wichita | M | A. M. Carr Bic. Works Model - Lady Wichita | Wichita | KS | 1896 |
| Wilhelm | M | W. H. Wilhelm Co. | Hamburg | PA | 1895 1896 |
| Willett's Special | M | George E. Willett | Chicago | IL | 1898 |
| Wilson Special | M | Harry Wilson | Doniphan | NE | 1898 |
| Wilton | M | Thomas Mfg. Co. | Springfield | OH | 1896 |
| Winchester | M | Boston Mach. Co. | Boston | MA | 1896 1898 |
| Wind Cutter | M | N. Hoffman | Chicago | IL | 1896 |
| Windle | M | Windle Cycle Co. | Worcester | MA | 1896 |
| Windsor | M | Sieg & Walpole Mfg. Co. | Kenosha | WI | 1896 1898 |
| Windsor | M | Mead Cycle Co. | Chicago | IL | 1910 1914 |
| Winner | M | Indiana Bic. Co. | Indianapolis | IN | 1896 |
| Winner | M | Telegram Cycle Mfg. Co. | Milwaukee | WI | 1896 |
| Winona | M | Svensgaard Bic. Mfg. Co. Also manufactured a tandem | Winona | WI | 1896 |
| Winslow | M | Boston Wheel Works | Boston | MA | 1898 |

| Bicycle Brand | Manufacturer or Distributor | Company | City | ST | Date of First Notice |
|---|---|---|---|---|---|
| Winton | M | Winton Bicycle Co. | Cleveland | OH | 1894 1898 |
| Winwood | M | A. M. Sheffey & Co. | New York | NY | 1895 |
| Wisconsin | M | Cribb Carriage Co. | Milwaukee | WI | 1896 |
| Wissahickon | D | Wallace & Engard | Germantown | PA | 1896 |
| Witch | M | R. H. Robson | Salem | MA | 1893 1898 |
| Wizard | M | Witch City Cycle Co. | Salem | MA | 1895 1898 |
| Wizard | M | Indiana Bic. Co. | Indianapolis | IN | 1896 |
| Wizard | M | B. C. Klein | Chicago | IL | 1898 |
| Wizard | M | McIntosh-Huntington Co. | Cleveland | OH | 1898 |
| Wold | M | Wold Chr. & Co. | Boston | MA | 1898 |
| Wolfe | M | Wm. H. Wolfe | Binghamton | NY | ---- |
| Wolff American | M | R. H. Wolff & Co. | NYC & Syracuse | NY | 1895 1900 |
| Wolverine | M | Adams & Hart | Grand Rapids | MI | 1896 |
| Wonder | M | Lindsay Bros. | Milwaukee | WI | 1896 |
| Wood | M | J. L. Wood | Morristown | TN | 1898 |
| Woodland | M | Bowersox & Kemmerling Bowersox & Beck in 1898 | Cleveland | OH | 1896 1897 |
| Worcester | M | Worcester Cycle Mfg. Co. Model - Royal Worcester | Worcester | MA | 1898 |
| World | M | Arnold, Schwinn & Co. | Chicago | IL | 1895 1918 |
| Worth | M | Chicago Bic. Co. | Chicago | IL | 1892 |
| Worthington | M | George Worthington Co. | Cleveland | OH | 1896 |
| Wright & Ditson | M | Wright & Ditson | Boston | MA | 1892 |
| Wright Special | M | Wright Cycle Co. | Dayton | OH | 1898 |
| Wulfruna | M | W. G. Schack | Buffalo | NY | 1892 |
| Wyandotte | M | Iroquois Cycle Co. | Chicago | IL | 1898 |
| Wyeth | M | Wyeth Mfg. Co. | Geneva | OH | 1896 |
| Wynnewood | D | A. M. Sheffey & Co. | New York | NY | 1896 |
| Wyoming | M | Wyoming Cycle Mfg. Co. | Cheyenne | WY | 1896 1898 |
| X Ray | M | Blanchard & Hooker | Binghamton | NY | 1898 |
| X-L | M | Luburg Mfg. Co. | Philadelphia | PA | 1892 |
| Yale | M | Lindsay Bros. | Milwaukee | WI | 1896 |
| Yale | M | Yale Bic. Co. | Battle Creek | MI | 1896 |
| Yale | M | Kirk Mfg. Co. | Toledo | OH | 1897 |
| | | Kirk-Young Mfg. Co. in 1896. Kirk Mfg. Co. in 1898. | | | |
| Yale Model 40 | M | Lindsay Bros. | Milwaukee | WI | 1896 |
| Yankee | M | Schultz Mfg. Co. | Chicago | IL | 1895 1896 |
| Yankee Flyer | | | Buffalo | NY | ---- |
| Yarnell | M | Moore Carving Mach. Co. | Minneapolis | MN | 1898 |
| Yellow Dog Racer | M | Fulton Mach. Works | Chicago | IL | ---- |
| Yellow Fellow | M | E. C. Stearns & Co. | Syracuse | NY | 1896 |
| Yosemite | M | Yosemite Mfg. Co. | San Francisco | CA | 1896 |
| Young America | M | Bradshaw Mfg. Co. | | | 1893 |
| Youth's Companion | D | Montgomery Ward & Co. | Chicago | IL | ---- |
| Yucon | M | H. C. Tillotson & Co. | | | ---- |
| Zenda | M | Zenith Cycle Co. | Binghamton | NY | 1898 |
| Zenith | M | T. W. Van Tuyle Canada | Petrolin | ON | 1896 |
| Zenith | M | Zenith Cycle Co. | Binghamton | NY | 1896 1898 |
| Zephyr | M | East Side Cycle Co. | Buffalo | NY | 1896 |
| Zephyr | M | Lindsay Bros. | Milwaukee | WI | 1896 |
| Zimmy | M | Zimmerman Mfg. Co. | Freehold | NJ | 1895 1898 |

| Bicycle Brand | Manufacturer or Distributor | Company | City | ST | Date of First Notice |
|---|---|---|---|---|---|
| Zion Special | M | Salt Lake City Cycle Co. | Salt Lake City | UT | 1896 |
| Zwerg Brothers | M | Zwerg Brothers | Rochester | NY | 1898 |

# Index

# Pedaling History -
# the Burgwardt Bicycle Museum

P edaling History – the Burgwardt Bicycle Museum, features one of the world's largest collections of antique and classic American bicycles. Over two hundred bicycles and thousands of items of cycling-related memorabilia are on display, presenting the technological, manufacturing, art, and social history of the bicycle. From the pedal-less wooden walk-about, through the elegant highwheels and the balloon-tired classics to modern high-tech racers, the museum offers you the chance to experience 175 years of the bicycle's evolution.

## PEDALING HISTORY –
## THE BURGWARDT BICYCLE MUSEUM
The museum's collection includes:
- 1860s Velocipedes
- 1880s High Wheel Bicycles
- Rare High Wheel Safety designs
- Classics from the 1950s and '60s
- Pneumatic-tired "safety" bikes from the Gay Nineties
- Racing bicycles, trophies, and memorabilia
- Harley-Davidson and Indian bicycles
- The only surviving 1880s Floating Marine Bicycle
- WWII folding paratrooper bicycles
- Racing and Courting Tandems
- A Bicycle Built for Five
- Children's antique bicycles and pedal-toys
- Military Bicycles
- Life-size displays, including an authentic turn-of-the-century bicycle shop and a Victorian cycling family's parlor
- Candle, acetylene, kerosene, and electric bicycle lamps
- Advertising posters and catalogs
- Bicycle-themed postcards, coins, and stamps
- Bicycle art and photographs

Colonel Albert Pope presides over the High Wheel section.

A marine bicycle floats over the Memorabilia. You ride the High Wheel!

Portraits of famous racers watch over the Racing section; interesting safeties line part of the right wall.

# G. Donald Adams

G. Donald Adams has had a major role in shaping the character of antique bicycle collecting in North America. He is the founding editor of *The Wheelmen* magazine and an internationally recognized bicycle historian and curator. Currently the External Relations Officer for Greenfield Village–Henry Ford Museum in Dearborn, Michigan, he has served as consultant on bicyle history to several American museums. His writing continues to influence museums and individual collectors worldwide to follow sound practices in preserving historically important bicycles and to interpret how these bicycles and their users shaped nineteenth century social, cultural, and technological history.

# Collecting and Restoring Antique Bicycles

*FINALLY, THE MOST AUTHORATATIVE AND SOUGHT AFTER REFERENCE BOOK*
for the antique bicycle collector is AVAILABLE again.
A *COMPREHENSIVE SOURCEBOOK* for everyone from the beginning hobbyist to the advanced collector, this new second edition provides a complete overview of these marvelous machines. Over 400 pages, packed with 350 illustrations and photos, this book covers the development of the bicycle from the earliest 1816 hobby horse, through the elegant high wheelers, tri- and quadri-cycles, to safety bicycles and interesting 20th century models.

- Tips on locating antique bikes, determining their authenticity and condition … even what kind of prices to expect!
- Advice on restoration versus preservation, including when and how to strip and re-paint, and how to find replacement parts or people to make them.
- How to ride the several varieties of high wheel bicycle.
- The antique bicycle club movement, and the growing interest in collecting antique and special interest bikes.
- Detailed information on early manufacturers, models, and design features.
- The first appearance of drive shafts, rack and pinion steering, differential gears, multi-speed gearing, band brakes … all invented for the bicycle!

*THE SOURCE for everyone interested in antique cycles…*
*…admiring them or riding along in style!*

---

## Collecting and Restoring
# Antique Bicycles
by G. Donald Adams

*Send to:*
Pedaling History Bicycle Museum
3943 North Buffalo Road
Orchard Park, New York 14127-1841
e-mail: bicyclemus@aol.com

ISBN 0-9649537-0-6 Hardcover: $32.50     *Quantity* _____     *Total* _____

ISBN 0-9649537-1-4 Softcover: $22.50     *Quantity* _____     *Total* _____

S & H: $4.50 first book, + $1.50 each additional to same address     *S & H* _____

*Subtotal* _____

*Check* ☐     *NY residents add Sales Tax @ 8%* _____

*VISA* ☐     *MasterCard* ☐     **Grand Total** _____

*Card Number* _____ *Expiration* _____

*Signature* _____

*Your Name* _____

*Organization* _____

*Address* _____

*City, State, Zip* _____

*Phone* _____ *Fax* _____ *e-mail* _____